MY STRANGLED CITY

AND OTHER ESSAYS

ALSO BY GORDON ROHLEHR

Pathfinder: Black Awakening in "The Arrivants" of Edward Kamau Brathwaite
Cultural Resistance and the Guyana State
Calypso and Society in Pre-Independence Trinidad
The Shape of that Hurt and Other Essays
A Scuffling of Islands: Essays on Calypso
Transgression, Transition, Transformation: Essays in Caribbean Culture
My Whole Life in Calypso: Essays on Sparrow

GORDON ROHLEHR

MY STRANGLED CITY

AND OTHER ESSAYS

Here, right at my feet
my strangled city lies,
my father's city and my mother's heart

from Martin Carter, "Not Hands Like Mine"

PEEPAL TREE

First published by Longman Trinidad Ltd in 1992
This new edition published in 2019 by
Peepal Tree Press Ltd
17 King's Avenue
Leeds LS6 1QS
England

© 1992, 2019 Gordon Rohlehr

ISBN13: 97818452324379

All rights reserved
No part of this publication may be
reproduced or transmitted in any form
without permission

CONTENTS

Author's Preface: A Requiem for Two Decades	7
Articulating a Caribbean Aesthetic: The Revolution in Self-Perception	9
History as Absurdity	23
Literature and the Folk	52
Sounds and Pressure	80
Once in a Blue Sun: *Review of The Harder They Come*	88
West Indian Poetry: Some Problems of Assessment	98
Afterthoughts	120
Blues for Eric Roach	128
A Carrion Time	131
My Strangled City	149
Songs of the Skeleton	234
"Man Talking to Man": Calypso & Social Confrontation in Trinidad 1970 to 1984	279
Acknowledgements	294
Index	296

DEDICATIONS

This volume is dedicated to my parents, Iris Elecia Rohlehr and Herman Johanis Rohlehr, in honour of their Golden Wedding Anniversary (August 1988); and to my brothers and sisters, Herman Godfrey Rohlehr, Gloria Rosalind Cummings, Iris Gertrude (June) Rohlehr, George Victor Alexander Rohlehr, Julia Christina Gwendoline Kollinger, and Geraldine Agatha Rohlehr.

AUTHOR'S PREFACE

A REQUIEM FOR TWO DECADES

> But that's what this country is about:
> the burning of flesh and cane:
> the ash
> of effort
> ("Ash Wednesday", Victor Questel)

I seem to have lived life always on the edge of upheavals, the borders of catastrophe. My early high-school days at Queen's College in Guyana of 1953-1954, took place opposite Eve Leary, a military camp which housed British peace-keeping troops – Royal Welsh Fusiliers, Black Watch, Argyle and Sutherland Highlanders – whose bag-pipe energies failed to prevent racial and political fracture and friction, and civil war in the early sixties. Second term first-year lectures at UCWI, Mona, Jamaica in 1962, were often punctuated by news of looting and burning at home. Wood burns well, and by the time I set out in 1964 for the neuter void of three years at an English university, a good part of the business area of Georgetown had been erased by fire.

None of these essays has come out of that period. But the years 1970 to 1990, which gave them birth, have been a continuation in a turbulence, enacted in Jamaica, Guyana or Trinidad, the three Caribbean territories to which I most closely relate. 1970 saw the Black Power upheaval and army mutiny in Trinidad. Essays such as "History as Absurdity" and the title-essay, "My Strangled City", grew directly out of 1970. At the very centre and core of these two decades, in mid-June, 1980, Walter Rodney, my classmate from Queen's College days and colleague at UCWI, was blown to bits in Guyana. 1990 was made memorable in Trinidad by the barely credible insurrection of armed Islamic sans culottes who, with the anticipated moral support of various opposition elements, invaded Parliament, held members of the Government hostage for six days, employing in the process methods of torture common to modern terrorist groups throughout the world. Another city has pointlessly burnt as my Caribbean drifts blindly towards atrocity and anguish.

All the fires, the political speeches from one side or the other, the racial rivalry in distress, the looting, the waste of energy and time, the "ash of effort" as Victor Questel once termed it, now seem to me to be the same catastrophe that I have been witnessing all my life. These essays are nothing but testimonies of that witness – offered to all who care – by a spirit which has been a channel for the urgencies of these two decades. They deal with thirty or so writers and singers, exploring linkages or spaces between sensibilities. They are concerned both with the interior silences, voids, black holes of our making, and with the rage, frenzy and noisy futility of our politics. They seek to show how both of these factors condition the poems we shape, the songs we sing and the novels we write; the balance of negativity and affirmation which we bring to our historical moment – a moment that has been made intense with the painful efforts to dismantle the mental structures of our inherited colonial state, and the equally anguished attempts to construct a new architecture of Spirit.

These essays are about the movement of the Caribbean folk from village to city, the disintegration and formation of life-styles, the in-search, frustration, energies and rebellion of urban people over two decades, and the emerging Caribbean aesthetic that has been the result of these processes of change. These essays are, above all, a journey between two catastrophes and two awakenings, 1970 and 1990. They consequently are a continuous exploration of the relationship between catastrophe and awakening, both as a central phenomenon of Caribbean history and as a recurrent feature of our traumatized present.

Often in these essays, the notion occurs of history as a duppy – a malign, unburied and unplacated spirit of time past. The writer or singer then assumes the burden of laying to rest the duppy of the past, so that an enlightened and humane community may live with balance and sane composure in the present. These essays are also a sort of laying to rest; the interment of twenty years of concerned engagement with the burden of making sense of our Caribbean vortex. I think of these two volumes of statements as a requiem for two decades. May these two decades of ferment, farce and phenomenal unchange, fold up, fade out and sink to rest.

Gordon Rohlehr, August 29, 1990 & November 26, 1991.

ARTICULATING A CARIBBEAN AESTHETIC: THE REVOLUTION OF SELF-PERCEPTION

During the period of slavery in the Caribbean, the "selves" of master and slaves, white and black, were prescribed by the rigidities of slavery and the plantation system. These were really imposed selves, hardened by the fact that the system endured for over three centuries and was thorough in its methods, most of which were directed towards the restriction of human potential and the reduction of people to tools, objects.

The limits within which Caribbean people lived were visible in every area of life: in the economics of primitive capitalism which shackled the fragile island economies to that of the metropole; in the class stratification which resulted from the economic system, and was reinforced by the factor of race; by the various slave codes or laws, which anticipated the psychology of the modern concentration camp by several centuries. But the limits within which Caribbean people lived were most clearly visible in the need, which the dominant race, class and civilisation felt, to create and perpetuate stereotypes, systems of coercion (laws), and propaganda which reinforced stereotypes (education), both during and after slavery.

There is no doubt that much was destroyed, much lost or obliterated. Many minds were shattered, most accepted and adapted to the limits which had been placed on human potential. Hence we have the role-playing Black, the jive-ass Black, the Uncle Tom stereotype, and the dozens of other well-known stereotypes which have existed since slavery and have gone through several cycles of permutation since Emancipation. Du Bois in several of his works, Ellison in *Invisible Man*, Kamau Brathwaite in *Rights of Passage*, have all dealt with the phenomenon of the enduring stereotype. Frantz Fanon has given it psycho-philosophical definition in his now seminal testament *Black Skin White Masks*.

The "revolution of self-perception" began with the inner resistance of the slaves to the self imposed on them by the plantation system and slavery. In its most fundamental form it was the refusal to be a thing, an object, a tool, mere chattel: the *negation of a process of reification.*

The positive aspect of this revolution involved the *constant affirmation of the validity of the submerged self*, the self – to borrow Kamau Brathwaite's phrase – in maroonage; the marooned, submerged and often subversive self. This *self-in-maroonage* was affirmed in infinite ways:

a. Rebellion and constant resistance on the plantation (suicide, malingering, rioting, the Haitian Revolution, Cannes Brulées, etc.)

b. The preservation of religions with an African base, or the adaptation of these under pressure of the plantation system/structure during slavery. After Emancipation, several religions existed in the face of constant harassment from the law and pressure from the established churches. The anthropological work on African-Caribbean religions is beginning to constitute an important body of literature. Offhand, I can list a number of concerns which have emerged from the study of these religions.

(i) The continuity of West African heritages in the Caribbean. Factors instrumental in such continuity have been the isolation of some communities; the inadequacy of the education system; the fact that during the post-emancipation period communities of "liberated Africans", who had never been enslaved, were settled in various islands (Trinidad, e.g.).

(ii) The notion of a continuum stretching between religions with the greatest "African" content and those with the greatest "European" content. Donald Hogg in *Jamaica Religions: A Study in Variations* advances this thesis for Jamaica. Continuum theory allows for overlapping, syncretism, conflict and consensus, and leads to a notion of religion as lived process within the framework of a total society, rather than as static, fixed structures.

(iii) The syncretic blending of West African and European proletarian heritages, in religions such as Zion Revival, Pukkumina, Rastafarianism in Jamaica, and the Spiritual Baptists or Shouters in Trinidad. Vodun in Haiti reveals another dimension of syncretism, including a post-Medieval Catholicism and a Dahomean cosmology in a single seamless theological system.

(iv) The relationship between religion and social institutions, such as communities and political parties. The cult/sect and charismatic or authoritarian political leadership. The cult/sect as an exploitable reservoir of popular lumpen-proletarian faith and emotion.

These are some of the concerns which have emerged from the study of Afro-Caribbean religions. That these religions are capable of leading scholars to such fundamental questions is the surest testimony of their vital and vibrant existence as the ground of being for large numbers of Caribbean people. It is also the clearest evidence of the survival of the *self-in-maroonage* after so many years of hostile laws, education, economic suppression and the cultural contempt of the white, brown and black servitors of the establishment.

c. The survival of folktales, proverbs, rhetoric, patterns of performance, and the capacity to create style, are further evidence of the continued existence of the *self-in-maroonage*. If the original folktale has almost disappeared, the capacity for storytelling has not. Hence the storytelling tradition is maintained in the calypso, Paul Keens-Douglas, Abdul Malik, Brathwaite's *The Arrivants,* and a growing corpus of short stories and anecdotes. This exactly parallels what has been taking place in the Afro-American tradition.

If the original propensity for proverbs and aphorisms has been modified, a tradition of moralising still exists, and is evident in the weighty didactic element in some reggae and a few calypsos: the desire to instruct through art.

The revolution of self-perception, then, is process, is on-going *self-affirmation* which, in the face of the unchanging rigidity of oppression, generally means self-assertion. In asking what that revolution means today we are in fact attempting to assess the quality of our self-affirmation in all the areas of our conscious living. These include:

d. Politics and the on-going class struggle.

e. Literature and that constant, complex exploration of the no-longer-submerged inner self; the no-longer-marooned personality.

f. Music – blues, jazz, gospel, calypso, funk, reggae – and the lifestyles, both sacred and secular, which sustain the music. Hence we shall have to ask ourselves what is the meaning of our capacity for celebration, dance, carnival on the one hand, and the trauma, agony and constant struggle which celebration masks. For our music, whether created by 'Trane, Sanders, Tosh, Marley, Chalkdust, Black Stalin or Bird, is connected with the phenomenon of survival. Sometimes as with 'Trane, it seeks to energise and humanise a city of stone and steel. Sometimes as with Chalkdust, Valentino, Marley and Tosh it cries out against, attacks and erodes a stone-deaf politics which, like the old plantation system it has succeeded, still regards people as things, objects, tools.

The body of my paper will be an outline of some of the trends in West Indian literature in English, which together constitute part of the on-going revolution of self-perception. For purposes of convenience I have arbitrarily divided my time-period into three interlocking phases: 1920-1950, 1950-1960 and 1960 to the present.

1920-1950

The twenties was the period of Garvey, Claude McKay and the Harlem Renaissance, to whose political and literary aspects both of these outstanding Jamaicans contributed. The thirties saw C. L. R. James's *Minty Alley*, his play *Toussaint L'Ouverture* (1936). The novels of Portuguese author Alfred Mendes (*Pitch Lake, Black Fauns*) and the short stories of Seepersad Naipaul, *Gurudeva and Other Indian Tales*, indicated the multi-ethnic nature of the Trinidad experience. The forties were a period of steady growth in which regional periodicals such as Frank Collymore's *Bim* and A.J. Seymour's *Kyk-Over-Al* emerged. Louise Bennett, whose creative acceptance and dramatisation of the language of the Jamaican people was in itself a revolution, had begun to write her poems in the late thirties, and had by 1950 become an artist whose work was known throughout the archipelago and in Panama. One of her contributions to West Indian letters was to establish the fact that the little people had not only a voice, but a way of seeing, placing and reducing the world of their social superiors.[1]

The calypso emerged during this period from the traditional structures of *kalinda* and *sans humanité picong*[2] to a flexible medium capable of accommodating narrative, social and political protest, scatological humour, and celebration. An entire and virtually unexplored body of oral literature exists in the calypso. It is a literature which has intimately reflected social change, and can provide the scholar with a documentary of the changing attitudes of grassroots Trinidad.

The literature of this period was being accompanied by serious inquiry into the roots and heritage of the people of the African diaspora. There had already been the substantial work of Edward Wilmot Blyden (*Christianity, Islam and the Negro Race*, 1887). In America this work was to be built upon and augmented by W. E. B. Du Bois (*The Souls of Black Folk*, 1903). The impulse to understand, explore and vindicate an African heritage was politicised by Garvey, whose *Philosophy and Opinions* (1923) is one of the few Afro-Caribbean publications which have survived the rigid censorship of that period.

Equally remarkable was Norman Cameron's The *Evolution of the Negro*[3] (1929). Cameron was a Guyanese student of mathematics at Cambridge, whose vocation to teach in Liberia impelled him to find out all he could about that country. This awakened in him an appetite to know more about Africa itself, particularly in the pre-European period. He read all the collected works of all the early travellers. He augmented these with French translations of Arab and Moorish documents. He developed a keen interest in African art and sculpture which led him to those museums in England which house artifacts stolen from Africa during the scramble. Thirty years before Basil Davidson's now famous *Old Africa Rediscovered* (1959), Cameron had already posited the link between Egypt, the Western Sudan and Africa south of the equator. He had already refuted the then current notions that excellence in African sculpture in bronze, iron and gold was the result of European influence.

He was interested in other things besides. In Chapter 11, on the Mali Empire, he showed an interest in oral traditions such as the drum and elephant horn orchestras; the praise songs and use of poetry for the recording of oral history. He felt that our poets and playwrights ought to be interested in such things and wrote poetry and didactic plays himself, in some of which he consciously sought to include an "African" presence and ethos. Forty years later in Kamau Brathwaite's *Masks* (1968), there at last emerged a Caribbean poet who could give impressive shape to identifiably West African oral traditions: the drum, atumpan, mmenson, the idea of masks, as well as the history, old ceremonies, dances and aspects of Akan cosmology.

Cameron, in his introduction, anticipated the criticism that there was nothing worth studying in African history. He also anticipated the now current accusation that to be seriously concerned with the African past is to be atavistic or nostalgic. *The Evolution of the Negro* was based on the idea that the past should explored as part of one's duty to oneself. One doesn't free oneself from the trauma of history by forgetting the past. One needed, instead, to accept past struggle as the basis for a self-confidence necessary for facing the present and creating a future. Thus, besides the descriptions of the pre-European kingdoms of Africa, Cameron dealt with the effects of contact with Europeans, slave life on the plantations and the abolition of slavery and emergence of the Afro-Caribbean person.

If his reading suggested the destructive nature of slavery, his vision was directed towards what was or would become possible if Afro-Guyanese people were to discover their roots. Thus *The Evolution of the Negro* sought to define these roots. Cameron spent some time describing the layout of villages as well as social institutions, laws, aspects of local government in Africa. He was interested in things such as cloth designs and hair styles, things which did not re-enter popular black consciousness until the 1960s.

Cameron's book, which went into two volumes (1929 & 1934), was about history as continuity, and the historian as healer, bridger of hiatuses in our knowledge and consciousness. But the conscious or unconscious aim of education in the English-speaking Caribbean was to divorce the Caribbean person from issues and concerns of central relevance to his knowledge of self and milieu. Thus Cameron's profound and scholarly work, self-published and distributed, reached only a few people, went out of print to resurface in 1970 when it was reprinted in America. Unlike many other such reprints, it hasn't appeared on the shelves of Caribbean bookstores. Garvey's vision, too, remained in the borders of our consciousness and was for years beyond the reach of our curricula.

This is essentially what we are up against, then, a *tradition of discontinuity* by which our most crucial perceptions and discoveries are relegated to the margins of consciousness. *The Black Jacobins* (1938), C.L.R. James' great study of the Haitian revolution, took twenty-two years to be republished (1962). George Padmore is still a name. Sylvester Williams remote, despite Owen Mathurin's fairly recent publication. Robert Love is virtually unknown. F.E.M. Hercules has scarcely been heard about. This is probably why an era which produced work such as Garvey's, Cameron's and the early work of Eric Williams, should have produced artists who were generally little more than excellent observers of the surface of actions and recorders of manners.

The creative sensibility of the period was largely divorced from the creative thought of the period. One of the obvious reasons for this was the fact that Caribbean people were not in control of their political destinies, or of their economies. This point had been made over and over again in the polemics of the 1930s and 1940s. It resurfaced in the various discussions about the possibility of a West Indian federation. One of the most interesting blueprints for a federation was Arnold H. Maloney's *After England – We; Nationhood for Caribia* (1949) which examined the potential and the limitations of the region as a whole, and envisioned a multilingual federation, and the emergence of a "cosmic race". Maloney was one of a family of distinguished Trinidad scholars, resident in the United States.

1950-1960

The period of 1950-1960 saw the evolution of a substantial body of literature. Mais, Lamming, Selvon, Salkey, Carew, Hearne, Mittelholzer, Harris, Reid, Carter, Walcott, V.S. Naipaul, Keane, Roach and Brathwaite all emerged in this decade. Denis Williams and Kamau Brathwaite lived in Africa during this period, as had Peter Blackman (*My Song Is For All Men*). Reid, without having actually lived there had written in *The Leopard* (1958) an imaginatively impressive novel, set in Kenya. The theme of African continuity or conversely of divorce from Africa appeared in the poetry of Roach and Walcott, while Brathwaite was writing plays for Akan school children, and had by 1962 already given shape to the first half of *Masks*. Denis Williams' *Other Leopards* (1963) explored the split sensibility of the Caribbean *omowale* and left his schizophrenic hero in a desert, almost stripped of his old self, and savouring possibilities of growth in an inscrutable future.

The writers of this decade had a better opportunity to draw on a body of emerging thought and scholarship than had those of the generation before. In anthropology alone, for example, there was the work Melville and Frances Herskovits, George Eaton Simpson, M.G. Smith, Raymond Smith, Andrew Pearse and Daniel Crowley. Afro-Caribbean folklore, religions, folkways, folktales, rhetoric and patterns of performance suddenly became "visible", and we find Kamau Brathwaite in an early essay, "Sir Galahad and The Islands" (*Bim*, 1957), suggesting that in these discoveries lay the basis for a new and alternative aesthetic.[4] We also find him writing reviews of West Indian literature while in Ghana, suggesting, as Cameron had done earlier, that a knowledge of African oral traditions would help Afro-

Caribbean writers in defining and using their own still vibrant oral traditions.[5] He was, in addition, a contributor to radio programmes in Ghana and, as an education officer, part of the new thrust towards the indigenisation of education there, in that early post-Independence period.

In history, the impact of Eric Williams' *Capitalism and Slavery* (1944) began to be felt on the Mona Campus of the University of the West Indies. Elsa Goveia's *A Study on the Historiography of the British West Indies* (1956) provided those who were interested with a means of locating most of the current notions about the history and potential of Caribbean peoples in their historical context. George Lamming read and was deeply influenced by the ideas of C.L.R. James.

Horizons widened during this decade. Lamming's "The Negro Writer and His World" (1956),[6] for example, moved far beyond the normal stereotyped discussion to suggest the complex situation of the Black as diasporan, as twentieth-century man, and as one who had to refashion both for himself, and for the benefit of the Other, that image which the Other had imposed on him. The artist is seen as rebel, as adamic refashioner of word and world, as lonely descender into private hell, and as illuminator of social and political reality. Lamming, who had read Richard Wright's *Black Boy* (1945) years before, was aware of himself as one of an international group of New World writers who were involved in a process of transforming the historic stereotypes which had been imposed on Black people, by speaking from within the self-in-maroonage. Significantly, "The Negro Writer and his World" was a conference paper read at the First International Conference of Negro Writers, held in Paris in 1956. James Baldwin also attended that conference, and provides a perceptive account of that crucial period in one of his essays, "Princes and Powers" (*Encounter*, 1957).

1960 to Present

Janheinz Jahn in *Muntu* (1958) had helped lift Afro-Caribbean literature out of its solitude and to locate it – often erroneously – in a wide Pan-Africanist context which had existed before in the dreams of a handful of scholars. His main concern was the literature of the Francophone Caribbean. Gabriel Coulthard's *Race and Colour in Caribbean Literature* (1962) began for the Anglophone Caribbean the crucial business of comparative Caribbean literature. As we have seen, this was taking place while the writers themselves were, through exile, in the process of widening their horizons and deepening dimensions.

The Pan-African context was, however, but one of the possible contexts within which the literature of the diaspora could be placed. V.S. Naipaul was an outsider to such a context. His position of outsider/insider enabled him to mock it, caricature it, critically analyse it. Never for one moment could he be fully part of it, however much of it was part of him. For "seepage" from the world of Creoledom was viewed by him as violation and chaos.[7] Naipaul, after a decade of wrestling with the problems confronting the *Asiatic* presence in a post-colonial society where the Afro-Creole presence was only just beginning to be defined and accepted as such, wrote *The Mimic Men* (1967). In this novel he posits that the violations of history have impaired both the public and the private selves – both what I have termed *the imposed self* and *the self-in-maroonage*. Because of this each ethnic group is seen as festering in its separate cell, while the public forum of school, parliament or business provides them with no real possibility, no common ground for dialogue. "Mimicry" in that novel is more than simple copying of other people's stuff. It is the result of the attenuation and destruction of will through historical process, the loss of the capacity for choice and the possibility of self-hood, and because of these things, the openness of the psyche's shell to every chance, opinion, fashion and style, and the replacement of willed choice by role-playing.

Derek Walcott could not be satisfactorily placed in a Pan-African context either. His stance, which he eventually defined as "mulatto",[8] was one of Janus-faced ambivalence which could at one and the same time theoretically reject and accept both Africa and Europe in the Caribbean. Lamming, indeed, notes ambivalence as one of the major aspects of the Caribbean sensibility, particularly when it faces the dilemma of affirming an "African" presence.[9] Walcott's seminal work seems always to grow out of this ambivalence. He has called it "making creative use of schizophrenia". In practice, this has meant the display of considerable strength in the affirmation of a European presence in the Caribbean sensibility and a considerable bitterness in confronting the resurgence of an African one.[10]

Just as Naipaul is able to deny the validity of the inner self-in-maroonage, Walcott is, in "The Muse of History", able to reject all the manifestations of this inner self – the drums, music style, rhetoric, religion, symbolism, etc. – as the basis for a new aesthetic. The difference between the outsider/insider position of the "Asiatic" and the "schizophrenic" position of the "mulatto" is that the latter is generally forced to affirm whatever he denies. Hence Walcott accepts the drums, music, style, rhetoric, folklore, dance and so forth as a viable basis for the construction of a New World drama, and has recently included in his poetry some of the very elements for which he has roundly abused a host of unnamed other Caribbean poets.

Wilson Harris could not be fitted into a Pan-African context either. He started with the notion of the Caribbean and New World sensibility as "the latent ground of old and new personalities" – a meeting place of the crumbling old world and the unborn new one. In the unnamed, untamed, osmotic heartland of this New World – aptly symbolised by the virgin forests, black inland rivers, and extensive savannahs of Guyana – all primal cosmologies, mythologies, dreams of civilisation and conquest meet, intersect, echo or parallel each other, creating tension, conflict, and at the same time infinite possibility. Yet the vessels within which these cosmologies meet are an odd collection of rum-guzzlers, murderers, delirious pork-knockers, moneylenders, whores, cattle-ranchers, rustlers, land-surveyors and psychotics from the coast of "domesticity and lights", who find themselves like white America's newest Thoreau, Jim Jones, in the Guyana forest of the night. There, all these people find nothing but themselves; the self stripped of its social, ethnic or economic props; and the result of such encounter is disintegration and the possibility of transformation through lived ordeal.

Harris's preoccupation with inner quest and cosmic issues had its base in a very particular sense and knowledge of the Guyanese political scenario. There, more than anywhere else in the English-speaking Caribbean, was the visible evidence of that plural, schismatic society, which the sociologists were trying to define in the sixties.[11] There is no doubt that the break-up of the PPP and with it the African and East Indian coalition in Guyana (1954-57) is partially responsible for the themes of Harris's first four novels, *Palace of the Peacock, The Far Journey of Oudin, The Whole Armour* and *The Secret Ladder* (1961-65). In these novels – the first two in particular – history is ordeal, a legacy of bitterness and guilt. It has maimed the psyches of both coloniser and colonised, and established brutal authoritarian and materialist patterns, not only in Euro/Afro-Creole society but also within the world of the indentured East Indian peasantry and their descendants. The ghost of this legacy of guilt, materialism, brutality and psychic crippledom cannot be laid by amnesia or evasion, but by confrontation and atonement, and since the crippledom exists within the psyche and has been maintained by ex-colonial peoples long after the physical withdrawal of the colonisers, then confrontation and atonement have to occur within the psyche.

Where Naipaul's people remain paralysed before their crippledom, and Walcott, faced with the maimed remains of history, at one point advocates amnesia, Harris, like the Hindus or the Buddhists, involves the psyche in terrible and agonising Karmic processes in which the intolerable burden of history has to be borne and worn because it is our own burden. Time has to be imaginatively re-entered and relived until one becomes worthy of reprieve or movement beyond. The price of becoming a person in the sense that Harris understands personhood requires a *movement through history*, then *movement beyond history*; a gradual peeling off of the old personality, a divestment of the props of colour, status, race, power and authority. Walcott eventually adopts a similar position in his play *Dream on Monkey Mountain* (1970) which owes much conceptually to Harris.

By the mid-sixties, then, the Pan-African paradigm had proven inadequate in the face of the multifaceted complexity of the total Caribbean experience. It was qualified by the notion of an ethnically plural and culturally diverse archipelago; by the idea of a mulatto heritage in which European and African elements are blended; and by the notion of an emerging indigenised Caribbean tradition which was flexible, complex and had grown, or was growing, out of the confrontation, competition, intersection and collapse of several peoples, lifestyles and cultures over a process of time and under pressure from a rigid, authoritarian and exploitative system.

If Harris's work suggests the interior dimensions of this shift in perception, Lamming's *Of Age and Innocence* (1958) was the first serious attempt to deal with its political aspect. Coming in the wake of the collapse of multi-ethnic politics in Guyana, this novel reveals the deep sense of schism running through West Indian society, as well as the desperate or resolute hope of unity in an open and ominous future. Secrecy and communion constitute the opposite poles of this novel. True political liberation can only be based on open dialogue, shared experience and communion both within and between ethnic groups; and communion requires trust, absolute candour and honesty between the leadership and the people, and between the different ethnic groups in a culturally diverse society.

But these qualities of openness, trust and candour have never been permitted existence in a colonial situation such as the one described earlier in this paper. Thus secrecy and mistrust permeate the relationship between Africans and Indians, the major ethnic groups in *Of Age and Innocence,* and become the catalyst for the tragic divisions which occur towards the end of the novel. If *In the Castle of My Skin* (1953) ended with a perception of the complexity of the African heritage, and an emerging vision of the spiritual and emotional oneness of the Black experience, *Of Age and Innocence* ends with the more complex vision of a multi-ethnic society in which the African heritage is only one of the many heritages competing for visibility and political presence, and Pan-Africanism a source of strength or a prop only to one segment of the population. *Of Age and Innocence* also ends with the embryonic dream of the younger generation; a dream – like Martin Luther King's – of openness, graciousness, cultural exchange in a world where there are no secrets, only a sharing of modes of living and seeing. It is the single hopeful possibility Lamming permits in a horizon of omen and smouldering catastrophe.

The intolerable wrestle between dream and reality has intensified since the mid-sixties. Far from achieving dialogue and communion among the oppressed, Caribbean societies have deepened the divisions of class and race. Central to this development was the Black Power movement in America which, forty years after Garvey, reopened the questions about the self-perception, economic position, and real presence of Black people in America. These questions had to be reopened and, viewed positively, the profound reassessment of the situation of Black people in the diaspora has led to a deepening of consciousness both in America and the Caribbean. There are far more people who are aware of their history and of the continuity of struggle, survival and creativity. While the system still seeks to marginalise Black people in general, there are far more people at every level of life who are articulate, resolute and conscious. There is far more publishing being done, more to read.

But it is also true to say that in places such as Trinidad and Guyana, the situation which Lamming explored in *Of Age and Innocence* still obtains. In those two countries, the two major races view each other as competitors and thus view each assertion of racial presence by the other as a threat to self-hood. The masses of both African and Indians remain exploitable, divided and open to manipulation by politicians who, because of the deepening of ethnic consciousness, have had, for the last twenty years, to project themselves as charismatic, ethnic culture heroes. Elsewhere in the Caribbean, politicians have even manipulated the religions of the oppressed, drawing on the fervour of the cult for political support, which at points reaches fanaticism. This is true of Jamaica and Guyana and was true of Grenada and of course Haiti.

What one is dealing with in the 1970s, then, is no longer the denial of racial presence to Afro-Caribbean people, but the exploitation of awakened racial consciousness by Black political leaders. So that the deepening of consciousness, which could be a strength, has ironically become the basis of fresh exploitation. Attempts to transcend racial and class divisions have taken the form of (a) verbal nationalism (b) a renewal of Marxist/Leninist ideology. The struggle for both of these ideals is just beginning, and promises to be long, paradoxical and bitter. Nationalism, for example, can easily become traditional insularity, which renders the region as a whole even more vulnerable in the world. Marxism/Leninism is, so far, advocated in a rigid and doctrinaire fashion, which seems to me to ignore the multifaceted complexity of the Caribbean situation. It isn't surprising that, in both Trinidad and Guyana, the cleavages along racial lines have remained and been most pronounced even in parties that have proclaimed a universalist Marxist ideology.

Since the mid-sixties, various "directions" have been evident in the literature. Kamau Brathwaite's trilogy *The Arrivants* (1967-1969) has been the mature fruit of an intense and richly various enquiry into the meaning of the African presence in the Caribbean and the Americas. One of his most important contributions has been his ceaseless experimentation with form, and his ability to use models drawn from the basic folk, folk-urban and proletarian cultural forms of Black people of the diaspora, and on the continent of Africa.[12]

What has happened in Jamaica since the late 1960s has resulted in an entirely different sort of poetry from Brathwaite, best seen in his collection

Black + Blues (1976). There, the poetry emerges out of the bleak mood which succeeded the assassination of the Black Power and Civil Rights movement in America and its collapse in the Caribbean. It constantly asks questions about the connection between revolution and consciousness. In "Glass", for example, the poet posits that revolution must be based on spiritual continuity with past revolutionary effort. But Blacks have inherited a tradition of discontinuity which, as Brathwaite had already illustrated in *Rights of Passage*, forces them to alternate between creative action and role-playing, revolutionary consciousness and the minstrel dance of death. How does one, beginning as colonials have had to begin, break the circle of repression/reprisal/retribution/revolution/repression? What creative action brings the necessary release from this wheel?

Brathwaite asks these questions with respect to a society which is half-urban and half-primal, facing the full stress of modern life with very few visible resources. Under pressure, this world begins to prophesy; to create song, legend, myth and dread omen out of the materials of everyday horror. Black people caught in the system, whether they jive in Harlem ("Glass"), or sharpen their ratchet knives in Kingston ("Springblade", "Starvation") become representative of all subjugated peoples, disoriented since the break-up of the Roman Empire and the formation of Western European civilisations. The Caribbean diaspora is placed in a long and vast historical context which has seen movement of peoples, disorientation, the extermination of millions of primal peoples in the Americas by the bearers of a superior technology of warfare, the confrontation of the materialistic West with the kingdoms of spirit in India, Africa and meso-America; the elevation of Western materialism into skyscraper, rocket, spaceship and mushroom cloud, until today the West predicts its own destruction, sees each new invention as an omen of catastrophe (*Silent Spring* (1962), *Future Shock* (1970), *The Greening of America* (1970), and longs for its now abolished sense of wonder, the reinstatement of its dead gods.

Brathwaite's problem becomes that of the entire New World sensibility; that of locating his ex-primordial peoples in this context of movement, disequilibrium and destruction. It is Walcott's problem, that of Lamming's last two novels (*Water with Berries* (1971) and *Natives of My Person* (1971)), that of Carpentier (*The Lost Steps* (1953), *Explosion in a Cathedral* (1962)), Harris and Fuentes (*Terra Nostra* (1975)). It involves a profound reassessment of the meaning of European history, which Brathwaite had already begun in some of his earlier poems, (e.g., "Heretic", "Judas of Barcelona" in *Other Exiles*).

The two sets of possibilities represented by Harris's *Palace of the Peacock* and Naipaul's *The Mimic Men* now become the poles between which our self-perception swings. On the one hand there is the possibility of rebuilding the lost kingdoms of the spirit whose ruins remain as reminders of who we were. How we are to do this becomes the basis of fresh debate. Is Tom's transformation into Ogun still possible? Can Makak really return to the green beginnings? Will Donne ever attain the palace of the peacock or Mohammed be purged by the refining fire of spirit? Naipaul's constant answer to this has been a resolute NO.

Brathwaite, with all his hopes for revolutionary transformation, has grave doubts. On the one hand, the ruined city man has created roots and prophecy, and his rumble of consciousness moves like an earthquake under the frail structures of "our mindless architects". But on the other hand, the city man is a victim who sees "vistas of rot only". Each new generation is "a new generation of clogged gutters", and constantly betrays its lightning flashes of intuitive vision: "the flash of dark into which I have carved no holy place" ("Caliban").

So that if *The Arrivants* moved with the faith of spiritual dialectic towards an equilibrium of negation and affirmation, void and structured form, silence and widening circle of sound, *Black + Blues,* constitutes a veritable *de profundis* of catastrophe. The landscape is more dreary, the manscape more ravaged. The result in terms of form is directness and plainness of statement, on the one hand, and a restless unfocused turbulence on the other. There is a greater intellectual width and depth and a burning intensity of inner search.

Fierceness and bleakness of vision are characteristic of the 1970s. Our poets at home have become furiously driven men. Walcott, Carter, Brathwaite, McNeill, Scott, Roach or Questel all share this "driven" quality, which is a direct response to the quality of chaos which exists in the contemporary Caribbean. One has travelled a considerable distance from the simple vision of the thirties and forties. The revolution of self-perception has always been taking place; and it continues, grows increasingly more complex and multi-faceted. It embraces now both the notion of ethnic heritages and their competition and confrontation in the contemporary post-independence Caribbean. It involves the relentless class struggle, and the survival of the structures and instruments of exploitation and repression. It hovers between the alternatives of adamic renewal or return, and existentialist sense of void. It challenges conventional notions of history and is part of a vast worldwide movement to relocate the submerged cultures of the devastated in the kingdom of human and humane achievement.

(Paper read at the Conference on "Caribbean Expressions: African Diaspora in the Americas", sponsored by the VisualArts Research and Resource Center Relating to the Caribbean, New York, September 18, 1979. First published in *Caribe: Report; Caribbean Expressions Festival 1*, New York, 1980, pp. 7-15).

References

1. Rohlehr, G., "The Folk in Caribbean Literature", *Tapia* Vol. 2 Nos. 11 and 12 (December 17 & 24, 1973).
2. Rohlehr, G., "Forty Years of Calypso", *Tapia* Vol. 2 Nos. 1, 2 & 3 (September 1972).
3. Cameron, N., *The Evolution of the Negro* (Westport Connecticut: Greenwood Press, 1970). Originally published in 1926 & 1934), Georgetown, Guyana.
4. Rohlehr, G., "The Creative Writer and Society," *Kaie*, (Guyana) No. 11, (August 1973) pp. 48-77.
5. Brathwaite, E., "Review of *Voices from Ghana*", *Bim* 30, Jan-June 1960, pp. 88-90.
6. Lamming, G., "The Negro Writer and His World", *Caribbean Quarterly* Vol. 5 No. 2 (February 1958).
7. Rohlehr, G., "Predestination, Frustration and Symbolic Darkness in Naipaul's *A House for Mr. Biswas*," *Caribbean Quarterly* Vol. X, No. 1, (1964) pp. 3-11. Also Rohlehr, G., "The Ironic Approach" in *Modern Black Novelists* (Englewood Cliffs, NJ: Prentice Hall, 1971), pp. 162-176.
8. Walcott, D., "What the Twilight Says: An Overture," Introduction to *Dream On Monkey Mountain and Other Plays* (NY: Farrar, Straus & Giroux, 1970); "The Muse of History", in Coombs O, (ed.) *Is Massa Day Dead?* (NY: Doubleday Anchor, 1974).
9. Lamming, G., "Caribbean Literature: the Black Rock of Africa," in *African Forum*, Vol. 1, No. 4 (Spring 1966) pp. 32-52, 1965.
10. Walcott, D., op. cit. For my comments on this aspect of Walcott's work see: Rohlehr, G., "My Strangled City", *Caliban* Vol. 3, No. 1, (Fall/Winter 1976) pp. 50-122, and in this volume pp. 149-233.
11. Smith, M. G., *The Plural Society in the British West Indies* (California: The University of California Press, 1965).
12. For a full-length study of Brathwaite's *Arrivants*, see Rohlehr, G., *Pathfinder: Black Awakening in The Arrivants of Edward Kamau Brathwaite* (Port of Spain, 1981).

HISTORY AS ABSURDITY

(A literary critic's approach to *From Columbus to Castro* and other miscellaneous writings of Dr. Eric Williams)

From Columbus to Castro purports to be more than just another history book. Its subtitle, "The History of the Caribbean 1492-1969", implies that it is the definitive study of 477 years of history in these widely scattered islands. Apart from this fantastic claim is the fact that the book was written by Dr. E. E. Williams, the Prime Minister of a country which has been for some years in a state of silent turmoil. Thus the reader is particularly interested in the views of its author on the Caribbean past; his sense of how the past permeates and defines the present; and the perspectives which he offers for the future.

Since, too, *From Columbus to Castro* is presented as the fruit of over eighteen years' experience and research, and succeeds an impressive list of books, monographs, pamphlets and lectures, it is of particular interest as the intellectual climax of a long academic and political career, and as the synthesis of a lifetime's experience in both the writing and making of West Indian history. Questions which engage the reader almost before he reads the book are, "What new things does Dr. Williams have to say about the Caribbean past?" and "How coherent will his vision turn out to be?"; "What, if any, is the connection between his scholarship and his politics?"

In addition to all this, *From Columbus to Castro* has already been used as the springboard from which the PNM means to jump into the era of the swinging seventies. It has been welcomed in by an exclusive dinner, which the publisher himself, Mr. Deutsch, travelled from London to attend; by an adulatory speech made in worship of the author by a minister of government who, from his lack of concrete references seems not to have read the book as yet; and by a meeting of the PNM at Queen's Park Savannah in which Dr. Williams, fulfilling his multiple roles of historian-politician and philosopher-king, unleashed on an unsuspecting public the party's new charter, which contains (and I quote) "the most profound concept in contemporary political social and economic thought." This seems rather like an attempt to oust Mr. Burnham of the Republic of Guyana in a game of Caribbean one-upmanship. Mr. Burnham had scored a first in the Caribbean by instituting the world's only Cooperative Republic in 1969. Now it is the Trinidad Magna Carta ushered in by a massive history book, which is certainly much more impressive than Mr. Burnham's *A Destiny to Mould*, which ushered in the Cooperative Republic.

From Columbus to Castro, then, is meant to be both the historian's bible for the new era, and the great work from which the national movement in Trinidad and Tobago will derive its intellectual dynamic against the deepening pressures of this age of neo-colonialism. It is Dr. Williams's titanic attempt to bring up to date such thoughts and perceptions as are his; to revise old insights, to include fresh ideas, and to assemble both the archaic and the immediate visions in a single massive volume. This would show once and for all how West Indian history can be impressed into the service of decolonisation; how the academic can become a politician and yet preserve his academic integrity, while at the same time reassuring former students of the now defunct University of Woodford Square that despite his years of hermit-like invisibility, the great brain is still solidly at work.

These days it is difficult to view without scepticism anything Dr. Williams has to say either as politician or as historian. His last two history books have been the objects of quite astringent criticism from professional historians at UWI. Dr. K.O. Laurence, for example, views Dr. Williams' *History of the People of Trinidad and Tobago* as an excellent "manifesto of a subjugated people", but criticises the author for a tendency to overstate his case, and to omit a number of things which would significantly modify his conclusions. Dr. Laurence mentions in particular Dr. Williams' failure to credit the contribution of Albert Gomes; to assess the work of the Abolitionists; to treat the system of Apprenticeship; to examine the effect of World War II and the American occupation on the islands; to consider the Moyne Report; or to see the long struggle for self-government as a continuous and unbroken process. He sees Williams' treatment of the post-1956 era as "frankly partisan" and ends with an implicit rejection of his methodology:

> However it is obviously desirable that the books which will dictate the view of their own history which the people of the Caribbean will possess for the next generation should be written as histories not as nationalist manifestos. Otherwise it will be necessary for later generations to unlearn much of the "history" which the first generation learned, just as in the United States, for example, it has been necessary to rewrite the traditional views of the emergence of that great country in the eighteenth.

Dr. Laurence then goes on to define the problem as an imperfect marriage between the historian and the politician.

> Dr. Williams of course is both politician and historian, and if it be said that it is the politician who gives the book its punch, it is certainly the historian who gives it its authority. That authority needs frequently to be challenged, for the nationalist politician has from time to time led the historian to swerve dangerously; but the book is a great achievement.[1]

One wonders whether the last statement is not defeated by all that precedes it.

Elsa Goveia's review of *British Historians and the West Indies*, first published in *Caribbean Quarterly* and since republished in John La Rose's *New Beacon Reviews, Collection One*, (1968), is in its calm way a devastating piece of criticism. She thinks that Dr. Williams has misnamed his book, and is able to show that he does not at all examine the work of seven or eight major British historians who wrote extensively about the West Indies. She mentions the "combination of omissions and hasty dogmatism which mars his present work", and concludes:

> Whether in education or history, good intentions are not enough, and the road to hell is paved with authoritative half-truths. No one is ever educated or liberated from the past by being taught how easy it is to substitute new shibboleths for old.[2]

She finds the book "disappointing and even somewhat irresponsible", and sees it as "just not good enough either for the people or for the students of the West Indies who are likely to read it." Later, she suggests that Dr. Williams write essays on the contemporary West Indian scene, which his experience as historian and politician could render valuable.

With these two warnings behind us, then, we cannot help but approach *From Columbus to Castro* with some degree of scepticism. Indeed, such scepticism is doubly necessary since Dr. Williams makes fantastic claims for the book, and has been prepared to use its publication as a means of bolstering up his political position in Trinidad and Tobago. Dr. Williams states his purpose in a preface.

> Few 'colonials' have to date extended their nationalism to the cultural field and dedicated themselves to the task of writing – or rewriting, where necessary – their own history.
> The present work is designed to fill this gap and to correct this deficiency. Its scope is the entire West Indian area, including the Guianas – whether their connections have been or are British or French, Spanish or American or Danish...
> Its goal is the cultural integration of the entire area, a synthesis of existing knowledge, as the essential foundation of the great need of our time, closer collaboration among the various countries of the Caribbean, with their common heritage of subordination to and dictation by outside interests (pp. 11-12).

From Columbus to Castro, then, has grown out of a belief that little is being done by West Indians in the rewriting of their own history, and its preface is a direct criticism of the History Department of the University of the West Indies. Dr. Williams has now come to rescue historiography in the West Indies from the doldrums, as he claimed in 1956 to have rescued Trinidad from the Crown Colony system and from political anarchy and immorality in public affairs. He must have been living in a hermit's cell somewhere, bypassed by time. He clearly has taken no account of the growing number of unpublished theses in West Indian history, the fruit of hard work, serious scholarship, and at times of nationalist pride. In this area, the lack of West Indian publishing houses willing to handle academic texts, is a felt one. Publishers know that relatively few West Indian historians will have Dr. Williams's ability to advertise their books on trips abroad, as well as on the local television and radio, since very few of them will be Prime Minister of anywhere.

Apart from its messianic urge, the preface expresses Dr. Williams's very commendable aim of working towards "cultural integration of the entire area". This indicates that he is one of an increasing band of creative writers in the West Indies who sense the essential cultural similarity of the area. Dr. Williams, despite his abrupt withdrawal from the Federation after Jamaica left, has been an advocate of regional cooperation since the mid-forties. In the fifties, when he was lecturing about the necessity for a Federation, George Lamming was producing *New World of the Caribbean*, a programme of readings from British Caribbean writers which was federal in perspective, growing as it did out of the optimism at the prospective British West Indian Federation. Now *From Columbus to Castro* appears while CARIFTA is in its embryonic stage, and while West Indian writers like Brathwaite and Walcott are annually widening their perspectives. Literature, history and politics are thus quietly serving as a counterpoint to each other, and Dr. Williams is certainly not alone in the great task which he says that he has undertaken. It is therefore good to hear Dr. Williams mentioning the names of some of the region's creative writers in his final chapter, and in his preface implying the identity of his quest with theirs, though it is by no means evident from some of his past and most of his recent political activities, that he has applied to himself their severe critique and rejection of our sterile politics and Afro-Saxon attitudes. It seems that he has read them to no end.

Dr. Williams's notion of writing history has hardly developed since *Capitalism and Slavery*. He still conceives of history-writing as the gathering together of a stockpile of facts to be hurled like bricks against dead and living imperialists. *Capitalism and Slavery*, like *The Negro in the Caribbean* (1942) was the product of the age when Black intellectuals first began as a body to refute the stereotypes of the African which Europeans had for centuries been vending. Those two early works were the academic equivalent of Césaire's *Cahier* and Damas's *Pigments* which the French banned and burned during World War II because this colonial had been able to show that France as a colonial power had been just as racist as Nazi Germany. Williams's early work was a significant advance in Black consciousness. The fact that it is largely a reaction to white prejudice explains its extremely factual nature. Williams knew that if he aspired to altering the past, he could do so only by a true rediscovery of fact. The meticulous citation of facts and figures was a necessary defence against the accusation, which is still being made about *Capitalism and Slavery*, that Williams as a Black man was simply trying to write history as revenge. It was self that he sought to vindicate – his own self and the racial one – and the completeness of this self-vindication depended on the authenticity of the facts. Dr. Williams at this stage couldn't afford to write too much propaganda, since identity itself depended on his telling a substantial part of the truth.

When the victim of colonialism begins to tell his version of the truth, he normally shocks the liberals within the ranks of the colonising race most. For the colonial, the study of his history is a journey into self rather than into time past; for the white liberal, it is more generally evasion of the deeper implications of racial and cultural contact under the artificial conditions of imperialism. Recently, Sylvia Wynter has argued that British critics of West Indian literature show a similar capacity for evading its central issues and agonies.[3] She identifies their failure as a failure to admit the part their people played in West Indian history, and to see how this produced the rebellion of the West Indian mind in both its positive and negative aspects. Her argument is that such rebellion leads to a totally different approach to art, which critics brought up in a metropolitan tradition of criticism judge from the standpoint of their own irrelevant or inadequate aesthetic. They therefore sidestep the judgement which West Indian literature passes on both their culture and their role in the sordid drama of Empire, by concentrating on the aesthetic flaws rather than the wider implications of this literature.

Significantly, as Dr. Williams realises, it is the Irish writers like Swift, Shaw and Joyce who come nearest to the corrosive irony which is the peculiar gift of the colonial experience. "I understood Britain's Irish policy and the Irish 'colonial' better after I had read Swift, Shaw and Joyce", he writes in Chapter Three of *Inward Hunger*. He also mentions with approval in *From Columbus to Castro* Swift's scathing satire on British imperialism in *Gulliver's Travels* (see p. 176). Whites who have known the pressures of colonialism themselves generally have an approach to history and to life which resembles that of their Black counterparts. Joseph Conrad, that Polish colonial, sailor and exile, in his *Heart of Darkness* was one of the few Europeans who realised an idea that is a first principle with Black writers: that in the imperial collision it was the West that was on trial – Western culture, values, mythology, scholarship, tradition, and reputation for humanitarianism. *Heart of Darkness*, a book which shows neither a love nor an understanding of the African, is nevertheless a macabre study of the decay of the West and ends up by expressing a profound disillusion at the process of history itself.

The Williams of *Capitalism and Slavery* was part of this international company of acrid ironists all bound together by the futility of their colonial status. His work most resembles Swift's in tone, in clarity of style and in acrimony. Indeed, since Williams thinks so highly of Swift, a brief comparison of the two men is not out of place. Swift's family had in the past seen better times, and he grew up with a boundless ambition for high office and aristocratic position.

> All my endeavours, from a boy, to distinguish myself, were only for want of a great title and fortune, that I might be used like a lord by those who have an opinion of my parts – whether right or wrong, it is no matter – and so the reputation of wit or great learning does the office of a blue ribbon, or of a coach and six horses.[4]

Swift, then, equated authority with respectability. An Anglo-Irish politician who would have liked to be a moving force in English politics, he was exiled instead to an Irish deanery because of his "subversive" writings as chief Tory journalist and pamphleteer. There he oscillated between contempt for the Irish whom he considered unworthy of a man of his calibre, and rage at the English who had banished him from his beloved coffee-house crowd, where he was a gentleman among equals.

Swift saw Ireland with a colonial's self-contempt as "this land of slaves" into which he had been dropped by accident.[5] His crowning ambition in Ireland was "to have none about me that denies my authority", and to live the "life of a king among slaves".[6] This, however, he regarded as a poor substitute for the attractions of high-level politics. His reaction was fascinating. First, he surrounded himself with minions, minor clerics, impoverished students seeking advancement, and later on with small businessmen and shopkeepers, over whom he exercised a more absolute authority than ever Lear could over his one hundred soldiers. Next he championed the Irish cause against a typically iniquitous piece of English legislation and was cheered as a national hero through the streets of Dublin by a people he detested. In his pamphlet against the introduction of Wood's halfpence, he all but stated the case for Irish Home Rule, and in his famous and macabre *A Modest Proposal* he equated the English treatment of the Irish peasant with cannibalism, which he set out to prove could more profitably be replaced by actual state-controlled cannibalism. The argument was that since England as an imperial power was concerned only with the making of profit, she ought to allow no moral scruples, no mere consideration of humanity, to stand in her way. In this satire, Swift also stated the principle of Buy Local, and in part blamed the Irish businessman for his lack of nationalist pride, and for the shoddy nature of his product. In *Gulliver's Travels*, Swift poured all his thwarted ambition not only into a rejection of British imperialism, but of the entire process of history and politics. In short, his life was an example of the now well-known colonial love-hate complex that binds the colonised to the coloniser, teaches him contempt for self and a twisted love for his people, and leads finally to the emergence of irony both as a quality of perception and as a psychological necessity.

This is, of course, nothing like a full summary of the life or career of Jonathan Swift. It is a simple isolation of the colonial experience insofar as it affected his career. There are several respects in which this career resembles that of Dr. Williams. In *Inward Hunger* Williams sees himself as the product of a largely irrelevant primary and secondary education who sets out to "conquer" Oxford. Chapter Three of this book begins with an extremely lyrical description of Oxford's broad academic tradition. Dr Williams' discovery of this heritage is seen almost as a fulfilment of self, a true discovery of identity. Then there is a latish discovery of the pain and irrelevance, the non-identity of being a colonial at Oxford – and a Black colonial at that. The second half of the chapter is decidedly less lyrical than the first. In it Dr. Williams describes how he moved from under the protective wing of his tutor and faced what he interprets as the racial prejudice of the institution as a whole, when he tried to qualify for a fellowship at All Souls. If a grim sort of humour informs his description of the ordeal of dinner-parties, teacups and choosing the correct teaspoon at the right moment, while saying precisely the correct piece of irrelevance that passes for wit in that incestuous world, it is a kind of naive outraged innocence that informs the narration of a passage like this one:

> The first incident occurred in the examination room. The examination included an oral translation from a foreign language. I chose French, Spanish not being available. The student had to enter a long room, in which he found some forty Fellows seated around a table. In the course of translation, I made a horrible mistake. The crowd roared. I received the distinct impression that the roar was aimed at me and not at the mistake. It sobered me at once, I lost all nervousness, I looked all around the room, at one individual member after the other until quiet had been restored. I felt like a schoolmaster upbraiding by looks a group of unruly pupils; some began to pick their nails, one looked out of the window, one twiddled with a book in front of him. When there was absolute quiet I resumed translation in a cold, unemotional voice. At the end I came to a passage of which I could not make head or tail. I declined to translate. The warden pressed me three times to have a go at it. I refused. To set the matter at rest, I told him on the final occasion that I did not wish to give rise to another such guffaw as I had already listened to. He thanked me for coming and I took my leave.[7]

This is a remarkable passage precisely because it reveals much more of Dr. Williams and the cultural predicament of the Afro-Saxon colonial than he admits. Beguiled by the idea that he had conquered Oxford merely because he had proved himself their best history student in years, he had dreamed briefly of joining that world of entrenched snobbery and tradition. As he saw it, the world had replied by laughing at his blackness and his ignorance of one of its languages. Like Swift, Dr. Williams found his ambition thwarted by the world towards which he aspired, and his dignity undermined. His rejoinder was also similar to Swift's. He stresses his moral superiority to his tormentors – "I felt like a schoolmaster upbraiding by looks a group of unruly pupils." The Oxford Fellows, though, probably saw him as a tiny little Black boy, whom they didn't want to torture too obviously. The entire passage is like Mr. Biswas's first appearance before the family tribunal of the Tulsis. There is a passage in Chapter Four of *A House for Mr. Biswas* which seems exactly to describe Dr. Williams' pose here: "Looking stern, preoccupied and, as he hoped, dangerous, Mr. Biswas became very busy helping the carter to unload." The incident has certainly taken its full toll, maiming part of the psyche beyond all redemption. Dr. Williams' entire life since that period has been partly an attempt to prove to the Fellows of All Souls that he is not only their equal, but their superior; not anybody's pupil, but everybody's schoolmaster.

How, for example, is the reader expected to take this account of the famous confrontation between Dr. Williams and Mr. Z of the Caribbean Commission, when, according to him, they were trying to use his book *The Negro in the Caribbean* as an excuse to dismiss him?

> Throughout the discussion I was conscious of two impressions (a) that Mr. X was literally flabbergasted. I doubt that he ever expected any colonial to write or speak to him like that; (b) that morally and physically I was his superior. That he should be evasive and apologetic I fully expected. But he was more than that. At times he was quite incoherent... when we were through he had had enough; I could have gone on (talking) for three hours.[8]

Here we find the daydream which the colonial always has of humiliating Massa, his longing to ply the castigating whip for a change. Beneath it lies the need to prove self and manhood, which can never be fulfilled unless there is an audience of squirming colonisers and a chorus of applauding slaves. There is a kind of triumphant pettiness about the passage which rings embarrassingly near to the core of the colonial psyche. All colonials have had the dream. It was one of the moving forces behind Swift's satire. In the case of Dr. Williams, though, a brilliant mind constantly satirises itself. The last passage quoted reveals all the bitterness of the infighting of the late Crown Colony era; the loneliness of the individual whose dignity had always to be asserted as limits were placed on personality. V.S. Naipaul, who came a generation after Dr. Williams and also attended Oxford, found it a distinctly different place from the one Williams described. In contrast to philistine Trinidad, Naipaul tells us, England has been the only place where he has discovered "generosity – the admiration of equal for equal." England must have changed after twenty years; but under the strain of the thirties, the divided Afro-Saxon colonial psyche could scarcely be expected to cope without a weird unpredictable oscillation between its component halves.

The victim learns to feel a simultaneous blend of love, hatred and contempt for both black and white, and he swings unpredictably between these conflicting emotions. Sometimes he expresses all of them at the same time, and in the same action. The result of this is generally irony of some sort, a peculiar rigour of mind, and a schoolmaster's desire to castigate and be respected.

This is perhaps what explains the similarity between minds as different as Dr. Williams' and Swift's. His habit of accumulating facts and figures and arranging them for ironic effect, and of sometimes summarising argument by an immense tabulation of detail is similar to a method Swift employs from time to time, to clinch his point for good and all. In the passage about to be quoted, Lemuel Gulliver receives the answer of that rational superman, the king of Brobdingnag, to his panegyric on European history and civilisation. The king's voice, which at this point is almost certainly Swift's, is the bewildered voice of the colonial rebel passing judgement on the myths which the colonising power has created for itself, and used in the process of controlling the minds of the subject people. Indeed part of Swift's Olympian laughter is at the fact that such a tiny immoral insect as Gulliver, European Man, should undertake the gigantic task of trying to change the customs and mentality of alien peoples.

> He was perfectly astonished with the historical account I gave him of our affairs during the last century, protesting it was only a heap of conspiracies, rebellions, murders, massacres, revolutions, banishments, the very worst effects that avarice, faction, hypocrisy, perfidiousness, cruelty, rage, madness, hatred, envy, lust, malice, or ambition could produce.[9]

What follows is one of the most famous passages in Swift where European Man is described as one of the most pernicious races of odious little vermin that nature ever suffered to crawl upon the face of the earth.

Now compare this passage from Dr. Williams' *From Columbus to Castro*, which is simply one of many in his work.

> One of the most vigorous of the abolitionists, G. Thompson, said that the immigrants into Mauritius were indolent, mendicants, runaways, vagrants, thieves, vagabonds, filthy, diseased, dissolute, immoral, disgusting, covered with sores; some were priests, some jugglers, some barbers, some wrestlers, some cooks, some grooms, some buffoons, some herdsmen, some peddlars, some scullions, bakers, tailors, confectioners, instead of agricultural labourers (p. 346).

It may be that Dr. Williams is quoting Thompson directly without benefit of quotation marks; or it may be that he is paraphrasing Thompson. Whichever is true, it is clear that he likes the pamphleteer style of the passage, which also appears in *History of the People of Trinidad and Tobago*. It may also be the vigorous polemical approach of such eighteenth century giants as Swift and Defoe that attracts Williams to their work. He is, like them, a polemicist of no mean order. The passage just quoted, though an extreme example, captures the main characteristics of Williams' style. Here can be seen his passion for making lists of words, facts, statistics – the passion for cataloguing experience in a manner reminiscent of Robinson Crusoe's diary. Even for the economic historian the passion is an extreme one.

In *From Columbus to Castro*, as in *Capitalism and Slavery*, one has the sense of a careful compilation and organisation of fact to suit the exigencies of a central purpose. Examples of this accumulation abound in both books – the later book draws heavily on material from the former – and are especially to be seen in the chapters where Dr. Williams shows how the slave trade affected things like shipbuilding, textile and iron industries in England. Here he mentions every minute article made from iron and used in the trade: fetters, axes, iron-hoops, handcuffs, stoves, tools, guns, and a host of others. This accumulation of detail, which at times threatens to break down into absurdity, is, no doubt, meant to convey the impression of the enormity of the trade, and is reinforced by a barrage of statistics, with which most other historians would have been satisfied. The device is semi-literary and semi-rhetorical.

One merit of this method of compiling fact, when, as in *Capitalism and Slavery* it is attended by direct reference notes, an adequate index and the meticulous citation of sources, is that it validates the work as a useful reference text, and enables other scholars to benefit fully from the scholarship and archivist activity of the pioneer historian. Indeed, G. R. Mellor, on checking Dr. Williams's *Capitalism and Slavery*, discovered that a few quotations had been taken out of context and edited to suit his main thesis, and concluded with the warning "that unless those who are engaged in research are very careful they will find what they are looking for."[10] When, however, as in *From Columbus to Castro*, absolutely no indication is given as to the sources of the majority of facts and figures, and there are few reference notes, the worth of the book is immediately in question. It cannot be safely used as the reference text it was intended to be, since the student has no immediate or remote means of checking either the facts or figures. He will never be able to ascertain, unless he duplicated research already done by Dr Williams (which would be rather a waste), whether the author is vending some of the same authoritative half-truths that both Drs. Laurence and Goveia have identified in his later work,

Lack of references must therefore be cited as a grievous flaw in *From Columbus to Castro*, especially since a substantial part of it is devoted to the presentation of bare statistics on the sugar industry throughout the ages. By constantly citing statistics without citing sources, Dr. Williams makes it impossible for the student to view these statistics in any context other than the one he himself provides. The quotation which he takes from Mark

Twain about there being "lies, damned lies and statistics" may well be true for his own work, for all the reader knows.

Another shortcoming is that at times fact seems to be indulged in for its own sake, until the pattern beneath the face of fact is obscured. Fact too often controls vision rather than vision fact. Perhaps this is because a sense of people as living complex beings rather than as economic, political or sociological abstractions, is generally missing from Dr. Williams's work. Elsa Goveia's comment on the West Indian historical experience is particularly apt here:

> It is essential for West Indians to grasp in all its complexity the nature of the influence which slavery has exercised over their history. But they will not be able to do this until they can see the white colonists, the free people of colour and the negro slaves as joint participants in a human situation which shaped all their lives.[11]

Dr. Williams would probably dismiss this, as he dismisses Mellor's thesis, as the "idealist conception of history" (p. 540), though all that Dr. Goveia seems to be asking for is "understanding of the basic pressures inherent in the situation". She would, perhaps, prefer to be regarded as a humanist historian, which is the category in which she, in her *Historiography*, placed all those historians who not only accepted the humanity of Indian and African, but tried to understand the complex human situation created by West Indian history.

Truly creative writing about the West Indian past and present, whether it has been accomplished by poets like Césaire, Walcott and Brathwaite, novelists such as Carpentier, Naipaul, Lamming or Jean Rhys, historians such as Elsa Goveia, the C.L.R. James of *The Black Jacobins*, or Walter Rodney of *A History of the Upper Guinea Coast*; or a psychologist such as Fanon, has always been concerned with this need to understand and explore "the basic pressures inherent" in the West Indian situation. It has always been a question of trying to understand self, of self-knowledge. The ultimate deficiency in the historiography of the West Indies has, for both coloniser and colonised, almost invariably implied a failure in self-knowledge.

In the case of Dr. Williams, there is at times, an almost deliberate abdication of the right to a self; an almost perverse reduction of experience to a rubbish-heap of statistics about sugar. In his work, people seem to be conceived of as the sum of the facts and statistics concerning their lives – certainly a limited vision of experience, not calculated to fill anyone's inward hunger. One of the features of Swift's writing that has had little influence on Dr. Williams's vision is Swift's passionate protest, most evident in *A Modest Proposal*, at the economists' tendency, real then as well as now, to reduce people to statistics. In this respect the irony of the colonial experience has certainly turned against Dr. Williams. In order to counter the numerous damaging stereotypes that white people invented about black people, Dr. Williams adopts a method of obsessive factuality, which in the end also drains Black experience of its humanity.

The true historian of the West Indies in this era will need to have a strong sense of the West Indian people such as is seldom evident in *From Columbus to Castro*. For in the case of the Afro-West Indians, more than even the poor whites and the East Indians, it was an entire race consisting of several peoples, which was stereotyped as inferior, and whose every aspect of being was invaded and violated. It is therefore necessary for the West Indian historian, who like Dr. Williams seeks to bring about "the cultural integration of the entire area" (p. 12), to do much more than present "a synthesis of existing knowledge" about the islands (which Dr. Williams does not do, in any case).

The historian of the seventies has a different role from the historian of the thirties, which Dr. Williams has remained. He has to be something of a social anthropologist, or a social psychologist, and to try to chart the enduring quality of mind that enabled people to survive the evil combination of circumstances. He will have to reject the idea that the Blacks were simply the objects, and never the subjects of their history, until comparatively recent times. The Blacks were the subjects of their history in so far as they negated the idea that they were less than human; in so far as they made repeated efforts at gaining their freedom; in so far as they took definite and unceasing action to help give their history its distinctive shape. They were its objects in so far as they were constantly at the mercy of their violators. Yet, as Dr. Williams himself notes, rebellion against their tormentors was as much part of the experience of black people, as submission to them. The exceedingly repressive slave laws, as he says, bear eloquent witness of this fact. In rebelling, the slave was both expressing and vindicating a self. It is not enough, therefore, simply to mention the fact that such rebellions did occur, and then to make a list of the corpses. It is necessary, if there is to be fresh vision, to do the same depth analysis of the dichotomy of rebellion and submission, as has been done of the economics of slavery and sugar.

If the historian neglects to do this, he is bound to sink into the simple fatalism that informs Dr. Williams's huge work, in which the images of death and destruction are as pervasive as in Conrad's *Heart of Darkness*. Some of the most icily impressive chapters of the book narrate the tale of the terrible wastage of lives, with a detachment that simply reinforces the blank brutality of the fact itself. Here, at least, the facts and figures are themselves frighteningly eloquent, and the factual method is fully justified in the face of the bleakness of the experience being described. In Chapter Four, it is the Spanish Empire and the death of the Indians; later, it is to be seventeenth century Barbados; then Jamaica and Haiti; then indentureship in Trinidad and Guyana with their phenomenal mortality rates; after that it is the malnutrition, hookworm and malaria of the twentieth century West Indies...
As the Guyanese poet Martin Carter puts it in his poem "Black Friday 1962",

> and everytime, and anytime,
> in sleep or sudden wake, nightmare, dream,
> always for me the same vision of cemeteries, slow funerals,
> broken tombs, and death designing all.

One does not have to travel far in West Indian literature to meet the image of death and abortion, though it is gradually being countered with images of the womb, birth, and resurrection.

It is as if the madness and eventual mysticism, which Dr. Williams describes overtaking Columbus, have also penetrated the very tissue of the historical experience of these islands. This is, of course, also a favourite idea with West Indian writers. Lamming writes in *In the Castle of My Skin*:

> A sailor called Christopher followed his mistake and those who came later have added theirs. Now he's dead, and as some say of the dead, safe and sound in the legacy of the grave. 'Tis a childish saying for they be yet present with the living. The only certainty these islands inherit was that sailor's mistake, and it's gone on from father to son 'mongst rich and poor [...]

This sense of fatality also informs Naipaul's *The Middle Passage*. It lies at the root of his irony, as much as it informs the acrid sarcasm which is part of Dr. Williams' response to the West Indian experience.

Time and again his conclusions about West Indian history closely resemble Naipaul's. As he traces the fierce international conflicts which took place in the sixteenth, seventeenth and eighteenth centuries, it is the irony that time and time again engages his mind. Consider this passage, one of several, for example:

> From the territorial aspect, the West Indian colonies assumed an importance that appears almost incredible today, when one looks at those forgotten, neglected, forlorn dots on the map, specks of dust as de Gaulle dismissed them, the haggard and wrinkled descendants of the prima donnas and the box office sensations of two hundred years ago. (p. 88).

Ironic, if even a trifle sentimental. The exploiters of this age preserve a much greater sense of propriety. But the bauxite of Jamaica, Guyana and Surinam, the oil of Trinidad and Venezuela, the sugar of Cuba, and even the sunshine and the beaches of most of the islands, still seem to be exploitable commodities, and provide the enterprising descendant of the slave trader and planter with his adequate pound of flesh. It is not the decline of the West Indies that should engage our sentiment, but rather their endurance as a perennially fertile hunting ground for everyone except the people who live there. There are several passages in Brathwaite's most recent poetry which make this point with a kind of despair. Reviewing the sterile economics and politics of the area, he concludes that:

> [...] the rope
> will never unravel
> its knots, the branding
> iron's travelling flame that teaches
> us pain, will never be
> extinguished. The islands' jewels:
> Saba, Barbuda, dry flat-
> tened Antigua, will remain rocks,
> dots, in the sky-blue frame
> of the map. ("Islands", *The Arrivants*, p. 205)

The difference between Brathwaite (who is professionally a historian, and is about to publish one of those books on West Indian history which Dr. Williams claims that few people besides him are bothering to write), and Williams or Naipaul, who seem to be paralysed by the nightmare of West Indian history, is one of emphasis. Brathwaite is as much concerned with the fact and idea of survival, as he is with the powerful fact of mortality and weakness. Naipaul, when, as in a *A House for Mr. Biswas* he does seriously consider the prospect of survival and rebellion, is concerned primarily with the interpenetration of rebellion and absurdity, of identity and nonentity in the West Indian response to experience. In Naipaul, the absurd West Indian situation leads to gestures at creative rebellion in the individual's efforts to arrange his meaningless world. These gestures may be Mr. Biswas's in his attempts to build a house, or Kripal Singh's in his attempts to be premier of a crown colony. In the small island, the barriers between plebeian and patrician are really superficial. All are caught in the circle of futility; thus rebellion itself, because it is conducted by nowhere people, culturally and economically both orphan and underprivileged, leads only to a further dimension of absurdity.

It seems to me that Dr. Williams, both in his writing and in his life, fulfils the Mohun Biswas syndrome. His sense of the absurdity of West Indian history has led to a most relentless and sustained rebellion. But as a book like *Inward Hunger*, or a pamphlet like *My Relations with the Caribbean Commission* proves, this rebellion remains painfully self-conscious, and at times betrays a longing to wield the same schoolmaster's whip whose lash still burns across his memory. The need to prove mastery returns him and his rebellion to absurdity. An example will, perhaps, make my meaning clearer.

Massa Day Done, a speech which he made on March 22nd 1961, has been considered one of his greatest. It had to be. With elections in the offing, C.L.R. James inexplicably fallen from grace, and the opposition forces growing daily more vocal, Williams needed to maintain his reputation for both rhetoric and intellect. Few Caribbean politicians would have found the former difficult. Dr. Williams began with a tirade of abuse against his political enemies which had the distinct ring of robber-talk and *sans humanité* picong, which are both forms of folk rhetoric and must have pleased the crowd no end:

> This pack of benighted idiots, this band of obscurantist politicians, this unholy alliance of egregious individualists, who have nothing constructive to say, who babble week after week the same criticisms that we have lived through for five long years, who nincompoops as they are, think that they can pick up any old book the day before a debate in the Legislative Council and can pull a fast one in the Council by leaving out the sentence or the paragraph or the pages which contradict their ignorant declamations – for people like these power is all that matters.

The ending of the paragraph is rather a rhetorical anticlimax, but the string of explosive big words rhythmically building up to a kind of climax would have sounded good to the audience. Here was Dr. Williams, the national schoolmaster, fulfilling his dream that had become an obsession since the days of his humiliation before the Fellows of All Souls Oxford, of castigating unruly schoolboys by a display of his intellectual superiority. It doesn't matter that professional historians have shown that Dr. Williams, too, tends to omit passages which contradict his argument; that was not the irony anyone would have been likely to notice at the time. Throughout the speech he stressed his intellectual superiority. To attack his ideas, he said, was to attack "twenty years of assiduous research", and to "jeopardise the interests of "our national community". He accused the opposition of "intellectual dishonesty" while he and his University of Woodford Square were "dedicated to the pursuit of truth and to the *dispassionate discussion of public issues.*" (Italics mine).

He then delivers a very fine lecture on the role of Massa in West Indian society. Massa was the one who historically brutalised black people, and who was always opposed to their independence. He sought power for his own ends just like the house slaves in the opposition party. In Trinidad, Massa met his match with the advent of the PNM (Dr. Williams' party) which had done so much to set right some of the major injustices that had been historically perpetrated by Massa. Next follows a list of the party's achievements in the areas of agriculture and lands, housing, health, education and so on.

The real surprise comes at the end when Dr. Williams boasts about the projected visit of Sir Winston Churchill to the island and expresses his pleasure that it is the PNM government which would proudly show him what local diplomacy had achieved in Chaguaramas, in begging him for "protection for West Indian products" and in "making representations to him in respect of West Indian migration to the United Kingdom." It is amazing how easily all the bombast deflates itself and, miraculously, still remains bombast. After the long litany which showed that Massa Day Done, Dr. Williams suddenly returns to the light of common day, where he depends on Massa's subsidies, and Massa's open door.

But the irony goes even further than this, because if Massa, by Dr. Williams' own definition earlier in the speech, was, black or white, a man who was ultimately opposed to the independence of the colonised, one couldn't choose a better example of Massa than Churchill himself. It was Churchill who was most adamant on the matter of India's Independence. He scornfully referred to Mahatma Gandhi as "a seditious Middle Temple lawyer posing as a fakir in dhoti", and asking for independence for his people. Churchill couldn't bear to think that anyone who studied in England should not be an Anglophile, or should identify with his own oppressed people. Race pride and *imperium in imperio* received their embodiment in Churchill, for whom Dr. Williams was proud to unroll the red carpet a few minutes after defining the Churchill-phenotype as the enemy of his people. This apparent right-about-turn would be inexplicable to anyone who did not understand Dr. Williams' Oxford experience. For him it isn't really a right-about-turn at all. It is yet another opportunity to prove to those invisibly grinning Fellows of All Souls how well he can translate French, and beat them at their own games of dignity and diplomacy.

Chaguaramas was not a PNM victory. Everyone recognised it as Dr. Williams' personal triumph... Everyone, that is, except C.L.R. James who saw it as primarily the people's, whose spokesman Dr. Williams was. To show Churchill Chaguaramas, then, was the last thing necessary to assure himself of his achievement. The achievement could not be real until it had received the applause of the right people.

But that was not the end of the speech. The more vehement and histrionic the early rebellion, the more relentless the late swing towards absurdity. After the passage on Churchill, the speech moves to its anticlimactic climax:

> It is *only* left now for Her Majesty the Queen to visit us. After all we are an important part of the Commonwealth, and if Her Majesty can go to Australia, to India and to Pakistan, to Nigeria and to Ghana, she can also come to the West Indies.[12]

Two interpretations are possible of this wonderful passage. The first is that Dr. Williams may have been welcoming the pomp and circumstance of a royal visit engineered by his own genius, as the ultimate proof of the greatness of his personal achievement, since it is difficult to see how he envisaged that the presence of the Queen per se could help the people of the West Indies in any way whatsoever. Indeed, he had earlier in the speech described the house slave:

> Always better treated than their colleagues in the field, they developed into a new caste of West Indian society, aping the fashion of their masters, wearing their cast-off clothing, and dancing the quadrille with the best of them.[12]

He even mentions post-revolutionary Haiti with its court, its titles, "its Duke of Marmalade and its Count of Lemonade, exploiting the Negro peasants". Indeed, nearly twenty years before, he had written of the coloured West Indian middle classes:

> The visit of a Prince of Wales, the honeymoon of a royal couple find them ready to display their loyalty to the throne, their affection for the mother country.[13]

Eight years after 1961, Dr. Williams accepted the award of Companion of Honour at the hands of the Queen, thus fulfilling both halves of the Afro-Saxon psyche, that of rebel and that of conformist to values which as rebel he despised – or rather, said he despised.

The second possibility is that Dr. Williams may have realised the deep love that his generation of West Indians, nourished on the buns, slogans and lemonade of countless Empire Day celebrations, have for royalty, and intended to use her unsuspecting Majesty as a gimmick to strengthen the devotion of his worshippers towards himself. Royal visits had provided excellent bread and circuses during the era of direct British rule, culminating in the fifties, when they had been relentlessly employed, first to prop up the foundering Crown Colony system, and, failing that, to effect a smooth transition from colonialism to neo-colonialism. One of the biggest sins of Guyana's PPP of 1953 was its refusal to pay even lip service to the throne. Some members had even picketed the Princess Royal, telling her "Limey go Home", in spite of the fact that her propinquity to the throne had been most carefully explained. Among the sedition charges brought up against Nazurdeen in 1953 was his alleged declaration "that the Queen was nobody but only a symbol of imperialism and that all the white capitalists in the colony (British Guiana) were her stooges."[14] Perhaps remembering the Ordeal of Teacups and Cutlery at Oxford which preceded admission to a fellowship, Dr. Williams realised that certain games had to be played by the rules. Trinidad therefore needed royalty to bless its Independence. Not surprisingly, the Independence games have retained most of the features of the Empire games.

Thus, absurdity has led to rebellion, which in its turn is a re-initiation into fresh absurdity. This is distinctly the Mohun Biswas syndrome, which demands that he forever leave and return to the colonial Monkey-House. The difference between Naipaul and Dr. Williams is that the former uses irony to probe and analyse the pain of his own loss, cultural orphanage, forced ambivalence and futility, while the latter exploits irony as a means of reassuring himself of his own moral and intellectual superiority. This has led to a failure in self-knowledge, an inability to reconcile the broken halves of the psyche, and the necessity either to retreat from a people growing daily in awareness, or to perform feats of self-justification over television and radio.

It is not surprising, then, to find Dr. Williams concluding from time to time in *From Columbus to Castro*, that West Indian history is absurd. Exasperated at the continual efforts which were being made to keep the planter class alive, he finally explodes:

> West Indian history is indeed nothing but a record of the follies and foibles of mankind (p. 229).

This closely resembles Naipaul's now famous passage in *The Middle Passage*, which states that "the history of this West Indian futility" can never be satisfactorily told, because "History is built around achievement and creation: and nothing was created in the West Indies."[15] *From Columbus to Castro* certainly reinforces such a conclusion. In it the West Indies are seen as a theatre in which word, deed, religious idealism, belief, morality, custom, the very foundations of humanity itself, rotted under slavery, sugar and the plantation system. Dr. Williams catalogues this decay, while at the same time trying to show that in West Indian history, the entire history of Europe stands condemned.

In this respect, he plays the role not only of schoolmaster, but judge – two closely related roles, since they both carry with them the dual joys of castigation and condemnation. Thus Dr. Williams judges the world as each country sends its actors across the West Indian stage.

> For over four and a half centuries the West Indies have been the pawns of Europe and America. Across the West Indian stage the great characters, political and intellectual, of the Western World strut and fret their hour... (p. 11)

The theatre-image is a trifle imprecise. Dr. Williams seems to conceive of the West Indies more as an universal assizes, over which he himself presides as grand inquisitor, using West Indian history as so much evidence for or against the whole of Europe. Concerned with the moral implications of slavery, he judges each personage according to how he relates to the African, acquitting him if he can acknowledge Black humanity, and condemning him if he shows any ambivalence in the affair. It is Lestrade's role in Walcott's *Dream on Monkey Mountain* that he seems to be fulfilling.

Thus in chapters sixteen and seventeen, Dr. Williams looks at how the entire cities of Liverpool and Manchester, built up by the proceeds of the slave trade and slavery, first support the trade, and then argue just as bitterly against it, on the grounds that it helps preserve the archaic mercantile system. Nelson, Britain's loftiest hero, is tried and defrocked as one who was against any sort of abolition (p. 261). Pitt the Younger is tried and found wanting. After examining Pitt's inconsistency on the issue, Dr. Williams concludes, "The great minister stood self-condemned" – which, of course, saves Dr. Williams the trouble of having to find further evidence to condemn him himself (p. 263). Hume, Jefferson, Chatham, North, Colbert are all guilty.

Cowper is guilty of weak sentimentality, Wordsworth of apathy, and the eighteenth century purveyors of the myth of the Noble Savage are duly ridiculed as absurd. Gladstone, in whose gentle footprints Dr. Williams himself was due to follow when he became Privy Councillor and Companion of Honour, is also sentenced, and with him, the entire flawed liberal tradition of which he was a cornerstone. The mortality rate is certainly high. Wilberforce seems to come off a little better than he does in *Capitalism and Slavery*, perhaps because Dr. Williams does not dwell so insistently on what his enemies had to say. But he is condemned as too wishy-washy and gradualist in his conception of change. Canning is berated for his attempt to serve humanity and mammon at the same time (p. 297). Among the few redeemed are Clarkson, Schoelcher and Adam Smith, who were reasonably consistent in their attack on the morality or economics of slavery.

But a peculiar danger generally awaits all Grand Inquisitors – a danger of moral self-righteousness. Two examples will suffice. First there is Williams's judgement of Canning:

> The British Government's middle-of-the-road policy of gradualism was explained by the Prime Minister, Canning. There were knots, he said, which could not be suddenly disentangled and must be cut. What was morally true must not be confused with what was historically false... It was not, nor could it be made, a question merely of right, of humanity, or of morality (p. 297).

But Canning, as Dr. Williams should know well by now, was simply articulating the dilemma of the Prime Minister anywhere, and the classic British conservative tradition of slow concession to change. Politics is, and has always been, a perilous sacrifice of morality to expediency in the pragmatist, and a painful conflict between morality and expediency in the man of conscience. Most politicians solve the matter by doing away with conscience and identity altogether. This is really the most elementary lesson in politics. Politicians become the world's most consummate comedians when, having renounced morality and identity, they insist that a moral interpretation be accorded their every action.

Then there is one of Dr. Williams's more damaging observations about Wilberforce:

> The British abolitionists relied for success upon aristocratic patronage, parliamentary diplomacy, and private influence with men in office. They deprecated extreme measures and feared popular agitation. This conservatism was largely the result of the leadership of Wilberforce, who was addicted to moderation, compromise and delay. He was a member of the secret committee of 1817 set up to investigate and repress popular discontent, in the days which foreshadowed the Peterloo Massacre (p. 298).

Wilberforce, like Canning, seems from this passage merely to have been a product of the narrow and undemocratic pre-1832 English tradition, and one ought not to blame him too much for his "moderation" and "compromise". If one judges Dr. Williams' regime in Trinidad by the same absolute, cold morality, one may be tempted to arrive at the same conclusion; that here is one who "deprecates extreme measures and fears popular agitation" — except, of course, that which he initiates himself; one who has between the mid-1960s and 1970, that is in less than a decade of Independence, set up committees and tribunals and passed laws "to investigate and repress popular discontent", and to enquire into subversion; one who compromises over change, believing, as he says he does, in gradual but distinct reform. The self-righteous indignation of the historically maimed mars his vision, which too often remains at a sense of outraged innocence at European hypocrisy to make him aware of the limits of his own rebellion. This is one of the pitfalls of protest politics as it is of protest literature of any kind. Rebellion, if immature, can lead to a defeat rather than a liberation of consciousness.

This criticism is also true of the last quarter of the book, which treats of more modern time. For example, Dr. Williams, to highlight the significance of the thirties, tabulates the unrest of that decade in an interesting passage, which, however, appeared before verbatim in *The Negro in The Caribbean* (see p. 93 of that work).

> The road to revolution had been marked out. The revolution broke out in the years 1935-1938. Consider the chronology of these fateful years. A sugar strike in St. Kitts, 1935: a revolt against an increase in customs duties in St. Vincent, 1935; a coal strike in St. Lucia, 1935; labour disputes on the sugar plantations in British Guiana, 1935; an oil strike, which became a general strike in Trinidad, 1937; a sugar strike in St. Lucia, 1937; sugar troubles in Jamaica, 1937; a dockers' strike in Jamaica, 1938. Every British Governor called for warships, marines and aeroplanes; total casualties in the British Colonies amounted to 29 dead, 115 wounded (pp. 473-474).

That paragraph, as it stands, was good enough for the forties, but hardly for the seventies. It ought to have been succeeded somewhere by a similar tabulation for the fifties and sixties, which would tell the reader something about the continuity of both distress and rebellion. Consider the chronology of these fateful years. Political, racial and social upheaval in Guyana, 1962-1964, followed by states of emergency, hunts for arms and subversive literature, the presence of British soldiers and warships, arson, labour disputes, long long strikes, looting, murder, mauvaise langue, the total poisoning of race relations on all sides, libel cases of all varieties, commissions of enquiry serving little purpose and evading essential issues, mass emigration of skilled labour, civil servants and graduates... Constant unrest in Jamaica... Poverty, weekly shootings by both police and Black youth, anti-Chinese riots in 1965, searches for arms, emergency in Kingston, restriction of freedom of movement and assembly; sporadic outbreaks of arson, strikes too numerous to mention, many of them quite serious, and culminating in a serious spate of labour unrest in 1968; the bulldozing of thousands of squatters from West Kingston to make way for a new industrial complex and flats for party members; the migration of these squatters to Maypen Cemetery from whence they are also driven by social workers, firehoses, policemen and soldiers; the celebrated Rodney Affair acting like a regional catalyst; riots and arson in October 1968; increasing use of the army as police force... Consider Trinidad of these times – which Dr. Williams, strangely, refuses to do... Strikes of all kinds... State of Emergency in 1965, anti-Communist witch-hunt, revealing hardly any Communist witches; the ISA to control labour through legislation unfavourably balanced to the advantage of the employer; demonstrations of all sorts; the Solomon Affair; Gas Stations probe; 1970; shootings; calling out of the army, marines; appeal to the British and the Yankees abused over the Chaguaramas issue, to send help now; treason charges, sedition, another state of emergency, murder, arson, Draft Public Order Act, Karl Hudson-Phillips... In the midst of all these things, an Independence... which few can take seriously... Obviously... Obviously...

The list can go on and on, since this is but a short catalogue of the bacchanal of the sixties. The total dead-and-wounded, the total minds shattered in the dark, the total teeth and ribs broken, the total homeless, have not been catalogued as yet. The total frustration hasn't been measured, though Dr. Williams probably has figures on that too, which he means to release before the next elections.

From Columbus to Castro, a work so rich in fact in its chapters which treat of the slave trade, the abolition, the decline of sugar in the nineteenth century, and the growth of gigantic companies in the twentieth, has virtually nothing to say about the post-World War II period. How is one to assess its worth? The first few chapters on Spanish and French imperialism in the West Indies, are old hat and can have been derived from almost anywhere. The chapters on abolition rehash arguments with which the student of *Capitalism and Slavery* is by now quite familiar. However, more details are given, though no one can say where most of these come from, since the writer declines the reader this privilege. The chapter on the Haitian Revolution, a clear paraphrase of C. L. R. James's *The Black Jacobins,* is like Dr. Williams's treatment of all Black rebellion, annalistic, rather than analytical.

As the book proceeds, the reader familiar with the rest of Dr. Williams's work finds himself wondering what is really going on. Passages he has read before, entire chapters almost, seem to repeat themselves. Chapter 18 is a simple paraphrase of Sewell's *The Ordeal of Free Labour* (1862), and adds little new to what Dr. Williams has already said in *British Historians and the West Indies.* Also, material that appeared before in Williams' book on Trinidad appears here once more. Chapter 19 on indentureship again repeats work done in *History of the People of Trinidad and Tobago.* Perhaps that is why it contains no close examination of indentureship in Guyana or Surinam, despite the regional scope claimed for the book. Here, as in the book on Trinidad, little attempt is made to assess the effects of indentureship on the society. Things like the problems of acculturation which faced Indian society in the West Indies, the questions of religion and language, of race relations and conflict are simply ignored, though one would have thought that some notion of these things was necessary in a history book whose object is "the cultural integration of the entire area". An opportunity is lost to examine human relations in Trinidad during this exceedingly rich late nineteenth century period, the latter-day struggle of French and English cultures for the souls of Black folk, the international spectrum of races, languages, currencies and customs that was nineteenth century Port of Spain. Thus *From Columbus to Castro* repeats here the main failing of the book on the people of Trinidad and Tobago – in that one never really sees the people of Trinidad or Tobago. Indeed, no one could ever guess from this book that the people of the different islands are profoundly different in temperament.

Chapter 20 of *From Columbus to Castro* contains passages which are almost a word for word transcription of passages in Chapter 12 of the *History of the People of Trinidad and Tobago*. Chapter 22, that hastily written chapter on the 1865 Rebellion in Jamaica, is a brief summary of what Dr. Williams has already done better in *British Historians and the West Indies*. Some of the succeeding chapters, especially Chapter 26, repeat huge chunks from *The Negro in the Caribbean*. Chapter 25 is an impressive sketch of the growth of American influence in the region, but this analysis is not carried beyond the early forties, so that the reader cannot gauge what the position is today. Indeed, the more one reads, the clearer does Dr. Williams' secret design for over three-quarters of the book become. The real aim is humanitarian rather than economic – to present a package-deal summary of most of what he has written before, in words as near to the original as possible, with a hundred or so new pages as a lagniappe, which at the modest price of twenty-two dollars and fifty cents, would save the already hard-pressed citizen the money he would otherwise have to spend, acquiring the separate volumes of Dr. Williams's most prolific career.

One's wonder widens as one proceeds. In a book which has been exceedingly rich in facts and statistics about sugar throughout the ages, the reader learns nothing, about Trinidad's oil or the bauxite of Guyana, Surinam and Jamaica, interests which are far more important today. There are works available on these things, some of them done by some of the very people whom Dr. Williams's preface apparently aimed to discredit. An analysis of the functioning of the multinational corporation in the area would have helped as a basis for understanding the perils that attend attempts at disentanglement of the regional economy from the metropolitan snare, and might have led to a less vacillating attitude towards the Castro regime in Cuba. Nothing much is said about tourism, though it is becoming of increasing importance in the lives of these islands, threatening to split tiny impoverished societies asunder for the nth time in history.

No analysis is offered of the political movement towards a nominal Independence. The emergence of trade unionism is barely mentioned. The formation and failure of the British West Indian Federation are hardly ever treated. Dr. Williams's real energies seem to have been consumed by his tremendous efforts at looking backwards. Thus he has little to say about the present. The struggle for the franchise and the important features of political consciousness which it revealed in the different islands are not treated. Marryshow, Critchlow, Manley or Jagan might never have existed, for all we are told of them in this book. Yet the book calls itself *The History of the Caribbean*, 1492-1969. It is probably meant to be the first volume of a really serious study.

Chapter 28 on Castroism is disappointing. It simply mirrors, rather than explains, Dr. Williams's ambivalence as a Caribbean leader on the only country that has seriously attempted to make Independence a meaningful concept. The chapter hinges on a series of quotations pro but more generally con Castro's Cuba. More often than not, Castro is depicted as an impractical dreamer who doesn't care for the economist, and indulges in "planless planning", which leaves his economy in a mess. While Dr. Williams does try in the final chapter to make up his mind about the meaning and implications of Cuba, he seems to be more concerned with stressing the superiority of his own, ironically, gradualist policy of steering the decidedly Anglican *via media* between the Cuban and the Puerto Rican examples. The last two chapters ought to provide the economists with a field day, since they will better be able to trace the disparity between what Dr. Williams says that he is doing, and what he is doing in fact. The least charitable of his critics see his late attempts to recognise Cuba, five or six years after he defined that country as enemy number one, as simply another elections gimmick, which is meant to indicate apparent concessions in the direction of socialism while the basic structure of the economy remains the same. The more generous of his critics see his new attitude towards Cuba as part of a genuine attempt to initiate gradual but definite change in Trinidad. Whichever is true, it is clear that the youth are not really with the Prime Minister, and that whatever efforts are being made now, have almost certainly come too late.

The most important thing about Cuba seems to have been the lesson which she has taught the rest of the Caribbean: that ideas about change are important; that some sort of rapport between the leader and the masses is necessary, and that, above all, self-criticism is an important feature in Independence. These are elementary lessons, but there is little evidence that they have been learned anywhere in the rest of the Caribbean. Dr.

Williams has had tremendous insight. A book like *Education in the British West Indies*, published since 1950 (written four years before), makes it clear that the entire education system needs to be restructured, and it lays down lines along which this restructuring should take place. There should be a greater emphasis on vocational and technical training. The area should understand the irrelevance of Oxford and Cambridge to local needs of agricultural development, an arrested urbanisation and the development of technical and commercial skills. A West Indian university would "consciously and belligerently undertake to guide its society along the lines marked out by the objective economic movement and in the direction to which the demands of the people are pointing."[16] The university will have to join the mass struggle, if its academic education is to have any meaning.[17] However, if it is to have direction, "the governing body should be controlled by the political representatives of the people."[18] Thus not only was the University to play a full part in nationalist politics, but politics was to control and shape the destiny of the institution.

Dr. Williams clearly did not envisage the possibility that both the politics and the academic endeavour of the area could be sterile; that the last thing post-independence politicians desire is that their authority should be challenged by either people or university. Everything which he wrote in the forties reads like a piece of bitter irony these days. Education has continued to be along the lines of metropolitan academism, churning out each year a fresh crop of GCE Ordinary Level students whom the Civil Service cannot consume. Education in agriculture was to have been accompanied by a vigorous policy of land reform, according to Williams' book. Fourteen years after his accession, there has been neither education in agriculture for rural areas, nor substantial land reform. The question of the sugar lands hasn't begun to be asked. The university as an institution has no obvious commitment to anything under the sun; and those few lonely souls who try to stop their own alienation by attempting to bridge the widening gap between the campus and the community, those who attempt to climb the fences which are being constructed with gruesome symbolism around the Campuses of the UWI, get caught up in the barbed wire. Lecturers have been expelled for alleged subversive activity, and in the Trinidad of 1970, university personnel have been detained on most fantastic charges and released because Dr. Williams himself, now in his disguise as Minister of National Security, could discover no adequate grounds upon which to hold them. Some university people, at times the most innocuous of souls, have received poison pen letters and phone calls from people who have eventually identified themselves as supporters of the Prime Minister of Trinidad, all because they tried to involve themselves at grassroots level. It is so throughout the area. Dr. Williams quotes Che Guevara's criticisms of Cuban economic policy, without noting that the most remarkable fact about these criticisms was that they were allowed to be made, and before both the Cuban people and the world. It is not possible anywhere else in the West Indies for one so close to the centre of power to admit failure.

But without self-knowledge, there can be no self-development. It is not therefore surprising that Dr. Williams in his last chapter is in constant despair about West Indian identity. The despair is probably as much personal as social. The passage that sums up his thoughts on a Caribbean identity is worth quoting in full. The region, he says, has indeed produced writers like Lamming, Walcott, Césaire, Fanon, Naipaul and Brathwaite.

> Nevertheless artistic, community and individual values are not for the most part authentic but, to borrow the language of the economist, possess a high import content, the vehicles of import being the educational system, the mass media, the films and the tourists. V.S. Naipaul's description of West Indians as 'mimic men' is harsh but true. Finally, psychological dependence strongly reinforces other forms of dependence. For in the last analysis, dependence is a state of mind. A too long history of colonialism seems to have crippled Caribbean self-confidence and Caribbean self-reliance, and a vicious circle has been set up: psychological dependence leads to an evergrowing economic and cultural dependence on the outside world. Fragmentation is intensified in the process. And the greater degree of dependence and fragmentation further reduces local self-confidence. (p. 502).

That definition of the vicious circle in which the region seems to be caught is one of the finest I know outside Naipaul. Recently, indeed, Naipaul himself has made a similar observation:

> The small islands of the Caribbean will remain islands, impoverished and unskilled, ringed as now by a cordon sanitaire, their people not needed anywhere. They may get less innocent and less corrupt politicians; they will not get less hopeless ones. The island Blacks will continue to be dependent on the books, films and goods of others; in this important way, they will continue to be the half-made societies of a dependent people, the Third World's third world. They will forever consume; they will never create. They are without material resources; they will never develop the higher skills. Identity depends in the end on achievement and achievement there cannot be but small. Again and again the millennium will seem about to come.[19]

This is the message of *The Middle Passage* taken to even gloomier extremes. It cannot be denied, though it can be qualified. No one anywhere can escape the tyranny of the mass media, and it is, perhaps, somewhat comforting to note that the entire bent of European literature suggests that the West Indies are not unique in their quest for identity. Identity depends in the end on self-knowledge, not on achievement. This is why people like Dr. Williams and his entire generation who have achieved so much, are still uncertain about their identity. It isn't simply a question of the poverty of the area; it may be more a matter of failing to recognise roots, whatever these are. If the education system is irrelevant, it can be changed at least partially, and along lines that Dr. Williams himself defined over twenty years ago. If increased tourism is to blame for a steady corruption of values, a more careful approach to the social effects of this aspect of the economy needs to be made.

For Williams simply to acquiesce in Naipaul's definition of West Indians as mimic men is, first of all, to fail to see that Naipaul was in that book talking particularly about West Indian politicians. As usual, Dr. Williams does not apply the lesson to himself, but sufficient has been said above to show that the statement does apply to him as much as it does to any part of the society. For Naipaul to state absolutely that West Indians will never create because to create one must have identity and to have identity one must create, seems to be a sacrifice of truth for absurdist paradox. Were Trinidad all that sterile, it could not have produced Williams, Naipaul, James, Padmore, Sparrow, Spoiler, Mannette and a host of others. Barbados, we have sometimes to remind ourselves, produced both Lamming and Brathwaite, whose contribution to our knowledge of self, and therefore to our identity, have been immense.

It is really quite naive to view our economic dependence as an insurmountable barrier in the path of identity; unless the only identity recognised were the economic one. In this respect, Dr. Williams's final definition of the Caribbean predicament is much more important than Naipaul's. His statement, however, needs to be qualified with the observation that the lower classes in the West Indies have always been most certain of roots, religion and self than the twisted products of a metropolitan education. When they mimic, they often make something of what they copy. Thus the Black Power mass movement of 1970 in Trinidad is very superficially interpreted if it is seen only as an imitation of the American thing. It is as Trinidadian as Canboulay, the Butler marches, Carnival and the brilliant political calypsos which were sung in 1970. The masses were transforming soul culture and international rhetoric and slogans, quite often improvising in mid-stride. The Rastafari Cult, visible symbol of the worst kind of colonial neglect, produced an artist such as Ras Daniel Heartman, a man with a deep sense of both tragedy and triumph, and has been a visible influence in the work of all serious Jamaican artists, including her talented musicians. Recently, Jamaica's substantial contribution to world jazz, as well as to her own musical identity, has been noted by James Carnegie.[20] All kinds of things are going on in the West Indies, which Naipaul and Williams seem not to consider important, although they do indicate that in spite of a terrible past, West Indians do possess considerable freedom of mind. The politicians are really some distance behind the people. Finally, what is always important about both Dr. Williams and Vidia Naipaul is what they omit, as well as what they say.

History, as a number of West Indian artists seem to be depicting it, is the study of human survival in the teeth of suffering. Naipaul the novelist has a more complex vision of West Indian history than Naipaul the social commentator, who tends towards an almost histrionic despair. A friend of mine describes Naipaul as a man who travels about the world looking for despair. The despairing vision of both Naipaul and Williams derives in part from their closeness to a European way of seeing. By not studying the West Indian people in any true depth, Williams ironically reduces their history to a Carlylean study of the lives of a number of significant individuals. Naipaul accepts the Froudian formula that there are no true people in the West Indies. Had Naipaul bothered with J.J. Thomas's *Froudacity* he may have qualified his opinion. Dr. Williams fails, not in not having appreciated Thomas, but in remaining too long in the late nineteenth century ambivalence towards the world of the coloniser which was very much Thomas's. Both Dr. Williams and Naipaul seem finally to regret their position as poor relations at the European feast.

The most unfortunate thing which could happen to *From Columbus to Castro* is for it to be regarded as the bible of the new era. It is distinctly a *fin de siécle* performance, a work that marks the spiritual end of a generation; the last will and testament of an era. The fact that Dr. Williams is much better at making statements about the past than about the present proves this. The very context in which the book was first welcomed to Trinidad also proves this. What was noticeable about Kamal Mohammed's panegyric was not only the adulatory 1956 catch-phrases which he showered on Dr. Williams, but his lament that he is the last survivor of that original young brigade. When Kamal told Dr. Williams, "Like a modern Moses you resolved to lead your people out of the house of bondage",[21] he may well have been aware that when Moses quit the scene the Israelites were still in the wilderness. He may also have been aware of the politically disconcerting tendency, which Dr. Williams shares with the Biblical cross-country walker, of disappearing for long periods from the people, to talk to his personal god, then descending from Sinai with a shining face and a mouth full of divinely inspired rhetoric to dazzle their eyes and puzzle their minds with strange new laws. This time, the long sojourn on Monkey Mountain has produced *From Columbus to Castro* and the new Charter, "the most profound concept in contemporary political, social and economic thought."

The real point of Kamal's speech was his consciousness of the fact that with the New Year reshuffle and the final dismissal of O'Halloran and Montano, the pillars of the business interests in the party, the fact that he was an Indian was the only real reason why he still remained in the cabinet. William Dumas, after all, is the real man in CARIFTA. Kamal, feeling his unimportance to the now empty nest and, perhaps, knowing Dr. Williams' capacity for loneliness and authoritarianism, was fairly lyrical with his praise. The climax to his declaration of loyalty is, however, slightly tinged with self-interest: "I feel a great sense of humility, pride, and thankfulness as the only Minister of Government who is still with you."[22] One wonders which feeling was strongest – humility which the moment required, pride at having survived where even the blue-eyed boys seem to have perished, or gratitude for benefits derived... Kamal's speech was, like *From Columbus to Castro*, more a funeral oration on the passing of the old régime, than a fanfare of welcome to a fresh setting-forth.

The last thing which needs to be commented on is the citation of the party motto – "Great is PNM and it will prevail" – as part of the dedication of the book to the party. This motto, cited in English in the book, is still cited in Latin as well on the front page of the party newspaper – "Magnum est PNM et prevalebit". Few examples of worse taste can be uncovered in the party's unwholesome history than the motto of the party itself. The original Latin motto has the word "veritas" (Truth) which the PNM have replaced by the letters PNM. In other words the implication of the motto is one of Orwellian *1984* absurdity – *The Party is Truth and Truth is the Party*.

Nowadays, with the nation itself daily questioning the credibility of the party, the party's epigraph is beginning to sound like its epitaph, and that of its philosopher-king. It is the fact that the truth prevails which has eroded the moral ground from under the party. It may win further elections, for want of an alternative, but it will be leading no one. In so far as Dr. Williams is concerned, two attitudes seem possible. One is tempted to pass on him the kind of absolute judgement which he has passed on all and sundry in both history and politics. In this respect, a quotation from Acton, quoted in Elsa Goveia's *Historiography*, seems particularly apt:

> A man is justly despised who has one opinion in history, and another in politics, one for abroad and another at home, one for opposition and another for office... [23]

This, however, is too absolute and implies that Acton understood neither history nor politics. The statement does not take into account the capacity of history itself to undermine belief, or of politics to defeat morality. It should not be a matter of indulged contempt, but one of austere silence, that the senior historian of a people, who has found Caribbean history, his own past, absurd, should have himself contributed so richly to the perpetuation of such absurdity. The 1930s generation has run its time, and is slowly taking its place as just another link in the common chain. The 1950s generation will soon begin its mistakes. The people of the forties seem to be quite bewildered, caught as they are between the embarrassing frenzy of an ageing rebel, and the terrific posturing of youth, who also cannot recognise themselves as simple common links in the chain. In the struggle for power which characterises the end of this era, as of any other, what is being lost is the sense of historical continuity. Regrettably, a deficient work such as *From Columbus to Castro* cannot restore it. It will help to integrate neither the people of Trinidad nor of the Caribbean area. If it does by mistake, then we are even more absurd than either Dr. Williams or Naipaul has imagined.

First published in *Tapia No. 11* (Nov. 29, 1970) and *Tapia No. 12* (Dec. 20, 1970). Also published in Coombs, O. (ed.) *Is Massa Day Dead*? (New York: Doubleday /Anchor 1974), pp. 69-108.

References

1. Laurence, K.O., – "Colonialism in Trinidad and Tobago", *Caribbean Quarterly*, Vol. IX, No. 3 (Sept. 1963) p. 53.
2. Goveia, E.V., "New Shibboleths for Old", *New Beacon Reviews No. 1*, (1968) p. 37.
3. Wynter, S., "Reflections on West Indian Writing and Criticism", *Jamaica Journal*, Vol. 2, No. 4, & Vol. 3, No. 1, 1968/1969.
4. Dennis, N., *Jonathan Swift* (London: Weidenfield & Nicholson, 1965), p. 17.
5. Dennis, N., ibid, p. 31.
6. Dennis, N., ibid, p.109.
7. Williams E., *Inward Hunger* (London: Andre Deutch, 1969), p. 46.
8. Williams, E., *My Relations with the Caribbean Commission, 1945-1955*, p. 11.
9. Swift, J., *Gulliver's Travels*, Book 11, Ch, VI.
10. Mellor, G.R., *British Imperial Trusteeship, 1793-1850* (London: Faber 1951), p. 447. N.B. On p. 540 of *From Columbus to Castro*, Williams does mention Mellor's book, with the dry comment that it propounds "the idealist conception of history", a fault of which Williams himself will never be accused; though the ironist, such as Williams is, is quite often a frustrated romantic idealist.
11. Goveia, E.V., op. cit., p. 34.
12. Williams, E., *Massa Day Done* (Port-of-Spain, 1961).
13. Williams, E., *The Negro in the Caribbean* (Washington D. C.: Negro Universities Press, 1942), p. 60.
14. *The West India Committee Circular*, Vol. 69 (1954) p. 48.
15. Naipaul, V.S., *The Middle Passage* (London: Deutsch, 1962).
16. Williams, E., *Education in the British West Indies* (N. Y. 1968), p. 75.
17. Williams, E., ibid. p. 77 (italics mine).
18. Williams, E., ibid. p. 82 (italics mine).
19. Passage from an article by V. S. Naipaul in the *New York Review of Books*, Sept. 3, 1970, quoted by David Renwick in "Why Constantine Resigned", *Sunday Guardian*, Trinidad, Sept. 27, 1970, p. 21.
20. Carnegie, J., "Notes on the History of Jazz & its Role in Jamaica", *Jamaica Journal*, Vol. IV. No. 1, (March 1970), pp. 20-29.
21. *Express*, Trinidad, Thursday Sept. 3, 1970, p. 5.
22. Ibid.
23. Goveia, E.V., *A Study on the Historiography of the British West Indies* (Mexico, 1956), p.174.

LITERATURE AND THE FOLK

George Lamming, in an attempt to grasp the meaning and implications of the new West Indian writing of the 1950s, wrote in *The Pleasures of Exile:*

> The West Indian novel, by which I mean the novel written by the West Indian about the West Indian reality, is hardly twenty years old. And here is the fascination of the situation. The education of all these writers is more or less middle-class Western culture, and particularly English culture. But the substance of their books, the general motives and directions, are peasant. One of the most popular complaints made by West Indians against their novelists is the absence of novels about the West Indian middle class.
>
> Why is it that Reid, Mittelholzer in his early work, Selvon, Neville Dawes, Roger Mais, Andrew Salkey, Jan Carew – why is it that their work is shot through with the urgency of peasant life? [...]
>
> Unlike the previous governments and departments of educators, unlike the businessmen importing commodities, the West Indian novelist did not look across the sea to another source. He looked in and down at what had traditionally been ignored. For the first time the West Indian peasant became other than a cheap source of labour. He became, through the novelist's eye, a living existence, living in silence and joy and fear, involved in riot and carnival. It is the West Indian novel that has restored the West Indian peasant to his true and original status of personality.[1]

Here, Lamming recognises three kinds of people. First there are the middle-class educated colonials, whom he later describes as having been educated "for the specific purpose of sneering at anything which grew, or was made on native soil".[2] Secondly, there are the lower classes, whom he later describes as "a mass of people who were either illiterate, or if not had no connection whatever to literature since they were too poor or too tired to read."[3] The third set of people are the new novelists, who, middle class in education and sometimes in background, chose to write, not about their group, but about the broad masses of the poor and untutored, whom Lamming terms the "peasants".

Later on, Lamming describes writers like Samuel Selvon and Vic Reid as "essentially peasant": "they never really left the land".[4] They write about and relate to a people, a definable community, authenticating their fiction with the rhythms of peasant speech. In this respect they are worlds apart from the contemporary metropolitan writer, who generally has no people to relate to, or speak about, "only large numbers of dwellers, vagrant or settled vaguely somewhere".

Here then, was the beginning of a theory about the "folk" in West Indian literary criticism, and about the relation of West Indian writers to their roots. Lamming's description of the "peasant" in the West Indies corresponds to Redfield's sociological definition of the "folk" type of society:

> Such a society is small, isolated, non-literate, and homogenous with a strong sense of group solidarity. The ways of living are conventionalised into that coherent system which we call "a culture." Behaviour is traditional, spontaneous, uncritical and personal; there is no legislation or habit of experiment and reflection for intellectual ends. Kinship, its relations and institutions, are the type of categories of experience and the familiar group is the unit of action. The sacred prevails over the secular; the economy is one of status rather than of the market.[6]

Redfield deliberately makes his definition of the "folk" absolute, because his purpose is to provide a sociological abstract, a theoretical society from whose imaginary pole social change could be measured. The abstract polar opposite to a "folk" society was an equally theoretical "urban" society. Real societies were seen as being in a process of movement somewhere along a continuum which extends from the "folk" to the "urban".

Lamming in his concept of the "peasant" society and the writers' relationship to it, and in the contrast which he points out between the West Indian and the metropolitan writer, is hinting at similarly abstract and absolute poles of "folk" and "urban". He does not, however, go far enough towards indicating that the real problem lies in capturing the complex movement of individuals and societies caught in the fluid continuum between the theoretically "peasant" and the theoretically "urban". Had he done so, he would have expressed less surprise at the fact that middle-class writers were preoccupied with lower-class people in defiance of earlier traditions of West Indian behaviour. It is clear that these writers, among whom can be included Lamming himself, had recognised a certain fluidity in their societies, which at times made it difficult to define differences between classes, behaviour, attitudes, language and other categories of sociological definition. Or rather, they had realised that genuine writing about the West Indies involved a grasp of how people, classes and attitudes interlocked at times, and retained their distinctness at others.

It is also possible to see the West Indian peasantry as less passive, inert and invisible than Lamming seems to believe they were before the advent of the West Indian novelist. Sewell, in the mid-nineteenth century, saw the peasants as people who were struggling successfully to maintain the spirit of emancipation, and to establish a certain independence from the plantation system.[7] Woodville Marshall, a Barbadian historian, has made the point that, for over a century since emancipation, the growing West Indian peasantry have been somewhat more than a cheap source of labour, as the stereotype invites us to see. Long before the novelist had even acknowledged his existence, the peasant had been working steadily, and against tremendous odds, towards an essential independence. The presence and "living existence" of the peasant found its earliest incarnation not in literature, as Lamming claims, but in what the peasant himself had, without benefit of middle-class intellect, been able to build for himself.

> Peasant activity modified the character of the original pure plantation economy and society. The peasants were the innovators in the economic life of the community. Besides producing a greater quality and variety of subsistence food and livestock they introduced new crops and/or reintroduced old ones. This diversified the basically monocultural pattern...
>
> The peasants initiated the conversion of these plantation territories into modern societies. In a variety of ways they attempted to build local self-generating communities. They founded villages and markets; they built churches and schools; they clamoured for extension of educational facilities, for improvements in communication and markets; they started the local cooperative movement.[8]

Marshall concludes that "peasant development was emancipation in action". His article, published in 1968, reveals that the role and contribution of the peasant had been under review since the late nineteenth century, and had preoccupied Caribbean scholarship since the late 1930s,[9] as well as having provided a few of the writers in the thirties with a subject.[10] The peasants themselves and their political leaders rebelled throughout the thirties, their efforts for self-definition extending into the seminal Guyanese situation of 1953. Not only the peasants, of course, were involved in those political upheavals, yet people like Butler and Jagan derived a large measure of support from agricultural workers in cane and rice, as well as from workers in industry and the unemployed of the towns. The point that I am trying to make here is that it was not simply the isolated efforts of the novelists, which in Lamming's words "restored the West Indian peasant to his true and original status of personality", but rather the efforts of the West Indian people as a whole which provided a dynamic powerful enough to charge the writers of the fifties. The writers expressed an awareness which had been there for some time, and on various levels; *reflecting* rather than *restoring* whatever finer quality had been immemorially there in the creative struggle, rebellion and movement of the West Indian people.

There are hints that Lamming sensed that the matter was far more complex than he could state it outside his novels. For example, he distinguishes between the Barbadian, Trinidadian and Jamaican.

> I would say that the Barbadian has much the same relation to Barbados which the Englishman has to England. They both have an inordinate pride in the look and feel of the land they call theirs. In the case of the

Barbadian I think I know the reason. The size of the island and the incredible density of the population has created his relation to the soil. To a Barbadian every square inch of land should be planted up.[11]

This contact with the land as a source of life from day to day is not evident in the Trinidadian. Trinidadians don't have that kind of land pride at all. The Jamaicans have it, but in a different way from the Barbadians.[12]

These two statements imply that one simplifies when one speaks of the West Indian writer and the West Indian peasantry without taking into account important variations and differences within each island, as well as between island and island. Also, the Indian peasantry in Trinidad manifest the land pride of peasants anywhere, and are to be distinguished from either the Afro-Creoles or the Indo-Creoles of Port-of-Spain. Since Selvon writes with equal facility about both types, it is a simplification to see him as essentially peasant, or as one who "never really left the land". Similarly, Mais's people are more normally the dispossessed of the towns, than peasants attached to the land. Sandwiched between the lane and the gully in their barrack houses, they have no land. What is important is Mais's ability to suggest that they are able to reconstruct a community in spite of the harshness of their experience, that the fragments of communal experience knit into a single tragedy, character flowing into character, as if the entire group were a single person. This accounts for both the fragmentation of form in The *Hills Were Joyful Together* and for the way Mais contrives to blend the disparate voices and modes into a single weighty philosophising voice. The nature of the society which Mais has to explore inspires a quest for form. The need to suggest the dichotomy of fragmentation and communion, expresses itself in the movement of the novel between anecdote and pseudo-philosophical chorus.

A similar thing happens in Lamming's *In the Castle of My Skin*, which would be very inadequately interpreted, indeed, were it to be seen as Lamming's treatment of the Barbadian peasantry, and nothing more. The book is about "the uncertain light one feels in the passage from sleep to conscious waking". Both the narrator and the society are in this process. Paradoxically, the narrator's growth in consciousness, in addition to his colonial education, results in a steady growth away from the land. Apart from naming his world, then, or capturing the stasis and continuity of an essential "peasant" society, Lamming is exploring the dichotomy of alienation and commitment, as well as the predicament of the exile of the intellectual from his remembered roots, which is central to West Indian literature.

As with Mais, Lamming's exploration resulted in formal fragmentation on the one hand, and in choric integrative passages on the other, this fluidity of form reflecting, one feels, something of the fluid variety of the West Indian personality. Consider some of the variety of narrative methods employed: There is a semi-autobiographical first person narration, which provides a skein of chronological narrative around which the rest of the book is constructed. There is a narrator whose function is partly to name a society which has not been named before, by constantly describing the village, its people and customs, or analysing the social structure of an impoverished colonial society. Most of these things are well done, although there is a tendency to overstate, in the manner of early Conrad, say, who Lamming says was one of his literary forebears. There is anecdote, especially in Chapter Six, which reveals early understanding of the oral tradition that still exists throughout the Caribbean. Then there are passages of choric writing, as in Chapter Four, where the Old Man and the Old Woman, examples of both continuity and a dying past, last survivors and yet ancestral voices, give the book an almost mythic dimension. In Chapter Ten, the separate voices merge into the single ancestral voice of the Old Man, who speaks in a dream. It is a lyrical meditative passage, whose theme is history, the entire historical process whose results Lamming has been portraying in the book. Here the Old Man, who has faded into an ancestral voice, is a persona for the author himself, who is delving back to roots within and beyond the village, while he warns the coming generation against sentimental self-identification with the African past.

The total effect of *In the Castle of My Skin* is one of growth and motion within a context of timelessness. The villagers seem to remain in a sleep, the stasis of colonialism, arrested history, arrested growth. The theme of sleep which pervades the book is important. As in a dream, all the characters are fragments of a single consciousness, so that character eventually flows into character, voice into voice, and all voices, natives of author's person, meet and melt into the single voice of history which speaks in Chapter Ten, outlining the past and warning against the future. Yet the village and the main narrator have both moved in spite of all the stasis; and the word has been spoken, the silence, symbol of colonial unconsciousness, has been shattered. There are all kinds of flaws in the work, mainly those of vagueness, heaviness, and a frequent insistence, but Lamming, like Mais, seems to have understood the need for an elaborate architecture, various enough to express that fluidity of personality which we have indicated is the product of a society in the continuum of movement between the "folk" and the "urban" poles.

Kamau Brathwaite in his early essays also probed the relationship between the West Indian writer and the "folk". At times, his usage of the term "folk" was as inadequate as Lamming's usage of the term "peasant". Indeed, sociologists and anthropologists seem themselves to have been in the throes of a debate as to the viability of the concepts of "folk" and "urban", and as to whether they were at all useful for the analysis of social change.[13] In an early article published in *Bim*, "Sir Galahad and the Islands", Brathwaite indicates a broad contrast between the "folk" and the "middle classes"; but finer distinctions are made in a paragraph contrasting the responses of Eric Roach and Derek Walcott.

> He (Roach) is in possession of a fact, a feeling that aligns him with "folk", with peasant tradition. This is the point of difference, too, between Roach and the 'Emigrants'. While Lamming's and Selvon's folk-sources are the city and the urban village, Roach's values are peasant values: acceptance, a sense of tradition.[14]

Brathwaite is at this point looking at Walcott's despair and terror at the poverty and barrenness of lower-class life on his island, and his sense of bitter helplessness in the face of this fact. Roach, who goes beyond despair, is able to do so because of his peasant roots. (Roach grew up on a Tobago homestead). One wonders, though, whether this is not too much of a simplification. Walcott describes his boyhood poignantly[15] and with an almost vehement intensity[16] as having been that of one whose circumstances were hardly better than those of the folk. Yet as a Methodist in a Catholic country, coloured among a black people, and "middle class" among the poor, he was classed and felt himself as an outsider. He fought hard, he said, to learn a love for a people whose hardy independence and reticence kept the stranger out. So like Joyce's Stephen Dedalus, one of his adolescent heroes, Walcott wavered between despair at the comprehensive penury of his world; courage to learn love and create; and a desire to impose on colonial squalor the remote mythology of the Greeks. His best work explores this schizophrenia, and his references to the "folk", or the "people" have generally been ambivalent. It is possible that if Walcott felt a greater sense of belonging, he would be a less interesting or corrosive poet. He would lose his wound, his despair, and his theme.

Brathwaite, while he identifies the "folk" as the peasants, also speaks of Selvon's "folk-sources" as "the city and the urban village". Here are three concepts: folk, city and, strangest of all, urban village. Yet it is not a simple matter of confusion, because in the West Indies all possible categories intersect, so that in the midst of a harsh experience in Jamaica, religious cultism flourishes, and identifiably folk genres fertilise the mainstream of urban music. West Indian society is in fluid motion, and often oscillation between the two extremes poles of the folk-urban continuum makes it difficult to define one's terms.

In his 1960 article, "The New West Indian Novelists", Brathwaite seems better to have grasped the complexity of the situation. There he notes Selvon's versatility, and senses the limitation of the term "folk" as a category in which Selvon's people can be placed. Selvon, he now sees, was writing about at least three different kinds of people. First there were "the folk, the East Indian peasantry in Trinidad", who appear in *A Brighter Sun* (1952), *Turn Again Tiger* (1958), a short story such as "Cane is Bitter", and the recent novel *The Plains of Caroni* (1970). Secondly, there are stories whose achievement is the "racy, humorous celebration of Trinidad's city-slickers found now both in Port of Spain and on the Portobello Road." Stories such as "Down The Main", "Wartime Activities", "Calypsonian", and a novel such as *The Lonely Londoners* or *The Housing Lark* fall into this category. Thirdly, there is "the soul-searching of *An Island is a World,* best seen, perhaps, in that novel, and in the story "My Girl and the City". To this may be added "Little Drops of Water", a short but very significant piece which appeared in *Bim,* 1967. There Selvon confesses to an exhaustion of creative talent, and at the same time attempts to articulate the meagre alternatives open to a writer whose world is withering into emptiness.

In *A Brighter Sun* Selvon examines the rapid semi-urbanisation of the village of Barataria during the years of the Second World War, and the corresponding emergence of the Indian peasant in a creolised culture. This he does by tracing a gradual expansion of the consciousness of Tiger, the central figure of the novel, and by understanding that the movement from a "folk" to a "semi-urban" situation is paralleled by subtle shifts in language.

Tiger's father is one of the last group of indentured labourers whose first language is Hindi, and whose Creole is cryptic, and entirely functional. Here, for example, he maps out Tiger's entire destiny in three curt sentences:

> "You gettam house which side Barataria, gettam land, cow – well, you go live dat side. Haveam plenty boy chile – girl chile no good, only bring trouble on yuh head. You live dat side, plantain garden, live good" (p. 7).

Tiger's speech oscillates between an early syntax pretty close to his father's to the free-flowing articulacy in Trinidad dialect, characteristic of the urban Creole, the linguistic continuum parallelling the sociocultural one.[18] Early in the book, in one of his many statements about manhood, Tiger says:

> "To my wife, I man when I sleep with she. To *bap,* I man if I drink rum. But to me, I no man yet" (p. 45).

This is not quite the syntax of the fully urbanised Creole. Tiger senses that part of the problem of adjusting to the changes in his society and status, and also of his quest for significance, is one of creating a language supple enough to deal with the growing complexities which accompany his loss of rural innocence. He undertakes this task in the traditional fashion of Creole Trinidad. Painfully learning to read, he creates a language of polysyllabic words culled from a dictionary, by means of whose impressive sound he seeks to assert the manhood which he believes is eluding him all the time. This makeshift language, analogous to the "signifying" of American Blacks, has been ritualised by the Carnival masqueraders in Trinidad called the Midnight Robbers.[19]

Tiger senses, or is made to feel by the ridicule he occasions, that "robber talk" is a false, or at least an inadequate language in which to conduct his quest for manhood, and one of the barriers towards self-liberation is overcome when he rejects his fabricated speech for one which genuinely expresses how he feels. In a splendid scene towards the end of the book, Tiger has occasion to reprimand two doctors, a Negro and an Indian, both of whom have refused to come out on a rainy night to attend to his wife.

> "I is a Trinidadian like yourself, and it was a white man who had come to poor Tiger hut to see he wife, while you and that other nasty coolie man who say he is a doctor too didn't want to come." (p. 188)

The passage is interesting for a number of reasons. Firstly, Tiger himself, through his very West Indian belief that manhood lies in beating his woman, has brought on his wife's illness after a particularly brutal and wrong-headed beating. He thus exposes himself to the equally brutal callousness of the Trinidadian doctors. Secondly, the phrase "nasty coolie man", a colonial epithet which has its parallel in phrases such as "black-and-ugly" or "stupid ole nigger" shows the keenness of Selvon's ear and the completeness of his control. It is precisely the phrase which a Negro might have used in abusing an Indian. Hence an ironic twist is given to the phrase "I is a Trinidadian like yourself". It means that the creolisation process is partly an exercise in colonial self-contempt, even when one is in the act of claiming one's rights as a full citizen.

The complexities of the Creolisation process were reflected in the insistent theme of race and racism, in the calypsos of the forties, the period which Selvon is covering in *A Brighter Sun*. On the one hand, there were a few people who viewed these calypsos as a sign of emerging nationhood. The politician Albert Gomes was one of these. In one of several articles on the calypso, he wrote:

> While so much of us are oblivious of the fact, the calypso singer has begun to announce in his songs that our ethnic "potpourri" is a reality, and that its many pots have begun to pour one into the other. The welding of our polyglot community is taking place before our eyes in the "tents" and the weddings of our culture are being celebrated right there. Indian and Chinese tunes are being woven into the fabric of our calypso, and as though to give formal acceptance to yet another fact that should be obvious, the jumping jive, the samba, the conga and the rhumba are becoming part of the music of the tent.[20]

More recently Albert Gomes, who has for many years been residing in England, seems to have revised this simplistic reduction of the Creolisation process to a fairly pleasant melting-pot experience. He sees himself as having been defeated by the "maze of colour" and racial prejudice which, he now says, had grown more and more pronounced from the late thirties to the late fifties – from Uriah Butler of 1937, to Eric Williams of 1956.[21] At least the later assessment, whatever it omits in its discussion of Gomes's political demise, does not simplify the complexities of the Creolisation process.

Neither did the calypsonians of the forties, whose songs reflected, if they did not analyse, the frequent harshness of the process of acculturation. Calypsonians mocked at Indians, Chinese, Baptists, Barbadians; sang about the lack of morals in white society; castigated Trinidad women for going out with American soldiers, even when, at times, they themselves were prepared to exist off the earnings to such women. In other words, calypsonians, the most extreme products of the process of urbanisation, provided a sounding-board by which all "intruders" on the urban scene were placed. Licensed eccentrics themselves, they mocked at what they saw as the eccentricity of others. This mockery, which took the form of "picong", a kind of wit based on caricature, reductive sarcasm and at times good humour, was a *rite de passage,* which ensured that creolisation took place on the basis approved by the urban Creoles themselves.

Hence, references to Indians and Chinese tended to be reductive, to stress existing stereotypes. Hindi and "Indian" melodies were mocked in the calypso. For the Indian peasant, the processes of urbanisation and acculturation tended to merge. Calypsonians noted this with what seems to have been scorn. Killer, for example, a calypsonian of the forties, noted the process of acculturation in Indians who rejected their Indian names:

> What's wrong with these Indian people
> As though their intention is for trouble
> Long ago you'd meet an Indian by the road
> With his capra waiting to take people load
> But I notice there is no Indian again
> Since the women and them taking Creole name
> Long ago was Sumintra, Ramnaliwia,
> Bullbasia and Oosankilia,
> But now is Emily, Jean and Dinah
> And Doris and Dorothy.

The prostitution unleashed on entire villages with the Yankee occupation of Trinidad during the war is noted with the usual cynicism. The calypsonian seems to envy the Indian women even their success as goodtime girls. In this field, too, the Indian was regarded as an outsider.

> Long ago you hadn't a chance
> To meet an Indian girl in a dance
> But nowadays it is big confusion
> Big fighting in the road for their Yankee man
> And you see them in the market, they ain't making joke
> Pushing down nigger people to buy their pork
> And you see them in the dances in Port-of-Spain
> They wouldn't watch if you call an Indian name

What one notes here is that the calypsonian is seeing Port of Spain as the centre of his activities, and regarding the Indian as a new arrival on the scene, who must be levelled. What is also interesting is that in

LITERATURE AND THE FOLK

mocking at the Indian, the calypsonian also reveals his own self-contempt, or lack of a self-image. While he notes the loss of name and customs among Indians in the city, he can still use the insulting epithet to refer to his own people, the "nigger people". This is exactly what is happening to Selvon's Tiger in *A Brighter Sun*. Several calypsos can be used as examples of what was happening during the forties as regards creolisation and race relations. Only one more will be cited. In "Moonia", sung by the Mighty Dictator, a courtship between an Indian girl and a Creole (Negro) is the theme.

> Well, I was in love with an Indian
> I was born in Jerningham Junction
> I couldn't see
> Eye to eye with her family
> So she said, "Me likes de kissing
> And dat Kilwal (creole) hugging and squeezing"
> The courtship stall
> When her mother jump up and bawl…
> "Aow yah! Ah beti! Aow yah! Moonia, Moonia
> Bap na like am Kilwali Moonia…"

The mother raises valid objections, by pointing out that the Indian peasant, Ramlogan, can offer cattle, a house and a reasonable match, while the Creole, (urban and most probably unemployed) offers nothing.

> Well, de mother jump up and mention
> "This is the height of provocation
> How baytee
> Coulda likam dat Kilwani?"
> She say "You know, Ramlogan house gat cattle
> The Kilwal can't gie am nutten."
> Beti a cry
> "Kilwal plantin' me garden, Mai"

And the father raises the final objection, with which the Creole seems half to agree. The Negro, he says, can offer only sexuality, which his "fast" daughter seems to value above all things.

> Arguing with her mother
> Her father jump in the picture
> Before my eyes
> He started to criticise
> This time he said, "What matter baytee?
> That kilawal […………] like donkey
> You gattam speed
> So you likeam dat nigger breed."

This transcription of the calypso is not word perfect. There are several places where the recording is unclear, and others where the calypsonian mocks at Indian accent and "Hindi", the dotted line being one of them.

What is clear is the unillusion of the calypsonian about the process of racial contact. Selvon, like the calypsonian, is clear about the implications of Tiger's "advance" from "Indian" to "citizen". He retains a fair detachment throughout the story, but would have shared Tiger's rejection of the false values of the Port of Spain city slickers. On the other hand, he does not reject the process of creolisation per se, as does, for example, V.S. Naipaul's Ralph Kripalsingh, anti-hero of *The Mimic Men,* who sees creolisation as holding the horror of miscegenation, as violation of Aryan purity. Selvon seems to view history and change as things which one must accept. In so far as Tiger does arrive at a solution for his existential problems it is this:

> "You don't start over things in life... you just have to go on from where you stop. It not as if you born all over again. Is the same life" (p. 209).

Much has been made of the calypso, mainly because in the calypso one has a permanent record not only of the passing phases of humour in Trinidad, but of how language was spoken, of the spirit of "ole talk", "picong", "mamaguy", abuse, from decade to decade. Selvon, in his stories about Port of Spain urban/Creole life, is relating to the same tradition of style and rhetoric which produced calypsonians like the legendary Spoiler, Wonder, Panther, Melody, Lion, Tiger, Invader, Atilla, Kitchener, Beginner and Dictator, all figures of the forties. These artists had a special language which involved heightening the mundane and humdrum into melodrama, or "bacchanal" as it is normally called. Gesture and mime reinforced speech. The language of the city was also the language of the small-time confidence trickster, the Brer Anansi figure who so often appears in Selvon's fiction, and whose method is to spin words fast enough to ensnare his victim, or, in the case of the calypsonian, to "captivate" his audience.

Selvon brilliantly captures the language of the Port of Spain *ole talk* in this passage about taxi-drivers, which appears in *A Brighter Sun:* The breathless prose, quicksilver fluidity of the passage can be compared with an excellent short story by Daniel Samaroo Joseph, called "Taxi Mister"[22], or calypsos such as Lord Melody's "Peddlars", or Panther's "Taxi-Drivers".

> 'Boy, dese taximen does have tings their own way too much. Some of dem does tell you dey leaving right away, and wen yuh get in de car, is because dey making rounds all Charlotte Street for more passengers, and wat yuh cud do? Nothing, because yuh in de car already. As for wen dey going down south! Boy, dat is trouble self. All dem touts by de railway station, from de time dey see yuh wid a grip in yuh hand, dey start hustling. "South, mister?" "Yuh going south? Look ah nice car here – it have radio. Leaving right away. South direct." And dis time, de smart driver have 'bout three tout sitting down, quiet as if dey is passengers (p. 86).

To clinch the point about Selvon's relation to an oral tradition of the streets, the urban "lime", the calypso (Selvon has a story called "Calypsonian"), I'll just quote bits of Panther's "Taxi-Drivers":

> You may be standing on any pavement
> Asking someone questions on the government
> All you see is taxis in a line
> And all you do is answering questions all the time...
>
> CHORUS
> An is Peeep – One to go
> You shake your head, you tell them no
> Braaaw – they blow again
> You shake your head you tell them no again
>
> And is, San Juan, Tunapuna, Arima, Sangre Grande...
> Madam, you going? I am de fellar who give you a lift in Toco last week ... You can't remember me?
> And they pointing their finger all over the place
> Somebody have a right to spit in their face.
>
> This happen to me up by Globe Theatre
> Ole talking, meself and the Tiger
> Tell you the truth I didn't want no taxi,
> In long and in short I was going to matinee
> Man, up comes a taxi driver
> "Panther! You going Point Cumana?"
> "Whe ah going deh for? I ain't got no fishing boat"
> He take a knife and nearly cut away me throat
>
> An is Peeep – One to go
> You shake your head, you tell them no
> Braaaw – they blow again
> You shake your head you tell them no again
>
> He say. "Panther, you're a old calypsonian I know along time. You mean to say when I want to go to Carenage you won't go wid me/ Whe is it at all? Anywhere you going ah carrying you Diego Martin, Four Roads, Tamana Buccoo Point, Uphill... any way at all..."
>
> Ah say, "You could be going down to Devil's Bay
> Leave me here! I ain't going no way."

The section in prose is spoken rapidly in the tones of the hustler above the rhythm of the calypso. The calypsonian regards the taximan as yet another smart man, who is using language against the citizen, rather than one who is trying to make a living. The language, an abstract from the language of the streets, is little different from Selvon's dramatic prose. Both Selvon and Panther relate to an oral tradition, but in this case it is a different tradition from that of the Trinidad folksong, say, having grown out of the process of acculturation in the town.

Since the epithet "folk" has been most insistently applied to the work of Selvon, one feels justified in spending the most time on it, to point out its variety, and consequently the inadequacy of the term. In *The Lonely Londoners*, the slickers of Port of Spain find themselves in a real city at last, the very centre of the Empire on which the sun seldom rises. It is in London that they realise the smallness of Port of Spain. There is a passage in *The Lonely Londoners* where Galahad is waiting for his girl in a subway where there is a huge clock which can tell what time it is in every capital city of the world. He looks for Trinidad to find out what time it is in Port of Spain, and succeeds in finding it only with the greatest difficulty. The point is well made, since Galahad regards this date as the first of his great achievements in conquering the big city. The passage symbolises the central encounter in the book between the parochial consciousness of the West Indians, and the vast chaos of London. Galahad, no doubt, may seem as insignificant and out of place in London as Port of Spain appears besides the great cities of the world. Yet Trinidad time is going to be imposed on the ponderous rhythms of Big Ben.

The "boys", as Selvon calls his innocents abroad, reconstruct the "lime" and the language of the "lime", and through imposing their language on the great city, they remake it in their own image. Sometimes they shrink it by the use of a reductive simile. Hoary Paddington slums reveal walls which are cracking "like the last days of Pompeii". The winter sun, symbol of the devitalised misery of megalopolis, is "like a force-ripe orange". The "boys", who have originated from a world of language, recreate in the big city a world of words in which they move, and through which they grope for clarity in the midst of experience as bewildering and vague as the London fog.

In a sense, catapulted into a strange world, their experience is as strange as was Tiger's in *A Brighter Sun*. They face a similar process of having to make sense of a bewildering milieu; like Tiger, the Creoles begin to ask questions about existence itself, about identity and manhood. But the "boys" remain fragmented, partial personalities. They continue to be identifiable in terms of idiosyncrasy; they have nicknames, not real names. Perhaps nicknames are an acknowledgement of individual richness of personality, but they are also suggestive of an incompleteness of self. This is definitely the case in Naipaul's *Miguel Street*, which seems to owe much to early Selvon. In *The Lonely Londoners*, it is the group that has a full self, that faces the wilderness and survives; not to belong is to be lost in the void.

The term "the boys" begins to gain weight as the book proceeds. It indicates not only the strange pre-moral innocence which Selvon's people seem to preserve wherever they are, but a certain immaturity, which persists because these calypsonians refuse to awaken to responsibility, even under the weight of metropolitan pressures. Thus Selvon contrasts Galahad's "grandcharge" (bluff) with Moses's growing gloom; the seemingly eternal youth of the group, with Moses's sense of time and inanition; their irresponsibility, with Moses's weight of life, the burden of consciousness which he has just barely begun to assume, as he absorbs each man's folly, failure and momentary triumph.

By the end of the book, Moses sounds more like Sergeant Pepper than the calypsonian Lord Kitchener. He is singing the genuine urban blues. He sees laughter as part of a tragic process. Like a Wilson Harris consciousness (it seems inadequate to speak of a Harris "character") he feels the weight of each man's experience.

> Sometimes listening to them, he look in each face, and he feel a great compassion for every one of them, as if he live each of their lives, one by one, and all the strain and stress come to rest on his own shoulders.

It is no accident that the boys gather at Moses's place "every Sunday morning... like if it is confession." Moses by the end of the book has a high priest's role: he greets the new arrivals and tries, reluctantly, in contrast to his Biblical namesake, to guide them through the wilderness. But near the end of the book, one sees him on the banks of the Thames, contemplating the aimlessness of things. Here, his function is similar to that of Lamming's Old Man in *In the Castle of My Skin*, in that he becomes a repository for group consciousness, a sort of archetypal old man, a Tiresias-figure. Is it accident or design that this technique of moving from a fragmentary form where several voices share the stage, to a point where all the voices are blended either in chorus as in Mais's *Brother Man,* or into the single representative voice of an archetypal figure, has occurred in all of these early writers? And what about the technique as it appears in Brathwaite's trilogy? How much is owed there to the structure of T.S. Eliot's *The Waste Land*, and how much to the instinctive groping for an architecture, appropriate to expressing the crucial tensions in West Indian societies between the group and the privacy of the individual soul, which these early writers seem to have done?

A continuum exists between a living oral tradition and a growing scribal one in the West Indies. It relates to the continuum which exists between the various West Indian Creoles and Standard West Indian English. Most West Indian writers seem to enter this continuum at several points. Selvon, for example, bridges the gap between oral and scribal traditions. When his works are read aloud to a group, and there is interplay between narrator and audience, they yield up ironies and subtleties which one can miss when simply reading the words on the page. There is a tendency in certain quarters to undervalue an oral tradition and the sort of criticism which it demands of the critic. Criticism of works which are meant to be performed can never be purely literary criticism, although it may borrow some of its methods. Louise Bennett's poetry, for example, depends so much on tones of voice, on the fluidity of the voice as it breaks out of the strict metrical limitations of the quatrain, that one ought to comment on the words in audible motion, rather than in their comparatively frozen form on the page.

A fair proportion of Brathwaite's poetry falls into this category. Since I have discussed his work extensively elsewhere,[23] I won't bother to do so now. I'd like instead to consider the work of Louise Bennett.

Mervyn Morris[24] and Rex Nettleford[25] have both written important essays in an attempt to begin discussion on Louise Bennett, while Dennis Scott interviewed her for *Caribbean Quarterly*.[26] In this necessarily brief enquiry, comparisons will be drawn, wherever possible, between the poems of Ms. Bennett and calypsos from Trinidad which treat the same, or similar themes. In this way, it may be possible to probe similarities and differences between the "urban" male mentality in Trinidad, and the "urban-folk" mentality of one of the most formidably accomplished women in Jamaica. Tentative insights may also be gained into the different positions occupied by two different sets of West Indian people, along the folk-urban continuum. Since, ultimately, the problem is in each case one of language, some comment will be attempted on the linguistic aspect of the issue.

From the very start of her career as an artist in the late 1930s, Louise Bennett decided to work in dialect, despite the initial discomfort, and even dislike, she occasioned in the middle class. She seems to have had a clear idea of her ends and, as early as 1944 in "Bans O' Killing", wrote a poetic defence of the language of her choice.

Her argument was that dialect and an oral tradition have provided the very basis of English Literature itself: that part of the process of self-acceptance was acceptance of one's most intimate language. The final stanza is a piece of verbal sleight of arm, very similar indeed to the method of several calypsonians, beginning with the Mighty Spoiler (Theophilus Philip), one of the masters of the late forties and the fifties. Louise Bennett is able to identify the precise quality of absurdity in the educated colonial arriviste, who assumes the accent and the accent-snobbery of the coloniser.

> And mine how you deh-read dem English
> Book deh pon yuh shelf
> For ef yuh drop a "h" yuh mighta
> Haffe kill yuhself.

The play on words (s [h] elf, sell) is brilliant, summarising the argument in the entire poem. Charlie, who wants to "kill" dialect, is in fact so unsure of himself in his acquired accent that he has to be forever on guard, lest he lapse into the old (natural) manner of speaking, and betray his lower-class background to the new world of arrivistes in which he seeks a place. Social, as well as artistic liberation, Ms. Bennett is saying, ultimately depends on self-acceptance. In her work, one recognises a consistent and intelligent attack on class and colour snobbery, especially in their linguistic dimension. The scanty critical attention which, according to Morris and Nettleford she has received, is probably the result, not only of middle-class Philistinism in the West Indies, but of the inability of the "Afro-Saxon" mind to dare understand the corrosive quality of Ms. Bennett's humour. They preferred to accept her as a "coon" entertainer, satire being, in a paraphrase of Swift, a glass wherein each man recognises everybody else's face.

The energy which sustained Ms. Bennett throughout her thirty years of almost unbroken and dedicated devotion to her art as poet, raconteur of Anansi stories,[27] actress and folklorist, could scarcely have derived from the educated or monied "middle classes". They were concerned with maintaining position and stereotypes – and few societies are more deeply encrusted with stereotyping than ex-slave societies which need to maintain their semi-feudal rigidity, or accept the possibility of a too rapid levelling-off. Louise Bennett, on the other hand, was primarily concerned with shattering stereotypes; with making the language of the people into a tool which could penetrate the barriers of colour and class, or at least point out their absurdity. It is, perhaps, for this reason that in her interview with Dennis Scott, she refused to be categorised.

> *Scott*: Your position in this country, it seems to me, Louise, is that of a middle-class professional entertainer. Or perhaps "professional entertainer of the middle-classes".
> *Bennett*: Oh, never that.
> *Scott*: Who then do you speak for in your poetry, and who do you speak to?
> Bennett: I think I speak to all Jamaica. In a performance, for instance – I don't want to talk about my *writing* – a large cross-section of the community from the Governor-General to the man in the street can react to the lines and the situations I present. So I can't feel that I belong to any class or that I write for any class.[28]

Scott, it seems to me, in attempting to describe the crucial relationship between the West Indian writer and his/her world, has allowed himself to be trapped in the very categories which, we have been saying, the very existence of the writer challenges. Ms. Bennett, on the other hand, seems to be arguing for what we have described as a fluid process of interlocked relationships, a continuum flowing between the various polar opposites which, for the sake of examining West Indian experience, can be imagined to exist.

On the other hand, Ms. Bennett's claim ("I can't feel that I belong to any class or that I write for any class") needs to be examined. Do the various types of people respond to her work in the same way, or does she, in spite of the supposed "limitations" of dialect, manage to make her appeal at various levels? If so, how does she do this? Such an enquiry will involve, in the first place, an examination of her people and their milieu and, secondly, an appreciation of the way in which she handles her masks, seeming to merge her voice with those of her personnae, while she retains such distance as is necessary to the pursuit of her central purpose.

Louise Bennett's people are largely semi-illiterates, caught in various stages of the transition from village to city. Had her formative years been the sixties rather than the thirties, she may well have found laughter difficult, the process of change more violent, and the dislocation caused in the transition from country to town more painful. There is little laughter in the folk-urban sounds of contemporary Kingston.[29] The transition in the thirties was probably less harsh. Or it may simply be that Ms. Bennett's laughter is her final mask. Her people are often bewildered by the rapid changes in their milieu. This deep perplexity is countered and almost concealed by solid common sense and shrewdness, which ignore the broad incomprehensible forces at work in the community, and reduce such intrusions as Mrs. Knibb's mass marriage campaign, a visit from the census taker, the chaos of politics and the remote machinations of Adolf Hitler, to manageable proportions. As we have seen, Selvon is depicting a similar thing in *The Lonely Londoners*. Between the innocents' bewilderment at the complex movement of local and world events, and their rooted understanding of the art of survival in their own little world, lies a wide range of richly comic possibilities, which Ms. Bennett explores.

In order to come to terms with their world, her people need at times to stretch language. Sometimes the result is brilliant. Universal adult suffrage, which does little to alleviate the accumulated ills of the society, is soon renamed "Sufferage". Mrs. Mary Knibb, who seeks to counter illegitimacy with mass marriages, becomes Miss Married Knibbs. Pedestrian crossings become crosses in the frightened gaze of the nervous chauffeur, whose language almost breaks down as he attempts to explain both his fear and his exasperation at the new zebra crossings which force vehicles to halt as pedestrians approach, but place no obligation on the pedestrian to give way to approaching vehicular traffic…

> De crossin a-stop we from pass meck dem cross
> But nutten dah-stop dem from cross meck we pass,
> Dem yah crossin is crosses fo true! ("Pedestrian Crosses" *Jamaica Labrish*, p. 74)

The question of what happens to the language of a people in a state of transition between village and city, who have to face dislocation and adjust abruptly to each new disaster, is one which needs to be investigated. There are sufficient signs in the popular urban responses – reggae, Rastafarianism and the new writing in Jamaica, whose basis is dialect[30] – that dialect is being stretched, both on the part of the educated writer who wants to "ground" with the "sufferers", and on the part of the "dispossessed" who are trying to come to terms with the intolerable. Such a situation will probably lead to the creation of a number of artificial languages whose makeshift improvisations in themselves explore nothing, explain little, but signal that a number of people of goodwill are trying a bridge a gap, seeking to belong. Perhaps, the success of the Jamaican deejay, with his peculiar patter of sound, his ability to link together incongruous phrases, more with a regard for their rhythm than for their sense, and the disarticulated structure of a number of exceedingly popular songs[31] are a sign of this. The immense popularity of people like U Roy, who have helped create a Jamaican equivalent of the jazz "scatting" for which Ella Fitzgerald and Louis Armstrong were famous, may be due to the fact that their destruction of language signals the points where the strain on dialect is too severe, while the vitality of their rhythms reassures the "sufferer" that all coherence is not lost, that life goes on in spite of all.

Louise Bennett seems to have sensed that when societies are in violent transition, sensibility and language, too, partake of the flux. Bewilderment and survival are two of the poles between which her people oscillate. Part of the technique of survival lies in the scuffler's use of language as mask. "Candy-Seller" and "South Parade Peddler" are two of the best examples of this. The higgler adopts the tone of voice which she feels appropriate to each customer, but showers abuses on those who refuse to buy. Examples of such abuse are omnipresent in West Indian fiction dealing with "the people". It is there in the novels, short stories or plays about the barrack-yard, and has been the lifeblood of certain types of calypsos, from the traditional *sans humanité* type, to the picong calypsos sung by modern exponents of the art.[32] A major part of the artillery of abuse in both Louise Bennett and the calypso is the simile. Examples from both make the point better than any exposition: Ms. Bennett's "Cuss-Cuss" is an example of a quarrel between two women, similar to what are called "Woman Bacchanal" calypsos in Trinidad. (The Mighty Duke – Kevin Pope – is the best contemporary exponent of this type of calypso).

> Yuh lip dem hang dung lacka wen
> Mule kean mack up him mine.
>
> Gwan, me an yuh noh combole
> You foot shapeless and lang
> Like smaddy stare far fling dem awn
> Ah meck dem hang awn wrang. ("Cuss-Cuss", p. 189)

The example from calypso is taken from Lord Melody's (Fitzroy Alexander) calypso, "Sparrow's Sister" (1959-1960). It was one of a series of picong calypsos exchanged between the two singers.

> Lie down on me rug
> With she face like a ole hedgehog
> And she smelling just like a swine
> And the hair on she head knottier than mine
> She don't use no underwear
> So imagine whe happening down there
> She so fat she belly lap
> Like a big wasteful bowl of sour pap

That last outrageously appropriate simile points to another quality which the calypsonian shares with Ms. Bennett: skill at caricature. Indeed, in both worlds, people are often defined in terms of their deformities. A long list of these terms exists in *Jamaica Labrish*: "Pulp y'eye Sue" (p. 90), "dry head Emma" (p. 90), "twist-mout Uriah" (p. 92), "nine-toe Berty" (p. 31), "duck-foot Imo knock-knee son" (p. 138). There is, however, a difference in attitude between the matriarchal good humour of Ms. Bennett, and the sort of insistent cruelties one can sometimes find in the calypso. Sharpness there certainly is in Louise Bennett, but little to match the reductive insistence of a calypso such as Lord Shorty's "Fat Pants Fathers", say, which is just part of a long tradition of anti-feminism in calypso.[33]

> This time he daughter face greasy like a fry bake
> She black like the pitch lake
> She hairy like a yam
> And under she arm smell like a uncook ham
> Sometimes worse than a poultry farm.
> She maga and dry, she have cross eye
> and looking stupid and dumb
> And when she open her mouth to smile
> She have in top and bottom plate o'gum.

"Fat Pants Fathers" is about the hypocrisy of retired lechers who are now trying to palm off their shopsoiled daughters as virginal. What is interesting is the excess of the abuse which the calypsonian calls into play in defence of his "manhood". Several calypsos of the early Sparrow are like this.[34] One notices the calypsonian's betrayal of his self-contempt in "She black like the pitch lake".

Louise Bennett's attitude to her people is summarised in the words of one of her personae:

> Lawd, ah pity po' Miss Matty
> But she is a real ole goat ("Hard Time", *Jamaica Labrish*, p. 120).

The difference is one of awareness. Anti-feminist calypsos seem to me to indicate the uncertainty of the male as to where his true manhood lies. Louise Bennett, in contrast, was certain enough about her femininity to mock indulgently at the missionary shortcomings of Mrs. Knibb's efforts at women's liberation ("Mass Wedding", "Bans O'ooman", "Registration").

Another point of contrast between Louise Bennett's work and a representative selection of the work of almost any calypsonian is the high degree of moralising in the former. This moralising is generally reinforced by frequent aphorisms and proverbs. It is really a quality of the religious tradition of the lower classes in Jamaica,[35] and the degree to which this tradition is being retained can be measured in the strong religious content of popular music in Jamaica today.[36] The calypso, on the other hand, is remarkable among New World art forms with African roots, in its almost total divorce from any folk-religious roots. More secular than even the blues, whose relation to the religion of Black America has been pointed out by Le Roi Jones and Charles Keil among others,[37] the calypso has been the result of the incoherent settlement of Trinidad by so many different kinds of people that there was no single religion strong enough to provide a solid moral basis for the kinds of people who created the jamette music of Port of Spain. Moralising calypsos are few, and generally sound thin. When proverbs appear in a Sparrow calypso they are generally wrenched out of context, and made to serve ends which are not necessarily moral. When, for example, Sparrow declares to Trinidad's good-time girls in "Jean and Dinah": "By the sweat of thy brow thou shalt eat bread", he is talking about sexual revenge. The religious undertones of the quotation are all lost.

Louise Bennett's use of the proverb is not always to reinforce a moral tradition. In a poem like "Dutty Tough", for example, the initial proverbs present the issue of the poem in general, and hence universal terms. They also control the structure of the poem, since the rest of the poem is an elucidation or illustration of the paradox which each proverb suggests. The poem begins:

> Sun a-shine but tings no bright
> Doah pot a-bwile, bickle noh nuff,
> River flood but water scarce yaw,
> Rain a-fall but dutty tough.

The third and fourth stanzas provide concrete illustration of the four related proverbs.

> Noh care omuch we dah-work fa
> Hard time still eena we shut,
> We dah-fight, Hard-Time a-beat we
> Dem might raise we wages, but –

> One poun gawn awn pon we pay, an
> We no feel no merriment,
> For ten poun gawn on pon we food
> An ten poun pon we rent.

Then the full implications of the proverbs are revealed in the sixth stanza:

> Cloth, boot, pen an needle gawn up
> Ice, bread, taxes, wata-rate!
> Kersene ile, gasolene, gawn up
> An de poun devaluate.

The poem, then, deals with the phenomenon of inflation/devaluation in the period of postwar depression; the paradox of increased wages and decreased purchasing power. Proverbs such as "River flood but water scarce", or "Rain a-fall but dutty tough", summarise the situation in an economy of language, giving concrete illustration to the abstract ideas of inflation/devaluation, and helping create a bridge of language stretching between the world of educated wage-earners concerned about the "economic situation", and the unlettered "folk" who create proverbs, and are the ultimate victims of economic policy.

It is through poems such as this one that Louise Bennett justifies her statement that she belongs to all classes, or none. It is not that class-barriers cease to exist, even for a moment, but that her art enables her to illustrate their irrelevance. In her best poems, she is able to preserve the mask of a forthright village matriarch who hilariously misinterprets events in the semi-sophisticated world of the town, while including her own sharp and not-too-simple commentary on things like race and politics. Two examples of this will suffice. "Problem" (1947) and "White Pickney" (1949).

In "Problem", she is dealing with the controversy which a film on Jamaica's problems occasioned. Under the guise of delivering a string of platitudes, she is able to suggest the real problems of race, colour and class which exist, and the lack of face, the spiritual nullity of the black/brown middle classes who have the material and educational equipment to deal with them.

> Yuh want dem show fe yuh big-house
> An yuh mota-car! A-oh!
> But dat noh Jamaica Problem?
> Dat a fe yuh poppy show
>
> Is no use wen stranger come, fe
> Sen yuh black gramma go hide,
> An show-off all yuh white gran-
> Pupa photograph wid pride!
>
> For de ole ooman kean hide weh
> An no matta wat yuh do,
> Dem won' se her eena parlour
> But dem se her enna yuh!

Here, it is obviously the "brown" man who is being addressed. The white grandfather is either dead or absent. His presence, which the coloured Jamaican traditionally has valued, is recorded in the photographs, and more visibly in the complexion of his brown-skinned grandson, and the privileges he has inherited of a big house, car, the values of materialism these represent, and the possibility of more rapid promotion than even his black peers. Yet, the brown man's black grandmother is still alive. The child she has borne the white man is, more likely than not, "illegitimate" (according to the white man's moral and civil law, and the blood-pride which he has elevated into natural law).

For the brown arriviste, then, the black grandmother represents a guilt which he prefers to conceal, not because he is particularly concerned with moral values, but because she symbolises the blackness in him, which the inherited slave-society values of race, colour, caste and material gain have taught him to scorn. She is a "problem" only because her grandson refuses to come to terms with the duality of his history, and avoids his own face. But, significantly, she has outlived the grandfather in a most vital sense; she is still there, having never had the opportunity to leave the new world, or return to the old. (Louise Bennett's 1947 poem, "Back to Africa", warns that there is no returning, that the Jamaican must accept his own broken earth, his burnt soil. "Oonoo all bawn dung a Bun grung/Oonoo all is Jamaican" (p. 214)). In other words, the black grandmother has now earned the right to the scorched ground that she has made home, while the absentee grandfather is fading into an image of the past. The grandmother, ground of being in the grandson, still has to endure a poverty whose existence makes possible the material prosperity of the latter. This, then, is identified as the real problem, the true soul-sickness of Jamaican society.

"White Pickney", like "Problem", was a product of the late forties, and deals with the question of war babies. The "voice" in this poem is the excited one of a semi-literate Jamaican woman who has just read a newspaper headline stating that five thousand black babies, the offspring of Negro American soldiers and white English women, are to be sent from England to America, the land of their fathers. With unerring logic, she concludes that the child of mixed blood assumes the colour of its father, and should be sent to the father's country. Hence, Miss Mary's mulatto war-baby, child of a white English soldier and a black Jamaican woman, is white, and should be sent to England. Also, in England, there would be a place for the seven mulatto bastards of Miss Fan, the wartime prostitute.

Beneath this mask, a rather more complex and acrid play of intellect is taking place, which gives the poem its inner tension and shape. There is, for example, a design for suspense. As in "Dutty Tough" the reader begins with conclusions. Arguments will be supplied in the heart of the poem, after which the conclusions will be restated, becoming, thereby, even more conclusive.

The conclusions of the first three stanzas are as follows: that Miss Mary need no longer worry to face the problem of providing for her child, since he can now be sent to England (origin of the problem); that the newspaper (which is gospel) says that her baby is white; that the headline reads, "Five thousand black baby dah-leff Britain fe 'Merica". None of this enlightens the reader as to what exactly is going on. The central stanzas – four, five, six and seven – do this. The final three stanzas – eight, nine and ten – restate the conclusions. In addition, stanza five contains the crucial paradox of the poem, the real core. Structure, then, is studied and flawless. A closer look at stanzas four, five, six and seven, the central stanzas, serves to illustrate all this.

Dem ya baby muma wite, dem
Pupa is black 'Merican
So dem teck de pupa colour
An gawn a de pupa lan.

> Dem half o' dis an half o' dat
> Dem neida dose nor dese –
> So since dem half-an-half, dem chice
> Watever side dem please.
>
> Ef dem deh baby muma call
> Dem "Black", den is awright –
> Since him pupa is wite-man
> Fe call fe yuh pickney "wite".
>
> An now yuh sure sey dat him wite,
> Yuh kean raise de pickney
> For him naw go able fit eena
> Yuh black society

Beneath the chop-logic of the "folk" voice with its conventional enthusiasm and gusto, lies the ironist's relentless intelligence. This results in a syntactic tightness and toughness, as can be seen in stanza six particularly, though it is a quality of the poem as a whole. It is the real logic, which the chop logic is meant to conceal, that accounts for the peculiar tightness of the line. In order to understand what the poem is really about, one must first bear in mind that it was written after a war which the youth of several countries, both black and white, had been told was against racism, Nazism, and the assumptions of Aryan blood-pride on which Nazism had been based. The rhetoric of the Allies had also stressed that the war was being fought to ensure international freedom and world cooperation. It had deeply humanist ends. There are several postwar calypsos which indicate that West Indians had been fed this rhetoric in no small measure. About the same time that Louise Bennett was writing "White Pickney", Raymond Quevedo, a calypso-singing politician, was berating the British for neglecting their colonies, in spite of the generous contributions West Indians had made in cash and blood, to the Allied cause during the war.

> I've tried but cannot understand
> The laws they've got in my native land
> In the war they told us we must fight to be free
> From the tyranny of Nazi Germany
> Where is the liberty of which they used to shout
> The freedom of speech they boasted about [38]

By 1950, Quevedo (Atilla the Hun) was asking Britain to give up the West Indies.

> In England the people live happily
> They get doctor, medicine and dentist free
> While down here three quarters of the population
> Dying out of diseases and malnutrition
> I'm warning Great Britain don't leave us for long
> Or they'll wake up in the morning and find these islands gone

If they won't help us in our difficulties
Why don't they give up the West Indies?[39]

That was the spirit of the forties. Calypsonians also commented on the war babies, but they tended to mock at the misfortune of their womenfolk, now abandoned by their American soldier boys. Sparrow's anti-feminism of the fifties derives from what had been a general tendency among calypsonians of the forties – to gloat over the "fallen" women. Louise Bennett's treatment of the same theme is generally deeper. In "White Pickney", she is, among other things, hinting at the failure of the white world to keep its bargain with black wartime allies. The Black American, as well as the Black Jamaican, returns to racial discrimination in his own country, having fought to end it in Europe. The same white blood-pride, which received its most degraded expression in Nazism, informs the opinion of the Allies, as regards the question of miscegenation. Even the white mothers of mulatto bastards call their children "black", not "white" or "coloured" – white being the colour of purity, the absolute which has been infringed, and black the colour of the child's bastardy, much more than it is the colour of the child's skin.

Far from mocking at the mothers, Louise Bennett hints at her sympathy for them. Behind the lines: "So dem teck the pupa colour/An gwana de pupa lan" lies a desire to make both sets of fathers responsible. In the fifth stanza, which I have called the core of the poem, she probes the central problem of what is to become of the mixed-race child, in a world where racial absolutism and the desire for purity of blood, still remain powerful factors.

Dem half o' dis an half o' dat
Dem neida dose nor dese.

The mulatto, the "half-an-half" man, mixed of all stuffs, both this and that, can also be neither this nor that, neither here nor there. Theoretically, he has either infinite choice, or no choice at all, since, despite the fact that he symbolises the very internationalism that the Allies claimed to be fighting for, everyone wants to send him away. He represents the guilt of the white mother, while the black mother, in an ex-slave, stratified society, realises that the mulatto has his niche in the class above hers. In other words, by the end of stanza seven, the irony has turned inward to hint at the presence of racial prejudice at home, the complexities of which had been dealt with in "Problem" (1947) and later in "Pass fe White" (1949).

This problem of colour in the West Indies is really part of the problem of being hybrid, the problem of living in a colonial society. As Walcott has been trying to say,[40] with varying degrees of clarity, the fate of the colonial, or ex-colonial, lies in his ability to make "creative use of his schizophrenia".[41] Louise Bennett's example seems to offer another possibility. One needs to establish a ground of being which will reduce the schizophrenia. "White Pickney" suggests that the mulatto quest for the land of his absentee father will be frustrating. Ultimately, it is not easy to "teck the pupa colour", or inherit his distant land. The alternative, which she offers elsewhere to the Jamaican, is responsibility to the black "grandmother" who has hitherto been neglected. It is interesting that the black poet who chose dialect as her medium tells her mulatto to understand and claim his black grandmother, while Walcott, who describes himself as racially and culturally mulatto, is more frequently preoccupied in invoking the memory, and justifying his quest for the white grandfather, in the face of what he seems to see as a growing chauvinism among the Blacks.[42] Walcott's long lyrical essay is too complex to be treated here, but what is fascinating is how a discussion of Louise Bennett has led us to Walcott, her polar opposite in terms of language, aesthetic and orientation, and should have revealed that they are at times dealing with the same complexities, even though they approach them from different directions. This sort of discovery is the most tangible proof of the existence of the various continua, the implications of which we have been investigating.

There is no space here for commenting on Louise Bennett as a political lampoonist, or to trace the development of her art in this area, from the early poems to the later astringency of some of her comments on Independence. Also, we have concentrated on the purely literary aspects of her work, but one who belongs to an oral tradition ought to be appreciated in the act of performance, where interplay between performer and audience can deepen the "meaning" of the work. On the page, Louise Bennett's poems assume a hymn-book monotony, and an apparent regularity of rhythm which could bore the reader who makes the mistake of hearing the poems as if they were meant to conform to conventional (Standard English) ideas of prosody.

As soon as one hears the poem performed aloud, especially by the poet herself, one begins to wonder how the ballad form can contain such energy and volatility. There are sudden changes in pitch and tone and speed, a complete departure from the stress patterns which the ballad form would seem to be imposing. The conventional notions about how verse is supposed to sound are soundly challenged, the listener realising that he is in an uncharted region. The problems of prosody haven't begun to be solved in the West Indies.

Rex Nettleford in his introduction to *Jamaica Labrish* relates her work to the calypso, to jazz and the blues: "What she sometimes does is to manipulate the tonal range of the language, setting the poems almost to music she patters along."[43] This is perfectly true. She uses her voice like a musical instrument; breaking lines, resolving stresses, playing infinitely with shades of sound while operating within the confines of metric strictness, and establishing a tension between metre and rhythm, like a good blues or calypso singer. I can sense a conceptual connection between the fluid improvisation which artists such as Don Drummond[44] were able to achieve within the rigidity of the ska, and what Louise Bennett achieves within the equally bleak rigidity of the quatrain.

This ability to explore a middle region between word and song, this exploration of tone and pitch, can also be heard in her rendition of Anancy stories. Anancy, the spider-hero and trickster, generally plays a double role.[45] The narrator has to indicate this by using different tones of voice for Anancy, and another for his victim, while preserving a neutral narrator's tone. Sometimes, too, the narrator has to sing in the story. The problem is how to do all these things without breaking the rapid movement of the tale and losing a created tension. Louise Bennett is able to do all this to preserve the relationship between voice and mask. Since this oral quality permeates her verse, one cannot argue too strongly for a criticism which is as hybrid as the work it considers, and as various in its approach as the artists are in their methods.

This paper has sought to identify the "folk", to identify some of their forms, patterns of rhetoric, music and attitudes, and to suggest possible connections between these things, each with the other. It has also sought of show how certain West Indian writers relate to these root forms, and to identify the "folk"-inspired element of their work. No claims have been made for the writer as belonging to the folk: indeed, the writers have from the start been identified as normally part of an educated class who, in exploring their roots, have achieved certain forms such as caricature; a disjointed, many-faceted approach to form, as seen in Selvon, Lamming and Mais; Brathwaite's sense of architecture and his employment of musical motifs; Louise Bennett's use of several tones of voice, and her ability to change mask, pitch and pace in mid-sentence.

This enquiry regards as irrelevant the question as to whether the artists examined are "folk" artists or not, based as it has been on the notion that most things in the West Indies are fluid, and most people caught in a series of interlocked continua, making it difficult to place anyone precisely – especially any "educated" person. Since West Indian writers inhabit various landscapes and milieux, few artists have been concerned simply with doing any one thing; most with either doing justice to their sense of schizophrenia, or with drawing creatively on a wide variety of richly agonising experience.

(Lecture delivered at ACLALS Conference UWI Jamaica, January 1971 and published in *Tapia* (December 1971/January 1972).

References

1. Lamming, G., *The Pleasures of Exile* (London: Michael Joseph, 1960), pp. 38-39.
2. Ibid. p. 40.
3. Ibid. p. 40.
4. Ibid. p. 45.
5. Ibid. p. 45.
6. Redfield, R., "The Folk Society." *The American Journal of Sociology,* 52, (Jan. 1947) p. 293.
7. Sewell, W. G., *The Ordeal of Free Labour in the British West Indies* (N.Y.: Harper and Bros., 1861).
8. Marshall, W.K., "Notes on Peasant Development in the West Indies since 1838", *Social and Economic Studies* (17, Sept. 1968).
9. Lewis, W.A., *The Evolution of the Peasantry in the British West Indies* (C.O. Pamphlet 656, 1936).
10. Gomes. A., (ed.) *The Beacon*, Trinidad, 1931-1933.
11. Lamming, G., op. cit., p. 215.
12. ibid. p. 216.
13. Miner, H., "The Folk-Urban Continuum", *The American Sociological Review,* 17, (Oct. 1952).
14. Brathwaite, E., "Sir Galahad and the Islands", *Bim,* Vol. 7, No. 25, (Jul. - Dec. 1957), p. 11.
15. Walcott, D., "Leaving School", Ch. VIII, *London Magazine Editions,* 1966, pp 114-136.
16. Walcott, D., "What the Twilight Says: An Overture", in *Dream on Monkey Mountain and Other Plays* (N.Y.: Farrar, Straus & Giroux, 1970).
17. Brathwaite, E., "The New West Indian Novelists", *Bim* Vol. 8, No. 31, (Jul.-Dec. 1960).
18. Ramchand, K., *The West Indian Novel and Its Background* (London: Faber & Faber, 1970), Ch. VI.
19. Crowley, D.J., "The Midnight Robbers," *Caribbean Quarterly,* Vol. 4, Nos. 3 & 4 (1956) pp. 263-274.
20. Gomes, A., *Trinidad Guardian,* Feb. 12, 1947.
21. Gomes, A., *Through a Maze of Colour* (Port of Spain: Key Publications, 1974).
22. Howes, B., (ed.) *From the Green Antilles* (London: Panther, 1971).
23. Rohlehr, G., "Review Article: *Islands*", *Caribbean Studies,* Vol. 10 No. 4, (Jan. 1971), pp. 173-202.
24. Morris, M., "On Reading Louise Bennett Seriously", *Jamaica Journal,* Vol. 1, No. 1, (Dec. 1967) pp. 69-74.
25. Nettleford, R., Introduction to *Jamaica Labrish* (Jamaica: Sangster's Book Stores, 1966).
26. Scott, D., (interviewer) "Bennett on Bennett," *Caribbean Quarterly*, Vol. 14, Nos. 1 & 2 (Mar.- June 1968), pp. 97-101.
27. Bennett, L., *Once Upon a Time: Jamaican Anancy Stories,* FRM, 129 Federal Records, Manuf. Co., Kingston, Jamaica.

28. Scott, D., op. cit., p. 100.
29. White G., "Rudie Oh Rudie", *Caribbean Quarterly,* Vol. 13, No. 3, (Sept. 1967); Rohlehr, G. "Sounds and Pressure: Jamaica Blues", *Moko,* Trinidad, Nos. 16 & 17 (June 6 & 20, 1969); Rohlehr, G., "West Indian Poetry: Some Problems of Assessment", *Tapia,* No. 20, (Aug, 29, 1971) pp 11-14; Rohlehr, G., "Afterthoughts," *Tapia.* No. 23. Dec. 26, 1971). Several examples of contemporary Jamaican writing can be found in *Savacou* 3 & 4 (Mar. 1971); One *Love* (London: Bogle-L' Overture Publications, 1971), and the Art and Literature sections of recent editions of *Jamaica Journal.*
30. Ibid. p. 69.
31. Ibid. p. 70.
32. Hill, E., "Calypso Drama", *Caribbean Quarterly,* Vol. 15, Nos, 2 & 3, (June - Sept. 1969) pp. 81-98, especially pp. 87-89.
33. Elder, J.D., "The Male/Female Conflict in Calypso", *Caribbean Quarterly,* Vol. 14 No. 3 (Sept. 1968) pp. 23-41.
34. Rohlehr, G., "Sparrow and the Language of Calypso", *Savacou,* No. 2, (Sept. 1970), pp. 87-99.
35. Hogg, D., *Jamaica Religions: A Study in Variations,* Unpublished PhD Dissertation, Yale, 1964; Beckwith, M., "Jamaica Proverbs", *Publications of the Folklore Foundation* (New York, 1925).
36. See note 29.
37. Jones, L., *Blues People; Negro Music in White America* (N.Y.: William Morrow & Co., 1963); Keil C., *Urban Blues* (Chicago: University of Chicago Press, 1966).
38. Quevedo, R., "Introduction", *Souvenir Collection of Trinidad Calypsos* (Port of Spain, 1949).
39. *Trinidad Guardian,* 17 January, 1950.
40. Walcott, D., See poems such as "A Far Cry From Africa", "Veranda", "The Train"; plays such as *Dream on Monkey Mountain* and *In a Fine Castle,* and "What the Twilight Says", see note 16, above.
41. Walcott, D., "What the Twilight Says: An Overture", *Dream on Monkey Mountain and other Plays,* p. 17.
42. Ibid. pp. 7-10. & pp. 26-27.
43. Nettleford, R., op, cit., p. 16.
44. See note 29.
45. See note 27.

SOUNDS AND PRESSURE

"Twist the music out of hunger
on a night like this..." (*Rights of Passage*)

Don Drummond died in the madhouse the other day. The reporter of his death described him as a criminal lunatic, which indeed he was. Some years ago he killed his woman and was confined to the asylum. But Don Drummond will be remembered as the best trombonist Jamaica has known for a long time, and one of her few artists with a genuine vision and message. Something in his work – a blend of militancy, despair, austere melancholy and tenderness and a profound loneliness – reminds me of the first two novels of Roger Mais, and suggests to me that Drummond's strength as a musician derived from his awareness of the extreme pressure which thousands of Jamaicans endure in the inferno of Kingston.

He was, perhaps, the most dominant figure in the early sixties, the years of ska. At that time, the latent creativity of the Jamaican people became evident in the rapid national growth of a fairly indigenous popular music. I say "fairly" because radio and cinema have made pop music universally acceptable, and it is now difficult to tell who derived from whom. In the fifties, American blues and ballads were extremely popular in Jamaica as they were throughout the West Indies, just as soul music is today's craze. But in the sixties, Jamaican musicians like Baba Brooks, Carlos Malcolm, Don Drummond, Roland Alphonso and Tommy McCook effected a transformation of a variety of external and local musical influences into a peculiarly Jamaica sound.

I believe that this transformation was partly due to the increasing pressure of life in Kingston during the sixties, and the musicians' increasing awareness of these pressures. The ska was an extremely aggressive and tedious beat, requiring a great deal of energy and producing a great deal of sweat. People danced it every weekend to the point of exhaustion, as if they found in its almost military rigidity both a perfect expression of their own unalterable position at the bottom of society, and an opiate, a release from the daily inferno of their harshly regimented lives.

Paul Oliver in *The Meaning of the Blues* has adequately illustrated that the American blues emerged from a people so suppressed that suffering appeared both irrational and absurd. For these people, the blues, with all its humour, its calypso-like sexual imagery, its defiant sarcasm, its melancholy and its stoicism, became a philosophy and a message to preach and moan. The blues achieved, for them, a real presence and became a person whom they could address as an intimate friend – the image of a suffering and anxiety grown so familiar that it was almost welcome. The Negro spiritual was the music of those Negroes who had fully accepted their suffering as a gateway to paradise. The blues was more complex – a mixture of submission and rebellion. There are several bad-john blues, just as there are several bad-john kaisos, and several rudie songs in Jamaica. For the blues was a tough secular form, the form of people who were forced to look at their own condition on the rubbish heap. The "good", spiritual-singing Blacks used music as an escape and referred to the blues as the "devil's music".

I stress the nature and origins of the American Negro blues, because I believe that a similar process took place in Jamaica in the early 1960s and has continued. Within a fairly short time, with the growth of the jukebox and the sound system, the beat spanned the entire island, revealing a unity of folk consciousness in the Jamaica masses, which all the weight of Seaga's flats, Matalon's industries and Ashenheim's concrete works were insufficient to crush. Kingston, like an extended tropical Harlem, seething in a perpetual long hot summer, achieved a raw jazz of its own. The people got the message. They understood that ska spoke of their anxieties in the same way that Pukkumina, or Kumina, or Rastafarian music, drumming and ritual did, or healing ceremonies and the other examples of religious ritual did. Nowadays, one has but to look at a crowd of people dancing the reggae, and one is struck by the similarity to Pukkumina. Jamaican music has been dominated by the steady and almost hypnotic use of the bass, and dance in Jamaica, like blues in the America of the twenties and thirties, is now both an opiate conveying oblivion and a kind of self-surrender, and a gateway to self-discovery. In a small city like Kingston, threatened by all the anxieties of alienation which are the mark of large metropolitan cities, the music and the beat are the only things which bring people together, and the dance is used as unconscious group therapy, as in Pukkumina, or Shango in Trinidad. Another general observation which I make to tie up the Jamaican reggae with Trinidad's kaiso and the American Negro blues, is the increasingly overt sexuality. I believe that in the case of America and Jamaica, emphasis on the joys and pains of sex is in part the other side of frustration and despair. Indeed, the word "pressure", which people were accustomed to use while referring to their depressed condition, for a short while was given directly sexual overtones. Songs like "Keep the Pressure On", or "The Pressure and the Slide" indicated the people's appreciation of how one kind of pressure leads to another. The sexual element in Trinidad kaiso does not seem to grow out of the same kind of despair. It is rather connected with the male pose of superiority, a pose so universal in Trinidad that it hints at a doubt as to where true masculinity lies, or rather, a doubt as to whether the proclaimed masculinity is real.

When the ska began to become popular, bands such as Byron Lee's, who had at the start refused to play the beat of "the subculture", began to act as if they had invented the thing. Aided and abetted by a certain Minister of the Government, Byron Lee went to America on national funds to promote the beat, and to make some more money for the recording company of which the minister was a director. This tediously middle-class act of appropriating a popular form and castrating it luckily did not affect the real artists in the society. In the instrumental playing of Don Drummond and the Skatalites one got a genuine sense of some of the urgencies and the anxieties of urban life in Jamaica.

With Drummond, playing ska was always much more than the exploitation of a popular beat. It was a courageous statement of the daily miracle of survival in that harsh world. Compositions like "Marcus Junior", "The Reburial", "China Town" or "Fidel" express an extreme frenzy, drive and anarchy, especially in the drumming and the use of the cymbals. Yet Drummond's solos in these pieces often bear little relation to this frenzy. He blows a slow and sometimes calm trombone, in a desolate abstracted minor key, as if he were part of the band only by accident. It is not that he is not in time or in tune with them, but his message is different. Perhaps his compositions reflect something of his own schizophrenia, the contrast between the disinherited and distracted consciousness, moving like Brathwaite's Rasta Man "through the streets of affliction" and the tedium and frenzy beneath all things.

In contrast with the rebellion of those compositions are the cooler pieces like "Eastern Standard Time", "Addis Ababa", "Further East", "Willow Weep", "Roll On Sweet Don", "Tribute to Don" – all of which make use of passages in unison, and of harmonies on long-extended, held notes. One can also compare a piece which he composed for the Jazz Workshop, and which appeared on the album *Jazz Jamaica*. The name of the piece is "Serenade in Sound". An effect of lamentation and an intense yearning for escape are expressed in these pieces. A study of the hymn-singing of Pocomania and other groups will reveal this selfsame use of the prolonged, held note, with the same effect of wailing. This too, like the frenzy and the rebellion, represents one of the poles of Jamaican lower-class experience. The Rastafarian mind spans all three phases – despair, rebellion, and the longing to travel further East back to the fatherland. It is my conviction that Drummond was steeped in the agonies and hopes of the Rastafarians.

One can tell from the names that Drummond chose that he was fully mindful of the Rastafarian personality. For example, there was "Beardman Ska", "Addis Ababa", "Marcus Junior", suggesting Garvey or his son, a Black Power leader in Jamaica; "The Reburial" suggesting a Pukkumina ritual based on West African rites, and referencing the actual return of the body of Marcus Garvey from London to Jamaica in 1964. Like the Rastaman he, too, identifies with the figure of Fidel Castro, and calls one of his compositions "Fidel". "Ghost Town" and "China Town" are slum areas in Kingston.

Drummond, then, was a representative figure, perhaps all the more so for his bouts of lunacy. Few people of sensibility retain pedestrian sanity in Kingston. Either they look away from the grotesqueness of things, or they go the abstracted way of Drummond and the Rastaman. The musicians all acknowledged his supremacy, and perhaps the best tribute paid to him lies in the fact that, after his confinement, all the trombonists and one or two trumpeters tried to sound like him. The most successful of these was a trombonist named Rico Rodriguez, who did some recordings with Prince Buster. There is "Barrister Pardon" and "Bone Yard".

Conditions in Kingston grew progressively worse. There were racial riots in 1965; the bulldozing in 1966 of hundreds of squatters from the West Kingston area; the growing anarchy of the dispossessed who were driven even from the cemetery; the organisation of violence along party lines in 1967. This disaster, anarchy and heartbreak created a perfect context for the blues. Out of this chaos emerged the rocksteady, a beat which resulted from the slowing down of the ska. It was almost as if a conscious attempt were being made to cool the country down. By some strange irony, the name "rock steady" was also applied to a special rubber truncheon which the police use the beat uncooperative citizens, so that the blows hurt, but don't show. In the midst of the frenzy, Prince Buster's reassuring voice told the fans, "Take it easy… No need to worry."

The rocksteady became popular throughout the West Indies. Unfortunately, despite the genuine talents of Alphonso and McCook, there was no instrumentalist of Drummond's stature and conviction to exploit this much freer beat. What is noticeable, though, is that the singers are now producing their own raw experience, and making deep, and sometimes bitter comments on the society. In the ska era, there were Rasta songs like Slim Smith's "The Time Has Come for I", and Justin Hinds' "Carry Go Bring Come", a song which commented on the adverse effects of rumour and "mauvaise langue" and was said to refer to Lady Bustamante. The rocksteady version of it is very moving, as the singer advises,

> Better to seek a home in Mount Zion high
> Instead of heaping oppression on an innocent man.
> But time will tell on you, you old Jezebel
> How long shall the wicked reign over my people?"

It is Drummond who plays the slow, sad trombone solo.

These songs, however, were mild in comparison with "Rudie" songs. Jamaica had moved from the era of Brother Man, the ritualist, to that of

Rudie, the anarchist. Far from being the violent enemies of society, Rastafarians are often like the good Blacks in America who sang spirituals or used religious delirium to exorcise hunger. The rudies, on the other hand, are like the early Blues men who sing their devil music... anarchists, who celebrate anarchy as the only true freedom left in the world. The term "rudeness" is used to connote a disrespect for authority in any form. But since the rude boys are most likely to come into contact with the judges, justice is the main theme of rudeboy songs. It must be noted that once rudie songs became popular, groups began to sing them simply to exploit the market. Yet some genuine tendencies can be noted.

Rudie tunes are sometimes about mock court trials, in which conventional justice is belittled. The rudie plays the part of both judge and criminal, in much the same way as in Ole Mas one ridicules some of the things or persons one dislikes by distorting their image in public. The idea behind these rudie songs seems to be much the same as that of Gay's *Beggar's Opera* in the eighteenth century, when the issue in England was also one of law and order as opposed to justice. Gay made pickpockets and whores act the part of lords and ladies, suggesting in the process that there was no essential difference between them in a system so obviously unjust. These rudie songs hint at an intense dissatisfaction with the process of justice, and especially with the lack of sympathy of those who judge for the people they are supposed to be judging.

In "Tougher than Tough", the rudeboy states his position. He is a bomb thrower, user of the ratchet knife; he is tougher than tough and, he says, he is free. This declaration is miles away in spirit from the bad-john pose of the Trinidad calypsonians, in kaisos like "The Return of the Bull", "Bull Pizzle Gang", or "Hangman's Cemetery", where the calypsonian usually depicts himself as a decent citizen, peace-loving, not easily moved, but when aroused, "ignorant" in the extreme. He is the quiet guy who is being harassed by "them hooligans", the bad-johns. He is no anarchist but can run amok if pushed too far. Nowadays bad-john kaisos are really out-of-date, because, although they do indicate the spirit of anarchy below the surface of society, and tell of the Trinidad of a generation ago, today they are for the most part grandcharge and melodrama.

The Jamaican anarchist is a much more serious person. In "Dreader than Dread" he dares justice and calls on all his fellow rudies to "Stand fast together and unite, to deal with one hundred or one thousand years." Here then is a music celebrating violence, and laughing at the sort of justice which makes violence inevitable, a music which calmly attacks the entire system. For those who are interested, Garth White has offered an analysis of the relation of the music to the society in *Caribbean Quarterly* (Vol. 13, No. 3, Sept., 1967). One notes here the complete difference in tone between rudie songs and those, say, of the Sons of Negus, a Rasta group whose songs are really hymns in praise of their King of Kings. If the Rastaman is detached, or rather attempts to detach himself in spirit from the system (there is a resemblance between the troubled lamentations of the Sons of Negus and the more melancholy side of Drummond) the rudies are in the thick of things, and prefer to confront them.

The lower-class hero of the towns, Rudie, is attracted to the dandyism of James Bond; hence the name "007" for Desmond Dekker's song on riots in Shanty Town. At the same time, the voice of the law-abiding citizen pleads with the rudies to "Stop your running around, making trouble in the town", in Dandy Livingstone's "Rudie a Message to You". The confusion in the minds of the lower classes is a genuine one. I discovered this in speaking to Prince Buster, whose L.P. "Prince Buster Fabulous" contains a fair number of rudie-type songs. In "Too Hot", for example, which tells of the state of emergency in 1966 when intensive and generally fruitless searches for guns were carried out, Prince Buster seems to be on the side of the rudies. "The police don't know what to do,/ Pound for pound, they say they ruder than you." "Rudeboys never give up their guns".

However, the record "Judge Dread", or "Judge Four Hundred Years" is more ambiguous. In some ways, I know of no more savage mockery of the idea of an inhumane system whose watchword is law and order, than this record. In Judge Dread's court, one is always guilty, and guilty of a multitude of crimes which no one man can possibly have committed, and the shortest sentence is one hundred years. To protest innocence is to show contempt of court, an offence punishable by a separate hundred years. Judge Dread epitomises, for the rudeboy, what justice has become in Jamaica – blind accusation and absurd reprisal. The rudeboy feels that the law-courts, like the rest of the society, have sacrificed justice to the creation of scapegoats. For him, law has become so repressive that justice has degenerated into a madness for power on the part of the judge. It is as if Prince Buster is predicting the moment when the authoritarianism of our societies will become megalomania, a moment which most Latin American countries have experienced.

Yet "Judge Dread" is not to be explained away in such a simple manner. Prince Buster told me that the disorganised activity of the rudies meant that they were simply shooting not only at each other, but indiscriminately at "Black people". Judge Dread, the epitome of repressive officialdom, was absolutely necessary in a situation of anarchy. Thus, in "The Appeal", he sentences the rudeboys to one thousand years, with the words, "Count how many Chinese are dying; how many White people are dying, how many other nations are dying; multiply them… and that does not amount to the number of Black people that are being killed by these rudeboys." Judge Dread therefore refuses them right of appeal, and also sentences the white defence counsel they have brought with them. Prince Buster argues that only a white man would bother to defend Blacks who had been killing their brothers. It seems, then, that the situation in Jamaica has become so bad that even the poor are looking for a more repressive operation of the law, rather than grass roots reform of a social system which makes both Rudie and Judge Dread inevitable. Such is the weird logic of repression. It breeds both rebellion and masochism.

Since the days of Judge Dread, social commentary of a more general nature has continued in song. "Everything Crash", by The Ethiopians, for example, looks at the situation in 1968 when several branches of the public services went on strike. "Look ya now, Pharoah house crash." The singers sound as if they rather expected this to happen. The system, they imply, was rotten beyond reform, and "Wha dam' bad a marnin' can't come good a' evening – Whoi!" Songs like The Kingstonians' "Sufferer" or Desmond Dekker's "Poor Me Israelites" or The Bassies "Things a Come up to Bump" record the common man's growing frustration with his lot. "Wake up in the morning, slaving for bread, sah/So that every mouth can be fed... Poor me Israelites". This implied comparison with the experience of the Jews, is of course, common among Blacks. This Desmond Dekker tune (he also sang "007") is at present high on the charts in Britain. There have also been songs like the Maytals' "54-46 That's My Number", which is really a moving comment on the madness for power which more and more commentators are noting as a marked feature in the country's police.

"Ah say to stick it up mister
Do you hear what I say suh?
Put your hands to your head suh!
Turn out your left pocket..."

It was the Maytals, too, who mockingly noted the crude way in which Dr. Rodney was banned from re-entering Jamaica in October of 1968. Their "Scare Him" is rather deficient in vocabulary, but it does hint that at least one section of the public interpreted the Government's action as a piece of almost childish absurdity. "See im there, see im there? See im there, see im there, don't mek im come back." There was also U Roy's song, "Babylon Burning", which not only anticipates the collapse of the system, but also points to the hopelessness of the poor man who asks, "Who can you turn to?"

A point which strikes one immediately about the language of Jamaican songs is the fact that, compared with Trinidad calypsos, they are naive, unsubtle and sometimes crude. Yet it is clear that Jamaican songs do not need the verbal subtlety or the evasive wit of kaiso. They communicate almost wholly through rhythm, choral effects; in fact, the music is meant to be danced, rather than listened to. Indeed, it can be further argued that the litany of under-privilege is a simple, direct and elemental one; that in Jamaica, the social, political and economic situation is so urgent that truth takes on the solidly crystalised form of the proverb. "Is carry go bring come, my dear, bring misery"; "Every day carry bucket to the well, one day the bucket bottom must drop out" etc. The poor in Jamaica know that there isn't much to be said anymore. The simple proverbs which occur so frequently in their songs gain a weight and meaning from the context of a lived suffering and experience out of which they grow.

Both the sounds and the pressure continue. The athletic and sometimes military nature of dance in Jamaica should not be overlooked. It often seems to the outsider that there is an organic connection between the kind of beat, the kind of movement which is made to it, and the silent inner rebellion and frenzy which possess anyone strong enough to look at the society face-to-face. The decent ordinary citizen in Jamaica, as submissive and conservative as the decent ordinary citizen in most countries, contents himself with dancing the reggae or "Strongman Samson", thereby dramatising and forgetting his impulse to rebel. His counterpart, the anarchist, climbs the hill to shoot and rob the rich. And the pressure continues to inspire the sounds; Orange Street will for a long time be shaking to the driving beat, each infernal day, each familiar blue afternoon.

(Originally published in *Moko*, Nos. 16 & 17 Friday 6th June 1969 and Friday 20th June, 1969).

ONCE IN A BLUE SUN: REVIEW OF
THE HARDER THEY COME

Just over one year ago, on June 5th, 1972, *The Harder They Come*, the first full-length Jamaican fiction film, was released in that island. Later that month, the film won a major award at the Cork Film Festival in Ireland, and its editor, John Victor Smith, received a personal award for the best edited film. The entire film was in Jamaica Creole, the language of Kingston's streets. This gave the actors tremendous self-confidence and power, by releasing energies which might otherwise have been consumed in self-consciousness about speech and accent, for the business of pure acting.

Perry Henzell, who collaborated with playwright Trevor Rhone in writing the script, and also directed the film, described his aims thus to Irish critics:

> I had a choice when I set out to make this film – to make a film for Jamaica, or to make a film for the rest of the world. I chose to make a film for Jamaica. Now that I have heard the comments about the film from its first non-Jamaican audience, it seems that I have managed to achieve both things. (*The Daily Gleaner,* June 22nd, 1972)

There is justification for Henzell's claim: for what strikes one about the film is both its rootedness in Jamaican reality, and the sense that it has moved beyond that reality. Its people are more genuinely alive than most of the people I have seen on the screen over the past year. It is interesting, too, that the Irish experienced little difficulty in understanding the Jamaican accent, which they found to resemble their own, and sent out a few queries to ascertain whether any gentlemen of Cork could be found floating around in Jamaica.

Normally, whenever a West Indian thing receives international acclaim, we begin to appreciate its worth at home and are eager to claim it as our own. This does not seem to have been the case with *The Harder They Come* – at least not in the Land of the Humming Bird Medal. The film has not yet been released in Trinidad, although (or because) its relevance to our situation is only too obvious. This review is prompted by the fact that some weeks ago I saw the film advertised in a city cinema, only to learn from a subsequent newspaper report that it had been seen by two censors, who had recommended that it be viewed by the full Board of Censors.

This did not surprise me, because although the film contains much less violence than we are accustomed to on the screen, and hardly any sex, its frank social realism and essential seriousness are no flattery to the usual image we project of ourselves abroad, of a fairly happy, good-natured, easy-going, tolerant and well-balanced people. This is, indeed, one of the things that struck Irish viewers at Cork. A newspaper report stated that:

> To the Irish the film is a tragedy made even more interesting by the reality and accuracy of its setting. Peter Cushing, star of several horror films, commented after the screening: "What a brave thing for Jamaica to have done, to have chosen so serious a subject for its first film. We often see the glamorous side of life in Jamaica and I think most of us are unaware of other aspects of Jamaican life."[1]

The Harder They Come, which opened on the night before the first sitting of Mr. Michael Manley's parliament, is in its way a symbolic commentary on the first ten years of Jamaican Independence, and an insight into the tensions of urban society in contemporary Jamaica. The euphoria of the anthem and the flag flagged as rapidly in Jamaica in the years after Independence, as it did in Trinidad. In Jamaica, a music of defiance and disillusion emerged in the mid-sixties and rapidly grew into a music of protest, violence and escapism in the late sixties and early seventies. In Trinidad, calypsos criticising the police, the government, the situation in labour relations and virtually every aspect of social life, began as picong in the mid-sixties, and widened into a flood of sometimes blue, sometimes corrosively humorous criticism, in the late sixties and the seventies.

The Harder They Come examines in a simple, fundamental and unpretentious manner the pre-political stages of this protest, and the context of unemployment, violence, hope, fear, frenzy and fantasy out of which it developed. It is by now a well-known fact that the 1972 General Elections in Jamaica were rich in the quality of political manipulation of popular response, through the employment of Rastafarian slogans, the symbolism and rhetoric of Afro-Protestant cults, and the urban protest music of reggae. Ironically, it was a minister for the conservative Jamaica Labour Party (JLP), Edward Seaga, who had promoted and exploited popular culture throughout the sixties. This manipulation had proved insufficient, and by 1970 the sentiments of a growing number of reggae songs were undoubtedly anti-establishment.

In 1972, Michael Manley came to power to the beat of Clancy Eccles's "Rod of Correction" and Delroy Wilson's "Better Must Come". Beneath these lay the heavier sounds of Junior Byles's "Beat Down Babylon" and Bob Marley's "Duppy Conqueror", and the furious though grounded rhythms of The Mystic Revelations of Rastafari. So it was interesting that the eve of the inauguration of the new government should also be the premiere of a film, which measured the pressures of the sixties, and related them to the creative flowering of the people's music in Kingston's dry desert of stone. It was perhaps even more significant, and probably prophetic, that on the afternoon of June 5th, 1972, Mr. Manley and most of his government and Mr. Shearer and the most of his opposition were attending the military funeral of a police constable who had been shot while on patrol duty. The situation had not changed one bit on the streets. A few days later, the police returned the compliment, when a policeman shot and killed a prisoner, who, he explained, had pulled a knife on him in a police car. And throughout June, the pattern of armed robbery and legal or illegal executions continued.

The Harder They Come makes it easy for us to understand why this pattern of repression/violence/reprisal, this vicious, wasteful circle of death, continues regardless of who is running and ruining the economy. Its straightforward plot tells about a country boy who is lured by the bright lights of Kingston to pursue his ambition to become a singer. Ivan (Jimmy Cliff) soon learns the city's grimness. He is only one of thousands of unemployed, "one of the uncountable miseries owning the land", as Carter once put it. Dozens of youths, most of them with no talent at all, want to add to the already saturated market of pop song, and line up outside the studios for the rare audition. A brief sojourn with a Baptist preacher (Basil Keane) ends abruptly when Ivan is caught making eyes at the teenaged Elsa (Janet Bartley), whom Preacher has raised for the glory of God and his own sexual gratification. This incident puts an end to Ivan's religious aspirations, which never seemed to be very strong anyhow.

Also, Preacher vindictively stirs up trouble between Ivan and a fellow-apprentice in Preacher's workshop, where Ivan earns a pittance. A fight ensues in which both combatants rapidly acquire weapons; one, a knife, the other, a broken bottle. Ivan gains the upper hand, cuts his opponent mercilessly across the face, and is hauled before the magistrate, who as an act of mercy to a first offender, decides that he should not be jailed, but that he should be severely whipped. This whipping, graphically captured in a brief vignette on the screen, remains as a nightmare in Ivan's mind, the symbol of his emasculation. The blows of the birch make him urinate like a little child. It is the turning point of his life. He has to leave the relative protection of Preacher's flawed church and workshop, and face the full frustration of the city. Refusing to allow himself to be robbed by the owner of a record company, he kills his chances of success in the world of popular entertainment. He joins a ganja-pushing ring, only to annoy his superiors by asking too many questions.

Among these are a clean-faced and successful detective (Winston Stone), who orders a patrolman to give chase to Ivan who is cruising on his newly-acquired auto-cycle. The detective's aim at this stage is simply to harass Ivan, but the hero is carrying a gun. Remembering the birching he received at the hands of the police, and afraid lest the mercy of the magistrate be meted out to him once more, he panics and shoots the policeman dead. The rest of the story is the inevitable manhunt. This section of the film is based on the life of Jo Jo Rhygin, a Jamaican bad-john of the late 1940s, who terrorised Kingston, melodramatically leaving "Kilroy Was Here" types of messages for the police, and was eventually shot on Lime Cay.

So that is the film's plot. What is there about it that should disturb our censors? Police corruption? We saw that and more mercilessly laid bare in films as different as *Z, The Godfather,* and the documentary on Martin Luther King. In *The Godfather* we were allowed to see an entire system flourishing beautifully in the manure of corruption, and becoming thoroughly respectable in a generation. The sensitive young hero explains to his non-Italian bride that a senator within the legalised political system needs to be quite as ruthless and corrupt as a gangster outside of it, and the ageing Godfather himself has but one regret – that he has not lived long enough to become fully accepted by the establishment. The next generation, he predicts, will become governors and respectable men of affairs. The corruption dealt with in *The Harder They Come* is, by comparison, petty, small-time, almost benign, though it spreads its crop of corpses across today's Jamaica with grim relentlessness.

What else is there to disturb our censors? Marijuana? The film at no point advocates its use. Addiction is not a theme here. It is merely incidental that the racket is weed and not something else, whiskey or electronics smuggling, say. The violent death of a lawman? This act is certainly not glorified in the film, and the bloodthirsty will be comforted when they hear that the state exacts full retribution by gunning Ivan down on a particularly lovely day, on a beautiful tourist-paradise beach. It ought to be pointed out, too, that Ivan is not presented as a Black superhero, a Shaft, a Slaughter or a Savage. As he progresses, he is shown as being more and more the product of a world of illusion fabricated on the fantasies of the Italian Westerns of Cruelty. *The Harder They Come* is as accurate a comment as Sparrow's "Gunslingers" (1959) or "Rope" (1972) on how such films form a real part of our world of illusion. The older Sparrow criticises the youth for not resisting the influence of these films; the younger Sparrow celebrated uncritically the make-believe, bad-john world of his day.

The Harder They Come was received with mixed feelings in Jamaica. Censors ordered the film to be cut in places, which one critic thought did some violence to its coherence and continuity. A television panel expressed enthusiasm for the film and sympathy for the hero, much to the chagrin of *Gleaner* critic Harry Milner, whose feelings about the film were most fully expressed in an article entitled "Crime in Films".[2] Milner began by praising the "high artistic quality" of the film, pointing out its "Jamaican background, fine reggae score, vital acting, brilliant direction, and Jimmy Cliff's star personality." He then went on to say that these things might not have been sufficient to assure the film's box-office success had its theme not been one of crime and violence, and felt that a truer image of Jamaica would have been transmitted had the film been about a youth who had worked his way to success despite the real pressures in his society, a youth such as Jimmy Cliff himself. Milner declared:

> I still think it is a pity that the first fictional movie made here for international circulation, and which through its quality, its sensationalism and its novelty is bound to resound abroad, should have been this film of murder, violence and crime, which is certainly these days an important part of our life, but in the long run not the most important, nor the most typical, nor the most endearing. The present figures for crimes of violence and homicide are at the present moment proportionately among the highest in the world, but this, I feel and hope, is a temporary malaise, like the vulgarity of the new rich, which only smears the real qualities of our people, the essential kindliness, humour, steadiness, commonsense and hospitality of all the classes of our people, which are always on tap when they are called upon.[3]

What he would have liked to see, he said, was a script more along the lines of Trevor Rhone's *Music Boy*, the 1972 Pantomime, which attempted to present some of those "real qualities of our people", although it treated of a similar situation as *The Harder They Come*.

A number of things need be said at this point. First the film is not sensational at all, although it attempts to examine sensationalism and a capacity for fantasy as real elements of our national life. Secondly, although Milner can admit that crime and violence are overwhelming features of Jamaican national life, he shies away from any attempt to say why this is the case. Hence, Trevor Rhone's and Perry Henzell's modest and responsible attempt to probe a major aspect of urban life in Jamaica is viewed by Milner with disapproval. Significantly, he does not say why he feels that a crime rate which, according to him, is "proportionately among the highest in the world." will be only a "temporary malaise".

To do this, Milner would have had to show where the gap between rich and poor was steadily closing, and the unfair system inherited from history was being significantly modified by the politics of independence. Mr. Milner does not do this. Indeed, he glibly anticipates this criticism in his next sentence when he writes:

> Included amongst our national virtues, too, is distrust of easy solutions and a healthy scepticism without cynicism which we have inherited from our former colonial masters with a tendency to trust the pragmatic and the empiric rather than the absolute.[4]

Here, as in the paragraph quoted above, critic Milner is peddling the well-known myth of Jamaica as being a single coherent nation, where all classes display the common virtues of "essential kindness, humour, steadiness, commonsense and hospitality", and an intelligent "scepticism without cynicism" about the politics of change. This is far from being the truth. There are also madness, frenzy, apathy, cynicism, and despair, existing at various levels in the society. Each of these attitudes has a different quality, depending on where in the society it occurs.

The *scepticism* of the poor about change is qualitatively different from the *complacency* of the rich, or the *nihilistic despair* of the academic, whose failure to see how analysis can ever be translated into action often leads to a paralysed irony, and a corrosive but helpless sense of absurdity. Violence and anarchy on the streets are quite understandable reactions to the existing system. In Jamaica, if one can trust the evidence of *dread* music, and the constant violence which is a product of the confrontation between repressive authority and despairing, directionless revolt, political scepticism, for a growing number of the poor, is coming to mean a total mistrust in even the possibility of a better life. When this mistrust manifests itself in the unemployed youth of the towns, the ultimate reaction is often crime and violence. When this mistrust manifests itself among the more mature or the more exhausted of the older poor, the result is often religious escapism to "a land far far away, where there's no night, there's only day" as the Abyssinian's song "Satta Amasa Gana" puts it. Or for those who cannot believe in the possibility of Zion, the result is often a stoical acceptance of the screw, accompanied sometimes by a profound humour of helplessness.

The attitude of one country woman I met in a taxi, towards the Empire Day (May 24th) Elections of 1971 in Trinidad, illustrates the point I am trying to make here. When asked why she refused to vote, she replied:

> "If I vote, I still got to lie down under the man. If I don't vote, I still got to lie down under the man. Well, is better I just go and lie down under the man."

For the poor, the screw continues regardless of who is running the country. Some opt out, others conform, others explode.

It is clear that Rhone and Henzell were not concerned with celebrating the traditional "folk" virtues of kindliness, humour, steadiness and hospitality, which Milner sees everywhere in his society, or with presenting the fortunes and misfortunes of the hardworking, long-suffering good citizen, who is sceptical without being cynical about politics. They were more concerned with showing how these qualities are stripped away as the young country boy experiences the inferno of the city, and the pastoral dream fades. It may well be that the urban experience of individualism, disintegrating communities and the erosion of "folk" values is today setting the pace and providing the dynamic for the rest of our Caribbean societies.

This is why the annual pantomime in Jamaica, which used to celebrate the rather stereotyped virtues of "folk" speech, "folk" vitality and music, has in the late sixties faced the problem of having to come to terms with the mood and philosophy of *dreadness,* the ongoing sound and quality of Jamaica's streets, which emerged as the youth in Kingston attempted to come to terms with growing pressures of unemployment, within a traditional framework of unequal distribution, and rigid class stratification. Milner would have preferred a film whose philosophy was similar to that of the traditional pantomime. He was presented instead, with one which attempts to examine the very starkness of tensions that the pantomime has either chosen to evade, or simplistically to resolve.

Because Milner would have liked a film which avoided the theme of violence, or at least depicted the triumph of sanity over chaos, he is too harsh in his assessment of the hero of *The Harder They Come.* Contrasting Ivan's career with that of Jimmy Cliff who plays the part of Ivan, he has this to say:

> The difference between the Ivan of the movie and Jimmy of real life is that the former, through his temperament rather than his upbringing, was impatient, self-centred in a stupid way, quick-tempered, vain, brutal, callous and after the quick buck; in fact, a rather typical criminal type.

According to this statement, Ivan is a walking catalogue of several deadly sins, a criminal by temperament; but the film seems to me to be examining some of the forces in society which combine to release in one person, the impulse to crime which is rooted in everyman.

The city is the domain of the scuffler, the smart man, the samfie man. Ivan begins as a naive country boy, whose first experience of the city is that of being robbed of his luggage as he stands bewildered at the chaotic country bus terminus. Preacher, whose religion can sustain an older person such as Ivan's mother, turns out of be vindictive and lustful. He tries to rob Ivan of his girl and his bike. The bike indicates the simple desires which are still Ivan's; his modest pastoral ambition to take his girlfriend out on a bicycle which he has fixed with his own two hands. Preacher gives this bicycle away to Ivan's fellow-apprentice in the mechanic's shop. As regards Ivan's quick temper, it should be pointed out that he did not seek the fight, and his cutting up of his opponent is probably no more than his opponent meant to do him. It was a question of survival of the fittest. So far, then, Ivan's behaviour can be seen as a reaction to his brief city experience.

Milner's answer to this is that the majority of Jamaicans endure this ongoing process, and more, with true uncomplaining grit, and that it is the struggle of the children of Sisyphus to push their stone of survival up the perpendicular hill of privilege, which ought to have been highlighted. What *The Harder They Come* does, instead, is to depict the rebellion of a youth who says "No" to the everyday heroism of bare subsistence, and "Yes" to the idea of the quick buck, and the illusion of the flashy sports car. Ivan does not accept his place or the possibility of a slow advance within the system. Nor does he articulate his protest against the system in political terms. What he does is to recognise the presence of illegality within the system. This convinces him that he can advance much more rapidly by illegal means. The lesson which he eventually learns, is not that law and order will prevail, but that law can become a tool in the hands of the powerful to castigate only such sins as meet with their disapproval.

After his birching, Ivan becomes an indigenised citizen of the town. He now has something to sing, something to shout. He has experienced the essential ingredient which strengthens the dread-beat of the city, and he composes a reggae song which is, in the words of Tony McNeill, his attempt to "learn the shape of that hurt". *The Harder They Come* does not simply have "a fine reggae score", as even critic Milner admits, it attempts to trace the connection between sounds and pressure. It shows how the energy behind rocksteady and reggae comes from the hard world of the street. Explosions of violence on the streets lead to implosions of violence in the music. Thus, in the spirit of the rude boy of the mid-sixties, Ivan puts all his fear, pain, bravado and defiance into his song:

> Yes they tell me of the pie up in the sky
> Waiting for me when I die
> But between the day you're born and when you die
> They never seem to hear you when you cry
> So as sure as the sun will shine
> I'm going to get my share, what's mine
> And then the harder they come, the harder they'll fall
> One and all

He goes on to say in a later stanza;

> But I'll rather be a free man in my grave
> Than living as a puppet or a slave.

That is his song and his hope and his tragedy. For Ivan is in the situation which the militant Black American saxophonist, Archie Shepp, defined so tersely to a white interviewer: "You own the music and we make it." The white Jamaican company owner *owns* the music which he cannot make. Ivan and his kind *make* it.

This white businessman symbolises the entire commercial system, and the way it functions with regard to anything which is saleable, including the grassroots sound. One notes that Henzell stresses not the *whiteness* of this exploiter, but rather what he illustrates of the spirit of an economic system. The exploiter knows the world he is exploiting. He speaks with the accents of the street, he understands the shifting tastes of the people. He knows what will sell, and when it will sell most abundantly. He has control of the media, too. The bigger disc jockeys are all in his pay. His sole criterion is market value, and although he can see the quality of Ivan's song, he also knows that Ivan, as an unknown, is exploitable, and so he offers him a ridiculously low price.

Human value against market value: that is the issue at this point. Ivan's song may be the product of blood, sweat and tears; it may contain the memory of his hurt, his experience of the emasculating whip, but the *owner* of the music is not concerned with this at all. He blocks Ivan's efforts to fight the system by promoting his song independently, and keeps the master-tapes of the record for future use. It is really this incident which finally convinces Ivan of the illegality and the inhumanity of the system, and the right of the individual to succeed by fair means or foul. It is at this point that he joins the weed-pushing racket, only to discover that here, too, the system is in operation, though it is impossible to say who wields the real power. All Ivan knows is that those who grow the weed, and those who run risks pushing it on the streets, seem to receive proportionately little for their pains.

Ivan is to learn how the ganja ring operates. Indeed, there is little to learn. At its lower levels, it consists of peasants who grow the stuff for a pittance, as an act of pure survival. If no one smuggles the weed out of the island, or if no one pushes it on the streets – that is, if the external and the internal markets collapse – the peasants will starve. The police know this, and threaten to clamp down on the trade whenever they want to blackmail the peasants into providing information about this or that suspect. This happens when Ivan is on the run. Indeed, a very effective scene takes place when the detective tries to elicit information from an old man as to Ivan's whereabouts. Just the look on the man's face tells one everything about the people's relative attitudes towards the police, and the fugitive. Although silence about Ivan's whereabouts has led to the police putting a stop to the trade in ganja, thereby increasing suffering among the peasants, they still prefer to identify with the fugitive, whom they regard as being closer to them than the guardians of the system's law.

At a slightly higher level in the ganja ring, one finds the distributors, such as Pedro (maturely acted by Rastafarian painter, Ras Daniel Heartman), or the Anansi-like Jose – Carl Bradshaw, who also played Ringo in Trevor Rhone's *Smile Orange*, is a brilliant smart man in the film. Word, gesture and facial expression, the entire stock-in-trade of the samfie man, his comic but sinister rascality, are all brilliantly captured by Bradshaw. True to his Anansi nature, Jose is a link between the pushers and the police. He is a small-time informer in the pay of the detective. At the middle level of the ring are people like the detective and the businessman. These are the socially respectable agents and middlemen for those invisibles who exist at the top level of the racket – an unnamed party in America, who flies the weed out by light aircraft. This is not sensationalism, but a well-known fact. So here again, as with the music, those who produce do not control distribution. Ivan rebels again, and pays the price for asking too many questions.

Ivan as gunslinger is, inevitably, an empty fantasy-ridden character. He begins to enjoy the chase in a strange way, and debases the spirit of his original protest by the triviality of his desires. Henzell rams the knife home by making the record company owner trade in on Ivan's notoriety, and issue his tune of protest – now that it is too late for such success to save Ivan from execution. It is an instant success, more because of the people's thirst for bacchanal and sensation than because of its own true intrinsic worth. For it is by no means clear whether the public recognise in the lyrics and tense rhythm of the song their own true cry, or whether public protest itself is just another commodity for the businessman/politician's market. If the product will sell, then sell it, regardless of whether it is music, dope or soul for sale.

Significantly, Ivan is much more interested in killing Jose than in tackling the businessman who, by robbing him, made him chose illegality. He is at the pre-political stage of revolt, where values are personal, and the rebel considers himself as a man alone in an unjust world. The result of this lack of political idea is that all the people who die in the film are poor, black and grassroots – policeman and criminal alike. Those who control the system are not even threatened.

The Harder They Come does not preach, moralise or offer solutions. It prefers to look at what is. If an idea emerges at the end, it cannot be summarised in any easy moral formula. When I saw the film I noted how completely everyone around me identified with Ivan, and particularly with his defiant pose in the face of death. They didn't notice, nor did they mind the element of fantasy in his defiance. It may be that under that mask they saw something of their own daily desperation in the face of a system where the extreme gap between rich and poor is still maintained by class-legislation, and the constant threat of coercion which sometimes materialises in physical violence, and often assumes the absolute form of death on the streets.

The *Harder* They Come may be no big thing, but it is the first West Indian movie which attempts to look at West Indian reality with sensitivity and frankness. It is imperative that it be released as soon as possible. It certainly will do us no harm to take a look at our own cracked features, once in a blue sun.

(Originally published in *Tapia* Vol. 3, No. 24. June 17th, 1973, p. 5-9).

References

1. *The Daily Gleaner.* June 22, 1972.
2. Milner, H., "Crime in Films", *The Sunday Gleaner,* June 18, 1972, p. 5.
3. Ibid.
4. Ibid.

WEST INDIAN POETRY: SOME PROBLEMS OF ASSESSMENT

The period between the late fifties and the present, between the short-lived West Indian Federation and the acquisition of Independence by some of the English-speaking Caribbean territories, has produced a great deal of writing and a consequently increasing number of anthologies. In poetry, there has been the hard-won maturity and painful craftsmanship of Derek Walcott, the fresh dimensions in theme, rhythm and technique which Kamau Brathwaite so lavishly offers the student of craft, and several anthologies of the works of individual writers, such as Seymour's *Selected Poems* (Guyana, 1965), Figueroa's *Love Leaps Here* (London, 1962) La Rose's *Foundations* (London, 1966), Charles's *The Expatriate* (London, 1969), A.L. Hendrik's *On This Mountain* (London, 1965), less known efforts such as Frank John's *Black Songs* (London, 1969), as well as Louise Bennett's *Jamaica Labrish* (Jamaica, 1966), whose excellences are yet to receive the detailed elucidation they deserve.

Apart from this there have been a number of general anthologies of verse, such as Seymour's effort in *Kyk-over-al* No. 22, 1957, the *Anthology of West Indian Poetry*; *Caribbean Quarterly,* Vol. V, No. 3, (1958); John Figueroa's two collections, *Caribbean Voices, Vols.* 1 & 2, which together are the most massive anthology of Caribbean poetry in English so far, representing, as they do, selections from the work of fifty-three persons. More recently, there has been Mervyn Morris's *Seven Jamaican Poets* (Jamaica, 1971) which contains poems by A. L. Hendriks, Basil and R.L.C. McFarlane, Edward Baugh, Dennis Scott, Anthony McNeill and Morris himself. There are also the periodicals, such as *Bim*, which continues to publish new writing; *Jamaica Journal*, which carries a section on the arts; Clifford Sealey's *Voices*, which still appears from time to time; and now *Savacou*, which grew out of the Caribbean Artists' Movement (London 1966) whose central spirit, Kamau Brathwaite, worked hard to keep the movement afloat in the late sixties, together with a number of other writers and critics, such as Orlando Patterson, Louis James, John La Rose and Andrew Salkey.

Brathwaite now edits *Savacou* in Jamaica, together with Kenneth Ramchand, while Salkey takes care of business at the London end. *Savacou* aims to erect a bridge between the disciplines of history and literature, and to provide a forum for literary critics who are concerned with establishing standards for the assessment of Caribbean writing. The third and fourth issues every year, are meant to be an anthology of current writing. *Savacou*

3/4 (March 1971), was the first of these double issues, and as such was highly experimental. Editorial problems immediately presented themselves, the greatest of which seems to have been whether an anthology, which is meant to be an annual affair, should contain only severely selected writing, all of which self-consciously seeks "greatness" or "eternity", or whether the editors should choose as broad a cross-section of what is actually being written, good or bad, so as to indicate as many trends as are current in the feeling, sensibility and creative effort of the period.

The editors of *Savacou* clearly chose the latter course. The journal contains an introductory essay, extracts from two diaries and five novels, short stories, translations of the Cuban poet Guillén, and a wide range of verse from the point of view of quality, content and style. Although writers from all over the Caribbean are represented, the journal gives the impression of being strongly Jamaican in flavour and orientation. This is only natural, since the editors live in Jamaica. An issue produced in Trinidad would no doubt have contained a great deal of such writing as is growing out of the hothouse atmosphere of political detentions, mamaguy, robber-talk and corruption, which constitutes the reality against which, and in which, the young Trinidadian is forced to live. Writers such as Winston Ganessingh, Anson Gonzalez, Victor Questel, Abdul Malik, Brian James, Alfred Fraser, Syl Lowhar and Ramdath Jagessar, all young, uncertain, and searching for a form supple and strong enough to contain the strong mixture of rage, grief and dirty blue laughter which permeates the society at this time, would have been generously represented.

There would have been room, I'm certain, for Malik's sense of urgency, love and death, Questel's "Down Beat", which illustrates the strange patchwork sensibility and the dangerous ungrounded impermanence of the limer, and Anson Gonzalez's "Cadence" which, employing the image of steelband, explores phenomena such as the erosion of folk culture, and the inroads which politics has been making into genuine sensibility. In "Cadence", the entire nation becomes a "Pan" side, about to perform for Yankee tourists on "Panorama" night and waiting for the maximum political leader who, in his pose as conductor, will provide the downbeat for the Carnival pappyshow to start. The beat comes, but the Carnival is over, so that instead of pan, one gets "panic" and "pandemonium". It is a political poem, which makes its point through the extended image, and the pun, techniques endemic to Trinidad, which one sees there in Questel's work as well.

Gonzalez wrote his poem *before* February 1970, which simply shows how deeply people were feeling the farce of the political gimmickry of the late sixties and sensing that the society was on the verge of pandemonium. The despair of the youth had been clear to me since Roger McTair's "Corners without Answers", (*Voices*, 1964), with its final lines,

> We sit on pavements dreaming our dreams
> Trying to invoke visions.
> No genie comes: disillusioned, we put bobs to buy another bottle
> To help us endure this transition of sadness.

It received eloquent expression in the 1970 calypsos of Creole ("Behind the Bridge"), Chalkdust ("Massa Day Must Done"), and Psycho, ("Jail Them"), and of course in the protest Mas of 1970.[1]

In selecting an anthology of current West Indian writing, then, I'd have tried as far as possible to determine how far that writing reflected and explored the tensions of the society, and would have used "genuineness of feeling" as one of my criteria. The question of form or shape is a much more difficult one to settle, since there is no common consensus anywhere in the world today as to what constitutes proper form. I myself admire a wide variety of writing, ranging from the overtly "dramatic" use of language, which may be concerned only with things like rhythm and tone, to the highly complex and concentrated use of images and symbols, and I welcome the presence of both elements in current West Indian writing. I welcome especially the confidence with which young writers are trying to shape ordinary speech, and to use some of the musical rhythms which dominate the entire Caribbean environment.

Yet it is precisely this that disturbs some critics of West Indian poetry. Eric Roach, for example, reviewed *Savacou 3/4* in the *Trinidad Guardian*.[2] Restricting his commentary to an examination of some of the poetry, Mr. Roach described his criteria for determining what was art, and what was good and bad poetry. In so doing, he joined a sharp debate which is going on about aesthetics, tradition, literary criticism and sensibility in the West Indies. This debate started quite long ago and involves English liberals such as Owens, Carr and Louis James, and just about every Caribbean writer and critic. A great deal of the recent debate can be followed in journals like *Caribbean Quarterly*, *Bim*, *Jamaica Journal*, *Savacou*, and to a lesser extent in *The Journal of Commonwealth Literature*, *New World*, and the Caribbean dailies. Then there are the pronouncements of West Indian writers on writing. The most prolific of these is probably Brathwaite, but Walcott has written considerably on the work of his colleagues, and has recently written a long essay, "What the Twilight Says: An Overture",[3] which deserves the closest attention for its strong autobiographical content, and its lacerating statements on current developments in Caribbean writing, attitudes, insensibility and politics.

Mr. Roach, then, a reviewer of long standing, is part of this debate. Without perhaps really intending to, he, in his review of *Savacou 3/4*, expressed the attitudes of his generation to what it sees as a number of unsavoury and alarming features in today's youth. In criticising adversely a number of the younger Jamaican writers, Mr. Roach also made clear his own assumptions about "culture" and "history" and expressed a particular disgust at what he saw as a tendency "to thresh about wildly... in the murky waters of race, oppression and dispossession, ... to bury one's head in the stinking dunghills of slavery." He seemed to me to be taking a firm stand against simple rhetorical protest which, he feels, retards rather than liberates. He stressed the artist's need to learn his craft and to write out of the fullness of his experience and found most of the poetry in the anthology bad, fanatical, boring and naive. On the other hand, he had every admiration for the work of Derek Walcott, Wayne Brown, A.L. Hendriks and Dennis Scott, of which he found too little.

Syl Lowhar sensed the assumptions about "culture" and "history" upon which Mr. Roach's review was based, and questioned these in the *Trinidad Guardian* (17, 18 July, 1971). Mr. Roach's reply on Sunday 18th July was that his review had nothing to do with racialism or nationalism, but with bad verse as against good, and with standards of judging poetry. He reiterated his arguments against self-consciously asserted racial pride, and said that the quality of the Black man's efforts in the task of survival is sufficient sign of his rich identity.

I do share some of Mr. Roach's reservations about the journal. Editing needed to be more selective. There were a number of poems of similar theme, some extremely simple, others much more complex in form and treatment. I would have opted for the more complex abstracts from experience, in preference to simple statement of it. I need to feel that a writer is trying to use language imaginatively – any language in which he chooses to write. I didn't feel that this was happening in all the poems I read. I don't, however, share all of Mr. Roach's reasons for wanting to exclude some of the writing. The abundance of publication from the late fifties onwards, the bewildering and often inchoate variety of forms, styles and techniques revealed, in spite of the frequent mediocrity of the writing, makes me a little less certain about standards than he seems to be. Intimate acquaintance with the pressures that exist throughout the Caribbean, and with the fact that some of the writers Mr. Roach rejects feel them even nearer to the bone than I, gives me pause in passing judgement on the sensibility of the youth. Having some knowledge of the sensibility which produces reggae, and the entirely different one which shapes kaiso, I cannot but wonder what forms will grow from these roots, and welcome every sincere struggle to make abstracts of the languages and rhythms which constitute the thews and sinews, the inner ground of our sensibility. These languages, ranging from Creole to standard English are often more various than is realised, and are all available for exploration.

Mr. Roach, however, and there are many like him, feels that West Indian poetry *must* be tempered by a concern for craft which *must* be learned from the great English poets. A closer look at the basis on which he accepts or rejects this or that poet, is revealing. He first gives his general impression on *Savacou 3/4*:

> Colour, trumpeted on so many pages, gives the impression that one is listening to "Air on the nigger string", or to the monstrous thumping of a mad shango drummer on his drum 'in sibylline frenzy blind'![4]

In the two succeeding paragraphs, the words "fanatical" or "fanaticism" are employed four times, so that one gets the general impression that a great deal of writing in the journal was black, bloody and bad – although Mr. Roach deals with none of the prose pieces and only a small fragment of the poetry. He makes no distinction between the style and treatment which different poets brought to bear on the same themes of deprivation, disillusion, and impending rebellion. He makes no mention, for example, of the Guyanese Marc Matthews's dramatic monologue, "For Cuffy", which is really about the failure of revolutionary effort in contemporary Guyanese politics and society. Cuffy, the great eighteenth century leader of a famous slave revolt, has been chosen by the rulers of independent Guyana as the country's first national hero. Matthews, in an exciting use of Guyanese Creole, contrasts the energy, movement and skill of the rebel with the dishonesty and indirection of those who, as a gimmick and gesture, have chosen him as their mythical culture hero. Matthews is also referring to Clement Cuffy, a convict whose escape from a Guyanese prison in the late fifties resulted in a relentless manhunt through swamp and backlands. Matthews seems to be suggesting that his society needs to understand and empathise with its poor, its criminals, and its rebels in a genuine rather than in a sentimental fashion. Indeed, this seems to be one of the common ideas to emerge from *Savacou 3/4* as a whole. Matthews's voice, far from being frenzied, or "demented" or "fanatical", is cool. His theme is not revenge or protest but the pathos of political and human failure. If there was any anti-protest poem, or one that looks at the danger of a sensational self-identification with the past, it is this one. Mr. Roach does not think it worth mentioning, although it makes his point with less exaggeration and more genuine control than he makes it himself.

The reticent and genuinely sad meditations of Anthony McNeill on his and his society's fate counterpoint Bongo Jerry's cool "dread", which I will try to explain later. "Saint Ras" and "Ode to Brother Joe" are really part of the same consciousness as "Sooner or Later" or "Mabrak". The two moods, modes and tones knit seamlessly into a single exploration of contemporary Jamaican anxiety and pain. I would have liked to see published McNeill's moving tribute to Don Drummond, a man whose music suggests that he was, like Saint Ras, trapped at the terrible crossroads of his fate. I believe that McNeill identifies deeply with the spirit of Drummond's music; that the image of the caged confused animal which appears in "Rimbaud Jungle" merges into the image of the wounded schizophrenic saint and musician, walking the back-streets of Dread City, and merges further into the sacrificial figure of the Rastafarian at Babylon's crossroads. Mr. Roach doesn't mention Mc Neill at all, although the latter is as gentle, reticent, and careful of craft as they come, and certainly a poet of deeper feeling than either Dennis Scott or Wayne Brown, whose work would hardly lose were it to include a deeper anxiety, a truer pain.

Questel's use of fragmented pan rhythms and the pun, his sense of cadence, innuendo and diminuendo, are perhaps part of a small talent, when compared with the moving elegiac power of Walcott's sculptured panegyric for Harold Simmons. But it deserves some mention. In my review of Walcott's *The Gulf* in December 1969, I remember stating that I believed his "Landfall Grenada", another elegy, was the basis for a new departure, since in it are combined both his early lyricism and his late restraint. The elegy for Simmons also has these qualities, and has, in addition, a controlled rhetorical splendour quite different from anything in *The Gulf*. It is a poem which by its strength, wholeness, full grasp of how the human spirit needs to affirm its life in spite of death and void, and its carefully channelled energy, criticises the self-indulgence of much that is written in the West Indies, including a great deal of Walcott's own work. One would have hoped that in dealing with Walcott, Mr. Roach would have noted the great variety of his style suggested even in eight pages in *Savacou 3/4*. How does Mr. Roach account for Walcott's attempts to blend the scribal with the oral traditions in "Statio Haud Malefida Carinis"? What does he have to say about the use of dialect there, and why does he believe that Wayne Brown also lapses into dialect in one of his poems? It may be that both Walcott and Brown, his best disciple so far, are trying to do justice to all the languages that they know and hear.

It is interesting that Mr. Roach hears *frenzied* drums in so much of the writing, and that he singles out the poetry of Bongo Jerry for comment. It is unfortunate, though, that he did not choose to illustrate the specific mood of "frenzy", and that he seems automatically to associate the drum with the monstrous, the animal, and uncontrolled emotion. He asks in some dismay,

"Are we going to tie the drum of Africa to our tails and bay like mad dogs at the Nordic world to which our geography and history tie us?"[5]

So Africa, too, seems to hold frightening resonances for Mr. Roach, as indeed, it did for people like James Froude or Anthony Trollope, and Charles Kingsley who was able to see a Negro worksong and satirical dance as signs of the animal-like depravity of the race, while he saw the fine Caucasian features of one native as sufficient sign of that Black's ability to lead his people out of captivity.[6]

For Kingsley, it was only necessary for the native to look different from the Caucasian to be damned, and for him to resemble the Caucasian to possess every potential for refinement, and every qualification for humanity. For Mr. Roach, who ominously claims to be Lowhar's brother under the skin, the drum of the Afro-West Indian is associated with an animalistic blood-lust, while "European culture" is most generously defined, and proffered as a means of Caribbean salvation. He writes, for example:

> We have been given the European languages and forms of culture – culture in the traditional aesthetic sense, meaning the best that has been thought, said and done.[7]

If by "we have been given" Mr. Roach means "we can take what we need from: we can assimilate or fruitfully relate to", fine. In this respect there is really no limit to what anyone can choose. The whole world is our schoolmaster. I am not quite certain, however, what is meant by "the traditional aesthetic sense". This implies that there has always been a universal conception of good taste, or sensibility, when, in fact, there is in the vast and complex tradition of Europe – not to mention other parts of the world – justification for just about every kind of writing, including the elemental naked statement of emotion which is what Mr. Roach says he deprecates in young West Indian writers, and the rhetorical use of local dialects, which Mr. Roach seems to view more as limitation than as possibility.

Mr. Roach's definition of "culture" as "the best that has been thought said and done" is also fascinating. European writers today are much less confident than he, and are busy trying to come to terms with the ironies of a culture which has produced both Wagner and Hitler, Nietzsche and the gas chambers of six million Jews. These and similar incongruities have turned many writers into nihilistic visionaries who are uncertain of everything, including the cerebration and rationalism on which their writing depends. West Indians, however, tend to romanticise Europe's staggering achievements, while they gloss over the constant barbarity which has been inalienable from them. It is necessary for the West Indian to acquaint himself, not with any one side of European achievement, but with the whole paradoxical movement of human history, precisely because the West Indies were in large measure a product of some of the worst aspects of all history.

I am with Mr. Roach when he sees the problems as one of rendering justice to the whole of our history. "We must write out of the totality of our history, our environment and our feeling." I don't see, however, how we can begin to do this if we deny the growing confidence with which our writers are exploring our speech and drum rhythms. Also, I don't feel that any one set of traditions will suffice in this business of doing justice to our experience, just as I can't see how any single set of standards will suffice in the assessment of the already varied writing of the West Indies.

Also, it seems to me that Mr. Roach, like so many others, is begging the question as to what constitutes the "totality of our history". Naipaul has already said that we have no history, and recently, Walcott has lamented our lack of "a tiered concept of a past".[8] But we have barely started to write this history, and to examine those admittedly inadequate records of the past. If there seems to be "no history", it must mean that a great deal remains to be written, not that nothing ever happened, or survived. I believe the sense of there being a void to be filled has led to a great deal of freshness, innovation and versatility in West Indian writing, and in Caribbean lifestyle, while it has also informed their underlying melancholy. Things get worse when the West Indian lives in Europe and discovers not only the tiered (tired) concept of the past and as many monuments as the book said he would find, but a greater despair, guilt and desire for self-mutilation than ever he knew at home. For while Europe's mausolea undoubtedly stand, not many Europeans seem to believe in them anymore. It is in Europe that Naipaul's Kripal Singh discovers "the final emptiness".

Not only must we guard against the assumption that we really understand what happened in the past, but we also need constantly to reinterpret our present in the light of every fresh discovery of the meaning of ourselves. Mr. Roach writes as one who is sure that he knows exactly what is good for us. But what *is* the totality of history, environment and feeling of a West Kingston Rastafarian? How is this to be expressed in language, and how will it transform the style of our writing when we learn what it is? No one really knows. Yet, the Rastafarian presence is a felt one in the popular music of Jamaica, which is colonising the Caribbean as surely as calypso used to in the fifties. It is also growing in Jamaican painting and sculpture, while the Rastafarian strength and dream provide the considerable army of the poor with some ground of hope, and the ability to translate hardship into myth.

This is perhaps why the editors of *Savacou 3/4* included Ras Dizzy and Bongo Jerry. I tried to show above how the Rastafarian becomes a symbol of sainthood for Anthony McNeill because the poet realised the sacrificial nature of the Rastafarian's life. He can see how Ras becomes the visible scapegoat of the society, how his pain releases the creativity of some, while it increases the need for absolution which so many others seem to feel. I also tried to show how Don Drummond achieved a kind of sainthood, through his loneliness, the inner schizophrenic wound which he bore, despite his crime in murdering a woman whom he seems to have believed to have been unfaithful, and the way that he expressed all of these tensions and made them sing in his music. A story about Drummond that has appalled me was the one that described how, in one of his fits of illness, he stood up in the middle of Cross Roads, his arms outstretched in the shape of a cross, and gazed into space. The whole thing was frighteningly symbolic.

The sensibility to which Drummond related was undoubtedly Rastafarian. A major voice in the development of Jamaica blues, he still dominates the city. One listens to the Abyssinians singing "Satta Amasa Gana" ("Land Far Far Away") and hears Drummond's "Farther East"; one listens to the various experiments with Rastafarian rhythms in the latest music from Kingston, and hears Drummond's "Johnny Dark" or "Addis Ababa". Moreover, one hears a host of instrumentalists still trying to get the peculiar Drummond sound, without quite realising that that sound was the inner cry of a whole lifestyle, and cannot be imitated.

I say all of this as introduction to an examination of Bongo Jerry's poetry, because I believe that that poetry has been deeply influenced by a whole style of rhetoric which surrounds the popular music of Jamaica. I believe, too, that Jerry shares Drummond's sense of "Dread", a brooding melancholy which seems always on the verge of explosion, but which is under some sort of formal control. It was Jerry who wrote the most moving obituary note when Drummond died in May 1969. I quote a bit of it from *Abeng*, and will try to relate its style to that of Jerry's poetry.

> *Don Cosmic* is gone to his *Garden of Love,* and though his twenty nine years in the Valley of the Shadow of Death gave us more music than we ask for, we hurt inside when we remember that he was pushed around, pushed about and then finally shoved out by Babylon.
>
> But Don Cosmic played a tune that has not ended: the melody of *Freedom Sounds*...
>
> ...by '59, they (Jamaica Jazzmen) had licensed and registered SKA or BONGO MUSIC in our name, the sufferers' name. And Don Drummond paid the registration fee.
>
> *Don de Lion* blew an iron that was black and blue, a Peter Pan to lost black man. A Pied Piper, more music in his right hand than Little Boy Blue too. More still in both hands, heart and mouth. Black Man's musical conscience; for he paid and played *"Tribute to Marcus Garvey",* and told of his *"Reincarnation";* He announced *"The Return of Paul Bogle"*... toured *Far East* at length, giving thanks and praise to the king of kings in *Addis Ababa.*[9]

The passage illustrates the point that I have been trying to make about how Jamaica translates her suffering into myth. The words italicised are all names of Drummond tunes which Jerry knits together into the text of his tribute.

This sort of thing relates, I feel, to a technique of knitting words and phrases together, which the sound system disc jockeys employ all the time. Jerry adapts this style to suit the mood of elegy. A particularly striking sentence is "Don de Lion blew an iron that was black and blue." The thing can be written in a kind of free verse form.

> Don De Lion
> blew an iron
> that was black and blue
> a Peter Pan
> to lost black man

>   a Pied Piper
>   more music in his right hand
>   than Little Boy Blue too...

This is disc jockey speech, especially appropriate because Jerry is talking about a musician. The rhyming prose, the reference to nursery rhyme or fairytale characters, the Rastafarian symbolism are all knitted together. Peter Pan could soar as Drummond's music did. He is also associated with a paradise of primal innocence, which Drummond's music reveals for his audience of "lost black man". Both Boy Blue (Drummond was immersed in blues) and the Pied Piper played music. Like Boy Blue, Drummond is asleep (dead) and his flock of people like Boy Blue's sheep and cows go astray for lack of guidance. The Piper, like Drummond, was left unrewarded for his efforts in freeing the people. Unlike Drummond, the Piper took revenge on the people; but Drummond, as "musical conscience" of the group, as prophet and priest for "lost black man" needed to continue his walk through "the Valley of the Shadow of Death", (i.e. urban Jamaica in Mais's *Brother Man*, Orlando Patterson's *Children of Sisyphus* and Lindsay Barrett's *Song for Mumu*), and finally to be "shoved out by Babylon" if he were to earn through his music, spiritual freedom for his people. It is this willingness to endure which earns him the praise name "Don de Lion", a Rastafarian salutation which is derived from the scriptures and the mythology of the early Protestants. The Lion is "The Lion of Judah", who, according to the Rastafarian hymn, "will break every chain, and lead us to victory again and again." He is a symbol not so much of reprisal (though that idea is suggested also) but of redemption.

Drummond's trombone sound was "black and blue" in precisely the punning sense that Brathwaite uses the phrase in the Prelude to "The Spades" passage in *Rights of Passage*, "just call my blue/black bloody spade a spade".[10] Walcott also employs the same pun in the poem "Blues".[11] "They beat this yellow nigger/black and blue". Drummond was both "black" and "blue", in the sense that he was a melancholic, that he expressed this gloom in a kind of pervasively minor blues, and that his music contained the hurt of his people, who are black. In Brathwaite's case, we have a grim pun on all four words "blue", "black", "bloody" and "spade". Brathwaite is trying to suggest the atmosphere against which the be-bop men created is that of the chain gang, the gambling saloon with its card talk, the prison, and the freedom of sounds. Brathwaite's chain gang is universal, and this is why his blacks swear in the accents of both the American Negro and the Jamaican in "Folkways", the passage that follows. This is why, too, "Wings of a Dove" appears in "The Spades" section of the poem alongside passages dealing with the Negro in the big cities, rather than in the "Islands and Exiles" section, where it also seems to belong. In Walcott's case, the ironies are complicated by the fact that the protagonist is a mulatto liberal, who is beaten "black and blue" by his "suffering" fellow-blacks.

What we have just seen, then, is how an apparently simple piece of writing has quite complex implications, which reveal themselves to people who understand the context of the passage. That entirely different abstracts can be made from the ethos of ska and Rastafarianism is evident from Brathwaite's "Wings of a Dove", Mervyn Morris's elegiac poem for Drummond, "Valley Prince", which appears in *Savacou 3/4* and Mc Neill's poetry, which has been treated above. If I remember rightly, Mr. Roach once told me that he did not understand the dimension of "Wings of a Dove" until he heard it read. He also said that he now knew why Caribbean leaders imprisoned people like the reader of the poem. I had found his second statement rather strange then, though I no longer do now. Mr. Roach seemed somehow to be afraid of the sheer energy of the poem, a work whose dramatic magnitude I myself never quite grasped until I heard Ras Mortimo Planno, a Rastafarian, read it. I understood then why Mr. Roach was afraid. Brathwaite had, like Mais, been able to capture some of the "Dread", the impending doom and silence of the brooding locksman. "Dread" is indeed a frightening quality; the image of naked elemental survival and the mythical sense of Apocalypse, with which the Rastafarian lives day after day, are indeed awe-inspiring.

Mervyn Morris, on the other hand, looks at the quiet pain of Drummond, his quest for inner silence while in the middle of crowds of horns and the chaos of cymbals, the way that he never "blow it straight", his unorthodox sense of phrasing which was part of his vision of a twisted world. I like the ominous pun on "blow me mind". Drummond was "blowing his mind" in the sense that he played as he thought and felt. At the same time, he was constantly staving off breakdown, his trombone being the thing that kept him sane in the national madhouse of noise and oppression. Bongo Jerry is nearest to the actual speech on which the music is based, and out of which it grows. In his "Sooner or Later" and "Mabrak", which I find to be more complex poems than either his "The Youth" or "Black Mother", Jerry relates very closely to traditions of preaching rhetoric and music which most Jamaicans can understand and identify immediately.

The rhetorical style of the disk jockeys has developed during the sixties, and has matured in the singing, talking "scatting" and clowning of people like U Roy. Gibberish, riddles, nonsense rhymes, proverbs and fragments of wisdom all combine in this form of rhetoric, whose aim, as Satchmo's or Ella Fitzgerald's was, is not to make sense in any syntactical way, but to fit words into the shape of a mood, or the fluid rhythm of a line. To understand "Sooner or Later" and "Mabrak", one must first have some sympathy for the tradition out of which these grew. Mr. Roach takes particular offence at the lines,

> so have-gots, have-nots,
> trim-heads, comb-locks, dread-knots
> is sheep from goat.
> find yourself, row your own boat,
> "be ready for the day"

which he sees simply as "claptrap". Perhaps, but this, when seen in the tradition which I have been suggesting exists, takes on a different complexion. The enumeration of stereotypes "have-nots, have-gots" etc. indicates impatience on the speaker's part. His aim is to get down to the fundamentals of self-knowledge and independence, "find yourself, row your own boat". The community for which this poem is meant would accept these aphorisms as meaningful bits of advice, wisdom which they can test by experience. The average reader of *Savacou*, however, comes from a world in which proverbs and aphorisms are meaningless. Yet one reads Louise Bennett's *Jamaica Labrish* and finds it saturated with proverbs, whose function needs carefully to be assessed. One listens to Jamaican pop, and finds again the prevalence of the proverb, the message, and at times, the sermon. One recalls the popularity of Justin Hinds's "Carry Go Bring Come", which was really a string of aphorisms.

> Is carry-go-bring-come [gossip] my dear, bring misery
> Running from town to town making disturbancy,
> Is time you stop doing those things, you old Jezebel.
> The meek shall inherit the earth you old Jezebel
> Me is no like to see you making disturbancy.
> Better to seek a home in Mount Zion high
> Instead of heaping oppression upon an innocent man.
> But time will tell on you you old Jezebel.
> How long shall the wicked reign over my people?

The Trinidad reader would probably be shocked to hear that these words were viewed as most effective political commentary, because the "old Jezebel" referred to was a lady of much influence in political circles, and that a move was made to have the tune banned. Don Drummond, incidentally, played the accompaniment to Justin Hinds.

Another thing about the passage from "Sooner or Later" under discussion is that it may be telling of the apocalyptic separating of sheep from goats, righteous from unrighteous, which the Rastafarian here interprets in social terms. While tired of cliché categories, he still secretly hopes that the "have-nots" and the "dread-knots", will eventually rise and defeat the "have-gots" and the "trim-heads", the "clean-face" men, decent, complacent citizens. But this is stated almost casually, in a language which sounds like jingle or nursery rhyme, and which apparently mocks itself. It is useful to compare the passage with another popular song, which was danced in Trinidad and Guyana merely because of its exciting beat and was incomprehensible even to a number of Jamaicans. Its name is "Bongo Nyah", sung by Little Roy in 1970. The tune is that of "Baa Baa Black Sheep".

> Baa Baa Baa Baa, have you any wool?
> Yes Jah, yes Jah, one big head full.
>
> Some for Breddah Hiah, Some for Bongo Nyah.
> But now me see them pork eater pass
> They shall burn with fire
>
> Fire redder than red
> Nyah dreader than dread
> How can you resist Jah
> When you have a bald head?
>
> Lick it back Jah
> Lick it back Jah
> Look, fram you deh yah
> You nuh know Bongo Nyah![12]

The first thing of interest here is the name of the song. Who or what is Bongo Nyah? The name "Bongo" has had a fascinating history. Le Page traces its roots in the Hausa word "bungu", which means "A nincompoop, country bumpkin" and is "often also applied to one of unprepossessing appearance". In Jamaica, the word retained these connotations, but gained the additional sense of "black-an-ugly", "illiterate", "very black", "stupid", "worthless", "African".[13] In other words, a word which in its original form meant simply "crude, ugly or loutish", assumed connotations of self-contempt in the West Indies, where ugliness was associated with blackness.

Not everyone, however, rejected his African roots and "Bongo" was a name adopted with pride by certain cultists who wanted to remember, or to cultivate a dream of origins. Members of the Convince cult are also known as Bongo men. In this cult, which resembles that of Pukkumina, the devotee under possession becomes the habitation of what he believes to be African spirits, or the ghosts of dead slaves, maroons and obeah men. In other words, they psychically reclaim a whole history which includes the sense of belonging to a tribe, resistance to slavery, and the rebellion of the Maroons and obeah-man. Bongo men under possession often seek to offend onlookers by cursing, fighting, and making gestures which are sexually suggestive. Insisting that their religion is African, they reject the notion of sin, and resist the influence of Europeanisation.[14]

Bongo men, as described by Hogg, seem to be concerned with the preservation of tribal memories in the face of a changing society. Because they are not understood by the rest of the community, they are forced to act the role of rebels, which they fulfil by attacking all the cherished mores of orthodox Christianity, the religion of those who consider themselves to be decent Jamaicans. It is therefore easy to see why Rastafarians adopt the title

"Bongo". In it they identify with the original purity of purpose and resolve of the Convince cultists, like whom they seek to incarnate the spirit of an African past in their being. It is also easy to see from this why Rastafarians have been able to invent a mythology. They have a profound realisation of history, and do everything in relation to historical precedent, preserving a sense of continuity which links Tacky to Bogle, to Bedward to Garvey and to themselves.

"Nyah" refers to the Niyabingi Order, a militant group of Rastafarians whose policy has been described as "Death to black and white oppressors".[15] Bongo Nyah, then, is committed to social justice in an extreme way; he is a total rebel who seeks the death of *all* his oppressors, black or white.

Since, however, there is very little likelihood of this dream ever coming to pass, most of Bongo Nyah's rebellion actually takes place in his head, where he converts it into a mystical conception of the ultimate struggle between good and evil. Years of successful police action have driven Bongo Nyah into a brooding silence until, to the rest of society, he appears to be simply a stupid Bongo man, black-and-ugly, who nurses a dead dream of Africa.

He is the society's "black sheep" (sheep implying both meekness and stupidity), whose wool (the Rastafarian's hair) the policeman is about to trim. The locksman's hair is his pride and, like Samson's, a symbol of his strength and capacity to endure. Jamaican policeman often try to humiliate Rastafarians by cutting off their hair. Hence the significance of the nursery rhyme opening of the song: "Baa, Baa, Baa, Baa, have you any wool?" The Rastafarian, as society's black sheep and scapegoat, is being taunted and badgered by the law into his age-old dream of the Apocalypse.

Contemplating the clean-faced society, which he abhors as pig-like and pork-eating[16] he explodes, "They shall burn with fire." He knows, too, that these people who mock his dream of a past, have no roots themselves, and are therefore afraid of fire, rebellion and the ultimate manifestation of *dreadness*.

> Fire redder than red
> Nyah dreader than dread
> How can you resist Jah
> When you have a bald head?

"Lick it back Jah" is really a phrase instructing the disk jockey to play the tune again ("lick it back"). Here it serves the purpose of reminding the dancer that he is really enjoying himself at a party, not burning down the city, and that he should not take his role of total rebel too literally. But the menacing possibility of Bongo Nyah's presence remains.

> Look from you deh yah
> You nuh know Bongo Nyah!

Translated, this means, "Consider how long you have lived here, and you still don't know Bongo Nyah!" It is precisely because the society has refused to face up to the necessity of creating an environment in which the Rastafarian can become a full citizen, that the unknown menace of Bongo Nyah remains.

The cryptic talent which produces songs like "Bongo Nyah" is very similar to the talent which lies behind Bongo Jerry's work, with its wealth of allusion to the apocalyptic imagery of "Revelation" and the fascinating, unwritten liturgy of Rastafarianism. One notes, for example, Jerry's usage of the call-and-response pattern, which is the root pattern of Jamaican work songs, and Rastafarian or sectarian preaching. A leader calls out a line and establishes a certain rhythm, while the gang, chorus or congregation, shouts sings or grunts a reply.

Take, for example, the well-known work-song, "Woman a Hebby Load".

> Leader: Woman a hebby load
> Chorus: Um hmm
> Leader: Woman a hebby load.
> Chorus: Um hmm
> Leader: Woman a hebby load
> Chorus: Um hmm
> Leader: When Saturday morning come
> Chorus: Um hmm...

Some of the best ska tunes were clearly based on the classic worksong call-and-response pattern. I think of Don Drummond's "Reburial", "Fidel", "Occupation", "Eastern Standard Time", "Stampede", "Street Corner", "Man on the Street", all of which are classic examples of his style. The soloists make their statements against the background of a continuously answering chorus. In Rastafarian sermons or even ordinary conversation, the group often answers the speaker with murmurs of "natural", "true word", "true story" and so on. In Bongo Jerry we hear and feel it time and again. Leader: "Sooner or later". Chorus: "But mus..." The importance of this pattern of call-and-response is that it tightens the bond between individual and group, and affirms their mutual acknowledgement of each other's presence.

The link between Jerry's oral poetry and Jamaican music is further illustrated by the fact that one of the versions of "Satta Amasa Gana", a current reggae meditation, is called "Mabrak". Song, sermon and drumbeat fuse in the reggae version of "Mabrak", as they do in Jerry's poem.

It is evident that Jerry's poetry makes its point effectively when read. Mervyn Morris had this to say about a recent reading of poetry from *Savacou*.

> The reason why Garth White was one of the most effective of the performers was that he seemed intimate with the rhythms of Bongo Jerry's poem (particularly "Mabrak") which had escaped me on the page.

Garth White used to be a bit of a deejay, and has grasped the significance of the cool menace of rocksteady Rudie tunes in his article "Rudie Oh Rudie".[17] He could therefore suggest in his reading something of the environment of the poem, and refer it to its true context in the folk-urban blues of today's Kingston.

A friend of mine who was at the same reading, had this to say:

> In "Mabrak" is a different kinda thing happening. Power *within* the people. Not so much high seriousness as *'dreadness!'* not prophecy and lyricism and spectral doom but *menace* and *cool* and *menace*. A different quality sound; and what makes it different is the humour in "Mabrak". The message doan just register, it resonates ... This sense of oneness is upsetting a lot of people.[18]

In an earlier letter, he had commented that the "dread" music of Kingston contained "more elemental honesty of rage and blues and menace" than any of the poetry he had heard emanating from the Mona Campus. This is no new thing. Drummond's "China Town", "Confucius" and "China Clipper", with their chaos of Chinese harmonies, preceded the 1965 riots against the Chinese. His "Marcus Junior", "Fidel", "Johnny Dark", "Reburial", "Man on the Street" and "Addis Ababa" were the forerunner to the upsurge of Black consciousness in the late sixties. The cool and menace were fully there in many of the rudeboy tunes of the mid-sixties. "Tougher than Tough", "Dreader than Dread", "Judge Dread" and "Ghost Dance", are ample example of this. What my friend is noting is simply the most recent example of an unchanging phenomenon.

For what really is "Dreadness"? The Rastafarian locksman claims to possess the quality his dreadlocks symbolise, both his leonine fierceness, and his inner strength. Ras Daniel Heartman's painting, *Daniel in the Lions' Den* makes this point. In it the *dreadness* of the Rastafarian's face makes the very lions seem tame. It is as if he has drawn the lions' strength and fierce energy into his own face, and yet the eyes are sad with perceived and felt suffering. *Dreadness* is all of these things – fierce energy, resolve and an underlying sense of the tragic. *Dread* is for Heartman part of a spiritual quality, and is bound up with his endurance. The rude boy associated *dreadness* with his defiant and rebellious stance against all authority, but, perhaps, he posed more insistently than the Rastafarian, since he may have lacked the latter's spiritual depth. Then Judge Dread,[19] who exercises power irrationally and without mercy or fairness, claims to possess the quality of *dread*. Judge Dread is the product of the ruling class's fear of Bongo Nyah, their ultimate answer to the locksman. (Judge Dread's shortest sentence is 500 years, and all are guilty). Something in the society has produced both Bongo Nyah and Judge Dread: the society's perennial failure to validate the Emancipation Act, the 1865 rebellion, or the spirit of Independence.

Dread is that quality which defines the static fear-bound relationship between the "have-gots" and the "have-nots". It is the historic tension between slaver and slave, between the cruel ineptitude of power on the part of the rulers, and the introspective menace and the dream of apocalypse on the part of the downtrodden. This is why dread remains a constant quality in Jamaica's creative life.

So we return to our original question which is, "Having identified this quality of *dread* as an inalienable part of our past and present, how do we fuse a form capable of containing it, and how do we assess such writing as attempts to do so?" People like Mr. Roach would have us forget the matter altogether, though this quality invests the society with a sense of the tragic and a capacity for myth. It may be, also, that similar questions are being asked all over the world, similar quests for form being made, and similar problems arising about standards of judgement. We can gain by identifying these areas of similarity. For example, familiarity with the Wright-Howe-Ellison-Baldwin exchanges[20] on "protest" fiction would redeem a lot of West Indian criticism from its naiveté. An understanding of how young Black poets in America are using rhythm as image to conjure up, as effectively as any word picture, the sounds and real presence of their environment, can enable West Indian poets, who grew out of a world similarly dominated by constant music and noise, to explore their own world in fresh ways by expanding our notion of technique and form.

Mr. Roach notes that "we are at the hinge of the Americas", but strangely uses this as a further argument in favour of our assimilating the techniques of England. His sole reference to the American presence in the West Indies is to:

> "the Afro-haired, dashiki-clad generation, maddened by its own simulated pride, by Negro-American acid rock and pot."[21]

Acid rock and pot are probably much more a white American/European, pop/hippie/yippie thing, but here Mr. Roach's point is well-made and timely. The youth of Trinidad are fed and accept a vast whirlpool of universal pop music, most of which is a reaction to tensions and sicknesses quite beyond their own anxieties. Very few of them understand the real and varied contexts of the music which dominates their existence, and breeds in them a scorn for their own thing. A knowledge of the pressures which Black artists have had, and still undergo, of the way records are made not to express "soul" at all, but to cater for the tastes of an exceedingly fickle market, can help youth in Trinidad to distinguish between the real and the synthetic products of America and Europe. It may also convince them that they are little more than the puppets of an international marketing system, whose final effect may well be to erode what little indigenous talent remains. For the pace with which the pop scene shifts in America alone is bewildering in the extreme, and the effect on local youth is to contribute to their deepening sense of instability, their lack of clear motivation, and their consequent desire to evade the task of transforming their own milieu.

The achievement of the NJAC[22] in 1970 was temporarily to channel the energies released by the message in soul culture towards political change in Trinidad. They were able to tap that unknown inner vitality in the youth, to bring it to the surface where immediately its energies became the greatest challenge which the politically sterile leaders of the country have ever had to face. They jerked the entire society into a long litany of self-justification, guilt and fear. The arrests, detentions, shootings and tribunals were an attempt not only to control social unrest, but to evade the challenge. The imprisonment of the legitimate leaders of youth not only restored ease and quiet, but drove the youth into themselves, heightened their desire for the opiate of music, drugs, saga-boy clothes, and easy slogans. The film *Woodstock* with its white liberal orientation and vagueness, its atmosphere of cliché and escapism, provided the youth with all the justification that they needed for retreat into the uneasy nirvana of weed and pills. And all sorts of people have encouraged Woodstock-type gatherings in Trinidad – from the businessmen who were planning a grand sit-in at Wallerfield in 1970, to the ruling People's National Movement, whose "Expression 1971" was a belated attempt to jump on the bandwagon of popular culture. Worse than this have been the misdirected attempts to control "folk"-consciousness, by a heavy-handed sponsorship of folk culture, the sickening political gimmickry which, unable to inspire, seeks to control every response of youth. One expects those who have recently been appointed by Whitehall to serve on its various committees for the promotion or discovery of national culture, to point out the vast inconsistencies which the country's rulers have betrayed in this area, as in most others.

One of the many questions asked by Mr. Roach concerns the possible fate of today's generation. His manner in phrasing it suggests that his age was in some way better:

> When today's whirlwind and whirlpool of race and colour in the Caribbean have subsided, where will all this soapbox street corner ranting and posturing of the younger poets be?[23]

But perhaps Mr. Roach himself is in a better position to answer this question than most people. The question he raised about standards of judgement and his unequivocal rejection of the rhetoric of this generation, sent me back to the earlier anthologies of West Indian poetry, in which a few of Mr. Roach's poems appeared. His declaration that:

> To be a Caribbean English language poet is to be aware of the functions and structure of English verse. At the same time one must, like a reptile,

> shed the skin of learning, disdain, while we revere that cultural dominance and strive for what we would like to call the West Indian thing. One must erect one's own bungalow by the sea out of the full knowledge of the architecture of the English places and cottages.[24]

made me reflect that at no point does Mr. Roach stress the need for the West Indian writer examining what he actually has in the West Indies, which, after all, is what he will have to come back to, when, like a soucouyant, he stops flittering about and returns to his skin, which history has already seared with salt, pepper and fire. Secondly, Mr. Roach speaks of "English poetry" rather than of "poetry in English", forgetting, no doubt, that the English language has long ceased to be the single property of any one people.

I therefore undertook to read his own poetry in the light of his statement about possibilities and standards, and was surprised to discover in his "I Am the Archipelago" not only the rhetoric of Marlowe and Shakespeare, but a bitterness and imagery reminiscent of some of Martin Carter's *Poems of Resistance*. Roach writes:

>   ...And now
> I drown in the groundswell of poverty
> No love will quell. I am the shanty town
> Banana, sugarcane and cotton man;
> Economies are soldered with my sweat
> Here, everywhere; in hate's dominion;
> In Congo, Kenya, in free, unfree, America.
>
> I herd in my divided skin
> Under a monomaniac sullen sun
> Disnomia deep in artery and marrow.
> I burn the tropic texture from my hair;
> Marry the mongrel woman or the white;
> Let my black spinster sisters tend the church,
> Earn meagre wages, mate illegally,
> Breed secret bastards, murder them in womb...

In many ways, this reminded me of Martin Carter. There was the general, rhetorical tribal "I", in which the poet sees himself as the spokesman for the group. He probes, catalogues and summarises the history of the group. Each line becomes a plain, self-contained statement or fact; it names, catalogues the distress, guilt, and rebellion of the group, like a political pamphlet, or the pioneer historiography of Eric Williams. The lack of *enjambement* is the result of this desire to catalogue. I can hear in those lines what it felt like to be a conscious young man in the last days of crown colony, when one could entertain the slender hope of federation and self-government. Moreover, in the very terms employed, I can hear the Geddes Granger of 1970, whose rebellion is simply the result of the persistence of crown colony consciousness, politics, actions and language in an age of so-called Independence. Because little has changed, the language of rebellion remains the same.

But this is not how the people who taught me English at UWI encouraged me to see the verbal rebellion of West Indian writers. Had Marlowe written those lines, they would have been viewed as part of a rhetorical tradition, part of progression from *Beowulf* and Kyd, which eventually achieved its fruition in Shakespeare and Donne. But unfortunately, the lines had been penned by Eric Roach. Their dramatic potential was completely ignored, though a poet like Mr. Roach springs from a society with a rich tradition of formalised rhetoric (e.g. robber-talk, *sans humanité* picong, all kinds of preaching, *Pierrot Grenade,* etc.) and may well have been attracted to the Elizabethans because their use of the language counterpointed forms which he knew, and which were alive in his own society.

Thus it was that R. J. Owens could divorce Carter's poetry from the Guyanese political trauma of 1953, and state simply that Carter confuses rhetoric with poetry. It would have been more rewarding to discuss Carter's use of rhetoric, with a view of discovering its sources, how it makes or mars his verse, and whether it opened any possibilities for Caribbean verse. Instead, Owens began with an *a priori* condemnation of rhetoric (just as many early white critics of music began with an *a priori* condemnation of jazz) and thus closed the discussion about the possibilities of a West Indian dramatic verse, even before it started. But it is a discussion which must remain open in island societies which oscillate between a rich oral tradition and a growing scribal one.

Owens was even more severe on Eric Roach's "I Am the Archipelago":

> Mr. E. M. Roach indulges himself in a breathless rhetorical rodomontade in *I Am the Archipelago.* The highflown tone and disarticulated movement turn the poem into a watered down version of minor Elizabethan blank verse.
>
> Mr. Roach is clearly an intelligent man and one hopes he will stop attitudinising and get down to refining the sensibility he shows in his *Seven Splendid Cedars.*[25]

Yet I have read these lines as an accurate definition of how the West Indian Negro felt about himself and his society then, and feels about it now. I have seen them as an intense summary of our entire social malaise.

Mr. Roach's article indicates that he has taken Dr. Owens's advice, to the extent that he too eschews the honest, if flawed, attempts by young West Indians, to come to terms with the similar harshness of both present and past. While Owens condemns the imitativeness of Caribbean writers, Mr. Roach criticises them for being too self-conscious and for their growing refusal to relate to an English tradition of great writing. Doubtless both extremes need to be avoided. Yet one cannot help feeling that Dr. Owens, in addition to stressing how badly the poets of Mr. Roach's time imitated their English masters, might have detected the emergence of characteristic ways of looking at Caribbean landscape and politics which are quite different from what had been taking place in the thirties and early forties. The reason why the poets of the forties and fifties so often provided descriptions, rather than explorations of experience, was that these pioneers felt the urgent need simply to name their landscape and give it some being.

It is no surprise that the characteristic mode of the sixties has been one of introspection, concentration, and sophistication of several of the techniques which the writers of the forties could only wield crudely. Seymour's and Carter's interest in history has taken a clearer and more definite shape in the work of Kamau Brathwaite. Shake Keane's interest in the musical rhythms of calypso and jazz has also found apotheosis in Brathwaite, and a growing number of writers. Walcott has learned how to speak with his own voice and to write a tight, concentrated, dense poetry in which he fuses public and private anxieties. Dr. Owens's hope for the emergence of a West Indian equivalent of Mark Twain, who would freely and unselfconsciously use his own local variant of "English English", had, in fact, already been fulfilled before 1960, in the work of Selvon and Lamming, though Owens seems not to have recognised this. What is important is that West Indian poets have.[26] Derek Walcott has pointed out the influence of Caribbean novelists on both his and Brathwaite's work. Strangely, Mr. Roach doesn't suggest that young West Indian poets can gain from a sensitive reading of the already substantial work of West Indian novelists.

In answer to Mr. Roach's question about the possible fate of today's generation of "soap box bards", I'd venture that in twenty years' time, their fate may be no worse than his. The experience of living in the West Indies is sufficiently chastening to temper most rhetoric into reticence. Carter burned out in five years into the sad blue "Poems of Shape and Motion"[27] whose doubt was much more movingly shaped into poetry than his earlier oratorical commitment. The weight of compassion, life and time which those poems contain tells me clearly as anything how our lives will, from generation to generation, be denuded slowly into grief, tiredness and silence. In twenty years, if spared by ganja, soul, cacapool rum and the widening barbarity of our politics, most of today's youth will be respectable citizens, without illusions, and terribly afraid of tomorrow's children, whose ears they will try to fill with fables of the swinging seventies.

(First published in *Tapia*, No 20, Sunday, August 29, 1970, pp. 11-14)

References

1. Before the Black Power marches of February-April 1970, there was considerable protest in the calypsos and Carnival of Trinidad.
2. Roach, E., "Review of *Savacou 3/4*", *Trinidad Guardian*, July 14, 1971.
3. Walcott, D., "What the Twilight Says: An Overture", in *Dream on Monkey Mountain and Other Plays* (New York: Farrar, Straus and Giroux, 1970).
4. Roach E., *Trinidad Guardian*, July 14, 1971.
5. Ibid.
6. Kingsley, C., *At Last, A Christmas in the West Indies* (London, MacMillan, 1871 [quotes from second edition, 1890]) pp. 16-17; p. 267.
7. Roach E., op. cit.
8. Walcott D., "What the Twilight Says: An Overture".
9. Bongo Jerry, *Abeng*, Vol 1, No. 16 (May 17, 1969).
10. Brathwaite, E., *Rights of Passage* (London: OUP, 1967), p. 28.
11. Walcott, D., "Blues" in *The Gulf and Other Poems* (London: Jonathan Cape, 1969), p. 34.
12. "Bongo Nyah": reggae song of c. 1970 performed by Little Roy.
13. Cassidy, F.G., and Le Page, R.H., *Dictionary of Jamaican English* (Cambridge: Cambridge University Press, 1967).
14. Hogg, D.W., *Jamaica Religions: A Study in Variations* Unpublished PhD Dissertation, Yale University 1964, pp. 262-270.
15. Smith, M.G., Augier, F & Nettleford, R, "The Rastafari Movement in Kingston Jamaica", *Caribbean Quarterly*, Vol 13, No. 3 (Sept. 1967) p. 7.
16. Rastafarians are not supposed to eat pork.
17. White, G., "Rudie, Oh Rudie", *Caribbean Quarterly* Vol. 13, No. 3 (Sept 1967).
18. Williams, N., Letter to G. Rohlehr (14th June 1971).
19. See Prince Buster's "Judge Dread", "The Appeal" and "Barrister Pardon".
20. See Irving Howe's "Black Boys and Native Sons", Dissent, 1963, vs. Ralph Ellison's "The World in a Jug" (in *Shadow and Act*, 1964) and James Baldwin's "Everybody's Protest Novel" in *Nobody Knows My Name*, 1963.
21. Roach, E., Review of *Savacou 3/4*, *Trinidad Guardian*, July 14, 1971.
22. NJAC – The National Joint Action Committee – which organised the 1970 Black Power demonstrations in Trinidad and Tobago.
23. Roach, E., *Trinidad Guardian*, July 14, 1971.
24. Ibid.
25. Owens, R.J., "West Indian Poetry", *Caribbean Quarterly*, Vol. 7, No. 3 (Dec. 1961) pp. 120-127.
26. See e.g. "Walcott on Walcott", *Caribbean Quarterly*, Vol. 14, Nos. 1 & 2 (Mar-June 1968) pp. 77-82.
27. Carter, M., *Kyk-Over-Al*, Vol. 6, No. 20 (1955).

AFTERTHOUGHTS

Since "West Indian Poetry: Some Problems of Assessment" was first published, I have received a number of comments from friends and associates. Two said that they liked the article itself much more than they did the material which it attempted to "vindicate". Now, I wasn't really trying to vindicate anything, and, in fact, have stated where I myself would not have chosen all of the material which appeared in the issue. What I was doing was simply an attempt to join a growing debate about the nature of the West Indian experience, and to describe the *context* of contemporary West Indian poetry, as I see it. This is probably why I spoke more about what was happening in reggae and in the folk-urban jazz of Jamaica than about the magazine itself. Mr. Roach's article convinced me that a number of people in the West Indies are prepared to talk about literature without understanding much about the context out of which such writing grows. If my article was attempting to do anything, then, it was to sketch in some of the background relevant to an understanding of the material in the *Savacou* anthology.

Another comment, which I ought to reply to, has been the feedback on the last paragraph of the article, where I said that most of today's strident youth will be little different from the last generation's once angry, now tired rebels, after twenty years have elapsed. This last paragraph was taken as a sign of my own despair. So it was. In my short life, I've already seen so much fraudulence and erosion of spirit through folly, absurd politics and naked dishonesty on all levels of existence that I cannot, with any honesty, be anything but a pessimist. Also, I feel that a great deal of West Indian writing is pessimistic for much the same reasons that my last paragraph seems to be particularly so.

That paragraph was meant as an answer to Mr. Roach's question as to the future of today's youth. What I wanted to stress was that there would be a continuity in the folly, powerlessness, deceit and grief which one can easily see in the people of Mr. Roach's age. If the rest of my article stressed the fact that there was a great deal of creativity in the West Indian people, it also stressed that this creativity existed *in spite of* Caribbean politics. I view with particular disgust the attempts which politicians are making throughout the West Indies, not to enhance, but to exploit art on all levels. This sort of thing can become tragic, when a folk art begins to be used as a tourist attraction, or to gain a few more votes for a party in office. Recently, here in Trinidad, Derek Walcott has been making a similar point. If in everything I've written I've affirmed a kind of faith in our capacity for survival, I've never underestimated the corrosive nature of absurd politics, or absurd history and historiography.

This is why I've seen the experience of Martin Carter as a paradigm of what will be the fate of most of the rebels in the West Indies. Because, if a finer spirit emerges from the carrion of our present, it will be won at the expense of individual defeat, sacrifice, tiredness of spirit and the sickness unto death, attenuation of faith and despair. This seems to me to be the meaning of both Carter's life and Walcott's. It also seems to me to be the experience of many a man who walks the street. I know that young people here feel it to the bone, and that most of them will simply seek one way or another of opting out of whatever struggle presents itself.

This is not to say that nothing will be created, but to stress the price at which such creativity will be achieved. In a recent article, "Calypso and Politics"[1], I tried to show how what is happening in Trinidad has produced a complex range of responses from a large number of calypsonians. On the other hand, there is the fact that 1970 has accentuated the youth's rejection of the calypso and of most things Trinidadian, for Lord knows what. Anyone who has lived through 1971 will recognise tiredness and despair as inalienable parts of the landscape here. My feeling is that they will increase, until the society creates new means of dealing with them, a new kind of indigenous soul equivalent to Jamaica's reggae, recognising both the similarities and the differences of the American thing. There are signs that the calypso is trying to adjust, to inject a deeper sense of blues into its traditional gaiety, to tackle the problems of this complex generation. I don't know, however, how long this will survive against the tourist-oriented Carnival season, onslaughts of sick Euro-American music and sicker films, the break-up of the lime, and the growing drugs racket. At present, the forces of decay seem to be so much stronger than those of creativity.

Jamaica is a different case. The forces of despair and erosion are even fiercer there than those in Trinidad. But Jamaica has a more coherent people and a more continuous line of history. Hence the dismay is counterbalanced by a tremendous vitality. Contemporary pressures in Jamaica seem to me to produce two types of response from the man on the street. The first is a rebellious urge to shatter the whole social framework, best seen in the rhetoric of Rastafarianism, the music of Rudyism, and more recently in the dread tunes of Kingston. The second is a desire to retreat into the self, and the dream of a land "Far far away where there's no night, there's only day". This is best seen in the hymns of Rastafarianism, (e.g. "The Lion of Judah", "Zion We Want to Go", "There is a Green Hill", by the Sons of Negus) and in more secular hymns such as Max Romeo's "Jordan River", The Ethiopians' "The Selah", The Abyssinians' "Satta Amasa Gana" and "Mabrak", and many others.

But these two responses are not opposites as some seem to think. They complement each other, intersecting at several points. The rebel is shot down or beaten and imprisoned. After a few years of this, his response is to retreat within himself, and search for new strength to counter this despair. The result of this retreat, this excavation in the ground of being, is a grounded music, whose basic beat, the ground-beat of survival itself, is as solid as the earth. Each new weight of pressure has its corresponding effect on the music, and the revolution is usually felt first as perceptible change in the bass, the basic rhythm, the inner pulse whose origin is in the confrontation between despair, which history and iniquitous politics inflict, and the rooted strength of the people. When such innovation takes place in the ground-beat, the whole trivial stream of popular appeasing-entertaining music is transformed. It acquires a new explosiveness which increases the dread and tension in the whole society, because the beat *dominates* the city. The rhythm of the basic bass is the grounded heartbeat of the city. So when the rhythm goes dread, the whole city feels the tension; and why not? After all, it was the cruel tension which determined that the beat should go dread in the first place.

Hence, the retreat to Ethiopias of the spirit returns to the sufferer the image of his own bleeding face. The inner journey takes him back to the outer hardship. It is this that the music of dread reflects. Hence in "Jordan River", we have first the dream of final release from horror:

> I saw Selassie – I stretch forth his hand
> to take I cross Jordan River
> I'm on my way to Zion

Then there is the other side of this dream.

> The man that hear the word of Jah
> and harden his heart
> shall be burned with fire

The dream of a final journey of the spirit is counterpointed by a dream that the wicked shall one day burn with fire. The same thing is true for Max Romeo's "Let the Power Fall on I, Fari", which is a prayer for physical and spiritual strength. A later stanza begins "Let the wicked burn in flames, Fari". The apocalyptic sense of the Jewish psalmist and his intense yearning for a final justice, a final vengeance, and ultimately transcendence of the whole sorry scheme, informs today's dread sounds from Kingston.

The image of a refining fire recurs in Jamaican music with a frequency which cannot but alarm those whose aim it is to preserve the historic scheme of things. One hears tunes with names like Niney's "Blood and Fire", Wayne Jarrett's "Brimstone and Fire", successors to "What a Fire" and Max Romeo's "Babylon Burning". Incidentally, "Babylon Burning" is the same tune as "Woman a Hebby Load", and recently "Nyah Man". Story carries the tune of this traditional folksong again. In other words, a folk song is carrying the burden of the folk-urban rebellion. This is an important point because it underlines the difference between Trinidad and Jamaica. It would be almost unthinkable for a calypsonian to attempt to use a folksong in order to convey his message. Calypso departed from these folk roots about three decades ago. While there was a sort of lime going in the towns, while legendary people like Polycar met in groups all over the city and created a style and a rhetoric all their own, the calypso retained its basic roots, or such basic roots as a small town is capable of providing. Today, however, Port of Spain is wide open to the world, and the character of the lime has changed. A lot of the rhetoric is imported, and the calypso, which depends on the richness of local idiom, imagination and gesture, and on the sense of a vital urban spirit in the lime, is suffering. An almost total lack of idea or continuity in politics has resulted in a bewildered society with a sense of void and sickness, and a demoralising directionlessness.

In Jamaica, the phenomenon has been one of urbanisation, a shift from the country to the towns. In Trinidad it has been more one of immigration, and almost automatic squatting in the towns, automatic unemployment, and loss of original roots in the process of becoming, not so much Trinidadian as a citizen of Port of Spain. This is why although there are so many roots in Trinidad, it is difficult to get to them. French eroded much of the Spanish influence, though evidence of it remains in the Parang. English education was first aimed at destroying the French substructure of language and the African basis of folklore and religion. The Church played a major role in destroying continuity in Trinidad culture, though the loss of the original language of Creole culture, that is Creole French, has had a lot to do with the sense of void and discontinuity in Trinidadian culture. This accounts in part for why the calypso has today moved so far away from what were regarded as its roots. In so doing, it has simply conformed to the general drift of things in Trinidad. Discontinuity is part of the national experience in history, politics and culture.

Jamaica, however, because of the greater integrity of its population, has begun to lay the foundation of a vital folk-urban culture. This is why Afro-Jamaican religion, mythology, rhythms rhetoric and music have begun to saturate the whole consciousness of the place. This accounts for the sound of *Savacou 3/4*, which I can see is simply a beginning. The folk-jazz group called The Mystical Revelation of Rastafar-I is another such beginning.[2]

When I heard the group in December 1970, they sounded like the most frightening awesome energy that I had ever heard in music. Marrying the agony of John Coltrane and Pharoah Sanders to the rooted cool and menace of Rastafarian drums, the Mystics, as they were then called, constructed the bridge between tropical and temperate zones of blackness. It was good to hear that Marina Maxwell was able to include them in her "Bongo Man A Come" programme of poetry and music. All sorts of things are jelling in Jamaica, which one needs to understand before one can begin to speak intelligently about consciousness or art.

All of these folk-urban manifestations have their roots in the syncretic Afro-Protestantism of Pukkumina, Bedwardism, Garveyism and Rastafarianism. At all times in the history of Black Jamaica, culture has had a religious basis. So also have politics, and the reaction of people to the depredations of politics and politicians has always had a nearly mystical basis. This is why it is difficult today to separate religious music from the music of open rebellion.

Take, for example, Bob Marley's "Duppy Conqueror", which was popular late in 1970. The singer begins by describing his release from prison:

> Yes, me fren,
> Dem set me free again
> Yes me fren, me fren,
> Me deh pan street again.

The next few lines are a statement both of defiance and religious affirmation:

> The bars could not hold me
> Walls could not control me
> They tried to keep me down
> But Jah keep I around

He goes on to say that he has to make a journey to "Mount Zion" and that no force either material or supernatural is going to stop him. "If you're a bull-bucker, well let me tell you I'm a duppy-conqueror". Normally, people in using the term "duppy-conqueror" deny that they are themselves duppy-conquerors, which today simply implies "hooligan". The words used to have a much stronger meaning, which Bob Marley seems to be trying to recapture in his song of defiance and faith.

A duppy is a spirit of the dead, whose burial rites have been incomplete. The spirit then wanders in a sort of limbo, and cannot take its place as an ancestral voice or protector of the group, but rather, if caught by an evil obeah-man, can be used against the group. In other words, duppies exist because one has failed to make amends with the past. In Marley's song, the whole oppressive system, which remains intact because of corrupt justice, becomes a duppy, a malignant spirit of the unplacated dead. This duppy of history, this corpse inherited from the colonial master, has been captured by judge and politician, evil obeah men, necromancers (or, to use Sparrow's word, *negromancers*) who employ their energies to destroy and gain personal power, rather than to make amends with the past, to heal history's wounds, or to increase the strength and coherence of the community.

The perverted leaders of the society, then, become the duppy which the man in the street must overcome. The duppy-conqueror is, in this instance, more than a hooligan. He is the myal man, the folk-priest who always appeared at critical moments in Jamaica's history. He usually claimed to have power over life and death, to be the true houngan, whose function had been perverted by the corrupt obeah men. In Marley's song, then, the man on the street is prisoner, sufferer, but also shaman, myal man, resurrected victim, who, because he lives within the grace of the Most-I (Most-High), cannot be suppressed by the gates, the bars and the prison walls which the privileged are compelled to raise up against him. In "Duppy Conqueror", the common man assumes the role of healer, defender of faith and consciousness, conscience, in a society which still consists of masters and slaves, judges and prisoners. In "Small Axe" the same spirit can be seen. I'll just quote a few lines to illustrate this point.

> Why boasteth thyself, Oh evil men?
> Playing smart without being clever
> So you working iniquity to achieve vanity
> But the goodness of Jah Jah I-ndureth for I-ver.

Now, this attempt to see the "criminal" as redeemer, as measure of the society's wound and power to transcend, is by now a commonplace occurrence in the West Indian literature. It is there in Mais, in Lamming's *Season of Adventure,* in Harris too, and appears as a major element of *Savacou 3/4.* The Guyanese Marc Matthews's "For Cuffy" is addressed not only to the slave rebel of 1763, but to Clement Cuffy, a convict whose jailbreak in the late fifties resulted in a relentless manhunt in Guyana's backlands. Moreover, both Cuffies, the rebel and the convict (same thing in the West Indies), are associated with the common man, the eccentric, the grotesque… Baldhead Barney, Top Hat, Charley, Banga Mary. In addition, all these people are seen as *the true preservers of conscience and sacrifice,* the real revolutionaries: and they are associated with their counterparts in Jamaica or Harlem.

It is with these that the poet, himself going mad, identifies, because he can recognise the fraudulence of those who lead the society, the degree to which they preserve the inhumane values of the original slave masters, whom Cuffy of 1763 made the fatal mistake of trusting, as Toussaint was to do later on. The protagonist of this dramatic monologue becomes like the eccentrics he is talking about. He assumes their fears, their schizophrenia, the fragmented rhythms of their speech, and like them he is an observer of the rest of the society as it waits for its deliverance.

> Ah stampin, ah stampin, ah stampin a whole heap o' groun' by de asylum, with truth in the morning just to keep me warm and ah see you waitin for a bus to come.

This desire to reclaim the "criminal" on the part of middle-class writers is partly an attempt to exorcise a guilt at having grown away from roots, or an emptiness at having never known them. It is also a positive attempt to create and deepen conscience in sections of society whose traditional response has been an automatic impulse to repress, to beat up, execute and imprison. As such it is to be welcomed. Half in guilt and half in self-vindication, the West Indian writer is declaring his identity with the West Indian people; in their shame, in their degradation, in their in-search, in their mythical eternal journeying, which so many Pukkumina hymns, Baptist hymns in Trinidad, and so much popular music in Jamaica are today celebrating.

Finally, then, this self-acceptance is the important thing. It is what Césaire's return really meant, a terrible affirmation in the face of an almost total despair, which, however, is how Kierkegaard would have defined real faith. Real faith, for the West Indian, will continue to grow out of despair, and in spite of the eternal recurrence of the betrayer, the boss man, all those bald-headed attorneys-general of repression, Césaire's great act of affirmation will continue to be made, even when it changes little or nothing.

> I accept... accept... entirely, without reservation...
> my race which no absolution of hyssop
> mingled with lilies can ever purify.
>
> my race gnawed with blemishes
> my race ripe grapes from drunken feet
> my queen of spit and leprosies
> my queen of whips and scrofulae[3]
>
> At the end of the small hours, lost pools,
> stray smells, stranded hurricanes, dismasted
> boats, old wounds, rotten bones, buoys,
> chained volcanoes, ill-rooted deaths, bitter cries.
> I accept![4]

It is this which is beginning to sound in the poetry of the "Commonwealth" Caribbean at the end of the small hours. Not surprisingly, some of us cannot recognise or accept the sound. On the political level, all over the West Indies the laws of censorship are being invoked, or, as in Trinidad, grim laws of sedition are being passed to kill this acceptance. On the level of literary criticism, one can still find the critic who believes that a thorough grounding in F. R. Leavis, an understanding of how he rescued English criticism from the Bradleyan doldrums in the thirties, will save us here, and help us to understand why Bongo Jerry writes as he does. But one will have to study the Caribbean people and to listen to them before one can learn to make important or relevant critical statements on the new writers. The critic's business is first to understand the contexts out of which the work that he is examining grows. Our context is simply not Leavis's. The critic, like the writer, will have to learn the meaning of self-acceptance. New day had already cleaned in West Indian writing.

(First published in *Tapia* No. 23, Dec. 26, 1971.

References

1. Rohlehr, G., "Calypso and Politics", *Moko* No. 73, October 29, 1971.
2. The Mystic Revelation of Rastafari were a Jamaica folk-jazz group of the early 1970s. Led by the drummer Count Ozzie, the group included saxophonists Cedric "'Im" Brooks and Kenny Terroade.
3. Césaire, Aimé, *Return to My Native Land* (Middlesex: Penguin, 1969), p. 80. Translated by John Berger and Anna Bostock. First published in French as *Cahier d'un retour au pays natal* (Paris, Volontés, 1939) and by Presence Africaine in 1956.
4. Ibid, p. 83.

BLUES FOR ERIC ROACH

> He flies and dreams
> His hard sure instinct beams him on
> While steep beneath him sleeps the green dark death
> That shall immobilise his viking wing[1]

The hawk and the rock appear as major images in Eric Roach's earlier poems, and the man himself possessed both the fierce energy of the hawk and the hard, stoical permanence of rock. One could not imagine, for example, that he was nearing sixty. His mind was amazingly ablaze, and he wrote to the last with the bitter energy of youth, counterpointed by a despair which never petered out into grey, self-pitying melancholy, but was somehow more compellingly alive than the easy indifference which most people mistake for hope.

Yet he believed himself to be out of touch with the spirit of the times, the more strident rhetoric of the youth, and doubted, Lord knows why, the validity of his own clean vision. I remember meeting him for the first time in 1969 at a reading of poetry where he was reluctant to read because, he said, all he had to offer that youthful gathering were "these cold, cold words". Often afterwards, when I questioned him about making a collection of his poems, he would laugh the idea away, because, he said, they were not good enough.

For his uncertainty we must blame both our own dumbness in failing to assure the poet of his meaning through sensitive appraisal of his work, and the vicious circle in which the poet whose work is scattered in a score of unavailable copies of *Bim* is bound to be caught. Because the work remains inaccessible to anyone but the researcher, it is unappreciated as a whole, and because it is unknown and unappraised, the artist loses the urge to have it published and may even begin to feel that its invisibility proves its worthlessness. This sort of thing has been happening to poets, calypsonians and academics throughout the West Indies for several decades now.

Yet Roach's work had been recognised by his fellow artists. Kamau Brathwaite has pointed it out in his essay "Sir Galahad and the Islands" (*Bim* 1957); Derek Walcott had put in pleas for collection and publication of Roach's poetry in articles published in the *Trinidad Guardian* in 1962 and in 1965; while George Lamming had focused on Roach's work in an article published in *Africa Forum* in 1965. In Trinidad, *Tapia* has, week after week, been opening its pages to the serious review of hitherto neglected artists and, ironically, a long study of Eric Roach's poetry which had taken months of preparation, had been completed by Cheryl Williams on the very day that the news of his death stunned us and converted an act of celebration into a note of obituary.

He wrote about the landscape and peasantry of his Tobago boyhood with regret for the absence of the values they lived in his new world of urban and suburban Trinidad. He wrote also about the paradox of beauty and spiritual aridity in our islands, and of his own rooted love and commitment to our little worlds. He looked for symbols of beauty, strength and creative leadership among the survivors of the crossing, celebrated the pride and skill of Black athletes, some of the first Black men to become "visible" to the sight of the world; wrote Cipriani's elegy; shared Lamming's hope in the Federation and disillusion at its break-up. He was never out of touch.

Indeed, he saw our failure with frightening clarity, and in his later work comprehended the annual death of each hero: Martin Luther King by the assassin's bullet; Butler, a lion converted by time and our studied neglect into a comedian; Williams whose failure in vision led us, in Roach's words, "back to barracoons".

Thus it was with bitterness that he addressed today's youth caught on its *via dolorosa*:

> Don't mock me about dreams
> I am too old.
> Don't sneer of prophecies
> count me among the numberless dead
> this grisly century.
> I've eaten so much history that
> I belch
> boloms of years to come.[2]

All his later poems contain this agony; this sense of the impotence of age, and more terrible, this intuition that the years to come will be as tawdry, as predictable, as penurious and as stillborn. All our poets have, at one time or another, had this intuition. Witness the ending of Walcott's "Laventille"; or witness Brathwaite's lament at the prospects of a new society whose architects have studied only in "cotton fields of Oxford":

> and the wheel turns
> and the future returns
> wreathed in disguises
> ("Trade-Winds" from *Islands*).

Eric Roach was caught in this vision of death. Ever since 1961 his mind was filled with images of death. Whereas in the poems of the 1950s his usual image for the poet was the Yeatsian one of the keen-eyed hawk soaring above the earth, daring to transcend the contingencies of his humanity, in 1961 the poet is seen as a purblind juggler of words and images of death. Roach seemed to feel his vision darkening and dying.

> He sees with blurred and dying eyes,
> Without regret, without remorse,
> With irony his own demise.
> He juggles images of death
> Sees disease sneaking into bone
> Till the worms come,
> And bone stripped bare
> Lies white and quiet in a fold
> Of sombre, unbreathing mould,
> Or drowned and sucked under the sea,
> Down to the never-never tide,
> Is swayed among the dark sea-stones
> And stroked by soft anemones.[3]

The intuition of death was there since then. It grew stronger as the 1970s dawned with their new marches, new hopes which he could no longer share, new dreadness. So in his last published poem, the one dedicated to Frank Collymore in *Savacou* 7/8, he speaks as one old poet addressing his elder brother-poet:

> the days stand up to bless me
> as I die
> bedded on my dying century
> dreaming the century's youth
> in a good place that's gone
> among the folk I love
> while my own death
> howls from a mangy dog
> haunting these barren streets.
> what's all my witness for?
> why do I wear the poor folk and the years?
> eh brother what's the score?
> is the game won or lost?
> will I know now
> at the breaking bitter last
> do old men know?[4]

(First published *Tapia*, Vol. 4, No. 21 May 26, 1974.)

References

1. Roach, E. M., "Frigate Bird Passing", *Bim* 13 (Dec. 1950).
2. *Tapia*, Sunday April 22, 1973.
3. "He Juggles Images", *Bim*, Vol. 8, No. 32 (Jan-June 1961).
4. "For Frank Collymore", *Savacou* 7/8 (Jan-June 1973).

A CARRION TIME

> Those miseries I know you cultivate
> are mine as well as yours, or do you think
> the impartial bullock cares whose land is ploughed?
> (Martin Carter)

Yeats once wrote words to the effect that out of quarrels with others we make rhetoric, while out of quarrels with ourselves we produce poetry. My reason for writing what may well seem to be a quarrelsome article is that Wayne Brown, who normally quarrels neither with others nor with himself, has suddenly chosen to quarrel with those who a few weeks ago wrote in Tapia[1] on the death of Eric Roach. His response to what he called their eulogies was an appropriately unnamed poem which was published in Tapia almost one month later.[2] I have interpreted this poem and other statements by Brown on West Indian poets and poetry as an extension of the debate on West Indian poetry which began in 1971 with the publication of *Savacou 3/4*, whose editor was chiefly Kamau Brathwaite. This debate involved Eric Roach, Syl Lowhar, Roger McTair and myself. The issues raised were so fundamental to West Indian poetry that it was always likely that the debate would continue in disguised form. Brown, as I hope to show, has reopened some of these issues, and has in the process of so doing commented on the work of fellow-writers such as Brathwaite, McNeill and Walcott, and provided us with statements on how he creates poetry.

The first seven lines of his poem for Eric Roach set the tone with a clarity unusual in Brown:

> Roach gone, the carrion
> who drove him, hurt hawk, from the echoing air
> with their hunger for bloodbath, their shrill caws
> of treachery,
> shriek with excitement
> Dead, and to them he is Hero.
> Carrion like them dead.

From this, one gathers that Brown is accusing the society as a whole and Syl Lowhar and myself in particular of having isolated Roach by popularising a new rhetoric of revenge and bloodbath, and by accusing him of treachery in not joining the blue blacks' klan. The difficult phrase "shrill caws" (cause) indicates that Roach's eulogisers are at one and the same time keskidees (shrill) and vultures (caws) who somehow have succeeded in harrying a hawklike spirit to death. Worse, having killed him, they trivialise his death, make it a topic for excited chatter. "Dead, and to them he is Hero." The society prefers its heroes and poets dead. Dead people bury the dead with dead praise. "Carrion like them dead." Not "Carrion like US", for Brown is somehow exempt from whatever communal responsibility a society needs to bear when its artists lose all hope in life. His own position as poet places him among the crucified rather than among the philistines, among the connoisseurs of suffering rather than among the indifferent.

Brown's reaction to anything is normally a weak echo of Walcott's, and one senses behind the beneath the poem those sections of Part Four of Walcott's *Another Life* which contain his reactions to the suicide of his friend, mentor and fellow-artist, Harold Simmons; to another friend's contemplation of it; to the traditional indifference of the society to the lives or deaths of its artists; to the twisted politics of the contemporary West Indies and to the penury of our intellectual death-in-life. In Chapters Nineteen and Twenty-two of *Another Life*, everyone is accused in the now tragic Assizes of Makak's schizophrenic mind. All are guilty and condemned, except, of course, Walcott himself, who is Grand Inquisitor here, not Judge-Penitent.

Is it deliberate that the opening lines of Chapter Nineteen sound like a grim parody of robber-talk, a counter-rhetoric whose aim is to show the vituperative what violence of the tongue really is?

> I enclose in this circle of hell,
> in the stench of their own sulphur of self-hatred,
> in the steaming, scabrous rocks of Soufrière,
> in the boiling pustular volcanoes of the South,
> all o' dem big boys, so, dem ministers,
> ministers of culture, ministers of development,
> the green blacks, and their old toms,
> and all the syntactical apologists of the Third World
> explaining why their artists die,
> by their own hands, magicians of the New Vision.
> Screaming the same shit.
> [...]
> and the academics crouched like rats
> listening to tambourines
> jackals and rodents featuring their holes
> hoarding the sea-glass of their ancestors' eyes
> sea-lice, sea-parasites on the ancestral sea-wrack,
> whose god is history. *Pax*
> Who want a new art,
> and their artists dying in the old way.
> Those whose promises drip from their mouths like pus.[3]

The people being tried and condemned include politicians, academics, historians who indulge in the horrors of the past, and literary critics who "pronounce their measure of toms, of traitors, of traditionals and Afro-Saxons." *Tapia,* I'm afraid, isn't spared.

> they measure each other's sores
> to boast who has suffered most,
> and their artists keep dying,
> they are the saints of self-torture[4]

Walcott's bitterness here has grown out of all the broken promises of the sixties when he made constant unavailing appeals for the recognition of the artist by state and people as "citizen, rather than as ruin revived for a season." It is the explosion of a deferred hope, which has stubbornly refused to wither, but can as yet ascertain little possibility of fulfilment. His angry outcry is also the response to the tidal wave of 1969/70, when politics invaded the private life, and the rhetoric of Black exclusivism forced him to counter the stereotype of the noble suffering savage with what he no doubt imagined to be the more viable stereotype of the tragic mulatto.

The burden of the passage is the well-known one: that while the complacent make a ritual of their petty mishaps, they do nothing for the artist who, as crucified man takes on, if even he cannot take away, the sins and pain of the group. The artist is the true conscience of the society. There is only one problem here, though, and that is that in making such a claim for the artist, the poet may be indulging in the same self-flagellation which he decries in the complacent. The tersest warning against this sort of tendency on the part of the hypersensitive once came from the mouth of a man on the street: "When you think you ketching you ass, you neighbour ketching 'e mudder-ass."

Brown has, as usual, caught the echo of Walcott's passion. What he has not caught, however, is the range and complexity of Walcott's response to our milieu. In Walcott, anger so rawly expressed is unusual. Contempt is usually contained by a capacity for praise and wonder, irascibility by wit and a broad humour which helps him maintain a sense of proportion. Were it otherwise, contempt, which is as double-edged a weapon as hatred, would eventually paralyse the artist's sensibility and reinforce the disease it was meant to cauterise. If one wants to see a quotidian workaday Walcott, one should go back to well over five hundred articles, essays and reviews on painting, cinema, calypso, carnival, drama and literature which were produced between 1960 and 1967, when Walcott worked as journalist for the *Trinidad Guardian.* Those articles, however their author may disparage them as being merely "a hack's hired prose"[5] reveal a rich, various, witty and scrupulous intelligence in which generous humour counterpoints acerbity. Knowledge of this aspect of Walcott's work is indispensable to any serious assessment of his poetry and plays, and it is time for a collection of these essays and articles to be compiled and published.

Brown's self-righteousness is as yet unearned. Intimations of a real pain do exist in his work, but what he has made of his anxiety is as yet vague and blurred. I believe, indeed, that Brown's reaction to my "Blues for Eric Roach" may have been prompted more by what I said in 1971 about the mediocrity of Brown's exploration of his angst than by anything he imagines me to have said to, for, about or against Roach. At that time I was commenting on the fact that Roach in his review of *Savacou 3/4* had praised the poetry of Walcott, Hendriks, Scott and Brown without mentioning the work of Tony McNeill:

> although the latter is as gentle, reticent, and careful of craft as they come, and certainly a poet of deeper feeling than either Dennis Scott or Wayne Brown, whose work would hardly lose were it to include a deeper anxiety, a truer pain. [6]

This statement, together with the fairly consistent effort which I've been making to identify the presence of a rich oral tradition in the West Indies, and to present it as spiritual acreage to be reclaimed by poet, playwright and novelist, would be, I think, be sufficient evidence for Brown to number me among the naive who are insensitive to "craft": craft being, of course, what he defines as such. But a close reading of his essays and poetry soon reveals that the poet for Brown is a man who descends into the fishpond of his private silence and emerges sounding like Derek Walcott. This parasitic apprenticeship to Walcott incapacitates him when he tries to respond to an entirely different talent such as Brathwaite's, in whose work he cannot recognise the presence of a shaping mind, a different sculpture, "carefully carved craft" and massive architecture.

Here, for example, is Brown's brief comment on Brathwaite's trilogy:

> Edward Brathwaite's *Islands,* the third part of his trilogy of long poems, appeared at the same time as *The Gulf.* It too was a great improvement on Brathwaite's earlier work, much of which was flat and only thinly disguised prose. *Islands,* in the terms of one reviewer, "resonates more consistently" than the earlier books, and it is apparent that Brathwaite in this book has begun to reap the fruits of his experiments with form and fiction. [7]

Although Brown here speaks of Brathwaite's development and his early "experiments with form and fiction", he cannot find anything positive to say about the whole *of Rights of Passage* or *Masks.* No mention is made of Brathwaite's use of jazz, from which he draws a whole network of allusions; or to how oral considerations have directed him to break his words and lines at particular places, which direct the reader quite naturally to place the correct stress on the correct syllables; or to Brathwaite's establishment of dialect as a medium for serious poetry, especially in "Wings of a Dove" and "The Dust".

Brathwaite's remarkable use of Akan symbols, oral poetry and ancestral elements, to which the Nigerian critic Asein has devoted a long essay,[8] Brathwaite's close reference to African theology and philosophy, to which Maureen Warner Lewis[9] has devoted forty-eight pages of the most recent *Caribbean Quarterly*, are dismissed by Brown, who neither knows nor cares about such things. Thus the experiments are condemned without even having been named, while their mature fruit in *Islands* is commended as a great improvement.

Like Roach in his review of *Savacou 3/4*, Brown can find nothing positive to say about the pioneer efforts of those who are seeking ways of building on the fundamental models and structures which exist in the folk-oral tradition. These writers are simply noisemakers to be avoided like the plague by the serious poet. The voice of the true poet must arise out of the depths of the subconscious, otherwise:

> everything you write is going to sound like polemic and harangue. I mean you see it all over the West Indies today: all these multiplying anthologies that we are told constitute a new poetic awakening and that are really vehicles for noise. By that I mean, that in most of them you will look hard to find a really authentic depth-voice speaking. It's as if people were mistaking frenzy for emotional authority.
>
> ...one has to avoid like the plague all this chest-beating in bad prose chopped into lines, and nicknamed "verse". You have to refuse to be trapped into making noise yourself. You have, I think, to be attentive; and silent.[10]

Most of what is said here echoes Roach's review of *Savacou 3/4*, in which, too, the speaking-voice in poetry was openly condemned. The presence of a speaking-voice points to the emergence of a dramatic poetry, the necessity for audience, chorus and a stage for performance. Brown as poet is a product of the romantic/existentialist aesthetic which began with the emerging individualism of the Renaissance period and fulfilled itself in the desperate moral isolation of modern man. As such he places less stress on direct communication than on descent into private silence.

It is no new thing to see the Caribbean artist as a kind of alienated Western man. This, for example, was how Lamming saw him in his first major statement.

> To speak of the situation of the Negro Writer is to speak, therefore, of a problem of Man, and, more precisely of a contemporary situation which surrounds us with an urgency that is probably unprecedented. It is to speak, in a sense, of the universal sense of separation and abandonment, frustration and loss, and, above all else, of some direct experience of something missing.[11]

Having thus described the Negro writer as archetype of alienated man, Lamming went on to describe the process of creating in terms quite similar to those Conrad used in his preface to *The Nigger of the "Narcissus"*, and to those used by Brown in describing how he creates. ("Century of Exile"). According to Lamming the artist's primary loyalty should be to:

> the world of the private and hidden self, a world which turns quietly, sometimes turbulently, within one man, and which might only be known after that man has spoken. Each man who becomes aware of himself as a separate existence shares this solitude; each man has had an experience, momentary or prolonged, of the meaning of being alone. I do not mean loneliness or any similar illness of certain self-important natures. I am speaking of the experience proceeding from the depths of one's being of *existing*.
> It is a moment marked by silence.[12]

Given a universe of alienated people, art naturally becomes the product of the disinherited mind, the expression of private tensions after the descent into private silence. The artist's task then becomes one of rescuing experience from the turbulence within, and investing it with verbal shape.

But Lamming is equally concerned with what happens when the artist ascends from the recesses of self to the world in which he moves among other men. If his ascent is successful, then art becomes an intersection of the private with the public, a marriage of the surreal with the concrete and the quotidian, and a blend of the unconscious with the conscious. Each artist works out for himself what is to constitute the relationship between these complementary poles of his experience. In Lamming both exist, and yet they remain curiously separate. There are the vast public themes of history and politics and national possibility, on the one hand, and the private desolation which seems to overtake most of his people, even, or moreso the committed, on the other. Private desolation, the inability of the individual to transcend the barriers which separate him from others and even from himself, often leads to despair, madness and ultimately to suicide.

It was Brathwaite who in his 1960 essay, "The New West Indian Novelists", pointed out the growing atmosphere of solipsism and silence in which Lamming's people were moving; the breakdown of conversation and communion, which he interpreted as a symptom of the failure of Lamming the artist to make the necessary journey back from psyche to society:

> As Lamming's work goes forward, we come to understand that the title of that first book (i.e. *In the Castle of My Skin*) is not a signature of colour, but a symbol of personal isolation. Standing alone in his isolation, the individual, Lamming says in *The Emigrants*, is unable to communicate with his fellow man. The harder he tries, the more completely is he misunderstood. Misunderstanding is the theme of *The Emigrants*.[13]

Lamming, according to Brathwaite, was arriving at "the logical conclusion to the journey of the self-regarding mind."[14] The sense of alienation has intensified in later Lamming, as the metropole ceases to provide the spiritual sustenance necessary for the artist. In *Water with Berries*, a group of West

Indian artists try to erect a frail sense of community against the incursions of London's grey wilderness, a crippling poverty, and the sense of their own irrelevance both to the islands they have left behind and the wilderness of their adoption. Each artist desperately needs the other, though each is locked in on himself. Teeton is the only one who has a personal and political commitment to the future of the island where he once failed. But this is a commitment which he is destined never to fulfil. What I am interested in here are the images of disaster and failure, of death by violence, fire, and suicide. Is suicide a result of a loss of commitment, or a loss of contact with community, or a solipsist approach to art and life, or the original barbarity of life in the West Indies? Or is it the ultimate result of the shattering of any illusion that life elsewhere has a special fineness which it lacks in the West Indies; that psychic integrity may be won without grounded faith?[15]

Brathwaite, in most of his essays from 1957 to the present and in his own poetry, has sought to define the nature of the relationship between the artist and society in terms other than that of Renaissance/Romantic Existentialist theoretics. He summarises the issues quite well in a 1971 essay entitled "Art and Society".

> For a long time now, we have been accustomed to see 'the artist' as a lonely, talented individual (Keats, Shelley, Mozart, Kafka), more or less alienated from his society (Gauguin, Van Gogh, Dostoevsky). A man, in a sense, who was wiser than his society and who was misunderstood, even hated, because of this. A man, too, who was compelled to be an artist, whatever the pain, disease, circumstances (Charlie Parker); who needed paint, pen, piano, not money; who could – and did – starve in the garret. Then there was the picture of the exiled artist (Joyce, Rimbaud, George Lamming, Naipaul), who for a multitude of sociocultural and socioeconomic and/or political reasons and pressures could not exist within his own society.[16]

Brathwaite regards these ways of looking at the artist as being intimately linked with "a way of seeing that conceives of society as a community of the elite; inheritors of a Great Tradition." The artist thus has to be "elaborately and expensively trained in the graces of the inheritance". Art becomes "a very learned and self-conscious procedure", and the artist eventually becomes, in the words of one "underground" poet, "an academic talking to academics".

Brathwaite then goes on to suggest alternative ways of seeing both society and the artist, and to suggest the possibility of a different relationship between them. Using Kapo, a Jamaican sculptor, painter and cult-leader as his example, Brathwaite writes:

> But there is another way of looking at the artist and at society; and this is a view which begins by looking upon society as made up of elite and the masses (the people or folk); in according them an equality of consideration, an equilibrium of attention. Within this more balanced

framework, priest, politician, judge, critic, artist, inhabit the fulcrum of our consciousness, mediating that gap and gulf between the one and the other, creating a continuum between elite and folk, requirement of a healthy society.[17]

The artist here becomes not *isolato,* but moderator, mediator, and medium, bridging the gap between psyche and society, and between the elite and the folk. He becomes "both participant and director, shepherd and servant", whose aim is to render equal justice to the visible and the interior universes, to explore both individual and social tensions. He becomes preoccupied not only with descent into private silence, but with the journey back from "eternity to season" (Wilson Harris), from the secret chaotic forest of the heartland's unconscious to the "domesticity and lights" of conscious waking life and society.

There is a third type of writer who sees his role as being purely social, and whose writing grows out of direct, and often disastrous contact with politics. He generally aims at immediacy, the poet becoming both priest and politician, the audience congregation and brotherhood. Poets such as Winston Daniel (Lasana Kwesi), *Giving Back to My People* and Abdul Malik (Delano De Coteau), *Black Up,* both products of NJAC and 1970, fall into this category. So did the early Martin Carter, who used to recite his poems at street corners in the early 1950s. According to Brown, such naked encounters with politics leads only to frenzied polemic. But that will depend on the poet, on how deeply he realises that every experience needs to be given shape; on how conscious he is of the existence of working models in the oral tradition throughout the region. Malik, for example, makes brilliant use of Shouter-Baptist sermon technique and rhythm and imagery derived from the steelband in his "Pan-Run" poems and is at present working on new ways of exploring antiphonal call-and-response patterns fundamental to the oral tradition. He works as hard at shaping his poems, and has as exact a notion of how they are supposed to sound (which one cannot predict until you hear the man read his work), as Brown has of his own work. He is also aware of the shortcomings of rhetoric and of the necessity for form.

Brown, however, can see only the limitations of this sort of writing. He regards commitment to a cause as dangerous to the poet, since such commitment may lead to the falsification of truth, and prevent the poet from making that all too necessary encounter with self. While Brown does not completely dismiss history, political science and economics, he nevertheless finds the types of reality they offer to be extremely limited. In his poems, he says, he tries to deal with something more basic, primal and instinctual, something fundamental to human response and behaviour. All writing, in order to exist for Brown, must contain this honesty of encounter. Even his own prose pieces, which are mainly literary criticism, fill him with disgust soon after he has written them, because they are an evasion of inner truth, a kind of lying. He doesn't feel that way, however, about his poems.[18]

It may also be that other people's prose, especially when it can come to no real terms with Brown's poetry, fills him with an even greater disgust than his own. In his opinion, far worse than the poet whose work is directly related to politics must be the critic who ventures to relate aesthetics to society. Such a person Brown calls – and here he at least creates his own expletive – a diarist. Hence, in reproaching Lowhar and me for our eulogies on Eric Roach, he declares:

Diarist, there are matters
best left to these birds and the sand's blowing.
Walk softly here

The "diarist" in this context, is a kind of newspaper reporter insensitively jotting down his notes on each personal tragedy – a dead, unfeeling man whose aim is to excite a public hungry for scandal as an antidote to the boredom of their lives. He is the opposite of the suffering, silent, alienated poet, and the ally of the public (bad) poet bawling for "bloodbath". Both the gutter-journalist and the poet-politician trade on the automatic stock-response of the mob, and are thus the servitors of decay (carrion). It is these people who murder the impulse to true statement in the Caribbean, as typified by Eric Roach.

I hope that I am not doing Brown an injustice by attributing too great a dimension of meaning to his lines. If, however, my interpretation is accurate, then my next problem is where did Brown get the idea that I, who once saw my own city disintegrate (Georgetown, 1962-1964), am possessed of a vampiric lust for bloodbath? The answer must be sought once more in the debate over *Savacou 3/4*. Mr. Roach had singled out Bongo Jerry's "Sooner or Later" and "Mabrak" as examples of the worst things the anthology had to offer. Both Roger McTair and I had pointed out that the poems related to the vocabulary, sermons, music and symbolism of the Rastafari brethren, and that their failure or success should be determined in relation to this fact.

It may well be that Brown identified me as sharing in Jerry's beliefs in the Apocalypse and Black redemption, simply because I had stressed as a first principle of criticism an understanding of the context of what one intends to criticise. The notion that those who opposed Mr. Roach in the *Savacou* debate need to satisfy their quite ordinary lusts with blood may have come to Brown from a misreading of two lines of "Mabrak":

for the white world must come to blood bath
and blood bath is as far as the white world can reach

Brown evidently has taken these words as an expression of the conventional desire among Black people to see the destruction of the "white oppressors".

While this meaning is no doubt present, it is not what Jerry is stressing in the poem. I take these lines to mean that the white world will inevitably destroy itself ("come to blood bath") and will then be unable to transcend such self-destruction. In England during the mid-sixties, most of the campaigners against nuclear weapons probably believed the same thing. They saw themselves as being engaged in a struggle to save the white world from itself. Bongo Jerry chooses the Rastafarian way – the way which requires first, the disentanglement of the Blacks from the lunatic perversities of Western civilisation; secondly, a grounding of self in roots and rhythms, sights and sounds; and thirdly, a movement away from the egotism and alienation implied in "I" towards the acknowledgement of and identification with brother-man implied in "I-and-I".

Interestingly enough, Brown himself senses the need for such roots as protection against the cerebral loneliness of Western intellectualism. Commenting on the growing loneliness and coldness of Naipaul, Brown says:

> I think this kind of alienation is a peculiarly Western invention (if one can now generalise about the Western World), and perhaps it's the corollary of conquest: the notion of man as the subjugator of nature. Now, there are certain things going on in the world today that are swinging the philosophical foundations back towards the sort of position I have been maintaining. Sciences like ecology and anthropology are all working in the direction of highlighting our inter-connectedness with the planet and its non-human life.[19]

Which, of course, ought to direct Brown towards Carpentier, Mittelholzer, Harris (from whom he derives the idea in the first place) and Brathwaite, (who has been making this same point since 1957); as well as towards Afro-Caribbean and Indo-Caribbean religions with their secretions of mythology, and towards the grounded sensibility which the Rastafarians have been talking about for decades now. There are many more ways of illustrating the inter-connectedness of life than exploring the imagery of the seascape, which Brown, a poetic skin-diver, combs for his images.

In his own way, Bongo Jerry is on a quest for a different and more interconnected life. "Mabrak" is a protest against cerebralisation of the word. Mabrak is defined as "black lightning", a strange concept in a world which has for so long denied the possibility of light coming out of darkness. It is the Black world's rediscovery of its vision. Mabrak is a retreat from ambiguity, word games, "hiding behind language bar" and "crossword speaking when expressing feeling". It requires a quality which Brown claims to value highly – inner honesty, a "straightening" of the tongue, an abandoning of mask and pose:

> delusion, name changing, word rearranging
> ringing rings of roses, pocket full of poses.

a reclaiming and a recreation of "sight, sounds and meaning to measure the feeling of Black hearts – alone."

Here Jerry's desire to disentangle the Black psyche from the cerebral distortion of psyche which Brown describes as a "peculiarly Western invention", is most evident. The urge towards cultural separatism is much stronger than any desire for revenge. Although the poet ends up by praying for the destruction of "Babylon" and the desolation of "Jezebel", these words should be seen as carrying the same metaphorical weight as they did for Milton, Bunyan and the Puritan millenarists. "Babylon" is a portmanteau word which conveys the notion of an unfair system of distribution; commercialism, and the subjection of human value to market value. "Jezebel" represents the whoredom of sensibility which is the inevitable result of the presence of Babylon. Brown himself would probably like to see the end of such things.

So much, then, for carnage. Brown's other great point was that Roach was cast out by the younger breed with their "shrill caws of treachery". Now, it is quite true that in a general sense youth in Trinidad have been rejecting the senior generation, and that there is a dreadful lack of continuity between generations. This is an illness which I observed for myself soon after I arrived in Trinidad in 1968, and which I tried to identify in my first article entitled "The Generation Gap" and published in *Moko*.[20] I have, in one way or another, written a fair amount about it since. But it is not true that Roach the individual was singled out for any special rejection by the younger generation. His disillusionment with public affairs dated much further back.

If his poems are any clue, his pain started when the Federation collapsed in the early sixties. He resigned as a P.N.M. journalist, losing his faith in the 1956 movement. This happened around the same time that C.L.R. James was forced to return to metropolitan exile. Both within the party and throughout the archipelago whose fusion Roach had dreamed ("I Am the Archipelago" and "Fugue for Federation",) schism reigned. When Brown, quoting Roach, writes:

> Love overgrows a rock
> but not a raftload of schisms

even a slight knowledge of the politics he condemns should have taught him that today's schisms are the results of yesterday's failures. Roach, who had been teaching primary school in rural Tobago when he was asked by the party to write for them, was right there in 1961 when the people learned the new mathematics of division – "one from ten leaves none".[21] Roach's rage was more against the failure of his generation than against the confusions of ours.

Nor was he outlawed by a younger generation crying "Treason". On the contrary, those who did recognise him at all, regarded him as being more committed than Brown to changing his world. He used to attend meetings of the short-lived "Pivot" which grew out of the New World movement sometime in mid-1968. A group of the younger members of New World became tired of the economic/political line of the parent group, which had recently emerged from the Carifta debates and public meetings. They decided to form a group which would place more emphasis on literature and cultural forms in general.

Pivot included Dion, Colleen and Roger McTair, Lloyd Taylor, Victor Questel, Syl Lowhar, Alfie Fraser, Dave Murray, Dave Darbeau, myself and occasionally Anson Gonzalez. Looking back at Pivot's cyclostyled newsletters, I realise how innocent those times were – gentle debates on Art and Morality; lectures on Drug Abuse, Naipaul and Sparrow; vague ill-researched articles on the *negritude* poets, the state of the nation, and the relevance, if any, of Black Power to the Caribbean. Even those characters whom I know now to have been police or political informers wore an aura of benignity in those amiable 1968/69 Sunday morning meetings in the old wooden building rented by New World which stood opposite Lord Harris Square until someone burned it flat in mid 1968.

The current of politics, from the Rodney Affair of October 1968 to the Bus Workers' Strike of 1969, caught many of the youths in its tide. It was their remu. Darbeau, Murray and Fraser were swept up, the jazz, reggae and kaiso sessions ending. They became foundation members of NJAC in 1969, and Murray and Fraser edited the UWI campus newspaper, *Embryo*, during the academic year 1969/70. Taylor and Lowhar helped form *Tapia* after the New World split late in 1968. Questel and Gonzalez were to become the best and most stimulating editors of *Embryo* in the crucial 1970-71 period. I became co-editor of the first eighteen (18) issues of *Moko*, whose first phase of publication ended on July 4, 1969.

Pivot could not survive the remu, though it continued to arrange public poetry-reading sessions in 1969, and the Pivot idea persisted well into 1971. Earl Lovelace, a good reader of his own work, participated in some of our programmes, and tested his new, and still unpublished novel, *Every Step is a Station*, before appreciative audiences.[22] Many of Questel's poems were first heard at Pivot sessions. Alfie Fraser's exceedingly abstract yet strangely compelling utterances, Roger McTair's blues, stood cheek-by-jowl with Cliff Sealey's short stories, and, in one reading at the Public Library, with Marguerite Wyke's poems, and Barney Ramon-Fortune's short stories. The people who had been writing in Sealey's *Voices* in the mid-sixties were mingling with the younger voices from Pivot, and they spanned both generations.

Roach generally contributed from the floor at Pivot Sunday morning sessions. Only once did he read, and that was at a programme I arranged at Tapia House on Sunday, August 29, 1971. By that time the House had become an open forum for this sort of thing. Since 1970 we had started blending poetry with related music, and by 1971 a number of us were aware of the unity of perception which existed among our musicians, singers, poets and raconteurs. Nowadays, after Ken Corsbie's and Marc Matthews's "Dem Two" and Walcott's dramatisations of Brathwaite's "Wings of a Dove" and "The Dust", the idea of performed poetry was rapidly gaining currency. The gap between the short story, the one-act play, dramatic monologue and the oratorical poem, was closing. Again, this was anticipated by Walcott's Theatre Workshop, which dramatised Sam Selvon's short stories (ballads and episodes) in 1969. But it was also anticipated by Kissoon's popular soap-opera type plays which were taken to the people, by all those excellent variety concerts in San Fernando, which are generally ignored by the press, and by the vast all-day NJAC rallies, which bring a variety of talent to the stage and provide them with one of the most serious of audiences in Trinidad.

The Kairi group, the latest descendant of the Pivot idea, have brought together a team of amateur writers and singers who call themselves "ISWE'", and have successfully dramatised their first programme, "Tanti Go See We". Questel is the only survivor of Pivot in Kairi, but "ISWE" can be seen as an extension of the 1968 idea. "ISWE", like "DEM TWO" have chosen poems from all over the region, and have seriously tried to study the style of each island. The poet as an academic speaking to academics is being asked to share the stage with the older figure of the poet as a man talking to men, or as people talking to people. In our islands, communal catharsis has always been as important as individual silence.

In looking back over all those meetings and readings, it seems to me that, collectively, the people I have been naming have done more to rehabilitate, not only Roach, but Carter (whom I included on the W.I. Literature syllabus at U.W.I. from the very first time that we did the course here), Louise Bennett, Sam Selvon, Don Drummond, who was unknown in Trinidad until we introduced him on the radio, at readings and at liming sessions): the forgotten work of countless calypsonians; and established figures such as Walcott, Naipaul and Brathwaite.

Our work has been to integrate, not to separate. When we chastise each other, it has generally been for the good of the group. For example, I was able to have a long discussion with Eric Roach after my 1971 article, in which we exchanged points of view, and when I did a twenty-six week radio series in 1973 on the calypso, *From Attila to the Seventies,* Roach, an established commentator on the calypso, was one of the first to tell me that the programmes had enabled him to see trends in the society, and in the shifts of style, humour and serious commentary which he had never noted before. Our work of rehabilitation is slow and arduous. Cheryl Williams, who wrote the long essay on Roach,[23] copied out in longhand what became sixty typewritten pages of Roach's poems from the Central Library's collection of *Bim*. She did not intend in doing so to pay respects to a dead man, though Brown's poem seems to suggest this.

Contrast, however, her painstaking effort with Brown's treatment of Roach in his series of articles entitled "West Indian Poetry of the Forties", which were published in the *Trinidad Guardian* during October 1970. Brown wrote:

> And finally, and perhaps most importantly, the poor man, the underdog, becomes in many of the poems of this period, the new hero. The peasant, who had almost never appeared in West Indian poetry prior to this, is now the focus of Cecil Herbert's "Lines Written on a Train"; of Roger Mais' "Road Menders"; of George Campbell's "History Makers"; of Eric Roach's "Homestead" which contains one of the simplest and finest lines of the period: "his life was unadorned as bread" – and a host of other poems.[24]

That and no more from Brown who considers us "carrion"; from this deficient diarist whose homework on the period was clearly confined to the poems anthologised in *Caribbean Quarterly,* Vol. 5, No. 3, (1958); from this connoisseur of fine responses who, having himself lumped Roach with other poets who spoke of the poor folk, now commands:

> And do not talk of the hawk on the air,
> or the plankton's release from its drifting.
> Spare him the folk he could not save
> Leave out the landscape he loved.

Brown has shifted from his 1970 ground, and is off on a pseudo-existentialist scene. "I have no home"; while the insane pattern of repression, reaction and revenge continues throughout the world, says Walcott in the title poem of The *Gulf and Other Poems* (1969); "I have no home" period, echoes Brown in the title poem of *On the Coast* (1972) three tired years later. Walcott doffs the castaway-mask after 1965, Brown dons it in 1972.

> And I am an orphaned islander,
> on a sandspit of memory
> in a winter
> of bays. I have no home.

Homelessness is, of course, one of the persistent themes of West Indian literature, and Brown is, perhaps, predestined to travel the same road as so many of his predecessors. The condition of exile often brings out, for six years or so, the best in a writer. I therefore expect Brown's poetry to improve soon. Already his criticism has done so. His review of Anthony McNeill's *Reel from the "Life Movie"* (*Savacou* 6), which he calls "Lyricism and the Anguish of the Clown",[25] reveals a deeper and more genuine response than any of his poems in *On the Coast*. I prefer to think of him as diarist, writer of that fine essay, than as echo.

One of his more striking points is the distinction which he makes between responses to pain and responses to grief in McNeill's work, and in the process of making this point, he discloses a fact of which I was unaware: that political militants fumbling towards vision, were laying claim to the poetry of McNeill. McNeill, one would have thought, was an eminently bad choice for this sort of purpose. Brown, however, offers an explanation:

> For pain contains (what the figure of the Clown also contains) incomprehension. It is therefore accompanied by (what the Clown is helpless to will) the rejection of itself, and what follows is anger. (While grief, based as it is on a notion of acceptance, which in turn arises out of a mythology of the world as orderly, of the Greater Plan, is manifestly non-revolutionary.)[26]

Out of one's perception of pain, he says, will spring rebellion; out of one's knowledge of grief, acceptance. Perhaps. But out of the perception of both excessive pain and excessive grief also spring lunacy, paralysis, doubt, despair, contempt when one has failed to shape pain and grief, self-righteousness when one begins to believe in the exclusiveness of one's suffering; and ultimately intellectual, moral or physical suicide, when one can see no resolution of pain or derive no catharsis from having endured it.

Suicide rather than rebellion is the direction in which McNeill's work seems to be moving. The image of the trapped animal, and of the incipient suicide, is even more frequent than the image of the Clown. Brown is clearly fascinated by this suicidal streak, though he never really places the object of his fascination. "Who'll See Me Dive", one of the poems which he cites as an example, of McNeill's exploration of pain conveys a sense of desperate incipient suicide. Other poems where the suicide theme appears are "The True Gage", "Suicide's Girl-Friend" and "The Compassionate Spider".

Brown glosses over this tendency with catchphrases – the only weak point in his essay.

> If I say that McNeill seems to me to be the first truly twentieth-Century, Western poet these islands have produced, it is this experience of pain, the experience of that time and that place, to which I am pointing. (This sense of pain surfaces in Walcott's poetry – see for example *A Map of Europe* or *A Village Life;* but he is finally rooted, and in a real landscape; while the sense of pain in Brathwaite's trilogy is, to my mind, more often rhetorical than enacted.)[27]

So the sense of pain is connected with an ultimate sense of alienation; its opposite is the sense of roots and a real landscape which Brown finds in Walcott, not, it appears, in Brathwaite. Towards the end of the essay Brown associates McNeill's poetry with the extremist anxiety of alienation, and contemplates that the hysterical madly sane Clown-figure will become archetypal, and his tragicomic mask crucially necessary as our societies continue to face the lunatic music of the future.

What is fascinating about all this, though, is that McNeill has penned two tributes to Brathwaite as a lonely innovator, who has rejected the "goggles of borrowed sight", and tried to use his own basic material of kaiso and reggae,[28] "Daring the sharks with a lonely reggae". Far from glorifying "the great illusive fishbowl" of the Western megalopolis, far from deriving any fulfilment from being "the first truly twentieth-Century Western poet these islands have produced," McNeill, caught in his careful circle and cage of snow, longs for the assurance of roots towards which Brathwaite has worked his way in the journey from the early placeless poems of *Bim* (1950-1964) through *Rights of Passage, Masks* towards *Islands*.

> Tonight, circled by snow
> in a foreign country,
> I praise one of the children
> who stood alone,
>
> hearing old drums
> under the bam-bam bangarang,
> who passed into man-
> hood through the eye of the sun,
> and smelted
> lonely calypsos & soul
> against the long morning of English rule[29]

The "long morning of English rule" refers here more to tyranny of form, concept and tradition than to political overlordship. McNeill understands the need for bridges to be built between the privacy of pain and a rooted sense of community, between the artist who borrows his goggles from the alienated West, and the other kind of artist who tries to work with what he finds right in his own backyard. Brown, I believe, for all his talk about the inter-connectedness of experience and the critique of pure reason which he attempts in his interview with Basil McFarlane, is at present fascinated with alienation, and its alternatives of desperate stoicism or suicide.

I suspect that this is why, after having less than four years ago presented Roach as a poet of the folk, he now wants us to see Roach as a man ultimately without context – "Spare him the folk he could not save" – a martyr whose life has brought and whose death will bring no redemption to the unredeemable. Roach, dead, has become the man that Brown now imagines himself to be, a man without context, caught in his lonely drift towards becoming the second twentieth-century Western poet that these islands will have produced; locked in the suicide which is the existentialist neo-romantic dream...

> Not free, free at last, Carrion,
> but locked
> in his tiring dream of destruction
> Within his head full of salt,
> his lost craft.
> nothing, his destination

These are the best lines Brown has ever penned, capturing as they do the tired eternal cadence of the sea, the slack, tideless drift, the exact sensation of one's body floating on waves. Thus Roach's death becomes the death of Brown, poetic skin-diver, lover of the sea, and by implication ours, a dreadful intimation of our drift into nothingness.

Yet even here one detects an echo of Walcott's voice as he imagines his own movement towards extinction:

> I wanted to grow white-haired
> as the wave, with a wrinkled
>
> brown rock's face, salted,
> seamed, an old poet,
> facing the wind
>
> and nothing, which is,
> the loud world in his mind.[30]

Here Walcott is communicating grim heroic acceptance, rather than drift into amnesia. Though Brown echoes the passage, the difference in rhythm and cadence between the two passages suggests that he has *begun* to find a way towards his own sound. This is something gained. Roach's death may have meant the birth of Brown. If so, I only wish that Brown would come back to his "no home"; for Roach's death is simply *one* of about twenty, which, if he cares, he can blame on the politics of independence and the enduring Philistinism of the purblind West Indian intelligentsia. And if one adds the victims of polio, typhoid and gastro-enteritis to those of indifference, Philistinism and politics, one would have a good five hundred or so corpses between 1970 and 1974 alone. What better fare for a self-righteous poet than such a fair field of carrion?

(First published in *Tapia* Vol IV, No 2, June 1974, pp. 5-8 & 11)

References

1. *Tapia*, Vol. 4, No. 17, (April 28, 1974).
2. Brown, W., untitled poem, *Tapia*, Vol. 4, No. 21, (May 26, 1974).
3. Walcott, D., *Another Life* (New York: Farrar, Straus & Giroux, 1973), Chapter 19.
4. Ibid.

5. Questel, V., in a brilliant triple-pun referred to Walcott's articles and reviews as his "axe fired pose."
6. Rohlehr, G., "West Indian Poetry, Some Problems of Assessment", *Tapia* Vol. 1, No. 20 (Aug. 29, 1971), pp. 11-14.
7. Brown, W., "West Indian Literature of the Past Year", *Trinidad Guardian* (August 31, 1970).
8. Asein, S., "The Concept of Form: A Study of Some Ancestral Elements in Brathwaite's Trilogy", *ASAWI Bulletin,* No. 4 (Dec. 1971), pp. 9-38.
9. Warner-Lewis, M., "Odomankome Kijerema Se", *Caribbean Quarterly,* Vol. 19, No. 2.
10. Brown, W., interviewed by Basil McFarlane, "The Century of Exile", *Jamaica Journal*, Vol. 7 No. 3 (Sept. 1973), p. 42.
11. Lamming, G., "The Negro Writer and His World", *Presence Africaine* (June - Nov., 1956), p. 329.
12. Ibid, p. 330.
13. Brathwaite, E., "The New West Indian Novelists", Part II, *BIM* Vol 8, No 32 (Jan-June 1961) p. 273.
14. Ibid, p. 274.
15. For a discussion of the theme of suicide in West Indian Literature, see Thieme, J., "A Style of Dying", *The Sunday Chronicle,* (May 5, 1974) Guyana p. 7.
16. Brathwaite, E., "Art and Society: Kapo: A Context", *Jamaican Folk Art,* Institute of Jamaica, 1971, p. 4.
17. Ibid, p. 5.
18. Brown, W., "The Century of Exile", op cit., pp. 40 & 43.
19. Ibid, p. 42.
20. Rohlehr, G., "The Generation Gap", *Moko* No. 2 (Nov. 15,1968).
21. Famous statement of Dr. Eric Williams after Jamaica's withdrawal from the West Indian Federation.
22. *Every Step Is a Station* was eventually published as *The Wine of Astonishment.*
23. Williams, C., "Eric Roach's Poetry", *Tapia* Vol. 4, Nos. 17 & 18 (Apr 28 & May 5, 1974).
24. Brown, W., "West Indian Poetry of the Forties", *Trinidad Guardian*, October 1970.
25. Brown, W., "Lyricism and the Anguish of the Clown", *Tapia*, Vol. 3, No. 13, (April 1, 1973), pp. 6-7.
26. Ibid.
27. Ibid.
28. McNeill, A., "Spring Poem: Brown's Town", for Edward Brathwaite in Salkey, A., ed. *Breaklight* (London: Hamish Hamilton, 1971), p. 209.
29. McNeill, A., "The Children", *Breaklight,* p. 221.
30. Walcott, D., *Another Life* (New York: Farrar, Straus & Giroux, 1973), p. 148.

MY STRANGLED CITY

(An Introduction to an Unpublished Anthology of Poetry)

> Here, right at my feet
> my strangled city lies
> my father's city and my mother's heart
>   (Martin Carter)

Nineteen sixty-four to nineteen seventy-five (1964–75) has been a period of traumatic awakening in Trinidad. At the very centre of the decade there occurred the Black Power demonstrations of 1970, which forced the society to contemplate its own face for two whole months of confession, condemnation, self-justification and self-righteousness. A general tendency since then has been for each citizen to shift the blame for the state of the nation on to other shoulders; to abnegate personal responsibility for the shape of the future while presenting themselves as a spokespersons for conscience and humanity. The state of the nation's conscience is nowhere more evident than in the troubled cataract of poetic statement which has characterised the decade. This collection of poems enables one to listen to a significant, though by no means a comprehensive, number of the people who have spoken and borne witness to the turmoil of our post-independence era. If it does nothing else, it will provide a window into the sensibility of this era, and enable us to trace as never before, the complex crosscurrent of feelings, ideas, intuitions and attitudes which all flowed into 1970. For while Bill Rivière, Lloyd Best, Susan Craig, James Millette, the NJAC and others have helped us to place the movement of this river of man in its historical, economic, social and political contexts, lacking has been any real statement on the spiritual dimensions, hidden currents of thoughts and feeling, which lay beneath the movement. But many people had been writing, for better for worse, before 1970, and many more have, for richer for poorer, spoken since; so that it will be possible to present this anthology, *Corners Without Answers*, as the complex chronicle of the conscience of this age and this people.

Bibliographical Notes to the Decade

Roger McTair was twenty years old in 1964 when he wrote "Corners without Answers",[1] the title poem of this anthology, and one of the young poets who contributed to Clifford Sealey's short-lived (1964-

66) but important publication, *Voices*. During the mid-sixties, *Voices* provided a bridge between different generations of writers, linking the statements of Marguerite Wyke and Clifford Sealey to those of Judy Miles, Wayne Brown, Earl Lovelace and Roger McTair. Volume One (1964-65) lasted for four numbers; Volume Two for three, the first of which appeared in September 1969 and the last in March 1973. Yet, despite the fact that *Voices* was to appear only occasionally, writers who had received their first exposure there continued to write and to grow. Roger McTair and Judy Miles published from time to time in *Bim*; Earl Lovelace went on to publish two novels and has completed two more which are as yet unpublished. Elliot Bastien has written more poetry and plays which, unfortunately, have not been seen in the West Indies. Wayne Brown published On *the Coast* (1972).

Towards the late sixties, a few of the younger contributors to *Voices* and a handful of even younger writers came together to form Unit 16 (1968), which soon changed its name to Pivot (1968-69). The political current of the late sixties and 1970 proved too strong for Pivot; the States of Emergency of 1970 and 1971 almost killed the taste of the young and serious for coming together. Only those who were already outlawed and scarred by the system had the courage to come together, and throughout 1971 and 1972, the NJAC organised vast all-day rallies, which were a mixture of variety concert, and political protest. One or two of the original members of Pivot appeared occasionally at these rallies, sharing the stage with protest calypsonians such as Stalin, Valentino and Chalkdust. Nineteen seventy-three to nineteen seventy-four (1973-1974) saw the emergence of the Kairi House group, whose team of young actors called themselves "IsWe". After a few moderately successful efforts, the group disintegrated, its most noteworthy ventures being now the sponsorship of shows at the Little Carib Theatre. It is the Kairi House group, spearheaded by Christopher and Judith Laird, which brought shows such as Dem Two/All Ah We featuring the Guyanese actors Ken Corsbie, Marc Matthews and Henry Mootoo. Astor Johnson has also sponsored the shows of Valentino and Stalin at the Little Carib (1975).

Since 1970, the volume of published writing has swollen beyond all measure, resulting in the joint publication of twenty poems each by Anson Gonzalez and Victor Questel, *Score* (1972); Abdul Malik's *Black Up* (1972) and *Revo* (1975); Leroy Calliste's and Selwyn Newton's *474 Years of Pain and Suffering* (1973); Selwyn Bhajan's *Season of Songs* (1972) and *Quest* (1975); Anson Gonzalez's *The Love Song of Boysie B* (1974); Lasana Kwesi's (Winston Daniel's) *Giving Back to My People* (1973) and *Poems of Rebellion* (1975); and Wayne Davis's *Old Oracle: Timeless Dream* (1975). Apart from these there have been the poems published in *Embryo* and *Themes* (UWI, St. Augustine), as well as those in *Tapia, Kairi* and *Corlit,* a literary journal produced by the students and teachers of Corinth Training College. And there has been Walcott's *The Charlatan* (1962 & 1974); *In a Fine Castle* (1970/71): and *The Joker of Seville* (1974-75).

There has also been a fair amount of criticism and cross (and I mean cross) talk. One has had, for example, Anson Gonzalez on Walcott's "Laventille";[2] Questel on Gonzalez's *Boysie B and Other Poems;*[3] Questel on Brown's *On the Coast*;[4] Brown on Brown;[5] Brown on Faustin Charles's *The Expatriate:*[6] Brown on Art and society;[7] Walcott on everything – poetry, theatre, race, Black Power, politics, revolution, 1970, aesthetics, vision.[8] Post-1970 statements by Walcott complement his five hundred newspaper articles and reviews written between 1960 and 1967 when he was employed by the *Trinidad Guardian* as a critic of cultural affairs and a variety of artistic forms.

There was also the *Savacou* debate in 1971, involving the responses of Syl Lowhar,[9] Roger McTair,[10] and Gordon Rohlehr[11] to Eric Roach's review of *Savacou 3/4*.[12] Obvious extensions of this debate occurred in Roach's subsequent reviews of West Indian poetry, such as his review of Wayne Brown's *On the Coast*[13] entitled "Conflict of West Indian Poetry" and subtitled, "Tribe Boys vs. Afro-Saxons". There was also his review of Questel's and Gonzalez's *Score.*[14] The *Savacou* debate extended itself on Roach's death, centring this time on Wayne Brown's response[15] to the obituary notes of Lowhar and Rohlehr.[16] In an article entitled "A Carrion Time", Rohlehr replied to Brown.[17] Of supreme relevance to this issue was Cheryl Williams's long study of the poetry of Eric Roach.[18]

Of special importance was the emergence of Victor Questel as a regular critic who published in *Tapia*. Apart from the reviews mentioned above, Questel commented on Malik's *Black Up;*[19] Walcott's *Another Life*[20] and has a considerable amount of unpublished material on Walcott's essays, poetry and plays. Questel's poetry, thoroughly misunderstood by Eric Roach in his review of *Score*, was recently the subject of a long and brilliant review by Winston Hackett[21] who had earlier written two short articles on the poetry and drama of Derek Walcott.[22]

This is, of course, only a selected list of poems and articles published since 1964; but it is sufficiently representative of the struggle of a generation for self-identification. Most of the writers under discussion are between the ages of twenty and forty. Older poets such as Walcott and Roach had been practising their craft for nearly twenty-five years, while most of the others are between five and ten years old as writers. Some have barely started. There is, accordingly, a wide variety of styles, much of which has only just begun to emerge.

The critic's role here is threefold. He must first chronicle the sensibility of his time, locating each poet within the landscape, and against the social background from which his statement emerges. He must next be able, by comparing the statements of different voices, to trace the drift or process of sensibility in his time. This second duty of the critic exceeds the first in that it moves beyond the simple chronicling of events and statements, and tries to determine their communal significance.

The critic's third task is that of commenting on the various ways of shaping language revealed by a variety of writers. This requires the close reading of individual poems, and a grasp of the principles operating beneath each style of saying. Given the embryonic nature of most of the writing here, the critic must have a sense of style and technique in gestation, in the process of becoming. This essay tries to do some of these things, and is, in the context of the many statements already made by various voices, simply an attempt to add to this river of man one more tributary of sound. One hopes that it will advance the debate about the nature of West Indian poetry and the new Caribbean person one stage further. If it fails to do this it may still be useful as a chronicle by one who knew most of these writers fairly well, and who has participated in their several journeys, which are merely the analogues of his own peculiar homecoming:

> were some who ran one way.
> were some who ran another way.
> were some who did not run at all.
> were some who will not run again.
> And I was with them all
> when the sun and streets exploded,
> and a city of clerks
> turned a city of men!
> (Martin Carter, "Black Friday 1962")

(II)

Voices: 1964-1966

Of the fourteen poems published in the first two issues of *Voices*, three seem to deserve one's careful consideration: Marguerite Wyke's "History Leaves No Memorials to the Poor"[23] and "Guyana",[24] and Roger McTair's "Corners Without Answers".[25] Mrs Wyke, a senator in the short-lived West Indian Federal Parliament, is better known as a sculptor. She had, however, contributed poems to *Bim* and *Caribbean Quarterly* during the fifties,[26] and was still producing occasional poems in the late sixties when *Voices* merged slowly with New World/Pivot, one tough decade after the federal dream had dissolved.

In "On Remembering Immortelles", Marguerite Wyke portrays the Caribbean in its oscillation between relative pastoral innocence and the poisonous reality of the H-bomb mushroom cloud. A mind which has known Nature's cycle looks back at a dead age where wonder was still a possibility and forward to the ultimate extreme of the technological world, the Bomb, whose scarlet flame may resemble immortelles, but is their anthropomorphic opposite. "Guyana" is her vision of an emerging nation sacrificed to the rigid demands of a parroted ideology, "scavenged from the frontiers of master-folly". That poem marks the beginning of what is now a tradition of bitter denunciation in Anglophone West Indian poetry. Like the Brathwaite of *Islands* or the Walcott of *The Gulf* and *Another Life,* she reacts to "the error of the corrupting word", "the grim crouched soucouyant in the fettered mind". Like them, too, she seeks out areas of sanity and innocence, which have so far managed to survive a mangling time. Thus she rejects both the Bomb's "thrust of flame" which results in "the spattered flesh and starched blood/Of weeping children", and abstract imported ideologies which produce minds narrowed to hand-me-down, unimaginative Western rationalism.

In "Guyana" one can feel the disillusion of a mind that has dreamed of federation, and hear its lament at the dismemberment of the archipelago, of which the civil and racial discord of Guyana was nothing but the most tragic symbol. In "History Leaves no Memorials to the Poor", we get the first of those brooding potentially explosive poems, in which the poet is removed from even the possibility of the pastoral dream. Here the alternative to the immortelles' flame is nothing so absolute as the mushroom cloud, or so distant as Vietnam's spattered flesh, but simply the dust and poverty of a Caribbean city. Mrs Wyke moved with this poem right into the heart of the sixties. It begins:

> History leaves no memorials to the poor
> Dulled by their galvanized dungeons
> In the step-steepled Laventille
> And the Caroni of their sorrows.

"History" here is employed in the sense that both the Naipaul of *The Middle Passage* and the Walcott of several articles and essays employ the term. It is the memory of the past whose concrete recording contributes to the sense that each life and each death matters, in that they add to an ongoing process. The poor are denied this sense of history as relevant process and movement-towards-fulfilment.

> But all their graves lie open
> And day by centuries' darkening day
> Someone throws in another primordial bone
> Or writes a cheque and looks another way.

The poor here are invisible, faceless and voiceless people, who at times, after overwhelming pressure, erupt into violence and visibility. They are the ultimate colonised people, imperialism being now defined as any form of human domination. The poem resembles, both in its despair and its compassion, Martin Carter's seminal "University of Hunger" and "I Come from the Nigger Yard".[27] Carter, earlier than most, had recorded that drift through time and space from plantation slavery to self-determination, and consequent upon this, from plantation village to rising steel city. Yet in those early poems, his thrust was outwards, from "the niggeryard of yesterday" with its burden of sorrow, towards the world of tomorrow with an affirmative strength and hope. By 1964, Carter had travelled a long way from that vision of a countervailing strength which could carry the poor beyond survival and sad music.

Eric Roach, whose experience in this period included the traumatic movement from rural Tobago to urban Trinidad, had temporarily dried up under the withering sun of the politics of the fifties and the sixties. More than any other he had expressed hope that the age-old divisions in the archipelago would be transcended by a politics of federation,[28] and more than any other he must have felt the shock of its dissolution. For eight years between 1962 and 1970 he published virtually nothing. The deepening trauma of the late sixties brought him closer to the assemblies of younger writers in Pivot, New World and Tapia, and eventually led to an explosion of creative statements in and after 1970, when, noticeably, his style became plainer, his imagery starker, his lines less regular, his sound more attuned to the atonality and dissonance of the age.

(III)
Derek Walcott: 1965–70

It is in Derek Walcott's two volumes of poetry of the sixties, *The Castaway* (1965) and *The Gulf* (1969) that the spirit of the decade is most rigorously, lyrically and consistently explored. *In a Green Night* (1962) is really a collection of earlier poems (1948-60) and is important as the record of an age of relative innocence and wonder. But it is in *The Castaway* that Walcott begins to write a poetry which focuses equally on country, seascape and waterless town, straddling the rural and urban poles between which Caribbean sensibility had begun to swing since the forties.[30] His "Laventville" includes and goes beyond the spirit of Marguerite Wyke's "History Leaves no Memorials", and was frequently read at Pivot and Tapia sessions during the late sixties and early seventies. It was the first of a growing number of poems which discuss the sociopolitical milieu of Port of Spain through the metaphor of a panoramic view of the city from the hills.[31]

"Laventville" became a metaphor of the sixties, summarising the themes of void, violation, loss and divorce from ancestral roots on the one hand, and the continuity in poverty, crime and spiritual enslavement on the other. Yet, as so often happens in *The Castaway,* the vitality of the language belies the message of helplessness and collapse. It is as if the "revolution" in which the society was to be caught up was already detonating in the poet's head. The "hopelessness and rage" of "Laventville" were the two poles between which the society itself would swing in the seventies. The terse sentence, "Action breeds frenzy" in the title poem "The Castaway", suggests the dichotomy which existed in the society itself, of inert paralysis and a molten passion of revolt seeking direction and an object.

As the sixties progressed, Walcott was simultaneously to claim his Crusoe's "happy desert" as home, to doff the castaway mask in an act of bitter acceptance, and to attempt a movement back to an "Adamic" world of wonder, greenness, the primal and "the bush".[32] But as the latter portion of *Another Life*, as well as the poems of this volume indicate, there is no way of avoiding the vision of the city or the whirlpool of politics. The difference between Walcott's political poems now and those of the sixties can be found in the greater plainness of style in today's poems. In *The Castaway*, political vision was, whenever it appeared, wrapped up in imagery. For example, the most compelling image of the future which Walcott then saw as facing the nation's youth, appears in "The Swamp".

> In the fast-filling night, note
> How the last bird drinks darkness with its throat,
> How the wild saplings slip
>
> Backward to darkness, go black
> With widening amnesia, take the edge
> Of nothing to them slowly, merge
>
> Limb, tongue and sinew into a knot
> Like chaos, like the road
> Ahead.

The "last bird" is, perhaps, the last scarlet ibis or egret to settle in the swamp's mangrove. But it may also be the vulture, which is the last bird because it presides over the dead. The "wild saplings" are the plants growing in the swamp. But we have been told earlier in the poem that the swamp in America's South is the "limbo of cracker convicts, Negroes," and that it has a "black mood" in that it constantly threatens a slow relentless death. The Trinidad reader would inevitably connect the Southern swamp with his own swamp, the swamp-dwellers of Shanty Town and Sea Lots, the La Basse on the foreshore, and the ethos of poverty and crime which surrounds the urban slum. The "young saplings" would in this context be a metaphor of the country's urban youth, or their bolom consciousness, receding stillborn to the darkness of the womb, or of the void, or of a past which is only absence and "widening amnesia".

It may be this failure to connect which leads the young, slowly but surely, to nihilism ("the edge of nothing") and an incoherence of language, effort and action ("limb, tongue and sinew"). Such nihilism and tangled incoherence combine to presage a chaotic future. There is every reason to interpret the metaphor of darkness and the fact that the youth go "black with widening amnesia" as statements about race and colour, and the emergence of "black consciousness" which was a result of the Civil Rights movement in the United States. During the early sixties, Walcott as an essayist and reviewer commented a number of times on the constant themes of race, return to ancestral roots, history and nostalgic longing for a romantic past, which were then quite prevalent in the West Indian novel.[33] At the time, he held that the West Indian had forgotten his past and had become accustomed to living without one. Thus in "Laventville", he depicts the experience of the middle passage as having been a "dull amnesiac blow", withholding Caribbean people from both past and future – "that world below us and beyond", This is the "widening amnesia" which he treats in "The Swamp".

At the same time, he criticised the growing preoccupation with blackness and Africa as escapism into nostalgia, and was particularly harsh in his rejection of such poetry as treated these themes. Hence in 1966 he declared that:

> Frankly, the bulk of West Indian verse is bad, only bearable if one forgives its origins and sympathises self-insultingly with its efforts. It has lagged far behind the novel; its structure is either sprawlingly 'modern' or embarrassingly imitative. It is weakened into rhetoric by such themes as national pride and racial peevishness.[34]

Yet Walcott had noted only two weeks before in a review of Clifford Sealey's *Voices* that

> Roger McTair's entanglement in his private vocabulary requires our sympathetic patience. The crammed, often confused shorthand of Wayne Vincent Brown will decode themselves eventually. Like all young poets they show a fury towards metaphor that is not merely decorative. More important they try to excise sentimentality and pathos from their poems.[35]

From this it would appear that one could be sympathetic without being self-insulting; that it was reasonable to expect that West Indian poets would eventually find form and technique appropriate to the sort of raw materials they were trying to shape; and that there was a new sound audible and a new spirit tangible in a handful of young writers which was worth encouraging.

The very next year was to see the publication of Brathwaite's *Rights of Passage,* and the next two that of *Masks* and *Islands.* Right away, a number of the younger poets, Questel, Gonzalez, McTair, Calliste and later Malik recognised in Brathwaite a careful and accomplished craftsman, and began themselves to experiment with language, sound, rhythm, song, dialect, and the performed word. They were attracted to quite different elements in Brathwaite: Questel to his skill at punning and association of related wordsounds, Malik to his ability to build on basic oral models such as the call-

and-response pattern, the sermon, the refrain; Calliste to the theme of Africa; Gonzalez to his use of dissonance and discord to create the verbal equivalent of jazz. Because of Brathwaite's seminal work, now republished as *The Arrivants*, Caribbean poets of the seventies are far more confident in their search for form based on models indigenous to their society.

(IV)
Transition of Sadness
Roger McTair; Judy Miles; Alfred Fraser 1964–1970

"Corners without Answers" expresses the trapped sense of hopelessness of a generation barely twenty years old in 1964. Like Europe's and America's postwar youth, they are disillusioned with the past and uncertain of the future.

> The road beyond is misty blurred
> The road behind we think was overrated.

But there is no energy here, no effort to confront or construct; only vision wasted;

> Watching dark rum drop in bottles; steadily
> Like barometers in bad weather

"Pseudo-prophets, not leaders and not led", these are, in fact, Selvon's wartime saga boys gradually awakening to the fearsome responsibility of having to define a future without any clear guidelines from the past. The youths are of the city, but they have not yet made something of it. As is the case with Selvon's limers, their laughter is fear of being alone.

> Through days and nights we form a crowd
> Needing people near
> And noise to shut out thoughts
> Of how we are alone, all drifting souls
>
> We sit on pavements dreaming our dreams
> Trying to invoke visions
> No genie comes...

The reference to "barometers in bad weather" indicates that McTair already has the intuition of the coming hurricane of revolt which was to break in the late sixties. It wasn't all intuition, though. By the third issue of *Voices* (March 1965), Elliot Bastien's "And Here You Are Now", which proclaims the realisation of the returned university graduate that he has a task of liberation to perform despite his "bent mind", appears opposite a notice announcing the end of a fourteen-day State of Emergency, in which a 6.00 p.m. to 6.00 a.m. curfew had been imposed on C.L.R. James. A few weeks earlier, Sparrow had been singing his famous "Get to Hell Outa Here", and Blakie his less known but equally trenchant "Doctah Ent Deh", the first two really irreverent calypsos to satirise the 1956 regime which was now beginning to reveal its cracks.

McTair understood his generation. It was he who, in an article entitled "What the February Revolution Really Was All About", first located the links between Black Power and Soul Culture; links which became painfully clear by the end of August 1970, when the same youth, now dressed in the weirdo outfits of Woodstock, celebrated Independence by a sixteen-hour-long soul session at the Perseverance club. For the rest of 1970, these sessions were encouraged by the establishment as a means of channelling dissent and, by 1971, all the various aspects of folk, urban and youth cultures were employed as gimmicks. There were free concerts advertised full-page in both dailies, and sponsored by various business firms. These went on until just after the elections when they ceased. Since that time, the youth have expressed no mass political loyalties, and may even be back on a scene similar to the one described in "Corners without Answers", with the slight modification that mild narcotics now replace rum as anodyne and escape.

For the individual who refused to be taken in by the shallow brotherhood of the lime, the alternatives were a desperate longing for apocalypse even to the point of self-immolation, or stark loneliness. In her first published poem, "The Holocaust",[37] Judy Miles contrasted the total commitment of Vietnamese Buddhist monks with the apathy and "stale, sour hatreds" of the Caribbean scene. In these monks, a chosen suicide indicates not failure to place value on life, but ultimate affirmation of an ideal worth the final sacrifice.

> But our faith is whirled, driven
> As dust in an endless drought
> Defying cycles.

The sound here is, perhaps, of Walcott's "Steersman: My Brother". The fixed image of drought belongs to the family of desert images which have acquired permanent residence in West Indian poetry.

"Lunch Hour"[38] examines the loneliness of one who cannot escape in crowds. People "suffocate" and "strangle" the city's main street at noon. Miles's Port of Spain is similar to Brathwaite's island/town of stiletto heels and formica tables, murderous ("stiletto") on the one hand, synthetic ("formica") on the other. Eating does not provide communion of any sort, or release the protagonist from a prison preferred to the falsehood of the city.

> They've tried to make
> that awkward dark cell
> below the staircase
> into a romantic alcove but
> eating there alone

> as she always does
> the young girl barricades
> herself behind a stare
> hard as old toast

The vision of Woodford Square is similar to that of Eliot's "Preludes".

> Going back
> the balding city square
> smells of dust, detachment,
> and passions discarded
> like chewed bones

As in Eliot, the eye is a camera selecting its images. Fancies curl around each image and cling. The seen world points to no reality beyond itself, but is precisely established and shaped by an eye which sees only its pain and the soul's irrelevance to anyone and anything outside of itself.

A bleak plain style had also surfaced in the poetry of Alfred Fraser whose work, confined to Pivot sessions and UWI campus newssheets, had begun in 1965. His unpublished "Woodford Square, Port of Spain" (1965/66) is "Corners without Answers" on solo trumpet, dry where the other is melancholy. The vision of the square is the same as Judy Miles's, though Fraser empties it of everything except its waterless fountain, himself and a pot-hound which, trotting towards him, somehow makes him "whole again." One man and his dog, without any meadow to mow.

Fraser's square is set in the dry heart of a city caught between a still visible colonial past (a Georgian library) and the uncertain modernity of the new Town Hall. The two buildings symbolise two eras, two styles, as well as two types of politics, which exist in uneasy juxtaposition. Style is a barren fountain with ugly statues. Stripped of its limers the square is made to symbolise a spiritual bleakness which in the seventies reaches frightening proportions in Judy Miles and Victor Questel.

In the five years immediately prior to 1970, Fraser, then in his late teens, was an omnivorous reader and a precocious experimenter who showed a dry relish for existentialist paradox, the avant garde jazz of Coltrane, Coleman and Dolphy, and the Beat/Pop scene from Ginsberg to the Beatles and Bob Dylan. Apart from "Woodford Square Port of Spain", a half-dozen or so of his pre-1970 poems stand out as indices of an individual talent which, however, needed its ground, its home, and a shaping discipline. These poems were "The West Indian" (1965/66); "Between Histories" (1966); "A Simple Nihilistic Philippic" (1968); "John Coltrane Is Dead" (1968); "Protoplasmic Consciousness/Cosmic Consciousness" (1968); and "Existentialism, Revolution and Death" (1969). There was also an untitled statement on the nature of art and the situation of the artist in the twentieth century[39] which summarised where Fraser himself stood just before the storm broke.

"The West Indian" is subtitled "An Imaginary Journey to Ghana" and is a drier version of Walcott's "A Far Cry from Africa", as well as a forerunner of "Negatives" (1969). Fraser's poem is a response to the idea of an Africa caught up in the traumatic violence of transition from tribal village to asphalt city, with all its apparatus for large-scale destruction of life. Exploitable, bewildered and shell-shocked, this Africa can offer no solace to the West Indian who has already gone through and survived worse holocausts. The voice in the monologue is still that of the lonely man sitting in Woodford Square's dry fountain:

> You'll find yourself in Africa
> they said
>
> I found myself lost in Africa,
> my dust mixed with the dust of desert
>   not yet dust
> my mud mixed with the mud of her rivers
>   defiling them
>   impure
>
> Chilled to the spine much more by the
>   midday rains
> than by the wet snow falling inside;
> chilled now to the spine by the minds
>   of these cold black people
>
> by the vastness of my own loneliness
>   of mine own
>   loneliness

Fraser preferred the loneliness of his own cold in-search, and looked askance at the very notion of return. The West Indian man he viewed as a sort of twentieth century Western man, who shares with his European and American counterparts, a sense of rootlessness and a disillusionment with history. "Between Histories" (1966) describes a search through labyrinths of the self in the familiar metaphors of a score of modern poets or novelists – the quest, the labyrinth, the Daedalus-like desire to "conquer the earth", the "Idea of infinity". The best lines of the poem are its driest and least derivative:

> And I looked for style but the only style I found was self
> So I bought style with eyestrain

and the wry conclusion in which Fraser acknowledges the futility of his quest for an art of classical symmetry and balance:

> Under the house of Sandburg
> somewhere under
>   I lie

> and gaze at the house of Macleish
> soberly painted and neat
> and wonder why
> not under there
> do I lie

For Fraser, then, there could be no escape either to a real or an imaginary Africa, or in Art as controlled introspective energy impressed into form. It is therefore not surprising that his initial reaction to Unit 16, which was the name that the founders of Pivot first chose for their group, was a poem called "A Simple Nihilistic Philippic" (1968) where he rejected the coming-together of young writers as yet another rumshop lime. If McTair in "Corners without Answers" had diagnosed heart-emptiness as the underlying reason for the communion of youth, Fraser, like Judy Miles, believed that it was more honourable to remain alone than to accept the illusion that atonement lay in crowds. Earlier than most, he understood how a common germ of escapism and desperate need linked the new era of Black consciousness to the ethos of Woodstock sit-ins, electronics and the obscure haze of psychedelia – to a new tribe, in other words, which was as unreal as the ancestral Africa of the negritude poets.

> games (naked in sandals, hidden behind beards, fleeing
> down the
> darkness behind the shades): all sat drenched in the negritude
> that poured from the speaker's mouth
>
> Tribal society! Tribal society! Don your loin cloths and
> thump your naked chests
> O! you see the hippies this year with their flowers and their
> chains
> and their unwashed bodies (as if that makes them hippies)
>
>   Chains that
> signify slavery (one way or the other) and their imprisoned
> minds
> follow in the costumes of their masters one year later

Fraser's reaction to this was a nausea which itself foreshadowed much of the post-1970 dismissal of the "February Revolution" as simply another species of masquerade.

> games: The eye grows in my stomach until it chokes me
> games

Yet Unit Sixteen/Pivot was more than a forum for negritude cliché, which, when it did occur, was criticised by people other than Fraser. Roger McTair, for example, in his review of John A. Williams's novel, *The Man Who Cried I Am*, praised it for its cool detachment and controlled passion, "its quiet depth rather than broad tortured surface." According to McTair, the novel's hero:

Michael Reddick is "I am! I am!"

He is not an Uncle Tom. But he isn't H. Rap Brown either. He is a man. A talented man who happens to be black and who is moving with his times and all the time. His revolution is the quiet one. Balanced. He won't start a war. But he isn't going to back down from one either. He is neutral in a positive sense. And he knows which side he is on even though he fights his battles alone.

Most of all he knows the vicious, ruthless, emasculating, genocidal, legal, cultural and economic overkill on the other side.[40]

Dave Darbeau's review of Carmichael's and Hamilton's *Black Power* was critical as well as sympathetic, while Ramdath Jagessar's "The New Discrimination"[42] presented the Afro Trinidadian as being as discriminatory and intolerant in his attitude to other races – the East Indian in particular – as the whites have been to the African. Questions raised in his article about racial attitudes in a cosmopolitan society, cultural dominance by an Afro-Creole oligarchy, cultural resistance by minority groups in the face of rising Black consciousness, would be repeatedly asked by numerous writers in the UWI campus pamphlet *Embryo* throughout 1969 and 1970, in UWI Caribbean Studies essays about race and politics, in scores of letters to the local press, especially since 1970, and at the first Conference on East Indians in the Caribbean held at UWI Trinidad, in 1975.

The point is that Pivot was capable of accommodating a number of divergent views, and this was a sign of health, rather than of the sort of sickness that Fraser had diagnosed. Indeed, the fact that he termed his "anti-poem" nihilistic implied his awareness of the necessity for politics, though it was clear that he could see no way in which the youth might arrive at a genuine political commitment. The "nakedness" which he recognised in their lives was equally his. Their evasion of face ("hidden behind beards") racial escapism ("fleeing down the darkness") and obscured vision ("behind the shades") would also be his as soon as he tried to make the leap out of his lonely silence into the whirlpool of politics. His reaction to the embryonic possibility which was Pivot, therefore, contained a fair measure of the same self-righteousness which was to be characteristic of the reaction of the society as a whole to the failure of the 1970 movement.

Between 1968 and 1970, Fraser's poems reveal two tendencies which are probably complementary: first, a movement away from crowds, meetings and the tedium of the human voice into the ever-deepening chaos of self, and secondly, an escape from inner incoherence into the dreadful simplicities of mass politics. The movement backwards into self is first seen in "John Coltrane Is Dead" (August/Sept. 1968).[43] Yet the fact that this retreat into self is presented in terms of the poet's response to a definite and significant event outside of himself – the death of 'Trane – results in a statement of far greater control and coherence than the poems which are to follow. A moving elegy to one of the greatest musicians of this century, "John

Coltrane Is Dead", employs the technique of disarticulated leap from idea to idea, so characteristic of the jazz avant garde of which 'Trane was a leader.

Coltrane is seen first as a magician who creates beauty and winged ascension ("butterflies") from the plainest and most banal of melodies ("a plain brown paper bag"). The second fragment of the poem contrasts the "truth" which the musician explores with the "real" world of affairs. The politician's truth is one of endless ole talk ("how long conferences"), of "gallerying" and further palaver. The phrase "how long", famous in the blues, suggests the spirit of the times in which 'Trane created – an age of debate, rhetoric, Civil Rights sermons and speeches in which patience was stretched to its extremity. 'Trane reacted to these things in his tense cry from the depths, "Alabama", and in "Reverend King", which moves from prayer to fury before it circles back to prayer.

The third fragment of Fraser's elegy focuses on the style of Coltrane: his bewildering flurry of notes, his "sheets of sound" technique. There is an indirect allusion to his composition "Giant Steps". For Fraser, 'Trane becomes Gulliver, other musicians mere Lilliputians beside him, as he with exhilaration "turns somersaults" in fields of semiquavers. The musician here is man/god, an image to recur in Leroy Calliste's "South Trumpeter". He is life-force, gaiety in spite of the barrenness ("plain brown") and ephemerality ("butterflies", "paper bag") of his world.

The final fragment focuses on the poet in his "cellar". The "cellar" – prominent in modern literature as an image of the inner self, and most notably in Dostoyevsky's *Notes from Underground*, Ellison's *Invisible Man* and in the dustbin, sickroom images which pervade Beckett's plays and novels, here symbolises the innermost region of the poet's mind. It is in this innermost region that Coltrane's death reaches him:

> A chill, feather-white wind blows through the window of my cellar
> and I hastily lock it in
>
> that the world be a bit warmer
> though I a bit colder

The poet needs this "icy intuition" – (as Walcott terms it) – if he is to warm the world: that is, make it a trifle more aware of its humanity and need for compassion. But the price which the poet pays for this is isolation, the state of being locked in with his cold vision of mortality.

In the late 1968 poem entitled "Protoplasmic Consciousness/Cosmic Consciousness" – (the second title is also the name of a late Coltrane album) – Fraser is trying to write down a series of incoherent impressions conjured up by the music. The music itself he listened to as an index of the turbulence of the times, the vortex of Trinidad politics in the late sixties, and the chaos of his own brain which now spun in bewildered circles, in the face of the necessity of choosing between the Scylla of self-obsession and the Charybdis of political commitment. If a statement about the nature of the relationship between the artist and society is any true guide, Fraser had strengthened his stand of exile from and opposition to his world. The artist is depicted as a necessary alien:

> Long before he lies naked in bed at midnight wrestling with ideas and pictures and words, he has to be alienated within his society. Only then can he examine the crowd from within and yet without; and only such an examination can change the individual innocent into such a Macleishian whore. Only said whore can be familiar with the intimates of society and yet be abstract enough to offer satisfaction to these suppressed needs. When I started to write I was lost somewhere between the supertechnicians, Walcott and Wordsworth. But the absurdity of it all was that I was writing seventh decade twentieth century, where rivers flowing had no relevance; blood flowing and sperm flowing had.[44]

Fraser is writing here with the arrogance of a man of the city and not even of homely Port of Spain, for he finds it necessary to assume the full deformity of megalopolis. His points of reference are, accordingly, Alfred Jarry, Lenny Bruce, the theatre of the Absurd, and the jazz avant garde; that is, precisely the points to which the youth "counter-culture" in Britain and America were relating.[45] He informs us:

> This I write after having heard Jacki Byard, David Izenon (formerly of the Ornette Coleman trio) and Elvin Jones (formerly of the late John Coltrane's Quartet) play an almost twenty minute piece in no set key or tempo. (I hope this group stays together, because only musicians of this calibre could make such music a success.) The three men created a full mosaic of chaos to wrench the (humble?) listener from pastel reality into that abysmal vortex of change.

Note how this merges with what Michael Horowitz says in his "Afterwords" to *The Children of Albion,* about the British and American Underground poets of the sixties:

> We've also joined issue with totally unscripted British, European and American freeform musicians – Dave Tomlin, George Kisch, David Izenon, Ornette Coleman – to unframe words and notes from all conventional meter, arrangement, mood, or conception of harmony, discipline, language. So that the music means something again and poetry speaks openly, to all.[46]

Fraser was clearly thinking along the same lines. But the question of relevance remained. If negritude was imported cliché, socialism and Black Power different costumes in the same masquerade, weren't existentialism and the Theatre of the Absurd, art as masochistic mutilation of sensibility and form, equally questionable imports? Fraser in 1969 felt not, and could therefore shut off his sensibility from the relatively unexplored Caribbean landscape with the declaration that rivers flowing had no relevance in the 1960s of chaotic cities and bloodshed. Adopting wholesale a post-existentialist notion of reality as chaos, Fraser produced his "Protoplasmic Consciousness" whose opening lines tell the reader that it is about:

> Nuances
> Resolution
> Revolving
> Questioning
>
> Being evolved not began
>   like the darkness disappearing
> Between the surreal and the unreal
> The life/snail going from extinction to extinction
> across the coral flesh

Beneath this poem lies the constant fear, real or simulated, of nuclear war, Vietnam's napalm, faces dripping with flaming caustic, the "plastic dimensions of the rain" of a new Hiroshima. It is this fear which seeks its release in fragmented images, the chaotic sub-world of surrealism, scatological metaphors, and sheer masochistic cruelty – an art of deformity for a deformed world.

At this point, Fraser might well have been one of the subway travellers in Walcott's "A Village Life", Simon and Garfunkel people caught amidst "the sound of silence".

> I watch that silence spreading through our souls:
> that horn-rimmed midget who consoles
> his own deformity with Sartre on Genet.
> Terror still eats the nerves, the Word
> is gibberish, the plot Absurd.[47]

Yet Walcott himself seems at this point to have been wavering between the perception of West Indian cities as replicas of decadent metropolitan ones, and a rooted knowledge of the villages, forests, rivers and peasants of his boyhood. We find him arraigning his company for their failure to be at home with Genet's deformity,[48] criticising the unnamed West Indian avant-gardists for lacking the power or the sense of decadence to produce a de Sade, a Grotowski, "or the madness of an Artaud",[49] and at the same time rejecting the "pastoral vision" of "reactionaries in dashikis", the tribalism of Black Power and Pan-Africanist groups, which Fraser had also dismissed as nauseating. On the other hand, we have Walcott talking about a return to the bush, a descent into the primal, Adamic man, the movement "back to the green beginnings of this world".[50] He obviously makes a distinction between his own pastoral vision and the weaker efforts of his brethren.

Fraser, rejecting the possibility of villages and turning away from even the confused potential of a small town such as Port of Spain, allowed himself no way out of this trapped vision of a deformed world. Thus when the chain of UWI campus-based protest – the Rodney, Michener, Anguilla, Camacho and Thomas affairs – together with the Bus Workers' Strike

(1969) impressed on him the necessity of political action of some sort, he had to justify his shift in position towards Black Power activism by a poem "Existentialism, Revolution and Death" (1969), whose very name echoes that of Camus's collection of essays, *Resistance, Rebellion and Death.* In this poem Fraser sees ultimate human choice as being between obsession with self ("self-consumption") and self-sacrifice to an ideal ("the self-consuming fire"). One must either learn:

> to exist in a world built on mutilation
> to love those so mutilated

or act to change such a world. Fraser, now accepting Fanon's justification of violence as a necessary stage in liberation, argues himself into an acceptance of destructive holocaust. The dream had existed in Judy Miles five years earlier.

> By fire I must create my dreams
> for only my dreams can survive the fire
> and become the reality of many tomorrows
>
> And them that are made of paper
>   Must burn! Must burn!
> And them that have stabbed
> with their sharpened icicles
>   Must burn! Must burn!
> And them that have left their scars
> on the psyches and hearts and bodies
> of my people, the mutilated,
>   Must burn! Must burn!

One year before he had seen through negritude, now he is saying:

> Let Blackness flow
> the thick black fluid of love
> over this septic, this sore that we die in,
> its cleansing reincarnation, its fire
> our birth, the destruction of this
> ugly city, the destruction of this
> ugly city

The voice has become incantatory, predicting the mood and rhetoric of 1970. Fraser has moved from the loneliness of "Woodford Square, Port of Spain" through several dimensions of void, towards incoherence, nihilism and desperate commitment to violent revolutionary reprisal for all that long history of mutilation. And in his metamorphosis we have the only really consistent and continuous measure of the city's subterranean drift from the melancholy of "Corners without Answers", through a transition of sadness, towards the strange mixture of soul, weed, rhetoric, and energy which broke in 1970. Fraser marched with NJAC in 1970 and was put on the list of those to be detained. He never was. One of my recollections of those days is of him walking across a dry field, through the brown dusk of an April evening, half an hour before the curfew and darkness, uncertain about whether he would get home.

(V)
The Mind Musicians
Anson Gonzalez 1969-1972

"With my blue note, my cracked note …my new frigged-up soul"
(Brathwaite)

There were, of course, other poems which chronicled the spirit of the pre-1970 period. One of the most direct of these was Anson Gonzalez's "Cadence" which first appeared in *Pelican* (1969). The poem talks about the "slime" and "stench" of a regime which, by undermining fundamental freedoms, allows its talent and manhood (such a gendering of political thought was a feature of those days) to drain away. The silence of opposition forces, the reluctance of public servants to disclose what corruption they have witnessed even though promised immunity, are alluded to in this poem. It explores the central image of a Panorama steelband frozen into silence by the "maestro massa". Its first line "The sound of silence", taken from the then popular Simon and Garfunkel tune, suggests the neo-folk scene of ballads and blues, and the reaction of America's post-Hiroshima youth to the tarnished American dream. Less intensely than Fraser, Gonzalez is aware of the wider context within which the movement of Caribbean youth might be located.

The political control of folk and folk-urban culture is conveyed through an image of dissonant pan music. "Cadence" depicts a nation caught in the act of masquerade, and is simply one of several literary statements where the metaphor of Carnival is employed to satirise political and national endeavour in Trinidad. Others are Walcott's "Mass Man" and "Junta", McTair's "Notes Towards a Final Belief", with its line "playing or going to mass, mas' is what they believe", Christopher Laird's "The Road", and much earlier than all these, Marguerite Wyke's "A Plume of Dust" (1958). The idea of masking and role-playing lies beneath Naipaul's *The Mimic Men* as well as Walcott's *In a Fine Castle* (1971). By 1970 it had become normal to refer to politics in terms of masquerade.

But if the establishment had grown sour, the protesting youth had, according to Gonzalez, developed no alternative vision. Older than people like Fraser or Darbeau by a few years, he protested bitterly against the emotional exploitation which was undoubtedly part of the 1970 movement. Two weeks before the February 26th March, he wrote in *Embryo* condemning the campus-based movement for its derivativeness.

The same violence with which the white man brainwashed me is now being attempted by my brothers. The same colonialism – this time from Negro-American sources. Instead of "Dan is the Man in the Van" they want to feed me *Soul on Ice.* Instead of nursery rhymes, they prefer to depress me with tape recordings of the rhetoric of Malcolm X and Stokely.

But then they sit in meetings and plan how to doctorise to the masses. Just as the white man, they decide what truths, what versions of the truth, the masses and importantly the student masses, must know. The same arrogance and hubris of which they accuse the whites, they themselves blatantly display.

The connivings, the strategy, the intriguing, the lies and the deceit of the other side, the white side, the establishment side, are all repeated on this side, but in this case Justice is on our side, they say.

And my friends – (with friends like these who needs enemies) – want me to take sides. I will take no effing sides with corrupt men – corrupt MAN. I have to live with you black and white effluvia of the Caroni swamp; but I do not have to like you. Leave me right there smiling at your antics. For I crave neither wealth nor power, only Freedom, and this you both wish to deny me.[51]

Gonzalez viewed 1970 solely in terms of the limitations of its leaders, and his poems on political themes concentrate on condemning either the establishment, or the opposition efforts or both, the poet holding himself aloof from contamination. He attempts to measure the extent to which people have suffered for the sake of empty slogans, as in "Decision"[52] where a voice chorus of the "committed" chants all the 1970 slogans to the rhythms of Lord Fluke's 1971 calypso about the Black Power Movement of 1970. Lord Fluke, eccentric and lovable, is one of those calypsonians who cannot keep time, and whose vision of reality is generally as incoherent as his words. Just as "Cadence" employed the metaphor of a discordant steelband to suggest the state of the nation, "Decision" employs the metaphor of a half-witted calypsonian to satirise the mass movement of 1970, the main object of attack being again the hypocrisy of the leaders and the betrayal of the masses to their pitiless enthusiasms. "Who Killed My Son"[53] dramatises the bewilderment of a parent at the indifference of revolutionary process to individual suffering, condemning such process as inhumane.

If "Cadence" lamented the paralysis of the present regime and predicted the discord of 1970, "Hey Alfie"[54] presents an image of the utter mental and moral collapse of the youth movement. It is one of Gonzalez's best thought-out and structured poems. The Alfie here is Alfred Fraser to whose activist phase the poem is addressed. The images, precisely chosen from jazz are appropriate to one whose first music is atonal, disarticulated avant-garde jazz.

> hey, Alfie
> as the cracked blue piano notes
> tinny off into cacophony

> of microphoned harshness
> through a beard,
> as the trumpet
> highpeaks Ujaama
> to Uhuru

Alfie had, as we have seen, accepted atonal music as a positive symbol of "the abysmal vortex of change" into which he had desperately plunged in order to escape the paralysis of empty waiting without hope. For Gonzalez, however, the "cracked blue piano notes" are the mind's sinews – (Alfie's, the nation's and his own) – giving way under tension. The fact that these cracked notes merge with the "microphoned harshness" of hysterical protest suggests that the leaders of 1970 were themselves breaking under the strain. The image of the cracked musician is strengthened by the fact that Gonzalez is referring here to a particular pianist who used to frequent the Students' Guild, UWI, during 1970, and spend hours at a time playing defunctive requiem music on a badly tuned piano. Alfie had defended the pianist as a true existentialist[55] in an article entitled "Musicians of the Mind". Gonzalez borrows the phrase, but twists it in his poem where it suggests not creative existentialist freedom, but the political manipulation of people's thoughts.

> hey, Alfie
> as the mind musicians
> compose in their
> concerthall void
> in this middle search
> emptiness of pool
> in their cadence
> of subliminal pain
> as limp-wristed drummers
>
> miss their beats
> while looking beat
> smiling beatific
> behind the glazed eyes
> of the committed

Several things are captured here: first a Queens Hall conference where the ruling party spoke for hours to rows of empty chairs – (*Tapia* loves to publish that photo) – then the beards, dark glasses and glazed eyes of fledgling addicts, failed revolutionaries, tired drummers; thirdly, the dual meaning of "committed": possessing conviction and certified as mad. The poem certainly contains the pain of 1971 with its Woodstock sit-ins, politically sponsored folk extravaganzas which filtered the protest of 1970 off in a haze of officially-endorsed marijuana smoke and masquerade.

"Nation's State" is a direct descent into the final circle of the inferno: a guerilla movement which has spent little time considering what McTair had described in 1968 as: "the vicious, ruthless, emasculating, genocidal, legal, cultural and economic overkill on the other side."[56] The poem alternates between the euphoric lines of the National Anthem and the reality of nationhood, which in 1973 is:

> The flower of our youth
> destroyed by the blight
> of powerseeking maskwearers.

These "powerseeking maskwearers" are not the police, whom some were describing in similar terms, but the guerillas. Gonzalez is again reaffirming his 1970 stance against Black Power, though it is only fair to point out that by 1973 the situation had altered. The guerillas regarded the Black Power movement as being passé and saw the NJAC all-day rallies and variety concerts as being an irrelevant "culture scene" in a situation where "the only solution is armed struggle".

Nineteen seventy cracked not only political alliances but friendships, by making the society aware of the reality of cowardice and betrayal. Thus both the Gonzalez of "Nation's State" and the Walcott of "A Patriot to Patriots" react violently to the use of the word "Brother" as a rallying catchphrase. Both also share the fear that any revolution based on a sense of racial exclusivism will lead to genocidal revenge in the West Indies. If Walcott is able to hear in the literature of "masochistic recollection" the hiss of Auschwitz and Hiroshima ovens,[57] Gonzalez hears in the crackle of Black Power microphones "the cannibalistic chantings" and "war drums" of (who knows?) "darkest Africa". Eric Roach had in 1971 heard the same sound in the poetry of Bongo Jerry.[58] Spokesmen from different generations could at least agree on some points.

(VI)
The Human Song
Syl Lowhar; Wayne Davis; Leroy Calliste

> Power is not enough to make us strong:
> The heart must also sing the human song.
> (Lowhar)

If 1970 left Gonzalez smiling bitterly at the antics of those caught up in the vortex of change, it deepened the commitment of Syl Lowhar who was, like him, older than the generation of Darbeau and Fraser. One of the early members of New World in Guyana, where he had been part of the Trinidad diplomatic corps during the early sixties, Lowhar had greater experience of active commitment than the newly-fledged members of the NJAC. In 1966 he entered UWI, St. Augustine, where he served on the Students' Guild Council, clashing on several occasions with Geddes Granger who entered two years after. I remember very well his solid contribution to the Woodford Square teach-in on Anguilla in 1969, the year when UWI was drawn into the whirlpool of mass politics. In 1968, when New World split, he became a founder member of the Tapia House Group, and was their chief spokesman in 1970 when the "February Revolution" exploded.

Lowhar, in a speech made on the night of April 20th, 1970, the eve of the declaration of the 1970 State of Emergency, explains the part he played in making the campus more aware of Trinidad society and the Caribbean Community:

> So when I went to St. Augustine as a student in 1966, I went with a sense of mission. I am sure that Brother Geddes would agree that it was both of us who had sounded the clarion call for Black Power in this new phase. We exploded the myth that students were complacent and apathetic. We agreed with the poet Derek Walcott that: "All its indifference is a different rage." We insisted on students' involvement in the affairs of the region which we defined to include Cuba, Haiti, Puerto Rico, Guadeloupe, Martinique and not those bogus definitions of the Caribbean given us by the imperial masters. We pledged to arouse the conscience of the Caribbean peoples against the evils of an iniquitous régime.[59]

Where Gonzalez ignores the historical context of 1970, Lowhar locates it remotely in the history of reaction against the plantation system, and more immediately in the new language of self-definition which had arisen since the 1930s to clarify itself in the New World Movement of the sixties, and in the protest of several depressed urban groups as the decade neared its close. Like Gonzalez, he warns against imported slogans, noting the tendency among Black Power leaders to simplify the formulations of thinkers such as Fanon, in order to suit their own immediate purposes.

Where Gonzalez in "Cadence" notes the growing silence with helpless anger, Lowhar asserts that freedom becomes a dead letter if it is not actively affirmed.

> The air is still filled with frightening rumours of States of Emergencies following signs of a military build-up. In this situation, sisters and brothers, the principles of democracy appear to be at stake – principles that are above party, above government, above the civil service. Every individual has a right, indeed, the obligation to stand up and speak out in the interest of freedom and justice. Every civil servant, every teacher, every public officer, every policeman, every corporation man ought not to be deterred to stand up and be counted in the struggle for freedom. Love of country demands this.[60]

Lowhar stood up and was, indubitably, counted. He was arrested on trumped-up charges and detained during the State of Emergency.

Members of the New World Group were generally more interested in politics and economics than in poetry. Lowhar, who was deeply influenced by the poetry of Martin Carter which he would read again and again at Pivot and Tapia sessions, blended poetry and politics. A Lowhar political speech generally moves freely between the two. His own work shows both the political concern of Carter and the lyricism of Eric Roach, whose poetry he deeply admired. "Bureaucracy" (1965) is, perhaps, the least regular of his poems, most of the others having something of the end-stopped pentametric rigidity of much Roach and some Carter. "Bureaucracy" was, no doubt, Lowhar's reaction to his own stint among Civil Service files, though its portrait of the bureaucrat who,

> Stern, stiff-collared, bolt-upright;
> Cuff-linked, pedantic, perpendicular
> With elbows squarely braced on lacquered desk
> Thumbs through the dingy mound of red-taped files
> And dips his pen in the blood of the people

may at the time have seemed a trifle grim for the cricket-playing Caribbean. Ten years later, what with sudden arrests, midnight searches, shoot-outs, sedition bills, laws against hair, gun courts and the rest, the picture seems, if anything, too mild.

In "To Martin Carter" [61] Lowhar intuitively grasps what lies on the other side of bureaucratic indifference to "the human song" – the constant imminence of apocalyptic upheaval. What is interesting are the terms in which Lowhar in 1966 expressed this rebellion. Carter's poetry becomes for him a Shango chapelle in which the spirits of the past are ingathered, particularly that of Cuffy, the Guyanese Akan leader of 1763. This spirit of rebellion ignites even the landscape, wind, wave, creek, forest. But 1763 contained the bitter lesson of betrayal as well, and of internecine struggle, the lesson which Carter himself learned as Guyana moved from the promise of 1953 to the schism of the sixties. Lowhar, however, ends his poem with fervent hope of renewal:

> If only Massacooram would come
> To avenge our murdered fathers
> And break these powered liners
> Arriving again for gold.
>
> Listen!
> There is a stirring in the leaves;
> A movement on the banks of three great rivers.
> Birds panic from trees into the sky
> Shrieking, shedding feathers.
> The drum beats louder, louder

> The echo deep inside grows clearer, clearer,
> I see a creature rising from the water,
>
> Whose eyes are torches of fire

What Lowhar foresaw here all came true barely four years later. What is interesting is how sojourn in Guyana led him so surely to landscape and myth, and the subliminal terror which lurks beneath the Guyanese imagination. Contrast Wayne Brown's description of the vague amorphous emergence of Black consciousness in the West Indies. Its womb is postcolonial void and inertia, not purposefully directed creative energy.

> some rage retreats from cheated eyes;
> some
> flung sperm spirals to the ocean's womb, where,
>
> born
> and grown
> and gathering now
> about its yellow stare,
> a hunchbacked Blackness wells and stirs [62]

And where the drum in Lowhar is a symbol of energy and renewal based on an awakened sense of the strength of the people in survival, in Brown it suggests only the monotonous cliché of past suffering.

> Waves,
>   unseen
>   heard only,
> thump against the sterile peer
> with the dull, unheeded, endless
> sorrow of an African drum

"Shanty Town", published first in February 1970 is Lowhar's first urban poem. Its regular iambic pentametric lines seem to be too rigidly ordered for the kind of stark picture Lowhar is painting here. The poem owes something to Walcott's "Laventville", as do so many poems on this theme, but lacks the controlled energy of the original, or the density of image. It does not move beyond straight description. What it does affirm, though, is the fact that these crab-people are the preservers of memory, religion and creative energy, the society's only source of indigenous growth. In this respect it differs from "Laventville".

"Dry River"[64] one of the few poems published by Lowhar since 1970, is a more successful poem than "Shanty Town". It is one of the first poems where the Dry River emerges as a major symbol of the withering of the primal life of the tribe. Owing something to Langston Hughes's "The Negro Speaks of Rivers", it sees the river as a symbol of history, the "green beginning" (Walcott) of the tribe. The Dry River which bisects the city, a miserable shrivelled concrete canal, is the ultimate limit of that journey away from water. Yet the instinct yearns for water, for flood. Somewhere beneath this poem is the drought and marching of 1970, and the Dry River becomes a symbol of a people's spiritual drought, seeking release in torrent:

> Comets are flashing flame across the sky
> While the Dry River speaks its language – thirst.
>
> The Canal cuts the city like a wound,
> Septic, yellow with pus, draining the life
> blood in the gullible sea
>
> Rage, rage Dry River
> Under the terrible flight of carrion-birds

Also caught up in "the abysmal vortex of change" was Wayne Davis, a lover of jazz, high school teacher, an idealist, dreaming of a more humane society. Together with a few people, he had been involved in the formation of UMROBI, a cultural group in San Fernando little different in its orientation from Pivot in Port of Spain. An idea of where Davis stood in 1970 is conveyed by his article on jazz[65] which appeared in February 1970. He viewed jazz as an intellectually and emotionally rewarding music which, rooted in the Afro-American experience, had moved beyond it to become a statement on "the mysterious nature of existence and of the Universe." Jazz, he said, was as important a statement on the modern world as modern poetry; and although he did not relate the form of some modern poetry to that of jazz, he did, in his comments on the music of Charlie Mingus, isolate some of the major features of avant-garde jazz:

> Now Mingus was a terribly alienated man. He was a loner. But he possessed a fierce burning integrity as a man and as a musician that is truly admirable. Mingus like other great artists has produced in "Black Saint and Sinner Lady" a musical composition that makes few concessions to the listener. The music that he has produced is disturbing, jagged, deliberately discordant. Melodies are shattered, chord sequences are disrupted and the emphasis is not so much on producing beautiful sounds as on producing meaningful sounds.
>
> All this is done quite intentionally because Mingus has tried to capture in his music the American nightmare, or rather the loss of the American dream. Mingus' work reflects the anguish, suffering, rage and confusion of the Afro-American. And it is an unremitting indictment of the harshness, cruelty and vulgarity of what essentially is a materialistic society.[65]

Davis's statement may be taken with Fraser's acceptance of atonal jazz as the representative sound of an era caught up in a whirlpool of change, and with Gonzalez's employment of cacophony to explore the growing mania of his society. It is also related to Brathwaite's experiments with sound in *The Arrivants* which will be a major textbook on technique for the next decade.

Dreamer and idealist or not, Davis was detained on Nelson Island in 1970. The poems by him in this volume relate directly to that experience of 1970,

MY STRANGLED CITY

though he has written others in which his interest in Hindu philosophy is included. It was after 1970 that he achieved his panoramic view of the city. "Squares" (1975) treats of the same fundamental situation as Walcott's "Laventville" (1985). Davis, who in "Dawn" describes himself as "a lonely/ embattled man/tinkling too harshly/with self-concern" becomes Hamlet in his "antic disposition", watching the play-acting of his city.

> Squares
> Antic sculptures,
> Of mellowed perfumed boxwood.
> And luminous metal banding
> And rust red tin roofs
> Asserting exotically
> Their absurd
> Jolting selves,
> Upon marvellous
> Plinths
> Of blue and white
> Veined quarry stone,
> Polished to delicate smoothness
> By the persistent bare feet
> of endless slave times.

The squares are first of all the houses of the poor. But they are also a metaphor of the prefabricated education which turns the brain into a box, or mass-produced prison cell. By the end of the poem they are the future, one of Pete Seeger's petty-bourgeois squaredom – "squaring off with the Joneses" in suburbia.

This vision does not move beyond Walcott's because the protesting voice reiterates its theme and explains its symbols instead of letting them work for themselves. Walcott's suburbs which shine "like pedlars' tin trinkets in the sun" shrivel to Davis's "Clogged/Indifferent/Fussing city". Walcott makes the point through image, linking the hopeless peddlers of. Frederick Street and Independence Square with the bigger peddlers of prayer, dope and cloth – the priests, merchants and middlemen. Moreover, "tin trinkets" echoes the "tinkling" steelband which the poet hears during his ascent to Laventille. Petty bourgeois emptiness ("tin trinkets") and castrated proletarian vitality ("steel tinkling") counterpoint each other in the nation's defunctive music.

What enables Walcott to achieve and maintain this fusion of sound, image and idea is a quality of imagination working on a rare mixture of intelligence and passion. As yet these qualities remain separate things not only in Davis, but in most of the poems in this collection. In the case of Davis, the passion is real enough – as "Prison House Blues" makes clear. Like Ferlinghetti, he can say "I am the man/I was there/I suffered." The intelligence is also there. But the fusing imagination manifests itself only at rare moments. Thus Davis is in "Prison House Blues" bound, like Roger

Mais, to the necessity of painting a sufficiently stark portrait of prison life to shock society into conscience. This he does, not by the downbeat restraint of, say, Victor Questel, who grew up in one of those "squares", but by presenting sadistic perversion as the normal and most corrosive features of prison life.

Prison is seen as the hell society creates to conceal its own deformity; as an evil secretion of the injustice and madness which society harbours; in short, as society's most compelling, real and terrifying image. With him one enters hell, at whose centre:

> The Devil
> Is a cracked concrete lavatory,
> Erect like a majestic marble
> throne.
>
> Giving an over-eloquent, ghastly
> yawn.
> Beckoning the other imps,
> the surly chamber pots,
> Weighed down by the mess of crime,
> To dance on, dance on

This is one point where image and idea are imaginatively fused. The reference to the lavatory bowl as "a majestic marble throne" reminds us, first of all, that the "Royal Jail" was constructed in 1812 during the reign of George the Mad. The ordure of Empire, then, is being maintained in an age of independence, and this is justified by the "over-eloquent" speeches of schizophrenic ("cracked"), heartless ("concrete") politicians ("lavatory").

The lavatory bowl also refers directly to the King Devil, who commands his lesser imps to "dance on, dance on". Davis here has smoothly blended his scatological imagery with the Carnival imagery of the Devil band and the Dame Lorraine schoolmaster. His method here is reminiscent of Errol Hill's *Whistling Charlie and The Monster* (1963) where traditional Carnival masks were employed metaphorically towards the achievement of keen political satire. In Dame Lorraine the schoolmaster cracks his whip and commands his pupils to "dance on", which they proceed to do with obscene pelvic movements. Here it is the authoritarian politician who is schoolmaster and the nation which becomes a masquerade band of depraved children.

The "chamber-pot" image is borrowed from Malik's poem, "Afro-Saxon 1970". Here it applies to more than Malik intended; the Chambers of Commerce, the Chambers of Law and the members of the cabinet. "Mess" on the literal plane is both the food served out to prisoners and the excrement into which it is converted. On the metaphorical plane, it refers to the state of the nation and the corruption which each confession from the lavatory seat of power reveals.

The Royal Jail of the poem thus becomes a metaphor for the nation itself, imprisoned by a dying and cracked regime *"pro rege et lege"*[66]

> It is the
> Living shells of men,
> Empty and dented
>
> Tin pan
> Shells of men,
> That I must weep for now,
> As I wept then

These men are old servants of the party who, when young, invested their hopes in what was called the national movement. Now, sucked dry by the system, they are dispensable.

> Old men who have lost
> Their heads,
> Because they have
> Lost their eyes.

Ironically, the society's purblind leaders are as much in prison as the society itself, which becomes:

> Men who sit
> Mesmerized
> By the mess of dotage
> And porridge,
> Spreading like the sour-mush
> Of wet bread,
> Embroidered with sour flies
> In an old duck pan.

If to the Mighty Chalkdust the gifts of the régime were no more than "a dead cobo"[67] and a sure sign of lunacy, to Davis, the promises and handouts after 1970 are no more than "the mess of dotage and porridge", by-products of the "mess of crime". The pun on mess is now made more horrifying by its association with both faeces and porridge – food for children gone sour. The children here are the nation's youth, McTair's sad young men, Fraser's alienated schizoids, Questel's tragicomic drifters, and Gonzalez's rabble deluded by power-seeking masqueraders.

Note too, the macabre accuracy of "embroidered" – linking old-time domestic warmth with the horror of decay ("sour flies"). The programme for the seventies – perspectives of the new society – turns out to be the same "old duck pan" of the fifties, but this time with more elaborate embroidery. If the circus was a carnival dance of animated chamber-pots, the "bread" is diseased mushy duck food. Together these images which function on both the surface level – since they refer to normal features of prison life – and at a subliminal level, indicate Davis's revulsion at the amazing contempt in which the ordinary people have been held. For it is ultimately they who become chamber-pots for academics, dotish politicians, businessmen and magistrates, and duck-pans to be filled with soft, sour, tenth-rate mush.

> But other ghosts inhabit Hades:
> [...] taut young men,
> Men whose eyes
> Are chisels,
> Cruel chisels
> That will chew
> Through smooth white bone
> Or rough grey granite beyond
> To gain their
> Wanted freedom

These are the potential anarchists who will level whites or blacks turned grey stone. Ironically, their humanity and promise ossify in the prison. Hence the epilogue which speaks plainly about the "spiritual distress" that the poet feels when he confronts

> The concrete fact
> Of a society
> That has learned nothing
> From slavery, but to
> Mimic murderously
> The style of outdated dictatorship
> And slavery

Leroy Calliste was also there in 1970, and on the verge of breakdown. His poetry trails off into wistful smoke, lament, pastoral retreat to rural pathway and nostalgia for an Africa which, contrary to a quite common belief, is relatively rare among the city's hard-boiled youth. It is not that the movement back to landscape in poets such as Selwyn Bhajan and Calliste is a bad thing. The problem is rather one of possessing the landscape with sufficient intensity and clarity so that description of nature ceases to be vague and generalised. Calliste, perpetually mourning lost innocence, does not do this.

His strongest poem, "South Trumpeter", should be compared first with Wayne Davis's "Kaleidoscope" and next with the elegies "Valley Prince" and "For the Don D" which Jamaican poets Mervyn Morris and Anthony McNeill wrote on the occasion of Don Drummond's death. Other poems by West Indians have been dedicated to music or musicians. The earliest of these are Shake Keane's "Shaker Funeral" and "Calypso Dancers",[68] Kamau Brathwaite's "Jazz Portraits"[69] which include an elegy for Charlie Parker, Walcott's "The Glory Trumpeter",[70] Alec Best's "Memorial Blues for Billie Holiday"[71] Wayne Davis's "Miles Beyond" and Faustin Charles's "Black Cat"[73] which, like "Miles Beyond" and Brathwaite's "Miles", is dedicated to the great trumpeter Miles Davis.

Calliste's "South Trumpeter" belongs to this growing family of music poems. Chancellor, the cracked trumpeter from San Fernando is, like

Drummond, elevated into prophet, man/god and icon of the cracked age, whose withering he has calmly foreseen. Like Morris's Drummond, he "blows his mind's fire." The difference is that Calliste's Chancellor becomes a symbol not only of trapped man/artist, but also of a society's yearning for the destruction of Babylon. Hence trumpet-bell lengthens to gun barrel, trumpet-blast explodes into gelignite and trumpeter becomes Joshua or the Angel of the Apocalypse blowing to fragments the kingdom of this world – the stone city.

> Down it comes, engulfing
> cities that crack and crumble, souls
> writhe, are raised, are freed;
> down it comes with each burst
> and the whole earth quakes,
> and prisons are broken
> by those staccato blasts.

This is the imploding dream contained in the Black music of the avantgarde; the dream which Davis locates in Mingus's *The Black Saint and the Sinner Lady* and Fraser in Dolphy, Coleman and Elvin Jones even as he himself moved towards it in his own writing. The dream exists in art, whether music or writing, long before it explodes into political action.

But – and herein lies the realism of Calliste's "South Trumpeter" – there is always the descent to strangled city and blues. Babylon remains as stonily unperturbed as ever; God as silent, the sky as "blue".

> But he alone knows
> that these piercing notes
>
> may be daggers too
> to touch a heart that's hard
> or rend that sky of blue.

Chancellor, it is said, went mad after some shocking betrayal in love. His "revolution" is personal, his music a reaching out to the absent hardhearted lover who, most certainly, will not return. It is ultimately an indictment, not of the time–limited political system, but of "the crossroads of time," not of the stony city, but of the blue neuter heaven.

(VII)
Prophet and Singer Malik 1970–1975

"...the dust-blown blood of cities..." (Walcott)

Malik was also there, speaking more urgently from the roots and from within the heart of the city than any other voice. More than any of the other poets here, his work has been the direct product of 1970. Most of *Black Up* (1972) was written in the Royal Jail where Malik was confined as a political detainee in 1970 before being transferred to Nelson Island. In a restrained and confident interview with Bruce Paddington,[74] Malik describes his experience as a product of both Grenada and Trinidad; his Laventille background, four years of secondary education in Grenada, and dropping out of school. More important was his compulsion to write a novel which led him to reading West Indian novels, and his overcoming of the fear of being considered odd, which was the lot of anyone who aspired to be a writer.

Malik's testimony of what gave birth to 1970 is important because it qualifies most of the other statements on this matter. Of all the poet-detainees, he was the one most "inside" the events of 1970. As a co-founder of the local Black Panthers, he was one of the first to relate the condition of the depressed peoples of Port of Spain to that of the Blacks in America's ghettos. The moving force in his awakening was *The Autobiography of Malcolm X*. It is this book, too, which led him to become a Muslim in 1968. He explains that:

> At the time, because of the economic situation principally I guess, in the Port of Spain areas especially, there were lots of fellas, the unemployed fellas mostly, who were becoming conscious of the struggle in America at the time. And to some extent a lot of those fellas were reading literature coming from the American scene, and one of these that was very popular was *The Autobiography of Malcolm X*.[75]

So there was a two-way movement taking place – complementary aspects of the complex social process which led to 1970. One aspect of this process we have already traced in our description of Fraser's gradual movement from existentialist aloofness towards grim acceptance of the necessity for "the destruction of this ugly city". This paralleled the drift of alienated intellect towards political vortex. The second aspect of this process may be observed in the countermovement of a writer such as Malik from a perception of the raw experience of the masses, through the anger and invective of 1970, towards a greater width, depth and maturity of vision. Discussing this movement in his work away from raw anger, Malik declares:

> All I know is that emotion is a transient thing, perhaps. Is that the word? But you know, you cannot sustain emotion on something like a political question. You can get angry, for instance, in the road; and that is your reaction. But, you have to contain that anger and channel it into some meaningful direction.[76]

This declaration was illustrated by the calm and gravity of Malik's performance in "The Bad Poet".[77] Jeremy Taylor, one of our more perceptive drama critics, remarked of that show:

> Some of his poems are songs, some are a dialogue between his voice and the musicians, some are spoken with a quiet drum backing, some are straight poems. He speaks them well, not chanting, not hypnotised by the sound of his own lines, as poets tend to be; he acknowledges with every breath that for him the poem is the meaning, the political message, the expression of his own suffering and frustration, and not just a literary form. In between he talks, very quiet and dry, in a throwaway style; there is power there, but it is kept in, the movements are languid, the voice very controlled, as if everything emerged from a terrifying weariness of spirit, rising only rarely to vigour.[78]

What Taylor is defining here is not simply Malik's performance, but the brooding tiredness and tense waiting of the city itself. Exactly the same mood pervades the poems of Victor Questel, the calypsos of Valentino,[79] the quite remarkable movement back to lament and the minor key in the calypso as a whole, index of a society's quest for its soul.[80] The mood is captured very well by Roger McTair in "March-February Remembering", and is there in the whole of Malik's *Revo* (1975). Its other side is Shadow's harsh, atonal rasp, his cracked voice and driving life-pulse,

A poem such as "The Zebra" conveys the vision of Malik in 1970. The New World Black is now a caged animal striped with white, seeking to reclaim an Africa which is romantically associated with free movement and instinctual life. White history is similarly stereotyped as being only the history of rapine and gluttony ("bloated waists"). The zebra must obliterate the latter if it is ever to recapture the strength of the former and employ it to "unsettle the settlers". Yet even in 1970 Malik is capable of moving beyond such simplification. "The Zebra" is less a poem of protest against Whites than an address and appeal to well-fed Blacks.

> Search me here
> to find – You –
> stripped naked
> of pretence
> and dust screen flattery,
> flashing black
> but dying in a
> western zoo reserve

This is atypical of the spirit of 1970 in that it seeks not to separate, but to reclaim the bourgeois brother whose rebellion, Malik senses, exists beneath the surface of his complacent exterior.

> Know me then!
> Know my fear
> Of being stilled
> In breaking the bond
> of speed.
> Let's run again

> Free!
> and far away
> our home with us.

This poem provides a fair indication of the countermovement of the masses towards their middle-class, privileged brethren. But it also indicates a certain confidence on the part of the rooted man. He is not appealing to his middle-class brother for leadership. He is rather inviting him to partake in the strength of a shared identity and freedom. "The Zebra" thus is the counterpart to poems such as Martin Carter's "After One Year" and Dennis Scott's "No Sufferer I" in both of which middle-class intellectuals claim affinity with the grassroots situation. Carter declares to the "rude citizen",

> Those miseries I know you cultivate
> are mine as well as yours or do you think
> the impartial bullock cares whose land is ploughed?[80]

and goes on to claim "I know this city much as well as you do."

Similarly Scott challenges his Rastafarian brother to "acknowledge I" since "there are types of poverty we share".[81] What has happened is that an educated elite, accustomed to judging, condemning, saying where there should be sympathy and where scorn, suddenly finds itself being judged and seen in all its nakedness by the rooted man. The result is self-justification. Nineteen-seventy was an illustration of the truth of Scott's statement. It proved that there were indeed types of poverty common to different strata in society; that concrete proletarian distress could momentarily merge with abstract academic angst, form part of the same river of man and detonate into the same rebellion; and then separate once more, each group seeking its camp and favourite obsession, the void in between filled with dread and imploding lunacies.

"Pan Run II" was written in 1971, by which time Malik had already moved away from simple anger towards the creation of a channel for raw emotion. This he achieved by adopting the persona of a pan man who serves as the poet's voice, but at the same time retains his own individual integrity. Malik is in this way able to dramatise personal experience, and employ the individual experience as a symbol of that of the group. If there is any influence on the shaping of this dramatic monologue, it is probably the poems of Bongo Jerry published in *Savacou 3/4* and Brathwaite's *Masks* and *Islands* both of which he claims to have fruitfully read.[82]

"Pan Run II" is the sequel to "Pan Run I", which traces the emergence of the steelband from a background of poverty, and ends with the pan man going to jail during the violent postwar days of bad-johnism. In jail the pan becomes a dream in the mind of the sex-starved prisoner; it is his woman whose portrait he, in an effort to retain sanity, carves out on the wall. This image is developed in "Pan Run II". The first evidence of careful shaping is seen in the use of refrain:

> Ah make 10 years
> 10 years an 12 strokes

Each lash, as in *The Harder They Come* leads to the emergence of the music;

> ...every lash
> scarring mih flesh
> like mih pan
> ah leff carve out
> on the jail wall

What is remarkable here is how effortlessly the link is established between the etching of the steel and the scarring of the skin, between creativity and crucifixion. As the rest of the poem will show, there is no masochism implied here: only a healthy acknowledgement of the necessity to move and grow beyond pain towards form.

The voice next becomes that of a Baptist preacher – "So ah crossing over now" – with his conception of life as a series of journeys across water and towards Zion. Then the speaker adopts the threatening language of the batonnier and bad-john slogans from Sparrow's "Gunslingers" (1959) – "clear de way/leh mih pass". Malik is employing a technique of allusion to place his speaker in time. The protagonist is a man of the postwar generation who, jailed for ten years some time in the fifties or early sixties, has recently been released from prison. He is still locked up in the language of his own era, whose catchphrases, the dynamic driving force of "Pan Run I", are dated in the seventies. If his language is outmoded, his experience is not; and in his monologue he makes a compelling demand to be heard and provides a detailed chronicle of the stages whereby the protest movement of the seventies came into being.

The way post World War II films helped shape and mar the sensibility of Trinidad's urban youth is suggested in the allusion to Audie Murphy's *To Hell and Back* (1955). Malik also has in mind of the lines from Sparrow's "Gunslingers" (1959):

> This time I ready to attack
> Like Audie Murphy in *To Hell and Back*

It is interesting to note that such films also played an important part in the formation of the sensibility of America's and England's postwar generation. According to Jeff Nuttall, the first reaction of the post-1945 teenager to the world of the H-Bomb:

> was one of formalized stoicism which we borrowed from the spivs, from demobbed soldiers, and from Hollywood movies, which we took and transmuted into a romanticism of toughness and aggression and subsequently wore like a suit of armour.

This led to the creation of:

> a culture of brashness, raw colours, hard gloss, discord, cold eyes and cruel rouged lips, a culture of the original comic-book superheroes, of SPLAT and BAM and ZOWIE; of spotlit trumpet sections standing up in rows, of exhibitionist, gum-chewing drum solos and bull-voiced tenor saxes, for somewhere in the middle of it all, this was the culture of swing, and somewhere in the middle of swing was jazz.

Nuttall goes on to describe this culture as escapist.

> It protected and disguised our vulnerability and it provided a formalized mode of behaviour to compensate for our own directional poverty.

It reduced language to tough monosyllables – "Oh Yeah…" "So what". "Girls were 'dames', impersonalised as far as possible, called 'it', worn on the arm, treated with a modish brutality."[83]

It is Naipaul who in *The Middle Passage* (1962) notes the connection between all that Nuttall describes here as being typical of the British postwar scene, and what was happening in Trinidad at the time, though he presents such brashness and mimicry as something peculiar to Trinidad. It is clear, though, that the culture of the zoot suit, bebop, cool and ultimately soul and rock, shared common roots with pop culture throughout the Western world. If the British and American youths turned to jazz, urban blues and funk, Trinidad had its equivalent and emerging urban sound in kaiso and pan. If British youth were reacting to all the carnage of World War II, and were expressing the sense of helplessness, hopelessness and rage of people whose assumptions about humanity, culture, tradition and civilisation had been thoroughly undermined, Trinidad youth were, especially after the departure of the American soldiers, reacting to the retrenchment of 20,000 workers, the renewed prospect of prolonged unemployment, the incredible density of population in the towns, and the absence of a language of self-definition and political organisations capable of channelling urban unrest and creating a true national movement. If Trinidad's youth seemed to mimic the styles of international youth, it is because they had similar needs and problems and an equal helplessness in the face of their anxiety.

It is the movement from the post-1945 era of directionless violence and void, towards the post-1970 situation of smouldering rage, blues and grim waiting that Malik traces in his two Pan Run poems. In "Pan Run II", the 1950's bad john, released from prison in the early seventies, now savours the slogans of the fifties with bitter irony, "To Hell and Back" thus becomes:

> to hell an back
> to hell
> behind the bridge

The situation has not changed in his ten years of confinement. Laventille is still "hell", and the movement from the Royal Jail to behind the bridge is a movement from one circle of Dante's *Inferno* to another. Note how the inferno image which is given intellectual extension in Wayne Davis's "Prison Blues" is present here in a different way. Malik's method is to proceed more by allusion than complex image. By letting us hear the unrestrained language of an insider, Malik creates a voice which is itself the testimony of the entire city.

"Hell" here is the "dustblown blood"[84] spilt in gang warfare, steelband clashes, police shoot-outs:

> an all we blood
> crawling cross de
> City like de dry river

There is a strange, and perhaps unintentional, irony that the blood of the poor should not only "crawl", but do so "like de dry river" which bisects the city into lifestyles. At this point the bloodshed is part of the sterility of a time that is spiritually dry ("dry river"). It produces no flood of revolution and it makes its way no further than from Laventille to Shanty Town with its swamp, its La Basse rubbish dump, and its vultures, black like so many of the urban poor who live off the shucked garbage from more affluent homes. Life ceases to be a motion picture or a kaleidoscope and freezes to a still, a fixed image of the La Basse.

> an ah keep seeing
> de la Basse picture
> Kobo black like we

Here is a far more precise description of the genesis of Black Power than we have so far encountered. The voice here is neither anonymous ("Corners without Answers"), dry lonely ("Woodford Square Port of Spain") nor melancholy ("Squid", "On the Coast"). It has moved beyond the lament of the sixties; for now the black crows dream of "shitting dong/white/people up in Cascade".

Hell next becomes "de dark/stinking manhole" of the "pit" in one of the city's cinemas. "Manhole" is both a hole which devours manhood and a sewer. "Pit" is cesspit, wooden outhouse, suggested by "shitting" and "stinking". (Scatological imagery is fairly common in the poetry of the seventies and may be observed in poets as different as Malik, Davis, and Walcott.) Note, too, the recurrence of the manhole/underground motif, linking Malik for a brief instant with Wright and Ellison. Hell is also the recurrent nightmare of the prison cell which Wayne Davis depicts as being an equally filthy manhole. Hence the screaming refrain arises once more:

> 10 years an 12 strokes!
> 10 years an 12 strokes!

Malik accurately notes how representatives from various segments of the society react to this voice from the sewerage/cellarage/underground. These people are placed socially according to where they sit in the cinema. The middle classes sit in the "house" which, like Biswas's, is still unreal and shaky. They are terrified by the voice from the "pit" because it is, as Malik observes in "Zebra", their own voice,

> stripped naked
> of pretence
> and dust screen flattery

"Blackness" for Malik, as for Bongo Jerry ("Mabrak") has to do with truth to emotion which they do not find among the respectable classes. The Black man in "house" is afraid of the cry from the pit for another reason. He is the man most likely to be attacked physically or undermined morally, being neither rich enough to afford the necessary steel bars, electrified fences and guard dogs, on the one hand, nor on the other hand, sufficiently callous or remote from suffering to ignore the call to conscience and commitment.

The upper classes – whites and high browns, tinged with a sprinkling of black – form a hard-core élite whose "balcony" status insulates and isolates them from the anguished voice from the pit. They neither hear the poor nor care about them, and hence experience neither the qualms of conscience nor the fear of being attacked which the middle classes feel. Hence

> ...dem others up
> in Balcony too far
> from mih mudder belly
> to see mih tossing
> in de night

The "mudder" here is the "habitual womb" of Walcott's "Laventville", the archetypal progenitor of the poor; – she may even be the city itself which gave him birth. The people in Balcony, sharing few ties of blood or experience with this mud or mudder, this ground and womb, cannot understand the nightmare ("tossing in de night") of the Black underground man.

In order to exorcise this nightmare memory of prison and sewers and to face the day-to-day hardship of life in the "stinking manhole", he drifts towards religion. But as in James Baldwin's *Go Tell It on the Mountain*, baptism brings no relief. When the mourner journeys within, he sees the same horrors he thought to have left outside:

> Blood like fire
> running cross de sea
> an all mih Mudder children bawling
> an drowning in
> dey own blood

MY STRANGLED CITY

This vision, induced by the texts from *Revelation* which tell of the apocalypse with its seas of blood, relates on the concrete level to the eternal internecine conflict among the "tribes". Today's gang warfare is simply the most recent version of this strife. The capital "M" in "Mudder" makes it clear that the reference is to Africa, both as the "mother" whose children crossed the middle passage, and as the scene of bitter civil conflict in these times.

The refrain returns, this time like the steelband echo in Walcott's "Laventville":

> And climbing past the wild
> gutters, it shrilled
> in the blood, for those who suffered, who were killed
>
> and who survive.

The difference is that while Walcott understands and can describe and suggest what the music is saying. Malik enters the music, becomes it in all its fluid phases from Baptist hymn to kalinda and kaiso; from T & TEC worksong ("Revo") to lament ("Fireflies"). The refrain "10 years an 12 strokes" is now bawled "in God ears", since no one from "house" has listened, and those in balcony can afford to be deaf.

But the journey to an Africa of the spirit and ablution in the blood of the Lamb bring no redemption because the traveller has to return to his daily destitution, where life itself is a gamble and redemption no more than a small loan from the wappie banker.

> no other fount
> I know buh de wappie
> Table an de Cassa
> saving mih when ah lorse

If anything, religious retreat and in-search make the pain of daily existence more intense, because they cannot exorcise the demons of hunger and cramped imprisonment. The result is movement towards rebellion:

> an mih blood flowing
> mad when ah broken
> like de dry river
> coming dong
> coming dong
> cross de City
> an lookin vex
> to kill

The images of blood and dry river occur here again, and now begin to form part of a consistent design throughout the poem. Here the movement of blood ("passion") towards madness is seen as a gradual development after infinitudes of frustration. This "blood" can be released as *sunsum,* soul's blood, in music; or as a revolutionary river in spate; or wasted in internecine warfare.

The protagonist has already seen too much of the third, and is not ready for the second. He therefore turns to his music for a secular salvation which religion could not bring. His pan ("woman") is what he has carved out of his pain. He recalls her birth, communal, squalid and public.

> all yuh know
> how mih blood
> did come in de yard,
> all yuh smell mih
> woman sweat
> after we did breed
> de fire under
> she belly

"Blood" here combines the idea of passion, lifeblood and the transmission of semen in an act of conception. Malik explains the symbolism of this passage in the foreword to *Black Up*.

> "Pan Run I" was forcefully inspired by a drawing on the wall of my cell, of a woman in the childbirth position giving birth to a Pan. The poem tells the human or sociological conditions that gave birth to the steelband. "Poonche" is a sexual term for the act when it was not private or exclusive. Everything considered, it was different to a rape because the woman knew where she was going and with whom. The tuning of the Pan is so symbolised.[85]

Here, then, is Harris's image of the "complex womb" of historical process in the Caribbean occurring in a writer who is probably his diametric opposite. Such things happen all the time in West Indian literature.

The idea that a drum is a woman and a voice, predominant in Akan oral poetry and restated by Duke Ellington in his *A Drum is a Woman* (1957), is richly expanded by Brathwaite in "The Making of the Drum", in *Masks*. The drum/woman/voice symbol is a bridge unconsciously linking Malik to both Brathwaite and African poets on the continent. Yet the symbol came to him not through his reading of Brathwaite, but as part of the living reality of his political detention in 1970.

The fact that the protagonist names all the fathers of pan –

> Fisheye – Batasby –
> – Jules – Ellie – spree man
> – Sarge – Bully – Mastifae

signifies that he has now returned to the group in the yard to find the "voice" which years before his "blood" had helped create. This voice/woman left him on "J'Ouvert morning". The J'Ouvert morning referred to here is the opening day of national awakening, the beginning of the carnival of party politics. It was indeed a new day for the pan man, who in the late forties and early fifties had been the object of considerable harassment. But it was also at this point (1956) that the politician realised the full extent to which this young folk/urban culture was politically exploitable.

Elections were a whe-whe game in which the police were anything but impartial[86]

> de whe whe man
> buss de mark
> an dem Police an
> all did play – Balisier

The national movement appropriated the wit of the calypsonians and the violent energies of steelband gangs – particularly Desperadoes and Marabuntas – who, encouraged by the partiality of the police ensured that the rural-based and increasingly East Indian dominated opposition party could not conduct meetings peacefully in the city. This was particularly true of the Federal Elections of 1958 when:

> de Shango man
> beat de Babu man
> out ah town

It is at this point that Malik, with a fine sense of the dramatic, suggests, rather than states how and why his protagonist went to jail. He had been one of those who had beaten the Babu man out of town, only to discover that the party encouraged violence and threats only insofar as these things seemed to be necessary for the censorship of the opposition campaigning in the city. Not only does the political leader not support his strong-arm man when he gets into trouble, but he suddenly becomes metamorphosed into Judge Dread, with whom he shares the same elitist class interest in law, order, decency and respectability.

> whu de smart man say?
> whu de doctor say?
> Crier man is
> 10 years an 12 strokes

This political betrayal is simply the beginning of an era of cynicism. Intolerance winked at in 1956 and 1958, maintains the national movement as two separate racial camps. In the midst of such schism the protagonist, now a prisoner, hears the new, comfortable words of his leader: "Massa Day Done".[87] He learns from his cell that the forces of obscurantism and colonialism are on the retreat; a message which echoes with weird irony against his prison walls. Confinement and betrayal teach a bitter wisdom, for he can now remember how thoroughly the youthful fervour of a city in search of its face and self has been exploited and drained away:

> de kaiso man did
> raise he voice too
> from de cage
> fuh all dem saga boys
> Jean & Dinah
> de Yankees gorn

In memory, Sparrow's "Jean and Dinah", itself composed, it is said, in prison, and, like the PNM, exploding on the scene in 1956, becomes a lament. For the Yankees have gone nowhere, and the music of 1956 is really a celebration of the impotence of a régime as emasculated, flashy and unsure of itself as any wartime sagaboy living off the earnings of his woman's prostitution to the U.S. Marines, satisfied with the leftovers ("The Yankees gone, Sparrow take over now") of imperialism. Pose, glitter and grandcharge thus become substitutes for planning and implementation. The artist is still in the cage.

This is why the protagonist is angry and cynical now; for the '70s can offer nothing better than the wasteful crash programmes of the '50s. These are accepted with a curse, because they are the only reward for service rendered ten years ago and his only chance of employment. Under this apparent compromise with the system, his aim is to wrest his music – that is, his psyche, his blood's issue, his whole way of seeing and feeling – from the dying clutches of the "ole man". The "ole man" is the old regime in which the pan man once invested total faith, but which has sold his pan to the tourist brochure, his dance to the Better Villages pantomime and his kaiso to the manipulation of Dimanche Gras and the poolside of the upside-down hotel.

Realising the enormity of the task involved in getting his "woman" back from the "old man" instinctively invokes the ritualistic verbal magic of the batonnier.

> Who is me?
> look ole man
> ah come fuh
> mih woman.
> Who is me?
> I is she master
> I is master
> of Iron an
> it in mih blood

What this self-identification signifies is grounded faith, cultural continuity the survival and endurance of what Brathwaite in "Ogun" calls "lost pain, lost iron". "Blood" here is the felt line of spiritual continuity between present and past. It is also the passion of the poor, aroused after a decade of betrayal and neglect: "...de blood yuh raising fuh 10 years."

Part of the protagonist's self-identification involves the recognition of ancestral roots and lines of creativity.

> Woman
> you is mih chile mudder
> an I is mih Mudder
> chile in nature

The pan is his "chile mudder" in the sense that, springing from the common and complex womb of folk-urban life, it in turn gives birth to the music which he has consistently presented as the issue of his soul's blood. He in turn is still in nature a child of Africa (Mudder). The word "nature" here suggests a capacity for instinctual life; the rooted, primal quality which Walcott identifies in Makak, his "ultimate peasant". Malik, however, is saying a different thing. His Makak is a man of the town, not the country. His icon is the Dry River, not the mountain waterfall; and he is not given any dream of a real or symbolic white goddess. He is instead feeling his way backwards to a line of continuity with the African past. Malik does not go as far as Fraser who in 1968 declared that "rivers flowing had no relevance" to the man of the seventh decade twentieth century, "whereas blood flowing and sperm flowing had".[88] He shows rather, how in the midst of the dry river, that is, of an urban life ostensibly divorced from its fresh sustaining natural water sources, there is still capacity for constant regeneration.

Walcott, on the other hand, is more preoccupied with the instability and exploitability of this urban man of the dry river.

> The revolution is here. It is always here. It does not need the décor of African tourism or the hip postures and speech of metropolitan ghettos. Change the word "slum" for the new word "ghetto" and you have the psychology of funk, a market psychology that, within a year of the physical revolution, has been silently appropriated: by Mediterranean and Asian merchants. Soul is a commodity. Soul is an outfit. The "metropolitan" emphasis of the "revolution" has clouded the condition of the peasant, of the inevitably rooted man, and the urban revolutionary is by imitation or by nature rootless and a drifter, fashionably so, and in time a potential exile. The peasant cannot spare himself these city changes. He is the true African who does not need to proclaim it.[89]

But on this point, as on so many others, Walcott has expressed an alternative and contradictory point of view.

When he is protesting against state exploitation of "folk" culture – (Better Village shows and the like) – we find him accepting the urban idiom as natural and inevitable, and pointing out links between the youth cultures of the Caribbean and America.

> One of the most dangerous signs of cultural fascism is the assimilation of folk culture in the policy of the State. This goes under the image of national identity and it manifests itself in folk parades, folk circuses, folk costume.
> Before the Nazis came into power the Nazi image was of Aryan blonde

German peasant girls strewing the streets with flowers. This, of course, is extreme but it was not extreme in the late thirties. Then the image of the peasant girl was to the German mind healthy and inspiring.

But it is the people who choose their image, not the State, and if the folk image of another generation now is Afro, Afros and dashikis, then that is the right image, and it cannot be intimidated or challenged by the State's insistence on the folk image. The present generation or coming generation has a right to be bored with the image of the previous generation. The present generation has a right to go after soul and rock and pop music, and it, therefore, has not only a cultural but a political right to align itself with its own generation in America. To obstruct that force politically is also to try to obstruct the flow of culture.

There was political obstruction last year, and I doubt whether there would have been so much violence if the cultural direction of a large part of the country was recognised. The cultural expression of the Black Power movement is a ghetto expression which is formulated in soul and funk. The folk expression projected by the Ministry of Culture is a pastoral expression. It seems unreal to project a pastoral image of the folk asserting its African roots when what one is principally confronting is an urban expression with the same roots. It is just that superficially the forms differ. Organically there is no difference in roots of pastoral folk image. If you repress the political expression of a succeeding generation which has the same roots you are therefore also trying to suppress the cultural direction of that generation.[90]

Although the first of these two statements was published in 1974 and the second in mid-1971, they were probably written around the same time. Orde Coombs collected his essays for *Is Massa Day Dead?* in 1971, the book taking three years to appear. The fact that Walcott was capable of stating such opposite sides of the same question with an equal intensity, tells us something of the whirlpool of contrary currents which 1970 could awaken in the same mind. It should also teach the critic patience in his approach to the confusion of the youth. Virtually everyone was, in fact, in a state of delirium, frenzy often wearing the disguise of cool, clinical sanity.

Malik's "Pan Run II" and Lowhar's "Dry River" suggest that the distinction between peasant and rootless urban drifter is not an absolute one in the West Indies. Both see the urban folk, sandwiched between quarry and swamp, as the preservers of values, the remakers of selves, symbols of constant hope and renewal like their American jazz counterparts. Malik's pan man could be an American jazz man. He has died and been reborn to several selves – Bad John, Convict, Baptist, Gambler, Musician, Rebel. Malik has as much faith in his stoicism, resilience, style and soul as has Ellison in his blues people of *Invisible Man*. Thus Malik's claim that his pan man has retained roots "in nature" beyond the Dry River and Atlantic:

> since from de Iron
> cradle of Benin and Ife!

> Yoruba thunder travel far
> in wood an tight skin

is not made with romantic nostalgia. It is rather an affirmation that the birth of pan is a reinterpretation in the New World of an age-old acquaintance with iron, wood and skin. Given the presence of Shango and Rada cults behind the bridge – even when these are greatly modified by the rigours of city life – one must accept his claim as a valid one.

Moreover, his voice is concerned not with moving back, but with celebration and moving on. It has humanised its iron city – "Lemmih hear de Iron scream" – as exuberantly as the jazz man tunnels through steel and rocks and glass to root and water.[91] Where Walcott in "Laventille" ends his poem with the image of prison, the theme of amnesia and the sense of birth unto death, Malik ends on a note of affirmation:

> now lissen to mih voice
> calling deep-deep from
> de dust pain drum
> an mih blood
> never stop running
> cross mih middle passage

One notes that he doesn't say "the middle passage", because here the middle passage has become a personal symbol. It merges with the Dry River down which his blood has crawled for so long, as an image of the separation which exists within Trinidad. The middle passage here is the divide which separates a man from a humane existence; it is the dry gulch of politics which has brought no more than a sense of betrayal; it is the gap between a man and his roots most acutely felt among our educated elite, and thoroughly understood by George Lamming since *In the Castle of My Skin* (1953), *Of Age and Innocence* (1958) and *Season of Adventure* (1960). The middle passage is also the gap which politics seeks blindly to create between the "Pan Man" and his "Woman" – that is, between the new emerging folk-urban man and his culture. It is these divides, all present in the poem and suggested by the constant improvisation on the "Dry River" and "blood" motifs, that the complex man of the city has spanned with his "blood" – in all the myriad senses of the word. For Malik, 1970 when the river came down, was a proclamation of this rooted faith which reclaims past in order to build in its present.

(VIII)
Between Timber and Termites
Victor Questel: 1969-1975

> somewhere in the corner of
> his skull
> your
> tiredness grows
>
> somewhere
>   (Victor Questel)

Victor Questel, one of the founder members of Pivot, made his first wry efforts at statement in "Reflexions" (1968) and "Down Beat" (1969). As existentialist as Fraser, his people were, however, recognisably men of Port of Spain who knew nothing of big city chaos; stoical drifters for whom all action and experience, whether it be unemployment, prison, sex, rape, music, cricket or violence, carried the same moral weight or weightlessness. Where Fraser's voices were often confused, self-indulgent, and unable to bring their vision of absurdity into precise intellectual focus, Questel's voices in this period were tempered by his restraint, dry wit, and ability to control morose self-absorption by humour. They are the warm human equivalents of Fraser's cold, disembodied, cerebral people, and through picong set themselves at a distance from the horrors of poverty and the vagaries of marital life; laughter becoming a technique of survival. It is worth noting that the 1970 Black Power leaders kept telling the crowds to stop laughing. They knew quite well that laughter and gaiety were what stood between stoical acceptance of one's destitution, and the sense of outrage which they wanted to awaken.

Apart from Malik and the experienced Walcott, Questel is almost the only poet in this period whose work shows consistent development. He watched the transition from the melancholy void of the sixties to the explosion of the seventies with a dry sceptical eye, refusing, like the early Fraser, to be taken in by pan-Africanism, the quest for ancestors, or the rhetoric of revolution. In "Torn"[92] he depicts his position: both ancestors are guilty, their wrongs merging into a single "wrong" and cancelling out for their poverty-stricken descendant.

> The wrong that are
> our ancestors,
> square the deal.
>
> I have no grief
> for words to
> flounder upon
>
> for the way lost

> is the way
> lost
>
> and revolution
> is the scandal
> of poverty
> sandalled to the
> dust of processions

One detects here ironic echoes of Walcott's "Choc Bay";

> All that I have and want are words
> To fling my griefs about
> And salt enough for these eyes

as well as of Brathwaite's *Masks;*

> But the way lost
> is a way to be found
> again

as Questel states his dedication to dryness. His definition of "revolution", in an economy of vision, encapsulates the shocking poverty of the city, its huddled lives flowering to endless scandal, or detonating to march, procession and sandalled pilgrimage; then crushed into dust. The "dust of processions" is both the frenzy of "demon/strations" (a Questel pun), and the funeral dust of Basil Davis's last ride, the largest procession of 1970.

Having grown up in the village of Gonzalez, Questel needs no vision from the hill. He writes, like Malik, from within the heart of the city. His obsessive punning in *Score* is really a sophisticated version of the normal verbal exuberance of the streets – an entry into the spirit of the calypso mentality by one who has never sought to wear the entertainer's mask. Questel's *Score* poems, as chronicle of one man's reaction to the blue post–1970 scene and as formal achievement, have been more than adequately explored by Winston Hackett in "Survival".[93] What Hackett pinpoints is Questel's "threadbare" sensibility, his starkness of vision, and the anguish in his laughter. The poems to be examined here are "Words and Gestures" (1973) and "Near Mourning Ground" (1975). The former takes the trapped paralysis of *Score* to its limit, as the poet journeys both within and without, but can find "home" nowhere. The latter is a new departure where the poet learns how to objectify personal quest by locating his experience in a fully developed persona. This is what Malik also achieves in the movement from the purely emotional protest poems of 1970 to "Pan Run II".

In "Words and Gestures" the poet begins by addressing a "you" who seems to be a lover with whom he can make no contact. Both people are imprisoned "behind glass" (the idea may have been suggested by a few Derek Walcott poems, e.g. "A Village Life") and "gestures ride the silence", since neither can hear, or hearing, understand the words of the other. The poet is doubly separated from the Other by his obsession with the void at the centre of the political vortex, and his immersion in a world of words. His sound shrivels to the dry weird comic crackle of a house lizard ("wood-slave") as he sits trapped in lonely repose between the solid organic certainties of the senses ("timber") and the patient erosion of his grounded faith ("termites").

The image of the "wood-slave" provides us with a direct clue that the "house" which is being destroyed by termites is the ancestral past as well, and the image may have been suggested by lines from Brathwaite's *Masks:*

> the termites' dark teeth, three
>
> hundred years working,
> have patiently ruined my art. ("Sunsum")

Questel, as educated grassroots man, can recognise, on the one hand, evidence of a solidly rooted self ("timber") and on the other, the riddled mask of the past. Like Fraser, he is trapped with his half-digested existentialist paradoxes. Like Fraser, too, he has come to realise the need for communion and love. These two passages, the first from Fraser's "Protoplasmic Consciousness" (1968), the second from "Words and Gestures", both express this need.

> Sitting there munching existentialist paradoxes
> Wind wind blowing through the falling rain
> If you believe him life is a suicidal tendency
>
> The thunder within me shakes my hand
>   and spills my drink – always
>
> My flesh is a searing mass
> 'How,' he asked, 'could those trapped within the
>   drum dance?'
>
> Sing me a tear a jewelled tear your only tear
> The tear that rolls along my parched tongue.[94]

Questel's voice is saner, but equally capable of leaping from fragmented thought to thought.

> Smash your pane or
> I'll burn out slowly between the lines
>
> Empty as an unshaded sketch
> shattered by the shot
> blank
> in your brain

Again the allusion is to Walcott's "A Village Life" where the pane/pain wordplay first occurs. Questel understands that it is necessary to break through the glass walls of the hermetically sealed self ("pane"). The alternative to such breakthrough is breakdown and withering of poetic statement; psychic suicide, as the void of one brain encounters the void of the Other.

(ii)

Section II begins with the slow journey of a snail across a garden. The poet's bespectacled eye ("windowed stare") follows the snail's journey. Here the borrowing is from Brathwaite's "Ananse", from *Islands*, and the snail, like the spider in Brathwaite, objectifies the poet's inner journey. Brathwaite, however, elsewhere employs the snail/spider images quite differently from Questel. Whereas in the latter they are images of retreat into ego and cranium, in the former they are images of psychic integrity and of organic growth from an individuated self where brain and belly, intellect and instinct are seamlessly fused. Writing about Kapo, Zion Revivalist cult leader, painter and sculptor, Brathwaite remarks that he is an example of:

> this other kind of artist among us; he, who is both participant and director, shepherd and servant, who *like the spiders or snail,* creates what he creates: shell, web, mahoe-woman from centre-self, from belly-head.[95]

Questel is not yet this sort of artist. Immersed in the undergrowth of his sub-self he enters a region where images begin to blur

> and colour
> runs along the darkening brain
> dripping shapes to the glare of
> half-blind eyes

Here, the external situation is that of the garden seen through the blurred lens of tears or a windowpane running with rain. Thus seen objects lose their precise shape, and colours run one into the other. By the end of this section the snail image becomes clarified as one of artistic isolation

> Possessed
> all I own
>
> are my scribal impulses
> learning like any snail
> that home is where I'm locked in

The poet is a man possessed, but he has no real possessions apart from an impulse towards statement; and no home except the shell and prison of self. Hence, no journey is real except interior descent, and no attempt can yet be made to break through the glass.

(iii)

"But/today is Carnival" – The shift is an abrupt one from the aloneness of retreat to shell/prison/self, to the noisy extroversion of carnival. (The poem was originally finished in February 1973). Carnival here is viewed as an inevitable and inescapable plague ("times falling sickness/season") where the heat, dust and sweat lead to influenza. The particular sickness being alluded to here, though, is polio, which in 1972 had forced the Trinidad Government to postpone Carnival to rainy May. Polio which cripples the young, becomes for the poet a symbol of the crippledom of a nation of masqueraders, who:

> [...] like their God
> shuffle between the crib
> and the cross
> crabbing their stations to
> prizes

Here, a number of things are being simultaneously suggested: firstly, the fact that carnival is a brief minstrel dance ("shuffle") between Xmas, the birth of Christ ("crib") and the beginning of Lent. This is even more so in Haitian Rara which extends from Xmas, through Lent and stops at Good Friday. Secondly, there is the slow movement of bands ("crabbing") over the Grand Savannah stage. "Stations", as Hackett suggests in elucidating a passage from Questel's "The Epileptic Boy of February", are both the Stations of the Cross which the society makes on its timeless *via dolorosa,* and the police stations in which steelband riot or political demonstration ends.

The crab image, so popular in West Indian writing,[96] is here an extension of the snail image. For, despite the poet's distance from the crowd, their slow, oblique crawl and uncertain crabbed movement are also his. The crab image suggests another even more complex one: that of the sea shell.

> the ocean's roars of their lifeblood
> sucked into the sunken shells of drums.

Every word here is loaded. The ocean here is the Atlantic. Questel agrees with Malik ("Pan Run II") that "mih blood never stop running cross mih middle passage" and accepts his affirmation that the urban experience has not destroyed the primal music which is reborn of the ocean. He would also agree with both Malik and Dr. J.D. Elder[97] that the steelband is the latest recreation of the ancestral African drum in the New World. In this respect, crossing the middle passage resulted in the channelling of the original music into other "shells" – "the sunken shells of drums". The idea of continuity is strengthened by the word "sunken" which could mean lying deep in the waters of the unconscious.

But Questel, whose vision is of both timber and termites, qualifies all this by making the same words work to suggest the opposite. Hence "shells of drums" suggests that what now remains of the original African consciousness is only an empty husk. "Shell" is also a reference to the conch shell of slavery which summoned the slaves to work or riot. It certainly is a reference to the extension of an imperialism built on slave labour, into the parasitism of today's multinational corporations. These corporations such as Shell and Texaco exploit ("sucked") Trinidad's and the world's petroleum resources. "Sucked" suggests the soucouyant, an image which Marguerite Wyke employed in a poem about neo-colonialism named "Tonight the Soucouyant" (1968). The "sunken shells of drums" are, in fact, both the empty discarded oil drums which the exploited people sink and etch to create their music – (at times under the sponsorship of the very soucouyants, e.g. Shell Invaders) – and the oil drums into which the country's economic lifeblood is sucked for an export that is far less profitable than it should be.

Questel is writing here with the density of image and complexity of wordplay and allusion characteristic of the Brathwaite of *Islands,* from whom he has obviously learned much. The next lines echo similar ones from his own 1970 poem "Pan Drama":

> their lifestyle
> caught in the glass eyes of cameras.

"Caught" is both "photographed" and "trapped" in the snares of tourism and endless old style. The fact that the cameras have glass eyes is an indication of the blind indifference of the people for whom the mas' man performs – soucouyants on holiday. Ellison in *Invisible Man* constantly employs glass and glass eyes as images of either the distorted vision of stereotyping whites, or of such Blacks as have accepted their "Invisibility". Similarly, Brathwaite's Puritan/capitalist god and empire-builder, Jah, lives in a world of glass.[98] So do Jah's humble servants, who are reduced to the role of trapped goldfish and perpetual performers. Questel's employment of the image suggests that the Caribbean man also is at one and the same time creator and minstrel, musician and clown, sharing with his Afro–American counterpart Jah's extended prison of glass.

If some of what has gone before suggests a mind which has responded sensitively and critically to Brathwaite's seminal work, some of what follows indicates Questel's thorough familiarity with Walcott's poems and plays. The lines:

> lost in this folk
> mass
> my cleft brain
> paces Papa Bois's
> heel

are clearly a response to poems such as Walcott's "Mass Man" and "Junta"[99] and the 1958 play *Ti Jean and His Brothers* which Walcott revised and rewrote in 1970.[100] There is the sense of schizophrenia ("my cleft brain"), powerful in Walcott's *The Castaway* and in some of his *Guardian* articles of the sixties. "Folk mass" has three meanings: "crowd of folk", "folk masquerade", and the mod-type religious services with which the Roman Catholic Church has occasionally experimented in the wake of the Black Power invasion of their cathedral in 1970. Spokesmen for reform in the Caribbean Christian community have advocated the localisation of the liturgy and church music.[101] There have also been calypso competitions in Roman Catholic schools which, two decades ago would have been sending their children on special retreat to pray for the souls of those who would be enjoying the revelry of carnival. The Eucharist and the Passion have been choreographed in a few churches since 1970.

Many have viewed the "folk mass" as another form of "ole mass", and Questel, sceptical about most things, becomes Walcott's Ti Jean, a paralysed intellectual contemplating the cloven hoof of the Devil, who may be the planter, the politician, the priest or the whole abstract academic tradition of the West which has helped produce so many sceptics in Europe and schizophrenics in the West Indies. Questel, therefore, questions the capacity of Caribbean man to confront the Devil with Ti Jean's innocence, wonder and mother-wit. Such qualities, he feels, are not recoverable, the way lost being for him the way lost. He thus drily mocks the chorus of a now defunct road march runner-up – "Play mas' in yer mas'"[102] and does his minstrel shuffle:

> like the rest
> marred by my own make-
> believe.

Thus Questel the maker, who, like the Walcott of "Mass Man", initially sought to establish his distance from the masquerade, realises that in an age of unbelief and spiritual paralysis, the poet's isolated quest for truth may itself be a harmful ("marred") substitution of mask for face, of style for verity. The separation of "make" from "believe" is a clear hint that the poet's "make-believe" is his poetry, the imperfectly fabricated issues from his cleft brain; fragile fictions in which he tries to make himself believe as he seeks substitutes for lost faith.

(iv)

In Section Four, the poet, like Martin Carter of "Not Hands Like Mine", contemplates "the people's slow/strangulation", seeking an image or creed capable of releasing him from his vision of death. He does not find it. His quest leads him deeper into the shadow-land:

> My uncertainty
> finds substance in shadows
> even the shadow of
> life

Conventionally, poets are supposed to find release in the marriage of their inner world with the concrete one outside their skull. But the dogged pursuit of craft produces no new images or even advertisements of a possible integrity. Instead, the "skeletal billboards" of "Prelude" (1970) recur and

> even Nothing
> now trapped
> between skeletal bill-boards
> has lost its profundity

If before Questel's sensibility had fed on existentialist philosophy of the Void ("Nothing"), and what has been termed "the rhetoric of No", he now grows tired of such insubstantial diet.

Turning his gaze once more towards the common folk of his society, whom he had formerly regarded as being little more than masqueraders, he can now perceive in them a richer, more positive and wholesome way of confronting death and Void. The bongo dance, performed at wakes, used to be the folk's way of celebrating the soul's passage from one plane of existence, life, to another, death. It is a symbol of the sort of reconciliation which the poet seeks – the unification or atonement of the schizophrenic city-bred sensibility with the rural Afro-Caribbean (bongo) mind;[103] the marriage of the isolated threadbare intellect to community, dance, the sensuous life of the instinct.

But to grow tired of saying "No" is not the same thing as to regain the faith to say an affirmative "Yes". The journey back from the deadly void of modern European cerebration towards an old-time innocence of pastoral celebration is hard for the city-bred Caribbean intellectual – though both poles are eminently possible in his society, some of whose citizens drift schizophrenically between the one and the other. For Questel:

> the search lurches tiredly
> like my first
> embarrassed
> bongo
> step.

Whereas Malik's protagonist becomes celebrant by re-entering the "Pan Yard" and reclaiming his "voice", "woman" and music, Questel's approach to "bongo" values is uncertain and dazed (lurches"). This is because he enters the yard with the tiredness of the modern intellectual, while Malik's pan man comes with the passionate blood of the rooted man.

(v)

The idea of the lurching bongo step suggests another – that of the "loss of balance" in the use of words. This is contrasted with the regular steady, mechanical movement of "iron mules in the oil fields". Technological man, the man, we are told, of the future, however sterile ("mules") his work may appear to the poet, is certain of his truths and satisfied with their mathematical rigidity. The multinational corporations need no other poetry than the steady rhythm and suck of these pumps, and the mulish sweat of the exploited nationals. The "green" poet, however, must face the insane chaos of the world inside, and recover for the page words which appear jaundiced ("yellowing") even as they become visible.

Love simply does not survive in this atmosphere. The act of lovemaking becomes part of the general absurdity, the poet as lover shrivelling into Ralph Kripalsingh or some cartoon figure,

> rasping with laughter
> as
> the comic artist encircles me
> in his lines
>
> while voices of mockery
> creep beneath my skull

The result of this attempt to communicate through dance, words and touch will be a further retreat into the skull's closed circle and the adoption of a self-defensive mockery.

(vi)

Section Six begins with an allusion to the myths of Adam and Crusoe current in the writings of Walcott since 1965.[104] According to Walcott, the Caribbean and American peoples are like Crusoe, inheritors of a new world which, like Adam, they have been accorded the sovereign privilege of naming. But Questel, like Walcott, is only too aware of the presence of the snake in this paradise of imperfection and historically congenital disease. His Adam is therefore another fiction of art ("painted"), and his protagonist finds himself

> Poised
> like a painted

> Adam
> frozen
> between flight
> and the sting of revenge,
> the dual attitude of both
> slave and citizen

The image may have been suggested by Walcott's use in *In a Fine Castle* of a painting by Watteau depicting a group of people fleeing from an island, but somehow nostalgically bound to the land they are trying to escape. This image also appeared in his discussion of the Crusoe figure in *The Castaway*.[105] There he noted the significance of the moment when Crusoe attempts to flee his island but cannot, realising that he is now the only truly indigenised citizen of his "happy desert".

Questel, in borrowing the Crusoe/Adam persona, suggests that Crusoe and Friday, citizen and slave, share a common characteristic of not having accepted the reality of self and landscape. He also suggests that they are one, but negatively and uncreatively, in their maintenance of the old dispensation. Crusoe, like Walcott's de la Fontaine family of *In a Fine Castle,* continues to oppress: Friday/Caliban continues to dream of revenge – revenge being no more than the other side of oppression. The "I" here is the poet, who now functions as mouthpiece for the masses who are, like him, poised and paralysed in an attitude inherited from history. The "painted Adam" image, then, invests our history of paralysis with the permanence and stasis of art.

In the second half of this section, the poet's eye shifts focus once more to the world outside of him. Someone, who is either a politician or a voyeur – most likely both – has just made another conquest

> as the country contemplates
> itself
> as a girl in her quiet hours

The conqueror here is clearly one who has taken advantage of the uncertainty and self-consciousness of the pubescent nation – politician exploiting a culture which has become self-consciously nationalistic for the first time; speculator exploiting the rising price of land; businessman capitalising on the instability of folk-urban taste – all parasites, all rapists. The poet as people's private eye and mouthpiece observes what is happening, but fear of reprisal and betrayal to the cowboy tribunals of 1970, 1971 and 1972 causes him to remain silent:

> I'll tell no one
> for the whispered word now
> could be the microphoned betrayal
> then

The fear was common enough in 1973 and found expression in a few poems which we will discuss later, as well as in Chalkdust's calypsos, "Ah Fraid Karl" and "Who Next?", Sparrow's "Sedition" and Kitchener's "No Freedom".

(vii)

In spite of this dreadful intuition, Questel presses on towards a definition of new objectives beyond the void. To escape paralysis he needs to convert gesture into movement and dance. This can come about only if he leaves the circle of his skull. He therefore chooses the stickfighter as his persona

> The stickman's sojourn on the hill,
> and
> the snail's lonely journey
> must both be mine; though walking
> a straight line is not the same
> as keeping your balance.

The stickfighter balances lonely eminence with an intimate communion with his drummer, chantwell and chorus. His poise is thus the alternative which the poet seeks to the stasis of "a painted Adam". But he also acknowledges the necessity for introspection and slow, painfully achieved meterage ("the snail's lonely journey") – a different movement and loneliness. His aim, then, is to marry introspection with extroversion, the private with the public, the loneliness which reaches out to chorus and community, with the loneliness which reaches inwards to hermetic, monadic silence.

The rest of this section is not nearly as convincing. Here the poet/stickman addresses a reluctant lover. But the fact that he as lover assumes the stickfighter's rhetoric suggests that he is still uncertain of his ability to perform. What he means by

> The circle is complete
> the violence is total

is unclear. Perhaps he means that the poem's circle is complete in that he has returned to his initial concern with his "wanton absence of experience" and his love of words rather than people. "The violence is total" suggests that he has at last committed himself to frenzied action, leaping, like Alfred Fraser, from existentialist impotence to grim affirmation of revolutionary violence. Questel was certainly preoccupied in the 1970/71 period with understanding what forces had impelled gentle youths like himself to make that extraordinary leap. His strange Ionescan play, *The Doctor He Dead* (written September 1970, revised August 1971, staged by the Kairi House Group in 1974), attempts to deal with just this problem and ends with its central figure, a youth named Davis who thinks by turns that he is in the General Hospital and the Mental Hospital, shooting the equally schizophrenic Doctor who is by turns Bill, "a failed politician posing as patient, but is the Doctor's secret agent", Eustace, "a patient who is determined to survive at any price", and whose obsession is silence, and the Doctor who is "a part-time practitioner".

"The violence is total," then, applies more to the engulfment of the youth in the whirlpool of change, than to the poet's own acceptance of the ethic of violent liberation. Indeed, his declaration that

It is the words
that are mad
the words

indicates a felt loss of control over his medium, language. Despite his stickfighter's boast, he hasn't gained "balance"; despite his quest for the snail's progress he does not walk a straight line. Rather, his thought moves circuitously with the psyche's irregular logic.

Thus the poem closes as it began, with the carnival image, borrowed from Walcott's "Mass Man"

And so
falling with every fruit
dropped by bats

my cry
rivals the wood-slave's call
when couched between timber
and termites
riddled
by its own gestures.

In "Mass Man", the following answer is returned by the poet to the carnival masquerader who invites him to join the dance:

But I am dancing, look, from an old gibbet
my bull-whipped body swings, a metronome!
Like a fruit-bat dropped in the silk cotton's shade
my mania, my mania is a terrible calm...

What Walcott sees in the image of a little child "rigged like a bat" and stumbling, is the young nation, withheld from its true freedom by a burdensome and hideous mask. He becomes the child by proxy, and the bat-image is smoothly metamorphosed, first, into that of the fruit-bat hanging upside-down after feeding – an image of parasitism and indolence – and secondly, into the more terrifying image of the slave, flayed and hung, keeping time like a metronome. The mask-wearing society still marks a time as old as the history of slavery.

It is to this image that Questel returns, though his focus is on the ripening fruit (the maturing nation), marred by bats (the politicians, professionals, capitalists, academics, its own people. As each fruit is despoiled (guerilla shot, policeman gunned down, school smashed up by vandals, mind blown by dope or simple frustration), his cry rivals that of the lizard ("wood-slave"); the old hewer of wood and fetcher of water, trapped between the hard labour of building something ("timber") and the certain knowledge of decay and waste ("termites"). "Riddled" contains the idea of both wordplay/conundrums and termites eating holes into the beams of the poet's house. It suggests mortality, in the face of which all art shrivels to gesture, desperate or comical.

"Words and Gestures" which won the first prize in the National Cultural Council poetry competition of 1973 is the beginning of a transitional period in Questel's poetry, where he tries to re-accommodate himself to the lifestyle of ordinary folk. From this long poem in which he tests his chances of returning to roots, Questel moves to "Only Believe" (1973), a poem in which he wavers between admiration for the fundamental rooted faith of the Spiritual Baptists and gentle mockery at their sectarian rejection of any other means of catharsis – Catholicism, the Jehovah Witnesses, the steelband – and at their evasion of politics. The Baptists function here as a mask for the poet who has diagnosed his personal problem as being a lack of faith in politics, words or action of any kind. Thus while the refrain "Only Believe" is a rejection of American capitalistic evangelism and the Puritan millenarian ethic of unbounded optimism, it is also an affirmation of the necessity for personal faith.

"Near Mourning Ground"[106] suggests in its very name that the careful journey back to ground has begun. "Mourning Ground" is an appropriately chosen symbol of the process which the poet needs to undertake in his act of reclamation. "Mourning Ground" in Spiritual Baptist ritual – Questel's closest relatives are Spiritual Baptists – is a ceremony whereby the pilgrim, after fasting, ablution and lying for eight days in the "tomb" or "sacred chamber" is, if fortunate, granted a gift from the Holy Spirit, and told what his life's work is to be. Questel acknowledges that he is near, not on mourning ground. He hasn't yet undertaken that dreadful journey in the spirit across land, across water, back towards faith and reclaimed roots.

He has, however, moved towards a closer association of his journey with that of an older and equally tired senior generation. In this poem he attempts to reclaim his "Uncle", who is the "Tom" of an earlier poem. Brathwaite's timid Tom, and Questel's real uncle, a Baptist preacher and stevedore, whose now half-inspired and half-doubting journey towards revealed or researched truth parallels that of the poet. Hence the print that "tightened beneath candle grease like the drumhead/of memory" is not only fine print of the Bible caught in the light of the preacher's candle, but the words of the poem taking shape beneath the poet's own candlelight of vision. Both journeys towards self-discovery are associated with the tightened drum of the cult, which functions as symbol and artifact, and as metaphor of a whole new phase of West Indian poetry.

Questel's allusion is to Brathwaite's "The Making of the Drum" and "Shepherd" as well as to Walcott's "A Far Cry from Africa" ("the tightened carcass of a drum").

The drum is the drum of memory because, on observing a Baptist meeting in Curepe in 1975, Questel recalls his own uncle years ago in Gonzalez. The performance of the Baptist meeting is polyphonic and polymetric. There is the Shepherd's voice; the background of sisters chanting in counterpoint; the interplay of word and song; the punctuation marks of the bell: the various movements which are themselves a counterpoint of swirling circles and staccato jerks; and the accompanying handclaps. Questel captures this in:

> as uncle swirled suddenly to balance a point on
> time
> to the bell's appeal

Sudden movement and balance are what the Shepherd has, and are qualities which the poet also needs ("Words and Gestures"). But as "Words and Gestures" illustrates, Questel is more comfortable with the poetry of isolation than with one of encounter and performance.

This is why his eye is welded to his uncle's movement and his Spiritual Mother's surrender to Jordan River. Both of these acts take him backward in memory to the time when he was a bewildered little boy not knowing what to make of all that passion. Now as poet he still does not know what the artefacts of the cult symbolise; though they do suggest a certain rootedness ("planted on the ground") and a strange flowering even at the street corners and crossroads of the city. Innuendo early in the poem suggests some sort of sexual relationship between Uncle and the Spiritual Mother:

> Shepherd my uncle,
> had seen her private vision,
> privately.

The poet knows, as Walcott does in "Pocomania", that the chanting of the sisters conceals "the sexual fires of Pentecost". But here this is noted with dry amusement; for the distance between preacher and poet is narrower. Each is trapped in the chasm between theory and practice, the ideal vision and the worldly reality. For both, truth has become oscillation "between poles of belief", paradoxical interplay of faith and doubt, affirmation and constant questioning.

> Thus Uncle no longer delivers "visions",
>   [...] but a text

mounted from the lost books of the bible

calmly prepared the night before by the arc
of the kerosene lamp.

Baptists are supposed to preach only when directly inspired by the Word of God, their sermons then becoming spontaneous and prophetic utterances under the spirit. Here Uncle is the old regime run short of master plans or vision, charisma replaced by something far more quotidian and even fraudulent. The word "mounted" suggests obeah, while the reference to "the lost books of the bible" indicates that the text is apocryphal and of doubtful authenticity. These "lost books", celebrated in reggae as the "Macabee Version that God gave to Black man",[107] link Shepherd's quest with Vodun, Shango, Santeria, Rastafarian, and Zion Revivalist quests for the lost history and culture of black people of the diaspora.

> Weekend baptisms
> constantly trying to cross water
> fasting
> eyes covered by several colours of seeing
> reduced

But Questel is not passing judgement on the Baptists, any more than he is condemning the Black Power movement which politicised this persistent quest for a lost "Africa". He recognises the shortcomings of charisma. The politics of spontaneous utterance is shortlived, suspect and corruptible. It ends up "hooking" (ancient slave torture) wayward souls to a new crucifixion which is presented as the one true light. Yet the uncertain journey of Shepherd – and here Shepherd is like Shepherd in Lamming's *Of Age and Innocence*, a mixture of cult leader and political visionary, Buzz or Daaga – across mourning ground, becomes the poet's own night journey across "water", the dark ocean of psyche. The seven symbolic bandages across the mourners' eyes are his. The obscurity of their vision, also his.

> But Shepherd is like any writer
> here,
> a lonely pilgrim going to meet himself
> a man burning on mourning ground
>
> grounded by a vision of flight and travel
> heat
> and fears
>
> reduced,
>
> returned and returning to the blank
> page
> trying to speak the vision clearly
> though he cannot
> without a text

Questel also realises that despite the ideas of escape and flight embedded in the language and symbolism of Rastafarianism and Shouter/Baptist liturgy, all those cults are rooted here, and their language as much the result of encounter as it is of the will to escape. Paradoxically, they are "grounded" by a vision of flight and travel. Their experience of persecution has indigenised them into the New World as only pain can. Because of

> [...] the private vision
> and the public pain,
> the heat and fears
> the stoning of the bretheren
>
> they had learnt that here
> it was more important to confront
> Jordan river than to cross it

This is why Uncle's feet are "concrete hard, scraping the cement". He has become one with the city's grit. Yet he has also known times (1917-1950) when, persecuted by law and respectability, the bretheren have had to "retreat to the bush". This quite literal retreat evokes echoes of the metaphorical retreat of "the bush" or the "green beginning" in Walcott.

It also parallels the poet's own snail-like journey through undergrowth. What is reality for Shepherd becomes metaphor for him. It is with this knowledge that he finally addresses the Shepherd, his alter ego, an elder maturer voice, possessed of the faith and sexual experience which he lacks, his lost Legba, more grounded in pain:

> Listen Uncle as the sisters hum us home,
> What tract yer pull
> traveller,
> mourner,
> man at the cross roads

What the poet seeks in vain is a tract; also a track, a clear pathway in the labyrinth; a message and talisman for this complicated age. ("Lord, Uncle, say the word"). One hears the echo of the centurion's entreaty as well as the priest's confession of unworthiness before inviting the congregation to Holy Communion. But Uncle, however valid his pain, has no healing word, in spite of the fact that like the Williams of Chaguaramas, he has been "preaching since the time the Yankees leave the base."

Uncle here becomes a representative voice from the older generation. He is "man at the cross roads" in that he is going through the crucifixion of middle age and all its problems of remembered passion and waning virility, and moving towards extinction. The poet, himself at different crossroads between faith and unbelief, intellect and flesh, seeks to connect his struggle towards faith with that of a defeated, disillusioned but dogged older generation. What he acknowledges at the end, though, is that despite the similarity of the struggle, doubt and defeat which both parents and children encounter, each age must seek its own language and way out of the labyrinth of words and woes.

(IX)
Icy Intuitions
Judy Miles; Wayne Brown 1970-75

Judy Miles's more recent work provides a clue to what happens when small-town loneliness fulfils itself in big-city alienation. If in 1965, Port of Spain could provide no context for the exchange of hearts, in 1975 it can generate no tenderness to break through the barriers between lives ("Suicide?"). Things are worse in the great white city, where a litany is about the inability to pray, the atrophy of wonder, and the consequent loss of a sense of holiness or innocence. In the metropole, the separation of the individual from communion is paralleled by the abstraction of the eye from the world it observes, which is other, alien, white and cold, caught in capitalism's deadly pendulum swing between time ("the clock") and the pursuit of material success ("the golden calf" in "Litany").

The big city is an artificial dance; the hasty overnighting of friends when neurosis becomes unbearable; a jester's mask without even the hollow carnival to give its grinning meaning; the desire to be noticed in a world where everyone is invisible; violated womanhood; Mary Magdalen searching hopelessly for Christ. All the images are quite ordinary, but, dislocated from their context, disconnected one from the other, achieve a Sartrean nakedness which is of the metropole. The city is measured, judged and rejected by the tropical eye which has rejected its own ground as well:

> I am chewing gum battered incessantly by
> gleaming dentures but never part of the system

The tropical eye, like that of Euro-America's now disaffiliated avant-garde youth, recognises the city as a symbol of Western rationalism, clean, antiseptic, sane, divorced from unhygienic Yahoo instinct, cerebral, pure

> [...] and eternally cold
> but glistening wherever touched by the triumphant
> spittle of the doctors.

Here, then, is that condemnation of intellect abstracted from humane warmth, that rejection of cold rationalism which is becoming more pronounced in Caribbean literature, as it seeks roots and energies, exploring its own landscape of rhythms.

But Ms. Miles is four thousand miles away from this possibility. Her poem "Black Out", with its suggestion of amnesia as well as power failure, is about the poet's encounter with primal truths. This, however, brings no release from loneliness. Seen through the uncertain light of a single candle – that is, the poet's vision – surface reality becomes distorted. The poet may attempt a dark descent into the mind's tomb to unearth a rich mummified identity which has been asleep for centuries. Or surfacing, the eye may cast such a savage light on the ordinary that it becomes estranged even further from the world perceived.

> and this light, savage as Khufu's
> torches along the Nile
> estranges me from my old home.

Here, then, vision does not heal or reconcile. It increases the distance between observer and object. Fraser felt the same way in the sixties.

Wayne Brown's "Soul on Ice" closely resembles a number of Walcott's winter poems such as "Greenwich Village, Winter",[108] "The Flock",[109] "God Rest Ye Merry Gentlemen",[110] and to a lesser extent "Cold Spring Harbour".[111] Here one encounters a situation frequently found in Brown; that of a careful shaping of experience where the better lines and images all seem to have been imported from another voice. Thus, as in "Greenwich Village, Winter" or "The Flock", poetry is making marks on snow; the empty snowfield is the poet's empty page or his equally empty heart waiting for epiphany as the sky awaits the return of Walcott's geese. Brown's "The syntax of solitude thickening" resembles Walcott's "weak vision thickening to a frosted pane" [pain],[112] which expresses the same basic idea and moves towards the same keyword. "The street's avalanche of bicycle bells" in Brathwaite[113] becomes "the city's avalanche of words" in Brown. To questions "What noise is that?" and "Shall I/die alone, away from the dog's hot/breath" which Brown asks, one almost replies in lines from Walcott's "God Rest Ye Merry Gentlemen"

> [...] What had I heard,
> wheezing behind my heel with whitening breath?
> Nothing.

The big city offers no elation. It is rather a place where all illusions collapse, and the poet – seeking Walcott's mastodons and Wordworth's "Characters of the Great Apocalypse", or, at the very least, a child's Xmas card dream of a winter wonderland – drifts into boredom. Wonder is dead for both the New World and the Old World person, who now join each other in the attenuated coupling of ape and ghost, Makak and his wraithlike white goddess, souls stripped naked at last of illusion:

> This is our pale vaudeville,
> so let us dance: the ape's skeleton, erect,
> and the ghost.

These are, in fact, the best lines of the poem, wry, self-mocking, naked. The final "Listen./It seems years..." is also very effective and conveys the sense of being buried under a burden of time which is often overwhelming in a great city.

(X)
Maledictory
Derek Walcott: 1970-74

Walcott's poetry since 1970, where it is not engaged in recalling the amber landscape of another life, shares in the bleakness and bitterness of the time. If in 1965 he had already diagnosed the dangerous void into which the country was slipping, by 1969 he was talking about the failure of revolutionary politics in Bolivia and the tragedies of Biafra, Vietnam and North America. Trinidad's situation was, in *The Gulf*, altered from one of stagnation to one of masquerade ("Mas' Man", "Junta"). *Dream on Monkey Mountain* (1968) was, among other things, a satirical rejection of the rhetoric of Black Power as being not only inadequate, but dangerous in that it concealed one's vision of the obscure process involved in self-acceptance, self-knowledge and inner integrity.

In his programme notes to the 1974 presentation of *Dream on Monkey Mountain* by the Theatre Workshop, Walcott summarises the situation in this way:

> Endowments, subsidies, scholarships, a building, state support, all of those things which might have happened have not. The last few years were full of the noises of revolution, but from neither side, the defenders or the upheavers, has there been any programme which goes to the heart of the problem: the culture of a people, the training and development of artists.

He thus concludes:

> The passionate promises of the radical: theatre. The leisurely enumeration of priorities by experts: theatre. The lies we send abroad about our cultural excitements: theatre. The old charred, indomitable stump of a man, that charcoal burner who has seen it all, Roman law, ghetto anarchy, centred conservatives, Afro-centred radicals, neither of whom seek to nourish his soul, that Makak, he is our main man. He is the Trinidad Theatre Workshop.[114]

But, of course, this tale of oppression, neglect and survival, so eloquently told by Malik in "Pan Run II", is the whole Caribbean present as it has been the whole Caribbean past, its grimness engulfing far more than the Trinidad Theatre Workshop. It is precisely this that made the 1970 Black Power movement inevitable.

Walcott, as we have seen, has made statements which both acknowledge the inevitability of 1970 and condemn what happened then as simply another form of masquerade. By 1972, his voice becomes vituperative after the sardonic style of Césaire's *Discourse on Colonialism* Where Césaire advises his comrade to hold as enemies:

> not only sadistic governors and greedy bankers, not only prefects who torture and colonists who flog, not only corrupt, cheek-licking politicians and subservient judges, but likewise and for the same reason, venomous journalists, goitrous academicians, wreathed in dollars and stupidity, ethnographers who go in for metaphysics, presumptuous Belgian theologians, chattering intellectuals born out of the stinking thigh of Nietzsche, the paternalists, the embracers, the corrupters, the back-slappers, the lovers of exoticism, the dividers, the agrarian sociologists, the hoodwinkers, the hoaxers, the hot-air artists.[115]

Walcott condemns to a hell of sulphurous self-hatred – "scabrous rocks" and "pustular volcanoes" – first all the members of the current political establishment:

> all o' dem big boys, so, dem ministers,
> ministers of culture, ministers of development

Secondly, the new academic opponents of the Establishment, whether they be Marxists or Pan-Africanists are dumped into a bath of hot pus hastily, before they get a chance to gain and abuse political power. These are:

> the green blacks, and their old toms,
> and all the syntactical apologists of the Third World
> explaining why their artists die
> by their own hands, magicians of the New Vision.
> Screaming the same shit.

The third group to be sentenced are all artists, historians and commentators who believe that a sense of racial history and heritage, a recognised continuity between the cultural forms of the ancestral past and the fragmented present is both possible and necessary in the Caribbean. These are:

> Those who peel, from their own leprous flesh, their names,
> who chafe and nurture the scars of rusted chains,
> like primates favouring scabs, those who charge tickets
> for another free ride on the middle-passage,
> those who explain to the peasant why he is African,
> their catamites and eunuchs banging tambourines
> whores with slave-bangles banging tambourines.

This is an overreaction to the new sound of drums, dialect, and music in West Indian poetry, and to the preoccupation of Black Power advocates with African history and slavery. It comes oddly from one who, in all his plays since 1970, has moved more closely towards an acceptance of popular idiom, folk song, bel air, kalinda, calypso, dance, Baptist ritual and rhetoric and, alas! in *The Joker of Seville,* tambourines and a Shango-cult drummer, Andrew Beddeau whom I once witnessed imperiously drumming in the Orisha in Tacarigua. The only possible conclusion is that when Walcott relates to such things it should be viewed, sanely, as an attempt – to use his own words – to "refine and orchestrate [...] the people's crude aesthetic."[116] When other writers relate to the same things in a different way, their efforts should be condemned as a form of bourgeois academic perversity ("catamites and whores") and an attempt to betray the folk.

Accordingly, the most impressive condemnation is reserved for

> the academics crouched like rats
> listening to tambourines
> jackals and rodents feathering their holes
> hoarding the sea-glass of their ancestors' eyes,
> sea-lice, sea-parasites on the ancestral sea-wrack
> whose god is history. *Pax*
> Who want a new art,
> and their artists dying in the old way
> Those whose promises drip from their mouth like pus. [117]

No doubt such academics do exist. But one wonders whether they are the same people as the small, impotent groups of guilt-ridden intellectuals throughout the region who display a certain amount of political consciousness. These, far from being allowed by the various regimes to feather their holes, generally receive short shrift. The greater number are banned from entering this or that territory, a few are denied jobs even in their native land, one was gunned down in broad daylight in Guyana, another beaten up and wounded in Jamaica. In short, they already know the sort of political harassment which Walcott recently predicted would be the lot of a truly radical theatre.[118]

For the feeling that basic freedoms are being threatened in the Caribbean, strong in some of Walcott's post-1970 poems,[119] is one which he shares with a large number of people. Along with this feeling there is the fear of being betrayed. "A Patriot to Patriots", for example, is addressed to those who seek from the poet open political commitment in an age when the police have been carrying out midnight house raids, one of which has happened to a leading member of the Theatre Workshop. The poet replies:

> Respect my quiet. I have seen revolutions turn
> into a barbarous, betrayed riot,
> I mistook such voices for the mountain rain,
> for a million tongues budding in flowers from asphalt.

What is striking is neither the caginess, the dread silence, nor the scorn

– all of which are quite typical of the spirit of the period. It is rather the fact that Walcott expected something to emerge from 1970, even though he had seen the 1960s in Naipaulian terms as alternating between "play-acting and disorder", stasis and masquerade.

Equally surprising is the poem "At Last", where Naipaul's attitude to the West Indies is now defined as being one of "contempt disguised as concern". The reaction seems to be that of one who has, like Trinidad's Indian population, sweated out the fever of his indentureship to produce fruit and flower from what Naipaul presents solely in terms of congenital and foreordained crippledom. Naipaul's statements to the effect that the West Indies "will never create" are seen by Walcott as a negation of his own effort, and that of the peasantry. "The Federalist", in terms of abuse similar to the ones we have just examined from *Another Life,* extends the attack on predatory publicists and politicians, and may have been evoked by the rum-and-roti campaigning of 1971.

"The Wind in the Dooryard" is an elegy for Eric Roach which focuses on Roach's sense of wonder and on the task which he performed of naming landscape and people. Walcott writes here with a clarity and simple lucidity reminiscent of Roach at his best. The poem, in fact, celebrates the life which Roach celebrated rather than talking about his death, which is only implied in some of the images. But urgent images of growth and freshness overwhelm those of failure and dereliction, as happens in all of Walcott's elegies.

(XI)
Valedictory
Eric Roach: 1970-74

> the city asphyxiates itself
> it has eaten too many daughters
> it has burnt too many hopes
> (Brathwaite: "Springblade")

If Judy Miles's journey marks the end of that long trek from village to big city, from community to isolation, Eric Roach's marks the beginning. Roach's poems after 1970 are those of a man who has lost the simplicity of his Tobago villages and can come to no real terms with Port of Spain. In his posthumously published article "Growing Up in Tobago", he describes the poles between which his life has swung, noting in particular the effect of a crown colony education on the village-reared sensibility.

> Just on thirteen, my father thrust me out of the warm organic cocoon
> of the village, not to fend for myself, but to take the six-mile daily journey
> to the recently started high school in town. It was a journey from the

past into the future, from simple tribal ignorance into the society of the world. Later I came to regard my journey as symbolic of the whole tidal movement of the Caribbean from its nineteenth-century morass of illiteracy, servitude, poverty and folk-customs into the glittering, heartless, murderous menage of twentieth-century western civilisation.[120]

To the "murderous" city he brought the whole sensibility of one who had known villages, trees, folk customs and relatively innocent and free love. He left Tobago to live in Trinidad relatively late – sometime in the early sixties – and worked for a short time as a journalist for the PNM. Later on he was to function as agricultural reporter and literary critic for the *Trinidad Guardian*, thus maintaining his link with the current state of arts in the Caribbean as well as with the countryside, whose neglect he often chronicled in his articles.

"Poem for This Day" (Dec. 1972) presents a vision of urban slums and "mouldering villages" in plain descriptive verse whose chief characteristic is its harsh consonantal quality. Words like "crawling", "maggots", "swamps", "clapboard", "rattling", "shanty" and "squatter" jar against each other. It is the sound of Roger Mais's *The Hills Were Joyful Together*, Walcott's "Laventville" and "The Federalist", Brathwaite's "Francina" and "Wings of a Dove": the dissonant dread sound of the city. In this essay we have noted the same sound in Gonzalez's "Hey Alfie" and Calliste's "South Trumpeter", where discordant music is related to mental derangement which finds release in a dream of apocalypse. In Roach, dissonance measures the psychic disruption endured in the journey from village to town.

Nor is there any village to return to. The people of "The Homestead" (1951) twenty years after are objects of pity or contempt to motorists "sneering at their gnarled and barefoot drought".

> you'd think the state too stern for mercies
> or the earth's blood, bitter as aloes,
> is too bitter to suckle these poor folk;
> that charity's atrophied in the heart
> too sterile for love's silken roots

So the drought which withers folk-life springs from the desert of the atrophied heart of the state, which Roach had once served. And the cycle of rural activity becomes a purposeless "bovine round/ of work, feed, sleep and blind begetting" – leading to exodus to "the sour slum", whose inside story is now being told by poets such as Malik.

> These slums are inhabited by
>
> those who've failed their hope
> like writers their weak talents;
> failed, failed lives
> failed spirit and failed love.

The lament becomes at once personal – an elegy for the talent which Roach sees himself as having lost – and the blues of an entire generation come now to the natural end of its allotted span, empty of promise, if still full of promises.

> and there it's all amen amen,
> save for the politician's cloven tongue
> his teeth rotting with foul deceits,
> handouts and handcuffs,
> the circus guarded with teargas and guns.
> all that goes free are rats and roaches;
> all left to liberty is abuse of power;
> all left to live is drunkenness and lust
> and mania for the bestial carnival [121]

It is Walcott's "Mass Man" updated by the events of 1970. The carnival now is not simply a stream of fantastic incoherent images, but a sinister circus hemmed in by guns, a symbol of the merry-go-round of economic privilege whose maintenance is the end of good government in the West Indies.

"City Centre '70", Roach's most direct response to 1970, appeared first in the magazine of the San Fernando-based Studio Arts Group[122] and two years later in A.J. Seymour's Carifesta anthology, *New Writing in the Caribbean*.[123] The second version, which is the one published in *Corners Without Answers* has an additional stanza which significantly alters the poem's meaning. In both versions, however, Roach identifies himself with the protest of the city's youth. The closing of Woodford Square for several months in 1970 symbolises for him the censorship of dissent and the death of the idealism of 1956 which had been shaped in that very square. It is the final contempt for popular opinion, the ultimate manifestation of the state's stony indifference to national distress.

But Roach defiantly acknowledges that the movement is not dead:

> that men do not die
> but grow in dreams of generations
> bitter and beautiful as cedar leaves

The cedar, a royal tree symbolising here the sovereign people, still grows with the self-regenerating cyclic energy of Nature and survives the drought of "the harsh comedy of history". The trees "imprisoned" in the chained square become identified with the citizens now detained on Nelson Island, the "Boca rock" of "the stone men". The laurels which "crown/their great immobile marathons" are laurels with which the poet would crown all those who went on those marathon marches to Couva, Charlotteville, Diego Martin, Arima, Laventille, Santa Cruz, Point Fortin, the hospital, the jail and the cemetery. So rooted is Roach that even rootless and directionless movement is expressed in terms of the rootedness of trees.

Having known villages, when he looks in the square he sees cedars; when Alfred Fraser, child of the city looks at the square, he sees an empty fountain; Judy Miles sees chewed discarded bones.

As with the trees, man's green hope which has withered to brownness will fulfil its cycle in rebirth. The people's brownness is "the earth's colour", the colour of roots which will spring to green as

>...the sweet
> cycle reaffirms itself
> rejoins eternity and greens again
> in the triumphant self-regenerating trees.

So, at least, Roach feels in 1970. By 1972, however, whatever hope he may have invested in the 1970 movement has disappeared in face of the already described aftermath of drugs, imported styles and costumes, and violence of armed conflict. In the light of these happenings, Roach adds the seven lines which now end the poem. These state that men are not trees who patiently reaffirm their cycle. The human drought explodes not in green leaves, but in the burnt homes of revolution's indifferent fire. It may also peter out in blues, as the old vicious circle of repression – reprisal – suffering – retribution – repression resolves itself in the old internecine murder.

> poor Abel tunes his threnodies, his blues:
> Cain's conscience smokes:
> Guilt sears his arteries like flame

When things come to this pass it does not matter who is Cain and who Abel. They are brothers and the guilt which begins to consume Cain is communal and national.

By 1973, Roach, writing now with hindsight, has lost sight of the symbol of the regenerating cycle. Thus "Hard Drought"[124] conjures up the possibility of a rebirth into life without hope, where history repeats its tired mistakes and the future is an aborted foetus hovering in limbo between life and death.

> Don't mock me about dreams
> I am too old;
> Don't sneer of prophecies
> count me among the numberless dead
> this grisly century.
> I've eaten so much history that I belch
> boloms of years to come.

It is with this version of unhope that Roach writes his valediction, "Verse in August" (1973). Here he reclaims all those songs, rhythms and memories which, "The Ballad of Canga Brown" notwithstanding, have seldom been a shaping force in his poems. Elsewhere, Roach explains why it is that the rich folk tradition of Tobago has been inaccessible to him as a poet:

> Although Cambridge school-certificated, we left school knowing absolutely nothing of ourselves, our country, its history and circumstance. We were adolescents lost between two worlds; one to which we belonged by birth but were educated to reject, the other we discovered in the books. We were, to coin a phrase, "exoticised natives".[125]

It was precisely this sort of background which had led him to reject out of hand all the poets in *Savacou 3/4* who had based their work on the oral traditions of the Caribbean – the call-and-response antiphon of folksong, worksong and sermon; concreteness and conciseness of proverb; the expanding concentric circles of Rastafarian sermon with its plethora of Bible-derived dread imagery.[126] Indeed, when Roach became forced to acknowledge the presence of these quite different formal models for serious poetry, he could see only an unbridgeable gap between writing in the Caribbean which is based on a study of traditional English poetry, and writing based on the Caribbean folk-oral traditions. Thus for him the poetic sensibility of the Caribbean became irrecoverably split between the "Tribe Boys" and the "Afro-Saxons". By January 1973, he is introducing his review of Wayne Brown's *On the Coast* in this way:

> Even before any worthwhile body of poetry has been created, poets of the English-speaking Caribbean have divided themselves into two schools. On the one side are the "tribe boys", the dialect, folk rhythm people, the black hell-raisers, the protest men. Afro-haired, dashiki-clad, they chant their rhetoric to drum beats, rapping to the brothers and sisters about tribal dispossession and the beauty of blackness.
>
> On the other side are the people of the Afro-Saxon élite group measuring styles and strides with North American and European poets. They do not turn their backs on the native landscape and environment but speak in aloof "proper" English voices. Their central concern is for the savants to say of them what is said of Derek Walcott, that they are among the finest poets in the English language.
>
> Each group regards the other with mutual contempt. The "tribe boys" claim to be creating "the New Caribbean verse", constructing a ringing rhetoric from the native patois for the new people emerging from the darkness of slavery and colonialism. The Afro-head and the beard, the dashiki and the drum and the vivid staccato free verse of this school are the visible pillars of its identity.
>
> The Afro-Saxon stance is that poetry is no protest weapon for causes or the barricades. It is just poetry, art or craft, as Dylan Thomas said, no more. Better still, it is one of the ways of writing in Western civilisation.[127]

Roach is correct in identifying at least two styles operating in contemporary West Indian poetry. What he simplifies, however, is the relationship between these two styles or traditions, and the people who write in them. In the first place, relatively few poets, then or now, have seriously attempted to shape dialect. One of the most successful of these, Kamau

Brathwaite, whom Roach is the same article calls "the Black Prince of the tribe boys", had been writing poetry for seventeen years in Standard English before he published *Rights of Passage* (1967), and has written only about 25% of his entire trilogy in Creole. Conversely, a writer such as Abdul Malik, who had been in the vanguard of the 1970 Black Power movement, is able to move with the greatest facility from Creole to Standard English, and from "public" to "private" poetry. Secondly, the criterion of "protest" is an unrealistic one for determining one's identity either as "tribe boy" or "Afro-Saxon". As we have seen, most of Roach's poetry since 1970 contains a high measure of bitter protest. Similarly, significant portions of the late chapters of Walcott's *Another Life* and a number of his poems since 1971 have contained straightforward protest, and are little different in sound, imagery or intent from much that has been written by people whom Roach might consider to be "tribe boys". Few in the 1970s have been able to escape the rigours of politics, which has forced tribe boys and Afro Saxons alike into a plain unmetaphorical speech, and a language appropriate to the dissonance of the time.

From what has been said above about people like Fraser, Questel and Malik, it should be clear that a far more complex process is taking place in the poetry of the time. Writers are relating to all aspects of their cultural background; integrating a sometimes ultramodern Western education with a concern for their own parochial situation; blending languages and forms; alternating, like Questel, between agonised statement of private pain and a slow healing movement back to roots. What is fascinating in all this is that Eric Roach, the most rooted man, has, according to his own statement, been educated only to deny his roots, while people like Fraser, who have grown up with a sense of urban rootlessness, urgently want to know and belong to the same world Roach has been educated to deny.

When Roach in his last will and poetic testament, "Verse in August", does reclaim his folk, it is in a spirit of defensive reaction to the shallowness of life in Diego Martin's suburbia – the world of his town-bred sons.

> Who'll dance my death farewell?
> who'll trample me a rhythm on my grave?
>
> > "bongo macedonia
> > viniway viniway bongo"
>
> not my tall sons
> they have not seen nor heard
> that macabre rime of death
> and if they did
>
> > i could not answer their disdain
> > they have inherited another season
> > in this uprooted suburb

> of folk from villages and slums
> where dusks breed secret hatred
> and faces are tight shut
> from love and friendship

This is different from the organic coherence of the life he used to know:

> my life began among kind folk
> whose barefoot indigence was whole
> as rocks and springs, whose love
> nourished life's roots.

The same folk, in short, whom Malik reclaims in his "Motto Vision" which is, like Roach's "Fugue for Federation" or "Love Overgrows a Rock", an affirmation of faith in the islands' capacity for union, love and integrity. "Tribe boy" and "Afro-Saxon" affirm a common faith and define a common need. The difference is that Malik has been nurtured in the town as well, and is therefore able to work towards a reconciliation with the sound of the city impossible to Roach.

Thus while "Pan Run II" and "Motto Vision" point the reader towards the future and stress that it is the responsibility of West Indians to make the West Indies home, "Verse in August" looks backward to the village past of Drag Your Bow masque, mime, jig, reel and kalinda, reclaiming it with fierce love and despair. The poem thus becomes the valediction to an age and a way of life.

> the days stand up to bless me
>   as i die
> bedded on my dying century
> dreaming the country's youth
> in a good place that's gone
>   among the folk i loved
> while my own death
> howls from a mangy dog
> haunting these barren streets.
>
> what's all my witness for?
> why do i wear the poor folk and the years?

So, it may be answered, that we may measure what we have lost without perhaps ever having learned to value it, in our trek towards what Roach terms "the glittering, heartless, murderous menage of twentieth century western civilisation." By juxtaposing the apparent extremes of Roach's memory of a coherent time with Fraser's descent into delirium or Questel's threadbare skeletal lines, frail as steel, or Judy Miles's icy severity, we begin to know a little of who we really are beyond all rigid categories.

(XII)
Future Mornings
Christopher Laird; Roger McTair

The response to 1970 contained more than rage. Several poems since then have been quiet and reflective. Others, such as Christopher Laird's "In Memory of Future Mornings", and Malik's "Fireflies for Beverley" have been elegiac. Others again, such as Malik's "Climb to Freedom" (1972), Laird's "The Road" and McTair's "March-February Remembering" convey a sense of waiting, remembering, hoping, counting the cost. In "The Road" Laird employs the carnival metaphor gently, and without the now automatic associations of mimicry which it generally conveys. The road is the symbol of freedom of movement, celebrated by Lord Kitchener in his calypso "The Road" (1963). "Walking the Road" is a conventional metaphor, hallowed by countless Black American spirituals and blues, of living one's life. The calypsonian's struggle for freedom to dissent is viewed positively by Laird as part of the process of "walking the road".

The poem begins in a post-1970 present, the era of Chalkdust, Valentino and Stalin

> sidestepping sedition
> to tell how men walkin
> this island of Trinidad

The panorama road march of the masses becomes a symbol of the poet's dream of a genuine mass political movement in harmony for the first time.

> Hear that rumble steel sound
> one hundred men beatin
> one pan
> one thousand foot shufflin
> Tokyo, All Stars and Invaders
> Harmonites, Starlift and Despers
> walkin the road as one

Laird dreams of all the bands meeting without steelband clash. This is the hope, despite mokojumbie leaders, social climbers "building they life on stilts", or the quest for ethnic identities separate from the national movement. Black Power, back to Africa and guerilla activity are rejected without rancour as being the rhetoric of midnight robbers, blowing whistles and speaking of journeys, doom and revenge.

For Laird, the struggle must take place here. Behind today's protest calypsonians – Chalkdust, Valentino, and Stalin – he can hear the echoes of

Atilla, Executor and Chinee Patrick, voices from five decades ago. What is sedition now was termed high treason then, but the protest must still be made if one is to continue walking the road. The masquerade contains its Devil as in Davis's "Prison Blues", its now chained dragon of protest, its burroquites playing the ass, its advocates of violence ("bois men") now shot dead and mocked by the white death mask of the King Pierrot. Yet, the poem ends in hope as a new mass movement takes shape and prepares to walk the road.

McTair also produces a dry-eyed, movingly-shaped elegy on the 1970 movement and captures that feeling of remembering and patient waiting, of onward-looking, onward-moving faith, which one hears in the calypsos of Valentino. Musing, he remembers that the marches of 1970 began in an unconsciously blossoming dream. The bad-johns and jive-ass saga boys – suggested by the name "Mandancing" i.e. "dancing man" – leave their razors at home to join a river of man whose destination no one knows. The spirit of the banned Stokely Carmichael marches with "the hard, not happy crowd", twinning the greater chaos of New York with the lesser one of Port of Spain. Irrelevant connection, said and still say some; inevitable bridge, said and still say others.

But the poem is about the aftermath and asks, "Where are the marchers of 1970?" They are silent again as in 1964, drinking or smoking weed, clinging to their bizarre cinematic identities and surveying again the corners without answers.

> In Boissière, Boothill stands, quiet;
> quiet the pacified
> streets, his head
> bad, smoke drifting in his mind, he
> on soft
> clouds.
> The world turns,
> slow, hazy,
> a hologram.

A hologram or holograph is a will or document written entirely in the handwriting of a dying man. The image thus suggests withdrawal into a separate silence where each mind doodles its scrawls, revolving around the blue-grey pain of its own dissolution. And this is indeed what happened to many who marched and to some who wrote.

(ii)

Reflecting on the march through Caroni, McTair recalls how it did not bring any unification of the urban and rural, because it served more to intensify than to dispel traditional African/Indian racial fears.

> Why your eyes Caneburn shiny black
> with fear?

> Why marching's rash certainty
> so clammy in your palms?

"Rash certainty" summarises the spirit of that march which was "rash" in its Quixotic assumption that the awful daring of a single gesture could even begin to erase divisions engraved by history. But it was "certain" of the necessity for creating a coalition between races, working people, the deprived of country and town. This certainty had grown out of the urban experience of the late sixties, one of whose significant points is now recalled by McTair.

> The house where Pivot, New World met, was razed;
> just moulds of twisted steel, charred wood and
> blackened stone.

This happened two weeks or so after the demonstration in 1968 on behalf of Walter Rodney, which by pure accident brought together for the first time UWI students and a handful of the unemployed of Port of Spain. The burning of the New World building was to be the political baptism by fire of a number of people who later featured prominently in 1970. The 1968 fire defined quite clearly the lengths to which the enemies of new language were prepared to go in their bid to destroy whatever this embryonic movement of young people represented. Now, five years after 1970, all the fires which have happened since that time smoulder in the memory of people and poet:

> the memory of marching flares in the Peoples' eyes
> Mandancing, Pinkeye, Boothill waiting,
> waiting –
> Waiting for the rhythms of moving feet; waiting
> to move

The spiralling marijuana smoke takes shape as "a hologram of memory", and moves the poet, traveller and citizen out of the isolation of his "bad head, away from the high of his blue heaven, back to earth and promise of "marching/side by side". It is this return to ground which enables McTair to move away from the nostalgic question "Remember?" to the renewed pledge of a maturer commitment based now on experience rather than the innocence of New /World/Pivot: "Remember!"

(XIII)
Other Voices
Alvin Massy; Faustin Charles; Selwyn Bhagan

Corners Without Answers is the first real anthology which seeks to do justice to the emerging urban sensibility in Trinidad. It is limited by this aim in that it does not really indicate the variety of responses which exist in the country as a whole. The urban sensibility, as revealed in this collection, is anxiety-ridden, restless, and falters between blind or studied commitment and nihilistic retreat to skull. It expresses itself in a plain style, demanding of the poet straightforward witness, a taste for blues, dryness and dissonance. At times it cracks into rhetoric, vituperation, scatology and self-righteous anger.

It is narrow of focus, hemmed in as it is by hill, swamp, La Basse, and all that steel and concrete. Many of these writers sound like people who have never seen trees, flowers, rivers or the sea. Exceptions here are Roach, Walcott, Brown, Massy and Selwyn Bhajan. Massy relates closely to the later work of Walcott and to early Césaire and Neruda. His "Tourist Brochure", prolix in its response to landscape, contains that unanchored angst and melancholy which we have noted as part of the spirit of the sixties. The eye of Massy's castaway-figure does not devour the seascape "for the morsel of a sail". It rather scans it for "the erased horizon of the past". Like Walcott's castaway, Massy's asks the question "Why does one remain?" Like Brown's he can find no answer.

> Like the seagull I search for reason
> to remain adrift
> over this wretched shore.

"Marooned on this archipelago of rocks", he is still trapped in that wandering gloom of the sixties, his talent exercising itself on the well-worn themes of history as amnesia, divorce from Africa, and the longing for a landscape more conducive to poetry. Missing here is the countervailing energy of rage which gives strength to Walcott's Castaway poems.

But other forces are already making themselves felt in Massy's work, transforming his "archipelago of rocks" into one of amoebae. Here Massy joins Césaire, Neruda and Carpentier in exploring the history and potential of the archipelago in terms of geographical, geological and biological imagery. The islands grow first as the amoeba multiplies its cells. They shed old doctrines and lives as tadpoles, black and water-born like the majority of the islands' peoples, evolve into amphibious frogs: at home on land, yet longing for their oceanic past. (Note how the same idea is present in Lowhar's "Shanty Town"). Massy points out the need to reclaim and understand this past, but at the same time stresses that history is an ongoing process which requires the discarding of dead doctrines "as moulted Plumage/or old skin"). The archipelago's poets are caught between rediscovery of the embalmed nightmare of history and the unformed inchoate language of a new age:

> My tongue
>   tastes you
> from its roots, eddying words
> still to be uttered,
> but your flavour is still
> indefinite as the years
> which leap at you
> trampling embalmed epochs
> your backs would prefer to forget
> as a lost life in a past of regrets
> and sudden vicissitudes

What will liberate us from this recurring vision of the past is "our own truths". Yet Massy doesn't yet say or know what these new indigenised truths are. Nor is he able to forget the past whose distressing evidence, after the style of Césaire's *Cahier,* he documents in the remainder of the poem. Indeed, the early images of metamorphosis are almost overwhelmed by the later (and more conventional) images of shipwreck, seawrack, crucifixion and erosion. It is, therefore, with a certain ambivalence that Massy ends the poem:

> I celebrate your slavery
> of sufferings
> your misery of misfortunes,
>
> your elemental evolution
> in a New World, a wider sky
> awaiting a fateful dawn
> under the blotch of sunset
> that hugs this embryonic era.

The future is both dawn and twilight, evolution and misfortune.

Faustin Charles is another poet who, working with elemental life-forms, seeks to portray "the wonders of becoming". In *The Expatriate* and *Crab Track,*[128] he begins with caterpillar, crab, fly, bat, earthworm, asphalt lake, sun and earth. But his poetry is at present inchoate and conveys the impression of not having been thought through or felt through so that these images are never established with any clarity. Charles seldom manages to connect biological with historical process. He falls midway between his mentor, Wilson Harris (*Eternity to Season*) and the more recent Walcott, lacking the former's capacity to shift fluidly from image to abstraction and back to image, and the latter's rigour, clarity and precision of focus on the visible. The advantage of poetry such as Charles's is that when successful, it can take one up, bear one along, the poem's "meaning" being contained in the act of being taken up. One is invited to become the experience – to enter the "bubble eyes" of streaming images. But Charles himself seems often to be abstracted from the process he describes – seems himself not to have been caught up at the time of writing, not to have entered the flow.

Charles's work, nonetheless, continues the movement away from pure reason which was there in Césaire from the start, and has resurfaced in Harris and Brathwaite. His interest in "cosmic consciousness", sun-worship, Caribbean cults and jazz links him with all those who seek to return the psyche of Western man to its lost kingdom of instinct. This in/quest expresses itself in terms of a new interest in African and Eastern religions and mythologies, as well as in the charismatic and Pentecostal aspects of Christianity. Such interest exists in the Caribbean not only as imitation but as memory and living force. It challenges, and is in places undermining the imposed superstructure of the plantation Church of bondsmen and bishops.

It surfaces in the simple sincere work of Selwyn Bhajan (*Season of Songs, Quest*), whose immersion in Transcendental Meditation and Maharishi's teachings is fully manifest in his two collections of poetry. In Bhajan one can see the beginnings of a countermovement in the poetry of the decade; a movement away from the city ("City", "Trini"), its politics and frenzy. His quest is for wholeness, oneness of being and inner serenity. He sees the poet as one who must live his truths. The only worthwhile writing is that which energises inert experience by the transmission of creative life-force and love-force.[129] This is similar to African Nommo: the word as power, as energy or energising spark and seed.

Bhajan's themes are mainly those of childhood, rural innocence and nature. Missing is the fierceness of encounter which one finds in the nature poetry of Walcott and Roach. Bhajan seeks instead either to merge with or move beyond the reality he perceives. His serenity is, however, qualified by the harsh challenge of the city, and, one suspects, by the problem of making his doctrine of universal love viable as an active force in the world of men. Those who have felt the need to humanise our strangled city believe that meditation and inner retreat to silence must lead to active encounter with the world outside; that love which accepts everything – even past crippledom and present dismemberment – is less universal life-impulse than masochistic perversity. Thus while Bhajan seeks the Buddha's way:

> To liberate myself
> Of worldly cares,
> Attachments,
> To rise above
> The measurings of time,
> The changing relative,
> To crave nothing
> Just to be
> What know I am
> To express my
> Self in fullness,
> Be one

With everything

Questel, Malik, McNeill, Davis, Judy Miles cannot avoid a terrifying encounter with whatever concrete reality their respective existences in cities uncover. For such, movement through is more important than movement beyond or rising above; and the price of movement through is acute anguish of the spirit, self-knowledge through inner pain, and in Eric Roach, the sickness unto death.

One welcomes lyrical/mystical poets such as Bhajan and Jagdip Maraj. Their work, relating as it does to an Eastern world-view, is a new thing in Caribbean poetry. Rich tensions are capable of existing between their conception of art as the movement of the soul in quest of oneness of being and the alternative idea of art as constant and lucid encounter with chaos, leading in the fortunate to catharsis. As the work of Harris has already illustrated, Eastern and Western-based aesthetics are by no means mutually exclusive of each other – least of all in the Caribbean where they are most likely to intersect invisibly.

Epilogue

If *Corners Without Answers* illustrates anything at all, it is the inadequacy of an approach to Caribbean poetry which divides writers into irreconcilable schools or camps. The sensibility of the Caribbean, secretly unified even when it seeks its poles, has already indicated its potential for either integrating, or exploring the continuum between apparent opposites. Thus if one of the lessons learned from the sixties and the seventies has been the danger of dividing Caribbean sensibility along the false meridian of Black and White, it is equally limiting to divide it along the even more perilous lines of art and polemic, scribal and oral poetry, private and public statement. All our writers have embraced both poles of style and statement. If this has made our writing restless and ambivalent, it has also kept it new and alive.

(First published in Roberto Marquez (ed.) *Caliban* Vol II, No 1 (Fall/Winter 1976) pp. 50-122, this essay was originally meant to be the introduction to an anthology of Trinidad and Tobago poetry entitled

Corners Without Answers. The anthology was never published; though several of the poems mentioned in the essay now appear in *Voiceprint*, Longman, Caribbean, 1989.)

References

1. McTair, R., "Corners without Answers", in Sealey C., (ed.) *Voices,* 1, No. 1, (Aug 1964).
2. Gonzalez A., "Laventille; Brown Man's Dilemma", *Arts Annual* 1, UWI, St. Augustine (June 1971), pp. 13-16.
3. Questel, V., "Stripping off the Masks", A review of Anson Gonzalez's *Boysie B and other Poems, Tapia,* IV, No. 10, (Mar. 10. 1974), pp. 6-8.
4. Questel, V., *Tapia,* III, No. 33 (Aug: 19, 1973), pp. 6, 7 & 9.
5. Brown, W., "The Century of Exile; Basil McFarlane Speaks with Wayne Brown", *Jamaica Journal,* V. 11, No. 3 (Sept. 1973) pp. 38-44.
6. Brown, W., "An Exciting Trinidad Poet", *Sunday Guardian* (Aug, 2, 1970) p. 15.
7. Brown, W., "Art, Artists and the People", *Sunday Guardian* (Aug. 9, 1970) p. 10. Brown, W., "Art and Reconstruction", *Sunday Guardian Independence Supplement*, (Aug. 30, 1970) pp. 12, 13 & 17.
8. Walcott, D., "What the Twilight Says: An Overture", in *Dream on Monkey Mountain & Other Plays* (New York: Farrar, Straus & Giroux, 1970); Walcott, D., "Conversation with Derek Walcott", *Sunday Guardian.* (June 20th 1971) p. 10, Interviewer, Therese Mills; Walcott, D., *Caribbean Contact* 1, No. 7 (July 1973) pp. 14 & 16; *Caribbean Contact* 1, No. 8 (August 1973) pp. 14 & 16, Interviewer Raoul Pantin; Walcott, D., *The Jamaica Daily News,* (Sun. Dec. 7, 1975) pp. 5-7, Interviewer Ulric Mentus. Walcott, D. , "The Muse of History," in Coombs O., (ed.) *Is Massa Day Dead?* (New York: Doubleday/Anchor, 1974), pp. 1-27.
9. Lowhar, S., *Trinidad Guardian*, (July 17th & 18th , 1971).
10. McTair, R., *Trinidad Guardian* (Aug, 18th, 20th & 21st, 1971).
11. Rohlehr, G., "West Indian Poetry: Some Problems of Assessment", *Tapia* I, No. 20, (Sun. Aug. 29th, 1971) pp. 11–14. Rohlehr, G., "Afterthoughts", *Tapia* I, No 23 (Dec 26th, 1971)
12. Roach, E., *Trinidad Guardian*, (July 14, 1971).
13. Roach, E., "Conflict of West Indian Poetry: Tribe Boys vs. Afro–Saxons", *Trinidad Guardian*, (Fri. Jan 12th, 1973).
14. Roach, E., *Trinidad Guardian*, (Wed. Mar 22, 1972).
15. Brown, W., Untitled Poem, *Tapia,* IV, No. 21, (May 26th, 1974).
16. Lowhar, S., *Tapia,* IV, No. 21 (April 28, 1974) p. 1. Rohlehr, G., "Blues for Eric Roach", ibid., p. 2.
17. Rohlehr, G., "A Carrion Time", *Tapia* IV, No. 24, (Sun., Jun 16th, 1974) pp. 5–8 & 11. See also *Bim,* XV, No. 58 (June 1975).
18. Williams, C., "Eric Roach's Poetry", *Tapia* II, No. 17 & 18 (Apr 28th & May 5th, 1974).
19. Questel, V., "Drama of the Streets", *Tapia,* II No. 13 (Sun. Dec 31st, 1972)

pp. 8–10.
20. Questel, V.. *Tapia* III, Nos. 51 & 52 (Dec 23rd & 30th, 1973).
21. Hackett, W., "Survival", *Tapia* V, No. 34 (Sun., Aug 24th, 1975) & *Tapia* V, No. 36, (Sun., Sept 7th, 1975).
22. Hackett, W., "Identity in the Poetry of Walcott", *Moko*, No. 8. (Feb 14. 1969). Hackett, W., "The Writer and Society", *Moko* No. 4, (Dec 13, 1968).
23. Wyke, M., "History Leaves no Memorials to the Poor", *Voices,* 1, No. 2, (Dec 1964), p. 11.
24. Wyke, M., "Guyana", *Voices*, Vol. 1 No. 1 (Aug 1964) p. 12.
25. McTair, R., "Corners without Answers", ibid., p. 8.
26. Wyke, M., "On Remembering Immortelles", and "A Plume of Dust" in *Caribbean Quarterly,* Vol. 5, No. 3. (April 1958).
27. Carter, M., *Poems of Resistance* (London: Lawrence & Wishart, 1954).
28. Roach, E. M., "Fugue for Federation", *Bim* VII, No. 26 (Jan–Jun 1958) "Love Overgrows a Rock", *Bim* VII, No. 25 (Jul–Dec 1957) "I Am the Archipelago", in Freath, Z., *Run Softly Demerara* (London: Allen and Unwin,1960).
30. Rohlehr, G., "The Folk in Caribbean Literature", *Tapia* II, Nos.11 & 12 (Dec 17th & 24th, 1972).
31. Other poems in this vein are Wayne Davis's "Squares", Abdul Malik's "Pan Run II", and Alvin Massy's "Pan".
32. Walcott, D., *Dream on Monkey Mountain and Other Plays* (New York: Farrar, Strauss & Giroux, 1970); Walcott, D., *Another Life* (New York: Farrar, Strauss & Giroux, 1972); Walcott, D., "The Muse of History", op. cit., 1974.
33. Walcott, D., Review of E.R Brathwaite's *A Kind of Homecoming, Sunday Guardian*, (July 22nd, 1962); Walcott, D., Review of Denis Williams's *Other Leopards, Sunday Guardian,* (Dec 1st, 1963); Walcott, D., Review of Austin Clarke's *Survivors of the Crossing, Sunday Guardian,* (Aug 23rd, 1964); Walcott, D., Review of O.R. Dathorne's *The Scholar Man, Sunday Guardian* (Nov 29th, 1964).
34. Walcott, D., Review of O.R. Dathorne's *Caribbean Narrative, Sunday Guardian* (July 3rd. 1966) p. 6.
35. Walcott, D., Review of *Voices,* Vol I, No. 6, *Sunday Guardian,* (June 19th, 1966).
36. McTair, R., "What the February Revolution Really Was All About", *Express* (May 31st, 1970).
37. Miles, J., "The Holocaust", *Voices* I, No. 4 (June–Aug, 1965, pp. 2–3.
38. Miles, J., "Lunch Hour", *Bim*, XII, No. 4 (June–Aug 1965) pp. 2–3.
39. Fraser, A., In *Pivot*, 1, No. 2 (Oct. 25, '68) (author's name withheld in original.)
40. Mc Tair, R., Review of John A. Williams's *The Man Who Cried I Am, Pivot,* No. 3 (Dec 1968).
41. Darbeau, D., Review of Carmichael's & Hamilton's *Black Power,* ibid.
42. Jagessar, R., "The New Discrimination", *Pivot,* II No. 1, (May 1969).
43. Fraser, A., "John Coltrane Is Dead", in *Savacou 3/4* (Dec 1970-Mar 1971).
44. Fraser, A., *Pivot,* I, No. 2, (Oct. 25th, 1968).
45. Nuttall, J., *Bomb Culture* (London: Paladin, 1970).

46. Horovitz, M., "Afterwords", from *Children of Albion: Poetry of the Underground in Britain* (London: Penguin Books, 1969), p. 333.
47. Walcott, D., "A Village Life", in *The Castaway & Other Poems* (London: Cape, 1965), p. 17.
48. Walcott, D., "What the Twilight Says", op. cit., p. 24.
49. Walcott, D., Ibid., p. 27.
50. Walcott, D., "What the Twilight Says"; "The Muse of History"; *Dream on Monkey Mountain.*
51. Gonzalez, A., in *Embryo*, II No. 17 (Mon. 9 Feb., 1970).
52. Gonzalez, A., "Decision" in *Score* (Trinidad, 1972).
53. Gonzalez, A., "Who Killed My…" *Themes* II, UWI, St. Augustine, 1970.
54. Gonzalez, A., "Hey Alfie", *Arts Annual* I, UWI, St. Augustine (June 1971).
55. Fraser, A., "Musicians of the Mind", *Embryo,* III, No. 17, (Undated prob. March/Apr 1971).
56. McTair, R, *Pivot*, 1, No. 3 (Dec. 1968).
57. Walcott, D., "The Muse of History," op. cit., pp. 8-9.
58. Roach, E., Review of *Savacou 3/4, Trinidad Guardian* (14th July, 1971).
59. Lowhar, S., "Black Power in Human Song", *Tapia*, Pamphlet No. 2, 1970,
60. Lowhar, S., Ibid.
61. Lowhar, S., *New World, Guyana Independence Issue.* 1966.
62. Brown, W., "Squid", from *On the Coast* (London: Deutsch, 1972).
63. Lowhar, S., "Shanty Town", *Tapia* I, No. 5 (Feb 1st, 1970).
64. Lowhar. S., "Dry River", *Tapia* I, No. 16.
65. Davis, W., "Voices in the Wilderness: A Statement about Modern Jazz", *S.A.G.* 1, No. 1 (Feb. 1970), pp. 16-17.
66. "*Pro Lege et Rege*" – Latin Inscription above the portals of the Royal Jail, Port of Spain.
67. Liverpool, H., (The Mighty Chalkdust), "Somebody Mad", 1973 calypso.
68. Keane, E.M., *L'Oubli* (Bridgetown, 1950).
69. Brathwaite, E., "Six Poems", *Kyk-Over-Al*, IX, No. 26, Dec 1960. Republished with the addition of two poems as "Octet", *Jamaica Gleaner,* (May–Dec., 1964); and as "Jazz Portraits", Nov., 1971 and as "Blues", in *Other Exiles,* 1975.
70. Walcott, D., "The Glory Trumpeter", in *The Castaway* (1965).
71. Best, A., "Memorial Blues for Billie Holiday", *New World Fortnightly*, No. 1, (30 Nov., 1964) p. 9 (Guyana).
72. Davis, W., "Miles Beyond" in *Old Oracle Timeless Dream* (Trinidad, 1975). p. 36.
73. Charles, F., "Black Cat", from Crab *Track* (London: Brookside Press, 1973) p. 48.
74. Interview between Abdul Malik & Bruce Paddington, *Trinidad Guardian* (Thurs Nov 6th, 1975). A fuller version appeared in *People* (Jan-Feb, 1976) pp. 113–117.
75. *Trinidad. Guardian* (Nov 6th, 1975).
76. *People,* p. 115.
77. "The Bad Poet". A performance by Malik at the Little Carib Theatre, Port of Spain, 6–8th, Nov., 1975.

78. Taylor, J., "The Man with a Message", *Express* (Wed. Nov., 12th, 1975) p. 9.
79. Rohlehr, G., "Beyond the Horrors and the Blues", *Tapia* V, No. 38, (Sun. Sept. 21st, 1975).
80. Carter, M., "After One Year", in *New World, Guyana Independence Issue,* (Feb., 1966).
81. Scott, D., "No Sufferer", in *Uncle Time* (Pittsburgh: University of Pittsburgh Press, 1973), p. 53.
82. Malik, A., *People*, p. 119.
83. Nuttal, J., *Bomb Culture*, pp. 20-21.
84. Walcott, D., "As John to Patmos", from *In a Green Night* (London: Cape, 1962).
85. Malik, A., "An Explanation"; foreword to *Black Up* (Port of Spain, 1972).
86. Gomes, A., *Through a Maze of Colour* (Trinidad: Key Publications, 1974), p. 237.
87. Williams, E., *Massa Day Done* (Port of Spain, 1961).
88. Fraser, A., *Pivot,* I, No. 2 (Oct., 25th, 1968).
89. Walcott, D., "The Muse of History", op. cit., p. 21.
90. Walcott, D., "Conversation with Derek Walcott", Interviewer, Therese Mills, *Sunday Guardian,* (June 20th, 1971), p. 10.
91. See Brathwaite's "Jah" for a poetic statement of this. The musical equivalent may be found in John Coltrane's "After the Rain", "Welcome" and "Kulu Se Mama", or Max Roach's *Lift Every Voice and Sing*, especially his rendition of the spiritual "Wait in the Water", which on the record is called "Troubled Waters".
92. Questel, V., "Tom", in *Score* (Port of Spain, 1972).
93. Hackett, W., "Survival", op. cit, (see ref. # 21).
94. Fraser, A., "Protoplasmic Consciousness", 1968.
95. Brathwaite, E., "Art and Society: Kapo: A Context", in *Jamaican Folkart,* Institute of Jamaica, Undated (prob, 1971), pp. 4-6.
96. See Lamming, *In the Castle of My Skin* and *Of Age and Innocence*; Walcott, "Sea Crab"; Brathwaite, "Crab"; Brown, "Crab"; Charles, *Crab Track*.
97. Elder, J.D., *From Congo Drum to Steelband* (Port of Spain, 1969).
98. Brathwaite, E., "Jah", from *Islands* (1969).
99. Walcott, D., "Mass Man" & "Junta", from *The Gulf & Other Poems* (London: Cape, 1969).
100. Walcott, D., *Ti. Jean and His Brothers,* in *Dream on Monkey Mountain & Other* Plays (1970). See also reviews of *Ti Jean*: (a) Lowhar, S., "A Struggle for Freedom," *Tapia* I, No. 8 (Sun., Aug 9th, 1970) p. 6; (b) Rohlehr, G., "Three Stages of Black Revolution", *Liberation* (Sept 1970), pp. 3 & 6. Author's name withheld in original.
101. Augustus, E., (ed) *Issues in Caribbean Theology* (Port of Spain, 1972/73); Hamid, I., (ed.) *The Troubling of the Waters* (Port of Spain, 1973); O'Gorman, B., "Introduction of Jamaican Music into the Established Churches", *Jamaica Journal,* IX, No. 1, (March, 1975) pp. 40-44 & p. 47.
102. Slinger, F., (The Mighty Sparrow), "Labour Day in Brooklyn", 1969 calypso.
103. For the etymology of the word "bongo" see Rohlehr, G., "West Indian Poetry: Some Problems of Assessment", *Tapia* I No. 20 (Aug. 29th, 1971)

pp. 11–14, and in this volume pp. 98-119.
104. Walcott, D., see the Crusoe poems in *The Castaway;* also "What the Twilight Says" and "The Muse of History".
105. Walcott, D., "The Figure Crusoe: On the Theme of Isolation in West Indian Writing", Unpublished typescript. UWI Library, St. Augustine, 1965.
106. Questel, V., "Near Mourning Ground", *Tapia.* V, No. 34 (Sun Aug., 24th, 1975), p. 10.
107. Romeo, M., "Macabee Version", reggae song of the early 1970s (Jamaica).
108. Walcott, D., "Greenwich Village Winter , from *In a Green Night* (London: Cape, 1962), p. 50.
109. Walcott, D. , "The Flock", in *The Castaway* (London: Cape, 1965).
110. Ibid, p. 44.
111. Walcott, D., "Cold Spring Harbour", in *The Gulf,* p. 61.
112. Walcott, D., "Nearing Forty", ibid, p. 67.
113. Brathwaite, E., "Dawn", from *Islands* (1969).
114. Walcott, D., Programme Notes to the Trinidad Theatre Workshop's 1974 presentation of *Dream on Monkey Mountain,* Port of Spain.
115. Césaire, A., *Discourse on Colonialism* (New York/London: Monthly Review Press, 1972), pp. 33–34 (translated from the original 1955 French publication by Joan Pinkham).
116. Walcott, D., "What the Twilight Says", op. cit., p. 35.
117. Walcott, D., *Another Life* (New York: Farrar, Strauss & Giroux, 1972).
118. Walcott, D., Interview with Ulric Mentus, *The Jamaica Daily News* (Sun. Dec., 1975), pp. 5–7.
119. Walcott, D., "Poem", *Tapia* I, No 17, (Sun, June 27th, 1971) p. 3; "A Patriot to Patriots" and "The Brothers" in *New Writing in the Caribbean* (Guyana, 1972).
120. Roach, E., "Growing Up in Tobago", in *David Frost Introduces Trinidad and Tobago* (London: Deutsch, 1975), p. 157.
121. Roach, E., "Poem for This Day", *Tapia,* II, No. 11 (Sun, Dec 17th. 1972).
122. Roach, E., "City Centre '70", S.A.G. I, No. 3 (Dec 1970).
123. Roach, E., "City Centre '70", in Seymour A.J., (ed) *New Writing in the Caribbean* (Guyana: Carifesta Anthology, 1972).
124. Roach, E., "Hard Drought", *Tapia,* (Sun, April 22nd, 1973).
125. Roach, E., "Growing Up in Tobago", op. cit., p. 157.
126. Rohlehr, G., "West Indian Poetry: Some Problems of Assessment", op. cit, 1971.
127. Roach, E., "Conflict of West Indian Poetry: Tribe Boys vs Afro-Saxons", *Trinidad Guardian* (Fri, Jan 12th, 1973), p. 4.
128. Charles, F., *The Expatriate* (London: Broadside Press, 1973).
129. Bhajan, S., "Art and the Artist: Maharishi's View," in *The New Voices,* No. 6, 1975 (also cited as Vol. 3, No. 5).

SONGS OF THE SKELETON

Kamau Brathwaite's *Black + Blues*

Part One
(*The Poetry of Fission*)

> But if to live here
> is to die
> clutching ashes
>
> the fist tight
> the skull dry
> I will sing songs of the skeleton
> (Brathwaite: "Eating the Dead")

Brathwaite's *The Arrivants* (1967-69) expressed the renaissance faith of the Black Nationalist movement in the possibility of reclamation, repossession and revaluation of spiritual and cultural ground, together with hope that new structures would be raised on this reclaimed ground of being. *Black + Blues*, which won the Casa de las Americas first prize for poetry in 1976, was written in the first half of the decade of the seventies; that is, in the wake of the assassination of the Black Civil Rights movement in America, whether it manifested itself in Christian, Islamic or urban guerilla activism.

This was also a difficult decade for the Anglophone Caribbean, and the poetry which emerged out of the turbulent seventies reflects the near-absolute gap between the measured fertile growth which the poet had hoped for his society ("green growing on green", from "Conqueror"), and the clearly observable ravages of the islands' political and economic reality ("the dungles of no hope").

Black + Blues depicts a movement from geological ("Fetish") to historical ("Conqueror") time. "Conqueror" provides a background against which the starkness of the contemporary scene ("Caliban", "Starvation", "Springblade") is placed. An omen of post-nuclear Apocalypse also broods over some of the poems ("Moor"). In spite of a pervasive vision of history as fatality – a vision which also was partially present in *The Arrivants* and which exists to a greater or lesser extent in most of our major writers –

Brathwaite ends *Black + Blues* on a qualified vision of possibility, one that is equally fervent though more cautious than the "green spreading opening day" on which all three books of *The Arrivants* ended.

The first sequence of poems, from "Fetish" to "Trane", is entitled "Fragments", and suggests that fragmentation has been the archetypal and aboriginal heritage of the archipelago. In "Fetish"

> The objects of wood, thatch and stone
> decayed relics, splinters, shell

are generalised images of ruin. They may be houses ("wood", "thatch", "stone"), and as houses they suggest ruined cultures, lifestyles and religions ("relics") – Amerindian, African and European, perhaps – whose fragments coexist on the static foreshore of the present. As Brathwaite states in "Caribbean Man in Space and Time":

> archipelago: fragments: a geological plate being crushed by the pacific's curve, cracking open yucatan; the arctic/north American monolith; hence cuba, hispaniola, puerto rico; continental outriders and the dust of the bahamas, atlantic africa pushing up the beaches of our eastern seawards.
>
> the history reflects the pressure and passage of lava, storm, stone, earthquake, crack, coral: their rise and fall of landscapes: destructions, lost memories: atlantis, atahualpa, ashanti: creations: fragments[1]

Yet Brathwaite feels, along with Octavio Paz,[2] that these fragments are not quite inert. They secrete a potential life which may be restored by research ("our problem is how to study the fragments/whole"), meditation and the creative exercise of the artistic imagination ("Contemplation restores them to our time"). One may, like Denis Williams' Lionel Froad,[3] leap in imagination from ruined artifact to recognised ancestor. *The Arrivants* was precisely such an imaginative, transfiguring leap from the inert "dust, glass, grit, the pebbles of the desert" and the fire-ravaged tree-stump of ancestors in *Rights of Passage*, to the living, uncurling tendrils, the embryonic growth and miraculously "living stone, living bone of coral" in *Islands*.

In *Black + Blues,* however, the poet constantly acknowledges that the history of fragments and shards has not been in any way transfigured by the light of creative contemplation. History in "Conqueror" has remained an unreal dialectic between the emptiness and nostalgic guilt of the conqueror/settler/plantation owner/merchant/landlord ("this empty house, these windmills turning, turning") and the menace, blues and ongoing rebellion of the dispossessed poor, whose crisp reggae percussion and chant proclaims the single machine-gun message:

> like a rat
> like a rat
> like a rat-a-tap tappin
>
> an we burnin babylone

The turning vanes and the steady grind of history's windmills, then, are controlled not only by the structures, strictures and systems of the conqueror (house, windmill, factory), but also by the constant rebellion of the subjugated.

In spite of this grim and unresolved dialectic, particularly evident in the recent history of Jamaica, the poet/historian can still proclaim a stubborn commitment to wiping out the obscurity and hopelessness in which his people move because of their uncertainty of self, and their ignorance of and inability to connect with their past; their leaders' absence of perspective; and the fixity of their inherited impoverishment.

Interestingly, the historian's final hope is for a dreamed-of movement beyond the dungeon of our historical inheritance.

> and the rope: whip tomb
> boulder
> that had bound you
>
> now talisman now twisted into
> prayer now shredded
> into timeless stars[4]

The hope here is that having walked "the four corners of [their) understanding" – a metaphor taken from the ritualistic movement of the Shango Mother to the four cardinal points in order to exorcise evil – the West Indian peoples will apprehend history not only as torture, ordeal and Sisyphean burden ("boulder"), but also as the accumulated and healing force of their own creative effort and spiritual strength. Such an apprehension of history will place them beyond its touch, or at least convert historical process into a talisman, endued with the magical power to protect them against future evil.

Such is the poet's enduring dream and the historian's unusual commitment in the face of the grim reality of the seventies. It is a dream which he shares with Walcott, even though Walcott speaks about the need to divest oneself of the lineaments or cerements of history, and to start from amnesia; and with Wilson Harris, even though Harris pursues the dream to the point where one arrives at that unlikely land above historical process, the "heaven/haven" of the *Palace of the Peacock*.

The question which the rest of *Black + Blues* poses is how does one extract a sense of the holy out of an ongoing history of evil? How does such a history become "twisted into prayer", when the very word "twisted" implies that the process of transformation will involve a mental, physical and spiritual torture traditional in the Caribbean experience? That question is given no direct answer in the poem, though the gunshot drum or reggae/rockers on which the poem ends, is a reiterated omen of the possibility of a revolution of the poor. Whether the poet endorses the prospect of such a revolution is an open question here, though far more definite answers are provided in a poem such as "Sun Song".

The poem "Glass" which follows is a description of present-day reality in the ghettoes of the USA. The people whom the poet sees through his bespectacled stare ("corneas of glass") are the diametric opposite to those of whom he dreamed towards the end of "Conqueror". Not only have they not gained a transcendent vision, they are history's most hopeless ruins. Scattered, internally divided, stagnating in the atmosphere of defeat which followed the assassination of the Civil Rights Movement, they have lost that sense of continuity and reverence for which the poet had hoped. Indeed, although he calls them "my people", the fact that he sees them through "corneas of glass," implies his distance and detachment from their condition. These people are centuries removed from the green of their ancestral potential:

> they cannot worship their dead,
> their ancestors' of centuries' steps,

Nor are they truly contemporary people, creatively in control of their present. Miseducated, they have been famished on a lean diet:

> those books you offer them: pink
> proverbs, blue eyed revelations [5]

The sisters, after the nine days' wonder of the Afro, remake-up themselves in the image of "your gentile venus". Yet they are not quite lost, since they retain both the creative "soul" of song ("arethas") and political potential ("angelas"). The grimmest vision is of the brothers:

> shadow boxing to the tune of needles
> angels of the fix
> bartering their sanity for trips
> around the skeleton

Vision distorted by dope, they now fight with shadows. They have lost the ability to grapple with the real enemy whom they beg "handcupped" for bread. Apart from suggesting "handcuffed", the shackles of the Mafia system in which these failed revolutionaries now find themselves, "handcupped" describes the gesture of Christian communicants at altar barriers, as well as the Islamic gesture of prayer before meals. The ideas of perverted prayer to the Mafia-gods of America's power elite, and futile religious escapism when such prayer fails, are thus combined with that of enshacklement.

The "tune of needles", like the word "handcupped", is one of those examples of Brathwaite's effortless wordplay. It suggests simultaneously the ravages of heroin, and the culture of sound-system, jukebox and discotheque phantasmagoria. But it does more than this. It links the two things together as they were combined in the lives of Charlie Parker, Billie Holiday and Jimi Hendrix, the latest and most sensational example of the Black pop idol who was play-actor, addict and victim of both his own excess and his self-abandonment in the mid-sixties to the most decadent crevices of the white cult world. Hendrix's early death from dope was a fitting symbol of the failure of Black consciousness in the sixties, and the perennial perversion of Black talent and the prostitution of Black creative force on the worst of white altars.

The reference to "boxing" is a reminder that boxers have shared the stage with musicians as visible symbols of Black talent, and that both have traditionally been under the control of the syndicates of capitalism. Moreover, as in the reference in "Negus" to Caribbean leaders and people praying to United States marines "by rattling [their] hip/bones",[6] there is the distinct suggestion that the ghetto Blacks of "Glass" are involved in the dance of death, the struggle with shadows. Pop culture has become palliative, escape and death-dealing barbiturate.

The phrase "angles of the fix" echoes the earlier word "angelas", and underlines the contrast between the example of Angela Davis in the seventies and the decadence of psychedelia and the Woodstock scene, which interestingly enough were promoted by politicians and businessmen in Trinidad soon after the 1970 "February Revolution", in order to drug the movement to sleep. "Angels" is also reminiscent of the motorcycle hoodlums who termed themselves Hell's Angels, and thus conjures up the whole cult scene from the Beats through the hippies, yippies, California Flower Children, Jesus Freaks etc. in which many Blacks became involved, particularly after the collapse of the Black Power movement and the mind-shattering experience of Vietnam. One can with hindsight reflect on the fatal nature of such involvement by recalling the murder in 1978 of hundreds of such Blacks by white cult leader Jim Jones in Guyana's El Dorado.

Brathwaite had with accuracy defined the predicament of *los angelitos negritos* in this poem of the early seventies. They are not the Black angels of whom Roberta Flack was singing at the time, but rather "angels of the fix". They remain fixed in their situation, in a fix even as they beg for their "fix" of heroin. Their drugged "trips" are thus entanglements, stumblings and ultimately voyages "around the skeleton" dances of death around white dry bones; the only rituals which have survived for these modern people, who would term ancestor-worship "primitive".

Having presented this devastating picture of contemporary Blacks in urban America, Brathwaite then sardonically remarks:

i hear them screaming
REVOLUTION

as the world revolves round
marcus malcolm mississippi memphis

Throughout *The Arrivants* Brathwaite touched on the theme of "revolution". His approach was usually cautious, marked by scepticism, a mistrust of slogan, and most of all by a consciousness of the slow workings of historical process, and an almost deterministic foreknowledge of history's betrayal. In *Masks*, even when new civilisations do arise after wars and journeys, they are termed "new world(s) of time and time's uncertainty". It is therefore very late in *Islands* that he explores the possibility of unleashing the leopard of revolt.[7] But even there, we are left more with the omen and potential menace of revolt; a sense of what lies in wait and will be averted only if our choices in the present can transform the structures and deformities inherited from the past.

Here in "Glass", Brathwaite defines attunement with past revolutionary effort (marcus/malcolm) and cultural continuity (mississippi/memphis) as the axis around which renewed consciousness must revolve. But these brothers have lost continuity in blood, passion, culture and tradition. Hence:

> but there ain't no vein
> of revolution
> only the blues
> and coltrane's gospel pain

Brathwaite is also saying that addicts and escapists of any sort, those who needle dope into their veins, are incapable of transforming their present, which is really the contemporary shape which a deformed and unredeemed past has assumed.

Unable to transform the present they are left with the blues, and the poet and posterity are left with the anguished music of John Coltrane, the truest and most articulate voice of the sixties, Baraka's "heaviest spirit", gospeller of the revolution in both consciousness and politics. But Trane was never a popular hero among Black hipsters, jivers and shadow-boxing addicts of the cult scene. They didn't and don't acknowledge him as their voice. He is the neglected artist/prophet/victim whose gospel is, like revolution, too hard and complex, and his music, as we shall see, becomes the poet's cry of pain, as he too begins to feel that he has preached, sung, shouted and groaned to no purpose.

Drought

The second section of *Black + Blues,* from "Caliban" to "Sun Song", is entitled "Drought". Drought is a symbolic journey through today's ravaged landscape, wasteland of the mind. It is Brathwaite's response to Jamaica of the sixties and early seventies, a fragmentary, disruptive poetry, a poetry of fission, hints of which had begun to appear in the later urban sequences of *The Arrivants*.[8]

In these poems the intelligence seeks to preserve its tenacious grip on observable reality. But the poet becomes so immersed in the chaos which he perceives, and into whose burning magmatic core he seeks to enter, that he at times fails to achieve single-minded and unified focus on experience. Images become dislocated, and don't always clarify reality. The eye moves restlessly from image to image; image gives birth to image, splits into two or three image-fragments as the aesthetics of fission seeks its shape. Brathwaite attempts to depict in "Drought" the process whereby the Caribbean is becoming relentlessly engulfed in the vortex of the late twentieth century. He is interested both in the historic sources of this process and in where it is likely to leave us, diaspora people who are neither in possession of our past nor in control of our present.

The Jamaica of the late sixties and early seventies, Brathwaite's point of reference, is presented as a trauma-shocked society, living under a constant state of spiritual emergency. It is a society which, as the poem "Conqueror" has already suggested, has remained rigidly fixed in its historical plantation mould of repression and rebellion, class division with its attendant attitudes of authoritarianism and subservience, acquiescence and secret subversion. Now in the seventies it threatens to crack under its tensions; and one is not surprised to find in the poems recurrent passages suggesting breakdown, upheaval and apocalypse. Such a sense of apocalypse was and is there in an overwhelming amount of reggae music since the late sixties, and strangely, the more deeply reggae has entered a whirlpool of impending chaos, the more popular it and the message of dread have become internationally and in the Caribbean.

Caliban

"Caliban", the first poem in this drought sequence, gives immediate evidence of the poet's shift of stance from that of the concerned sensitive Black traveller, for whom the Black reality of New York's megalopolis is a matter for empathy, not for direct engagement. Thus, while the poet's distance from the people he perceives – that abstract, general "my people" of the revolutionary sixties – is indicated in "Glass" by the "corneas of glass" through which he views them; here in "Caliban" the voice is more concerned with speaking from within a situation of tragic failure and frustration. The mode is that of soliloquy, indicating isolation. Yet it is an isolation which in the end draws attention to the communal nature of Caliban's experience as a "victim of the cities' victory", a diasporan product of New York, Paris, Kingston town.

"Caliban" begins with the image of "mabrak" or "black lightning", Bongo Jerry's image[9] of "the coming of light to the black world." This "coming of light" was seen as being part of the Rastafarian bequest as well as being the result of a sense of continuity of the African presence in the Caribbean. It was also catalysed by the Black Power movement of the sixties – the "black electric storm" which then generated hope of new vision and consciousness.

Writing in the early seventies and in the wake of the defeat of the sixties movement, Brathwaite now records that Black Power resulted in no lasting sense of reverence, no sanctuary of respect.

> The flash of dark
>   into which i have carved no holy place

Its single blinding flash illuminated only the scars of the past and the stark apocalyptic handwriting on the wall of the present for the historically maimed.

> the lightning of scars
> my flesh illuminated by the writhing of death

There are a number of clues that Brathwaite views Caliban here as a failed artist/creator, one who has made little use of his brief pentecostal light. The words "carved no holy place" remind us of both the carver Jake in Mais's *Black Lightning* who was presented as a Promethean figure, and Brathwaite's own carpenter/sculptor Ogun of *The Arrivants,* icon of the artist as spirit-filled enthusiast and energised creator-god. The word "writhing" contains the word "writing", thus sustaining the implication of creative activity. This idea, indeed, was also present in Bongo Jerry's "Mabrak", where the lightning is described as "sky-writing", apocalyptic illumination and calligraphy. Brathwaite now returns to the image with the bitter knowledge that whatever Bongo Jerry might have hoped for has remained unfulfilled. Thus "writing" becomes the "writhing" of a people in their final snakelike death-throes. The omowale had discovered since *Masks* that "beginnings end here in this ghetto", where the drugged shadow-boxers of the diaspora have proved incapable of harnessing the electricity of their own mabrak vision.

The forked, twisted movement of black lightning next becomes the writhing movement of a nest of black electric eels.

> my flesh illuminated by the writhing of death
> by the ideals of eels
> the gum tree writing its tears

Brathwaite with his image of shocking betrayal of energy returns to the spirit of the "Homecoming" sequence in *Islands.*

> And so without my cloth,
> shoulders uncovered
> to this new doubt

and desert I return,
expecting nothing;
my name burnt out,

a cinder on my shoulder.
No clan or kinsman turns
my self respect

into a claw, a tooth,
a dagger; even my skin
now sheds its shame;

like a snake
the eyes do not wink
away; whips do not flinch

from what they will destroy:
strips, strips of flesh, flash
of the black forked tongue

licking these scars [10]

Here the Stranger, newly returned from a harrowing encounter with the ancestral land, has salvaged not even a dashiki or a bundle from Africa. Even the chip on his shoulder has burned to a cinder. There is a kind of arid self-mockery in the picture, which is spiritual toughness of a kind, grit for the new home which must now be built. If in Africa the inability to belong was a matter of shame leading to self-laceration, here the land itself has lost the memory of its past. Moreover, there has been progress of a sort – a black skin is no longer considered a liability: "even my skin now sheds its shame". But the words here are double-edged: Black people have exchanged shame at blackness for pride in blackness as smoothly as a snake sheds its skin. Their vision, too, is treacherous vision, their acclamation the duplicity ("the black forked tongue") of the snake. The Stranger's scars, his private hurt, the genuineness of his pain, mean little to his brothers at home. Those who doglike seem to fawn, ("licking these scars") are in fact the most uncompromising flagellants, whose "whips do not flinch/from what they will destroy".

It is clearly to this milieu that Brathwaite returns in "Caliban" when he describes how rapidly the flash of black lightning turned into "the ideals of eels". "The gum tree writing its tears" is an allusion to Othello's final soliloquy, in which he describes himself as one

>   whose subdued eyes
> Albeit unused to the melting mood,
> Drops tears as fast as the Arabian trees
> Their medicinal gum.

Othello is at this point savouring both a sense of betrayal and self-betrayal, and can restore his tragic dignity only by a histrionic act of suicide. Here it may be that the poet views not only his people but himself as failed creators, and is expressing a sense of loss at not having been fully worthy of the proffered moment of blinding illumination.

A great deal of ground, then, has been covered in these opening lines, which are an illustration of how a single image splits into several image-fragments – what I have termed above "the aesthetics of fission". The next few lines illustrate the well-known personal/impersonal nature of Brathwaite's poetry, in that Caliban is simultaneously a metaphor of the reduced condition of the diaspora man in the city's wilderness, and persona for the poet writing/writhing in what he considers a trivial and insidious milieu.

> I have become lost in this forest of singing wires
> of grasshopper gossip
> of syphilitic cities of no night

For Caliban the urban ruin, the tangled lianas of the African rain forests of centuries ago have been replaced by the "singing wires" of civilisation, but there is no real contact of hands, hearts or minds here, even though the humming telephone wires might suggest communication and conversation. Similarly, the poet lost in the more genteel jungle of academia, finds real dialogue impossible.

> call my name: it is answered by the spittle of lizards

The lizard image is an extension of the snake/eel image and is meant to place the spirit of meanness and petty contempt against which the poet needed to struggle for his "holy place".

If the American Calibans had to face the system's assassination squad – a "phalanx of executioners" – or the general withdrawal of Black Studies programmes from universities in the wake of the defeat of the movement, the Caribbean Caliban confronts the traditional weapons which have been employed in the past to deface the Black image: scorn, contempt and hatred.[11] The only difference is that this contempt issues from the intellectual centre of the islands, what Lamming in *Water with Berries* terms the Mona Crematorium. The poet's reaction is violent.

> tirade of hate echoing out of the iron wells
> of my flesh
> the crystal water flowing upwards to drench me
> its sibilance devouring my eyes

The image of the well is probably taken from Eric Roach's 1953 poem "The Fighters"[12] where the image occurred of African history as an underground well, kept open by an instinct for freedom and struggle which remains alive in the Blacks of the diaspora. Roach in considering several generations of Black heavyweight champions sees in their strength, courage and excellence the outward and visible sign of all the qualities of human excellence which have grown and continually fulfilled themselves by attacking the barriers of prejudice:

> the wall which fear and fools
> Have built between two skins, and fantastic pride
> Rebuilds where it is worn and cracked and crumbled.

Roach concludes that the African bloodline was never severed:

> Deep down in the deep seam the water's clear
> And clean from the Black Rock of Africa.

Brathwaite criticised what he saw as a romanticisation of Africa, and a desire by Roach to escape from the "strenuousness of his barriered society".[13] He was, however, attracted to the image of the underground spring which occurs in several ways in *The Arrivants* as well as in *Mother Poem* where it is most pervasive. In "Caliban", however, Brathwaite is dealing with a man whose innermost being has been invaded by the city's iron. Hence the paradoxical "iron wells of my flesh", where the natural and organic "flesh" has been penetrated by the manufactured and inorganic ("iron"). Thus the health-giving runnels of the poem "Jah"[14] which flow upwards in spite of the city's rocks, steel and glass, now no longer perform their quickening function. A process of reversal takes place in which the fertilising waters from the underground of being are converted into waters of hate and thus lose their creative quality. Tainted by the poet's bitter response to spite, envy and "the spittle of lizards", the creative impulse/energy becomes destructive. It consumes vision, "devouring my eyes".

The next image is an Ogun/Shango image: that of the iron, fire and violent hurtling power of the locomotive. Brathwaite in his notes to *Mother Poem* states that:

> The god of lightning, Shango, frequently combined with Ogoun, god of iron, often manifests himself in the Caribbean as a locomotive engine.[15]

Here the image serves a dual function: in Prospero's mythology, the locomotive engine has served as a symbol of the triumphant Industrial Revolution and the mid-Victorian idea of Progress.[16] In Caliban's lost mythology, the same locomotive is associated with the loss of politics and war. Lost in the space between two mythologies, Caliban cannot control the loa of politics and rebellion which now possesses him. The loa is destructive. He causes trees to wither, silences the hummingbirds, bestows neither growth nor transcendent beauty. (Bird images in Brathwaite often suggest ascension/transcendence, movement beyond, flight of dream). Ogun, the god of politics and revolution, silences the hummingbirds (poetry? music? freedom of voice?). His thirst is insatiable. Huge clay jars of water ("monkeys") cannot contain it.

The rage of Caliban-turned-Ogun is, however, pointless and far less creative than the power of Tom-turned-Ogun in *Islands*. For while Tom's Sabbath enthusiasm is converted into shape and "emerging woodwork image", not only does Caliban's blind rage remain inchoate, but it has lost, or missed, or is incapable of destroying its object. It is a self-destructive, internalised frenzy. "But the cockpit is burst in a mabrak of madness". Shango is Spitfire aeroplane, anachronistic, and exploding with his own lightning. "The coal explodes inwards to furnace of darkness". Ogun is loco/motive imploding with his own thunder. To "explode inwards" is to implode, to be blown apart by internal forces which never reach the surface, as violent underwater currents, invisible on the surface of a stream, can sometimes split rocks. Caliban breaks down under the force of his own energy, and the life-sustaining fluid of his sensibility ("ichor"), the fragrance of which he was capable, the holiness which he sought ("Incense"), peters out.

Brathwaite is saying that energy can be creative or destructive. Invoked, explored and controlled, energy is cathartic. Channelled through form it becomes art – hence song, hymn, chant, shout, drumbeat and dance, dramatic enactment. These are the ichor and incense of the survival movement traditional in the Caribbean and Afro-America, and in *The Arrivants* Brathwaite was able to extract from the cathartic rituals still alive in the Caribbean various metaphors relevant to his own acts of poetic making. But, as we said above, the problem of form became extreme as the perception of fragmentation intensified during the sixties. This is illustrated by how Brathwaite uses the Shango/Ogun motif in this poem. The whole point of Shango or Vodun rituals is the control of energy. The houngan "ties fire", controls the powers which ascend from the underground up the lightning conductor of the poteau-mitan or central pole of the *hounfort*. The poet is supposed to be able to exercise the same control over whatever possesses him in the process of the poem. But here the rituals have gone awry, the moment of energy is wasted, the loa turns on the devotee who has proved an unworthy vessel for his containment.

Clearly "Caliban" is Brathwaite's attempt in the early seventies to find a metaphor for the direction in which sensibility had moved; his own sensibility, that of Jamaica, and that of the Black consciousness movement. If art faces new problems of form in the face of what Alfie Fraser once termed "the abysmal vortex of change",[17] so does politics. Brathwaite is concerned about both art and politics in *Black + Blues*. The failure of Caribbean politics in the decade of the seventies has been the failure to create a ground on which our energies might grow and find creative expression. Our politics has never been concerned with the inner person and creative capacity. This may be why Jamaica, Guyana and Trinidad waste down their youth, turn their energies so relentlessly inward, then explode under their own uncontained and yet unliberated force.

The final vision is of Caliban at the end of all processes: the ultimate big city man, "blind, tortured" like Samson among the philistines, twisted and bent like Legba the Dahomean cripple-god who aged in travelling west across the Middle Passage. Caliban is

> victim of the cities' victory
> victim of the cities' skin and trinkets
> wilderness of wind and shellac

Last skin-and-bone survivor on the warscape of ruin, the city's "skin and trinkets" replacing the traditional slave trade, there is not much left of Caliban in Prospero's meat mart.

The poem closes as it began – in unhope. If Prospero is to blame for Caliban's state, so is Caliban, who is as he is because he has betrayed his own black lightning. He now has nothing left but the dead Western cowboy heritage of desert ("cow's head"); rich America's consumerist excess which has been the greatest shaping force at work in contemporary times on the sensibility of the islands[18] ("glut"), and death ("skeleton") – what remains after the crow's feasting on those who failed to make it through the desert.

Part Two
(Poetry as Omen and Dread Testimony)

> "Now the crippled omens arrive on crutches of rumour"
>   (Brathwaite, "Springblade")

So far, we have been observing a process whereby the poet has been moving towards self-identification with the ruined manscape which he describes. The implied distance in "Glass" is reduced in "Caliban" where the poet's personal frustration merges with that of this "victim of the cities' skin and trinkets". It is, however, well worth noting that Caliban is as much the metaphor of a process as he is a person. The aspect of the Caliban metaphor explored in the poem relates to Trinculo's drunken dream in *The Tempest* of making easy money by taking Caliban home to England and converting him into a circus spectacle for "holiday fools".

> "Were I in England now, – as once I was, – and had but this fish [i.e. Caliban] painted, not a holiday fool there but would give a piece of silver: there would this monster make (i.e. the fortune of) a man; any strange beast there makes a man. When they will not give a doit to relieve a lame beggar, they will lay out ten to see a dead Indian."[19]

Brathwaite is observing the end – or by-product of this centuries' old coloniser's dream of making an easy fortune through human exploitation. Here exploitation assumes its subtlest and cruellest form: the exploitation of image which reduces a person to a stereotype, a freak, a dancing-bear, a monster in the muppet-show of the coloniser's civilisation. Brathwaite makes the point that exploitation of creativity and distortion of image exist not only in such visible areas as the world of sport and entertainment, but also in the world of letters. His reaction is a mixture of shame and rage, because he realises that part of the blame for his present condition must rest with Caliban himself.

As if to emphasise this point, Brathwaite focuses next in "Starvation" on a homegrown Jamaican ghetto, whose spokesman is not a hypersensitive and pessimistic intellectual, but one of the poor, a "reduced" man: one of those dwellers in the "dungle of no hope". "Caliban" located the black man in the white city and system. But Jamaica, as the Rastafarian sufferer declares:

> ... is no white man lan
> an' yet we have ghetto here.

Implied is a reversal of perspective. Behind the voice of this Jamaican Caliban, Brathwaite is saying that one would naturally expect ghettoes – either of Nazi extermination or the slower murder of exploitation, hunger and dehumanisation – to be in Trinculo's world ("white man lan'.") After all, Prospero and Trinculo between them invented the system, city and ghetto, and Jamaica as ex-colony can always claim that it has inherited and is no more than an extension of that system, the black shadow of the white manscape. Yet the sufferer refuses to accept such an automatic excuse in an age of independence. What he sees is the wilful preservation of colonial class structure symbolised in the identity of "barbican" and "babylon", as well as in the irony of

> de wayside cabin dem a-kall
> a bus stap, hadvertisin'
> SHERATON HOTEL

The two structures, bus-stop, which is temporary dwelling-place and part-time home for the homeless, and hotel, which is massive foreign-owned structure and temporary home for the well-fed, are the contemporary extensions of the shanty and Great House, the *senzala* and *Casa Grande* of Gilberto Freyre's famous study.[20]

The poem, in monologue form, becomes the Rastafarian's testimony of hurt and hope. The incident which triggers off this dread testimony is common enough: passing cars, symbols of privilege to the dispossessed, raise dust and splash water on people waiting for the bus under a covered bus stop. In Jamaica, waiting for the bus can be an eternal vocation, and often, after an hour of the most chastening heat borne in patient silence, the bus passes full, or refuses to stop, or isn't going where one had hoped. So that for the "sufferers" – a term current in the late sixties – waiting for the bus (Godot?) becomes a symbolic act. It flings the humiliating Gethsemane of their low status in their faces, with every cloud of dust or splash of water.

It is under such circumstances that one person will suddenly "burn through dis wall o' silence" which often accompanies such waiting, by uttering a spontaneous testimony which is generally addressed to no one in particular, but which articulates the frustration, bitterness and rage of the group. His voice then becomes medium for the general will and hope; his utterance becomes jeremiad and isaiaic prophecy, the poetry of omen and dread testimony.

A poem such as "Starvation" depends for its strength on the poet's ability to capture the authentic tone of the sufferer's voice. At its best it contains both the sufferer's intelligence and the poet's invisible eye and voice. Thus, for the rootsman, the seasonal drought is literally reflected in a physical drying up, as actually happens in some areas of Haiti, or more devastatingly in the Ethiopia of the Rastaman's dreams, where sometimes the only water children may know is their saliva, produced by sucking stones.

> we have place where man die wid im eye-water dry up
> where he cyan even cry tribulation
> where de dry river rocks clog im in

For the poet, the images suggest lost vision, lost sensibility, the incapacity for tears and hence the shrivelling of the "feminine" quality of compassion; the disappearance of the stream of ancestry which is now a dry river; the evaporation of *mogya* and *sunsum* – soul's blood. These images will, in "Springblade", be associated with the violation of the nation's anima, which is symbolised by a recurring female presence.

There are two types of omen in the poem. The first type is where ordinary actions attain unusual intensity, and ordinary objects or details become suddenly charged with fearful possibilities. Hence the passing cars, the waiting, the bus stop, the hotel, the dust with its oasis of potholes and the dry gully, all become omens of the emerging springblade of violence.

The second type of omen is where the marvellous, the non-rational and the incredible begin to become part of ordinary reality. We see this second type of omen in the allusion to:

> dis rage o' crow dem
> walkin' pan de coffin wid it wheels,
> stoppin' at de station, police
> station, haxin' for sargeant brown

It was in October 1970 that three crows are supposed to have appeared on a coffin mounted on wheels, asking for one Mr. Brown. The "incident" was recorded in reggae and by Ras Dizzy Bongo.

> Have you heard about the strange mistry in the city of Kingston, Jamaica, recently, of a Ghost going to police stations asking for one Constable Brown attached to the Police Department? Well when you listen to the action of a mistical Ghost in mistry about town. It was on Wednesday of October last that the big excitement hit up town West of Trench and Jones Town about a 'Walking dead Coffin' on wheel walking the city.[21]

Ras Dizzy's account is not easy to follow, but one can gather from it that large numbers of people believed or were attracted by the rumour; that a policeman who attempted to shoot the duppy fell frothing on his face; that the ghost coffin appeared at an elementary school and a teacher fainted.

Whether all this happened or not is not as important as the fact that people were prepared to believe in the supernatural, particularly when it seems to prophesy catastrophe. The story of the "Clashing of the Sevens" (on the 7th of July 1977) is a case in point. A false rumour was spread that Marcus Garvey – now a folk ancestral figure – had predicted dire upheaval when the four sevens met. It was sufficiently serious for the issue to be discussed on television, and for the government to call out the army as a precautionary measure against any citizen who might attempt to fulfil the prophecy.[22]

The point is that the society is perpetually on the lookout for omens of its own downfall. Every small action or rumour contributes to the hope for a final dissolution of Babylon. The sufferer in "Starvation", like his counterpart in "Wings of a Dove" feels that he will justifiably be called upon, by both God and History, to become the servant and instrument of the apocalypse. He retains a certain grounded faith in spite of the fact that earlier efforts to invoke a warlike *Nyabinghi* spirit have failed ("summon de nyah bingeh/but none-a dem come"). The allusion here is probably to the abortive Rastafarian uprising of 1959. The protagonist of "Starvation" believes that he will survive the downfall of Babylon.

> i waitin' here:
> one day the grass goin' green,
> de tyre dem goin' shred thru to the rim

The crash of the material world is symbolised by the immobilisation of the machine and by the hotel "resurrecting " itself "back down to gravel". On the other hand, the fact remains that the sufferer will still be "waitin' here" for that bus which never passes; that he will still be singing the blues – whether they be the Don Drummond blues of shattered minds, the Paul Bogle blues of historic though failed rebellion, or the broken bottle blues of the coming apocalypse. The picture here is still one of fixity, of no real change, of the recurring future: the unresolved dialectic of oppression and rebellion.

Brathwaite is in these Kingston poems – "Starvation", "Springblade" –

the most immediate in the collection, taking seriously all the omens in a society which is half modern (city, bourg) and half tribal (bush, folklore, ghost, zombie, duppy). He is asking a question implicit in "Glass", "Caliban" and "Moor": What happens when the semi-primal consciousness of the folk is faced with the asphyxia of the contemporary city – poverty, break-up, breakdown, advertising, aridity and junk? In "Starvation" – which was itself the name of a 1969 reggae song banned from radio by the Shearer Government[23] – the response is testimony, sermon and prophecy; the restatement of the biblical myth of the apocalypse in terms of the legend of the three crows on the ghost coffin.

Springblade

"I have heard in the voice of the wind the voices of my dim killed children"
(Gwendolyn Brooks, "The Mother")

"Springblade", the most central poem of the collection, suggests another possibility: that violence can flash out as swiftly and as lethally as the ratchet-knives of the yout'. The title is meant to convey two ideas: the hairspring imminence of violence and the transition from Rastafarian pacifism to Rude Bwoy militarism, which had taken place since the mid-sixties.[24] With this transition, politics in Jamaica took a new and tragic turn. The two major political parties, after the initial manifestations of Rudyism, moved to contain the violence of the yout' by institutionalising it. Officially, they took the usual steps against it: police and army campaigns, harsher legislation against crimes of violence, appeals to the public to bring in all firearms. Unofficially they exploited it, gave it a central place in the political system, and established the era of rulership by "balance of terror" which accounted for well over five hundred lives in the bloody electioneering of 1980.

Brathwaite in "Springblade" (1970/71)[25] explores this moment of transition, which he interprets as an omen of fearful possibilities. More insistently than in "Starvation", the derelict landscape becomes symbol of an internal disintegration and omen of an impending explosion. The placement of "Springblade" at the centre of the collection is deliberate. It is in every sense a watershed poem, the vision of a moment of transition. What precedes it is the futuristic despair of "Moor", where the ravages described in "Glass" and "Caliban" are projected into a future of post-nuclear ruin, and the sequestered tribes retreat into "what is left of the jungles", Kilimanjaro submerged by glacial Mount Blanc. What follows it, however, is "Sun Song", a new breath of spirit; a symbolic rediscovery of both flowers and fire in the bone-hard heart of drought.

"Springblade" starts with the assertion: "But there is goin' to be a revolution". The word "but" is ambiguous. It serves as a pointer to and intensifier of the statement which succeeds it. It also has its normal contrastive force and can mean "in spite of all: despite all evidence to the contrary". For the poet had in "Glass" "Caliban" and "Moor" presented urban Calibans as victims of a process which they could not control, and as being incapable of revolution because of their lack of self-knowledge and their disconnection from past revolutionary effort. Viewing his people through "corneas of glass" he had concluded then, "but there ain't no vein of revolution". Here in "Springblade" arises an alternate voice of resistance, which challenges the poet's scepticism. The voice may be his own submerged voice and spirit of resistance, the caged leopard of revolt which in *Islands* remains imprisoned by paralysing doubt, and can be released only by an act of extraordinary daring. What Brathwaite seeks to do in "Springblade" is to identify the exact texture of a mood, of a moment in time which contained both the optimistic fervour of the exploding yout', and the more defensive, cautious and desperate hope of maturer minds. These latter could affirm only an existential hope-in-spite-of. Both aspects of the mood are contained in the ambiguous "but" with which the poem begins.

The inevitability of revolution is seen in the evidence of universal corruption and decay.

> the garbage knows it
> festering the silver sidewalks

The "garbage" may also be Patterson's children of Sisyphus, human jetsam reduced to struggling with vultures for rotten meat, and ultimately becoming themselves fodder for corbeaux. The phrase "silver sidewalks" performs a number of functions; it is a reasonably precise description of the grey concrete pavements caught in the heat-waves of drought. They then gain sheen and glitter, and serve as an apt image of the mirage and veneer of city life, the illusion which conceals the desert. "Silver sidewalks" also reminds us of Brathwaite's beautiful praise poem to Kumasi in *Masks,* which begins:

> city of gold,
> paved with silver,
> ivory altars,
> tables of horn,
> the morn-
> ing sun of
> seven hills
> greets you best,
>
> knows you blessed.

The Kumasi which Brathwaite addresses is one steeped in legend. It is the central city of the Ashanti eighteenth century empire, and Brathwaite's language as poet/okyeame is appropriately heraldic.

But there is more to it than this simple contrast between Kumasi and Kingston. Kumasi's wealth during its period of greatness was substantially due to the slave trade.[26] Its power was due to war and the subjugation of its equally bellicose neighbours, and its tendencies were, like its neighbours', mercantile and expansionist. Most of the wars concerned the control of the traffic in gold and slaves. Kumasi was, in short, a city/state on the brink of being absorbed into and corrupted by the same nascent and vigorously expanding capitalist economy that created the Caribbean, and through slavery led to Jamaica becoming the home of so many Akans of the diaspora. The entanglement of Africa in an aggressive European economic system which she was powerless to control, and the effect of this on African societies, is one of the themes of *Masks*. This is the unromantic reality behind or beneath the mask of old ceremonial.

Kingston, born just forty years before Osei Tutu established the Ashanti Confederation, has emerged as a shining example of the system which produced it – a "city of gold, paved with silver" for the merchant and the landlord. But the metaphors have lost all of their heraldic associations, and were beginning to lose them, as *Masks* showed, even in the Kumasi of Osei Tutu. Kumasi, at the green beginning of historic process, and Kingston at the dead end, both manifest an intestinal corruption endemic in the system which has engulfed them both. Thus silver is here, as in Conrad's *Nostromo*, a metaphor of "material interests" and betrayal; bullion, mercantilism, monopoly, usury, betrayal, the market values of the bourg.

The mountains, once an image of truth, stability and faith, are now evidence of the ecological rape carried out by the burghers of the silver sidewalks.

> the mountains have lost their battle of innocence
> invaded by cut stone and crooks

"Cut stone" suggests diamonds as well as the structures of the *nouveaux riches*, built at the price of the castration ("cut stone") of the city's proletariat. Such castration has its counterpart in the metaphor of rape which, confined to the landscape here, will soon extend to the country's daughters/ mothers. Castrated sons, violated daughters, submerged mothers.

The nature of the predicted revolution is immediately in question. On what positives will it be based when all the evidence points to a loss of contact with earlier revolutionary effort? Here revolt (Cuffy, Bogle) maroonage (Tacky) religious organisation (Bedward) and the sustained idea of an African international (Garvey) are all impossible. As in "Caliban" the source of demoralisation is the city.

> the city asphyxiates itself

> it has eaten too many daughters
> it has burnt too many hopes
> with candle, with kerosene,
> with charcoal, with cigarette,
> with the dead voices of carbon.

As in "Manchild", the city eats at the very source of future life, the daughters. The poem, as we have already seen, conceals multilayered metaphor under an apparent plainness of description. This is one of Brathwaite's favourite modes, and has led to a number of superficial interpretations of some of his work. A complementary tendency has been towards an apparent obscurity of metaphor, where the words yield their dimension only after the closest scrutiny. This occurs in the phrase "the dead voices of carbon", where the initially puzzling word is "voices". On examination, the dead voices become defunctive popular songs, which constitute the transient poetry of the city. "Carbon" is in this sense the material from which the records are made.

But there are the additional ideas of cigarette smoke, carbon monoxide from exhaust pipes, the charcoal fires of wayside vendors scuffling hopelessly to make ends meet. The result of this assault on the daughters (that is, the muses of creativity and new birth, the nation's anima) is that no fresh vision can emerge. All birth here is abortion.

> a new generation of clogged gutters
> eyes fragmented by louvres
> vision corrupted by crevices

"A new generation" normally means hope, but "clogged gutters" suggest pollution of mainstream/bloodstream/*sunsum*, absence of grace and the mire of unhope waiting to absorb the newly born. Slave mothers were known to abort or destroy their children rather than let them grow up in such a world.

"[E]yes fragmented by louvres" again blends the literal with the metaphorical. The actual picture is the real one of Kingston's citizenry walled up in their dread-shocked houses, peering out apprehensively at the more than half-expected intruder, gunman, rapist or duppy. The idea conveyed is that of the split vision, the schizophrenic eye of a half-primal, half-contemporary people. Glass and metal are generally associated in Brathwaite with the city, and we are made to feel the glass's edge slicing into the fragmented eye.

The final statement before the theme is repeated also concerns diseased and betrayed motherhood. Clinics become concentration camps. Images of potential sensuousness are all reversed. In face of this, the repeated declaration, "But there is goin' to be a revolution", is now less ominous and more desperate, and the question of what shape the revolution will assume becomes a more urgent one.

> the yout' talk about it all day long
> it is inhaled with every spliff

But that makes it opiate, ganja-dream, and brands it with the possibility of uncoordinated re/action.

In spite of this possibility, there are signs of growth in the music of the yout' which, since the mid-sixties, had begun to crackle with anticipated explosion. Max Romeo's "Babylon Burning" (1968); Prince Buster's "Pharoah House Crash" (1968-69), The Pioneer's "Starvation", The Kingstonians' "Sufferer" (1969), Niney's "Blood and Fire" (1969-70), Jimmy Cliff's "Suffering in the Land" (1970), and Bob Marley & the Wailers' "Duppy Conqueror" (1971) are a fair sample of the music of the yout' during the period in which "Springblade" took shape. Hence the revolution "detonates in every system" – the explosive drums and bass rumble of the megawatt sound system – as well as in everybody's inner mechanism, both of which were beginning to be controlled by the gigantic emergence of Marley, Tosh and the Wailers. "Those wailing virgin voices" are the sound of the real and metaphorical rape taking place daily in the city – the outcry of the violated daughters/country. It is also a peculiar phenomenon that a castrated falsetto has since the sixties become popular throughout the world of pop music, including some reggae. Violated daughters find their counterpart in castrated sons – and unisex emerges.

The sense of an inevitable revolution increases as issues are trivialised into toilet-bowl gossip, or ignored altogether by the establishment media. "The margarines ignore it". The "margarines" are the magazines/newspapers controlled by the coloured elite, who are skilled at buttering up the unpalatable truth. Omen ignored matures into irreversible fact. Thus the background music changes from the elegies of Drummond (1960-65) to the outcry of Marley against imprisonment of flesh and spirit ("the duppy is the conqueror/the resurrection of the dread"). "Dread" is the unburied duppy of history which returns like an evil force to possess the society of the present. Slavery and plantation history, unburied, unresolved, resurrect themselves in the rigid class stratification, the secretions of authoritarian contempt and smouldering subterranean revolt of the present.

The daughter, violated anew on "the mattress with its history of sweat", metamorphoses into an image of the country itself on the verge of uncontrollable explosion. The woman here is Kingston herself, Slade Hopkinson's "Mad Woman of Papine".

> her veins clogged with the gutters
> her flesh dry and blotched with the gullies
>
> her blood full of dry-river boulders
> varicose, blood clart...
> my mother gleams from the ghettoes

These images of drought perform the same function as in "Starvation". The qualities associated with both manhood and motherhood are clogged and restricted by the same severity of spiritual drought. The Jamaican expletive "blood clart" combines the ideas of a drying up of *mogya* and *sunsum* (blood clot), and abortion or rape (blood cloth). Beneath the surface plainness of the images lies the Akan concept of personality and heritage, to which Brathwaite frequently refers in order to understand the transformation of West African sensibility under the pressures of transportation, slavery and their attendant systems of cultural control. As Danquah puts it:

> ... the Akan maintain that each individual is made up of three constituent factors: (i) blood (mogya), derived from his mother: (ii) an individual personality the 'personality-soul' (sunsum) derived from his father, and (iii) a life-soul' (kra), a divine spark which is associated with the life principle, identified with blood, derived from the moon, or later, one of the planets.[27]

In "Springblade", Brathwaite examines the results of a process of historic disruption, which has affected the balance between male and female and divine principles in the diasporan person.

The final stage of this process is arrived at in the mother's madness; the gleam in her eye; the fixed idea in which the will to throw stone or bomb, the fingers grasping those instruments of destruction and the instruments themselves are inseparably fused.

> her fingers cannot unhook
> from her will, they cannot unhood
>
> your compassion
> she will kill you tomorrow in a passion
> of wicks, she will toss the first brick, the first
> bomb...

Such was Brathwaite's description of the state of sensibility in Jamaica some months before the 1972 elections. In "Springblade", these impending elections provide the most dreadful omen of brutalisation of the anima. Political and sexual corruption go hand in hand. The police, indispensable to the preservation of the balance of terror, are themselves the instruments of corruption. Hence they are associated – like the politicians they serve – with the rape of the city's daughters, whose wailing "blue siren" voices merge with "wailing virgin voices" of an earlier line. The voices of the violated daughters and the castrated sons blend to create a music of prophecy which foretells, to all those who have not, like Ulysses' crew, deafened their ears with wax, coming disaster.

It is these voices which introduce the second type of omen. So far we have been dealing with that level of omen where ordinary reality becomes charged with extraordinary significance, and we have been noting the impact of this on Brathwaite's language, which alternates between surface realism and multilayered metaphor. Now Brathwaite is about to deal with omens of a more subliminal sort; omens which are the result of the penetration of the marvellous or non-rational into the world of normal reality. "Now the crippled omens arrive on crutches of rumour". These omens, though crippled, aren't the gift of Legba, the god of all beginning. They open no barriers, provide no answers to the riddle of the crossroads.

The first omen is a dream of the suicide of the city's daughters, venereally contaminated even in virginity – ("o syphilitic maidenhead") – and ultimately reduced to hysterical, disappointed brides. This omen suggests the failure of conventional religion, the collapse of its myths and symbols. No immaculate conception is possible here. No Christ will be borne, no second Adam of the New World, for no Mary exists to bear him. No divine bridegroom will arrive with his traditional gift of healing love and reconciling marriage.

The second omen follows from the first. It is an omen of death, guilt, judgement and retribution, and has been mentioned before in "Starvation" – the legend of the coffin with its three crows, a ghostly commission of enquiry into the nation's unforgivable crimes. Such a projection from the folk collective unconscious indicates the intensity of the popular dream of justice; a dream which, like that of the old Hebrew prophets or St. John the Divine, encompasses the final catastrophic destruction of the kingdom of this world.

There is, as in Mais's *The Hills Were Joyful Together,* the recurring need for miracle ("the loaves and the fishes") to feed the country's multitudes. But here the miracles work backwards. Water is not converted to wine here: wine turns instead to vinegar – a crucifixion image. The wedding songs of Cana become the outcry on Calvary, "I thirst". The Bolom, aborted foetus unable to be born, caught in limbo and doing the devil's bidding, becomes our most appropriate metaphor. He carries "messages from dead of wombs": he is the voice of the aborted muse, the nation's murdered or submerged conscience still trying to communicate from beyond the grave. Derek Walcott in *Ti Jean and His Brothers,* a 1958 play, revised and revived in 1970 and produced in Jamaica in 1971, brilliantly explored and extended the Bolom myth of St. Lucia. That play must have been at the forefront of Brathwaite's mind at the time of the composition of "Springblade".

It is at this point that the second reference to "the duppy conqueror" is made. This seminal Bob Marley composition raises an interesting question. Why does reggae at precisely this moment (1970-71) begin to delve into myth and folklore, the singer seeing himself as pitted against a diabolical system ("duppy") and claiming the powers of the traditional myal man (i.e. the duppy conqueror)?[28] It was at moments of extreme social stress that myalism emerged in Jamaica and claimed powers to confront a perverted obeah. Mais's *Brother Man* is a contemporary projection of the traditional conflict between myalism and obeah, Brother Man and Brother Ambo.

After this catalogue of omens, the mood of the poem shifts to one of elegiac lament as the poet contemplates what might have been, had the Caribbean fulfilled its potential of "green growing on green". The "psychedelic" culture of the youth is viewed as a betrayal of the effort, suffering and labour of the past, which has hindered our own attempts at a beginning ("big/inning"). A big inning requires patience, skill, application and tenacity of purpose, all of which Brathwaite, at this moment of gloom, sees as lacking in his people. The only possibility exists in what might have been:

And yet we could have had them: sons, dreamers
lovers
but we refused to see them
burned blind mirrors to them

depriving them of shadows
sucking them soulless
no broken shell in the history of generations, spill
less

What is lost, what is still sought even in this faint hope of what might have been, is the absentee bridegroom and lover, the rebirth of dream and compassion within the male psyche – the restitution of the disinherited anima.

"Springblade", we are reminded, is about the pitilessness of Kingston's yout' and the barbarity of the political leaders who manipulate them; the processes by which they lost compassion – whether they functioned on the side of authority (policemen) or on the side of revolt (rude bwoys). It is therefore about a tragically vitiated ethic of manhood, which seeks its fulfilment in rape and murder. The springblade in this respect is a perverted phallic symbol, as well as the rapist's favourite weapon.

This reduction of "mabrak" to the "psychedelic flashes of madmen" is the result, according to Brathwaite, of having blinded our vision to our own past. As in African philosophies, the past is not conceived of as an abstraction, as a series of remote events termed "History", but as the dead, the now inert life-force of the ancestors. Brathwaite alludes to the "catching the shadow" ritual which used to be part of Pukkumina/Zion Revivalist practice. One had to capture the spirit of the dead in clear water to ensure its final release from earth. The spirit thus released could work positively in the lives of the living. Otherwise, it hovered in a limbo from which it could be enslaved by obeah-men and forced to do their bidding. It was also believed that some obeah-men had the power to capture one's shadow even when one was alive, and only the myal man knew how to cure such shadow loss.[29]

Brathwaite is, of course, interested in the metaphorical potential of this ritual, rather than in its literal aspect. He sees us as having functioned like perverse obeah-men who have captured the shadows (souls) of our own children, and left them without vision. They have become zombies ("soulless"), without any possibility of regeneration, of being egg or secreting semen ("spill-less"). But since our children's "shadows" are extensions of ourselves – mother's blood *(mogya)* and father's *sunsum* – to render our children shadowless is to betray ourselves in the worst sort of way, and to render ourselves incapable of a future.

Brathwaite thus sees the Caribbean failure as being the same as that of the ruined American Calibans of "Glass", who have been unable to develop a sense of history as a living link of generations. He feels that we could have established that link, not only in terms of knowing how people lived and what they did in the past – (academic textbook history) – but by fulfilling their example through and in the pattern of our lives in the present.

> But their resurrection could have been of real flesh
> they could have burned seed to unshifting future

For Brathwaite, past life-force is handed down as a secret inner bequest of spirit, impregnating the present moment like the orgasmic shock of semen, and creating a grounded ("unshifting") and pregnant future.

Here, for the first time in the poem, the sexual metaphor is employed in a positive way, but only to describe what might have been and thus to deepen one's sense of the destitution of the present.

> We could have had these children...
>
> We could have rendered them painfully,
> respecting themselves through their fathers,
> surrendering themselves to their grandmothers'
> visions

The words "rendered them painfully" recall the phrase "twisted into prayer" ("Conqueror") and are a warning that though it would not have been easy, it would still have been possible to have had these children. The Akan ideal of a balance between male, female and divine essences in the psyche of the newborn child is again being alluded to here. It is precisely the loss of this balance, the castration of the male, the violation of the female and the attenuation of the divine that has concerned Brathwaite in these poems. This loss of balance is reflected in what is sometimes termed the male/female conflict in the Caribbean, which is characterised by anti-feminism in the man[30] and subterranean or overt contempt in the woman.[31]

If at the deepest level the life-force of the past is transmitted as a secret inner bequest, on a more superficial level it is done externally and consciously through oral tradition ("the tales of their ancestors"), legend, history book.

But such external history and folklore are really the visible manifestations of those inner and spiritual processes whereby an entire lifestyle and vision of the world – the *mogya, kra* and *sunsum,* the intimate soul-vibrations of particular peoples – are transmitted from generation to generation.

Brathwaite believes that the Caribbean people have cut themselves off from their source of deepest nourishment ("negating the nipple/that pout of love"). And having rendered their children soulless they:

> set them up here some to build crazy
> palaces, imperial shops, super
> markets that have become cages

The phrase "set them up" suggests betrayal as well as the act of establishment. "Supermarkets" indicates that the imperial values of the market sit above (super) everything else. But like the "crazy palaces", these supermarkets, today's Great Houses and the values they represent, have become prisons of the spirit, as well as refuges from the now equally crazy denizens of the shanties. Such are the two Jamaicas, two variants of lunacy, separated by the dry gully about whose symbolic significance we should now be clear.[32]

The poem ends with a vision of "dread" which can now be seen as the logical relationship between the two Jamaicas, whose separating chasm is bridged only by the violence of flash flood. "Revolution" here is perpetual, since the class issues have never been resolved. So long as the Duppy remains the conqueror, dread will always have its season of resurrection.

> ... repeat
> ing itself like yes like yes-
> terday with its sores, with its
> old scores
> to pay, with its rope, with its hope
>
> of revolution

Here the sense of "revolution" Jamaican style as a going around in circles, is strong. If the hoped-for revolution is predictably a repetition of the past, then it will also be a repeat of past failure. This is a recurring problem in Brathwaite – that of breaking history's cycle of apparent futility. Here he has posed his positives in terms of what might have been, but in this withering descent into the drought of contemporary (1971) Jamaica, the poet does not flatter himself with the slightest hope that what might have been is what can or shall be. Both the omen and the testimony are dread. Regrettably, in the bloody elections of 1980, the omen hardened into fact and the testimony achieved the stature of prophecy.

Part Three
(*Flowers of the Harmattan*)

So far this essay has concentrated on two dominant themes of *Black + Blues:* the predicament of marginalised and disinherited youth in cities incapable of sustaining them, and the situation of the creative mind in a turbulent landscape. Our focus here will be on three interrelated concerns: (i) the wasted potential of alienated labour, maimed by the machinery of the "status crow"; (ii) the possibility of a comprehensive revolution of the oppressed, based on a rediscovery, awakening and unleashing of their hitherto suppressed or passively dormant capacities and energies, and (iii) the problem of conscience and consciousness, the viability of the muse in the midst of spiritual and physical malnutrition.

Krow

The poem "Krow" is a cousin of Ted Hughes's "Crow", which Brathwaite in an early version of "The Love Axe/1"[33] mentions as a poem that defines without explaining the spiritually devastated condition of Europe. Brathwaite himself attributes this condition to Europe's having karmically absorbed into its system the dereliction which it has spread throughout the world. Hughes's "Crow" hovers in an atmosphere of impending holocaust. Brathwaite, too, is fascinated by this deathscape, and the possibility that the immense necrophilic power-structure that is Western Europe, North America and the Soviet Union, will eventually devour the carcass of the entire world.

The poem "Krow" is about South Africa whose system of racism, wage slavery and militarism is the poisonous fruit of some of the worst excesses of Western capitalism. It is constructed around two portraits: one of the founding father of the modern apartheid state, Paul Kruger, whose name is spelt Kreuger, so that its first syllable sounds more like "Krow" the other of the people whose labour has made possible the kingdom that Kruger rules. The portrait of Kruger, who in old age had grown gross and diseased, suggests decay and defeat beneath the mask of imperial control, the emptiness and spiritual nakedness of the conquistador, caught in a moment of diseased repose.

> Kreuger in his chair stark
> naked in his clothes, the hammer
>
> blow from blue fists soft
> as milk, open as a vice,
> a victory of cards collapsed

The focus then shifts to the workers, whose nameless labour is unrewarded ordeal, and whose fate is one of constant reduction, a burning-out and melting-down.

> sweat: fat fed like a flame
> on a wick of bone without name

"Krow" is "Work" spelt backwards, suggesting here the defilement of labour; the reversal of a fundamental principle and right. Unredeemed labour, the dialectical opposite of decadent power, is so thoroughly controlled by the oppressive system that it can barely dream of revolt.

> the fires rustle dreams only
> there is no light, no heat
> of destruction of wood

Lacking revolutionary zeal and deprived of vision (candlelight, "eyes of the vegetable oil"), exploited labour fulfils a purposeless round in which rest and work are two sides of the same coin, "liot instead of toil". The word "liot" does not exist except as the meaningless reversal of the word "toil", just as the word "krow" is the meaningless reversal, the hollowing-out of the word "work". If repose for Kreuger/Unprospero reveals an unhealthy grossness, repose for Caliban is part of, rather than release from, the bovine ménage.

Just as Kreuger's portrait suggests in the slow decay of fat flesh, the decadence of a structure based on pure materialism and vulturine greed, that of the alienated worker describes a gradual, horrible drying up, a spread of slow ruin.

>   clott-
> ing cobwebs growing into the corners
> of glass; nests
> of haemorrhage crowing in the grey brain: cap-
> illaries drying out drying out drying out, turn-
> ing to straw, stretched with the lack of rain

The images of dried-out bloodstream and cobwebbed vision, convey the central Brathwaite idea of the atrophied *mogya, kra* and *sunsum,* the dried-out bloodline of spirit. This death, this drying-up of *sunsum,* is Krow's most withering bequest to the primal peoples whose lives he has invaded. It is today most disastrously evident in the arid townships and sterile, starving "homelands" to which apartheid has condemned millions of used-up and discarded Black workers. But it is as old as the collision of Western Atlantic civilisation with the New World. This is how Brathwaite describes his conception of that catastrophe:

> The draining of the lake of Mexico... How many of us recognise that that is what happens when the stain of civilisation, the deterioration of Rome, reaches the New World? Montezuma, Tenochtitlan, Mexico City on a plateau. It is a confrontation of Mount Blanc. Mexico represents a

challenge to Europe. The Aztecs represent people as great as Caesar. What did Caesar do in the confrontation? The most terrible single action known to me: the draining of the lake of Mexico: complete extermination of culture, not only of people, but of their environment. A city on a lake is now a city in a dust bowl, the complete configuration altered.[34]

Thus we have all those images of the dry river, the gully, the desert; which are paralleled by the microcosmic images of blood-clot, dried-out arteries, dry brain-coral, "the ducts and factories sucking the rivers out" ("Coral").

Yet at this point, the poem suddenly turns. The human spirit is not defeated by Krow's mangling machinery. Miraculously, it not only survives, it stubbornly understands.

> and his stubborn understanding of this pain
> his fingers growing out of the knives of tractors
> his wrists crushed and clattered
>
> but the dream still/born, still alive in the fire.

The aborted, "stillborn" bolom dream is replaced by the dream which resurrects itself, in spite of all. "Still" and "born" taken as two separate adjectives suggest that the dream is simultaneously asleep and alive. They capture the wavering hope of this moment of transition, and move the poem forward to the affirmative "still alive in the fire", where "still" connotes continuity right up to the present time. The dream is still alive only because it never really died.

Harmattan Poems
1970-1975

"Sun Song", placed in *Black +Blues* at the end of the drought sequence, that is, immediately after "Springblade", was originally one of a sequence of "Harmattan Poems", dated April/August 1970 and published in *Black Orpheus*.[35] The poems in that sequence were "Spirit", "Kite", "Shak", "Sun Song/1", "Sun Song/2", "Suman" and "Crab". "Suman", "Shak" and "Sun Song/1" are omitted from *Black + Blues,* and the integrity of the original sequence of "Harmattan Poems" is thus lost.

In *Black + Blues,* "Sun Song" could easily have come after "Krow". Its central images are sun, drought and fire. Like "Spirit", it seeks to identify a hitherto invisible African presence in the Caribbean, whose symbol is the harmattan, the hot wind from the Sahara whose jet stream of fine dust sometimes carries across the Atlantic, twinning the skeletons of Ethiopia and the Sahel with those of Kingston and Haiti. In the Caribbean, the harmattan has, until recently been, like all things African, an unacknowledged presence, but for Brathwaite, who identified the dust long before the American weather satellite, it has become a major metaphor of that something "felt in the blood" which he has tried to communicate. As he said in 1975,

> Africa is being burnt by drought from the Sahara, and it is burning us too. It's the same wind, part of the whole, and unless we can absorb and understand that, we do not understand anything. When that wind blows, I can feel it in my nostrils and on the skin. You know that wind comes from somewhere. It is not just an accident. When you see the sunsets on the evening, those red sunsets, what do you think you're looking at but DUST. You're looking at DUST. [36]

That dust mingles with the dry season in the Caribbean, so that it helps produce a fire, not only of red sunsets, but of flowers: cassia, hibiscus, bougainvillaea, the burnt red leaves of the almond, which fall in February and March. The harmattan rides through the Caribbean between Christmas and Easter, Nativity and Resurrection. Brathwaite's "Harmattan Poems" are about this intersection of seasons, the marriage of Sahara and the Caribbean archipelago, the mergence not only of two landscapes but also of two modes of being and seeing, in the psyche of the poet. This mergence manifests itself in a quest for new metaphors, similar to the one undertaken in *Islands,* but by means of processes more difficult to follow.

Brathwaite's new metaphors are rooted simultaneously in a West Indian and a West African framework. For example, the central presence, the spirit which pervades the "Harmattan Poems", is the harmattan itself. It is associated with the ideas of desert, spiritual wilderness, dry season of the soul, wasteland, dearth of poetic inspiration. Since, however, dry season in the Caribbean is the time when canes mature and flower and most of our flowering trees are ablaze, it is not necessarily a time of despair at all. Ours is not the unchanging drought of the desert, but an interlude in the tropical shift and cycle of seasons. Harmattan precedes hurricane.

In addition, the Caribbean croptime drought has traditionally been associated with the canefires of rebellion (Cannes Brulées); or with bush fires which wreak considerable devastation; and sometimes with fires deliberately set by those who deforest and ravage our hills. The colour red predominates in drought, and can be seen in almond leaves, ripened fruit, flowers and fires. Hence, in the "Harmattan Poems", Brathwaite is preoccupied with the colour red, blood and fire and flower. Since Lent and Easter are both in the dry season, we have (as in Salkey's *A Quality of Violence*), the Christian concepts of wilderness, spiritual testing, the confrontation with the devil in the guise of Krow, or Judge Dread ("Dred"); sacrifice, imprisonment, crucifixion, and resurrection. Sacrifice and imprisonment are movingly explored in the beautiful and harrowing testimony, "Good Friday 1975: Kingston in the Kingdom of This World",[37] where the imprisoned prophet and muse cries out against Krow's systematic imprisonment of the human spirit, not only in Kingston where children have been fed to flames, but also in the kingdom of this world of "the status crow".

Good Friday, grim as it is in Kingston or Soweto, is still prelude to Easter, the season when the kite ceases to be a crow and becomes a symbol of the resurrection of Man/God. In "Kite", one of the "Harmattan Poems", the kite is crucified man, scarecrow, skeleton; yet it sings, soars, celebrates and dances at the end of its string. It resembles the bird and butterfly images which pervade *The Arrivants,* and is an example of how, by pointing a way out of the Slough of Despond, the "Harmattan Poems" counterpoint the desolation of poems such as "Bread", which is about hunger and the ordeal of creative conscience in a driven landscape of starvation; "Krow", which is about the reversal of Work as a creator of meaning and a validator of human existence, or "Labourer" which is about the mangling of a man's hands by the factory; the crippling of proletarian creative capacity into an inability to work or make the harmattan. Poems do this by celebrating the variety of ways in which the sensibility is nurtured and the secret means by which it grows; by reaffirming the principle of movement and growth in spite of; by asserting the connection between drought and renewal. They enact renewal in that they are metaphors of the process of making, showing how the New World sensibility synthesises and transforms the most disparate experiences, nurturing itself on the transmigration and intermarriage of images and concepts, the interweaving of the dry air currents of the spirit.

Sun Song: Shango

"Sun Song" is the most obviously political of the "Harmattan Poems". Its first eighteen lines are a memorable evocation of the sights, sounds and feel of drought. The opening line, "The drought has burned my tropic" first appeared as "The drought has burned my topic". One senses that both ideas are intended, and that the fire which is central in the poem is both internal and external. The poem, in fact, describes a journey from the external images of drought to a realisation of their inner significance. Brathwaite's drought has an almost ethereal quality, which is conveyed by images of gossamer fragility such as "termites' wings", "spindles", "grasshopper husks". There is also the delicate use of sound-echo in

> I walk the streets of easter's april
> welcomed by crickets
> the creak of cicada, grass dry as grasshopper husks

where we can almost hear the dryness in the thin sounds of insects. Water exists as mirage, or dream of torrent, the inverse of Harris's waterfalls and rivers: "kaieteur's curved crashing to dryness". We are then, at the heart of dryness.

The external drought with its memory of rain, points us to the state of interior expectancy, of waiting, which is prelude to the act of making or doing or commitment. The image of the stripped tree, prevalent in Brathwaite since *The Arrivants*, where it is generally associated with the despoliated tribe, surfaces here. Here, however, it is invested with hope and becomes a totem to which the poet addresses his prayer.

> deliver me cold skeleton
> branched like bare trees
>
> for journeys lit by stars
> my bones sing with dry honeycombs
> bees burrow in cinders and ash

The prayer is for deliverance, not from anything, but for night journeys, descents into self and memory. A great spirit of imminence pervades these "Harmattan Poems", which are the true foreparents of *Mother Poem*. It is the spirit of new songs about to be sung, of new shapes about to be released, of new language which, heavy on the tongue since "Eating the Dead", is now about to be born. The "songs of the skeleton" are being sung. Ezekiel's dry bones, cold since Eliot revived them in "Ash Wednesday", are invested with new life. There is also an allusion to "the bees in my blood's buzzing brain of memory" of "Negus". These bees, possible relatives of the honeybees which Yeats once entreated to "build in the empty nest of the stare", are an image of the poetic imagination which creates its own song and sweetness even in the city's cinders and ash, even among "the dead voices of carbon" ("Springblade").

Brathwaite saw this capacity for new song as the result of the sense of wholeness of heritage which had already given birth to *The Arrivants*. He identifies the source of his confidence in "Suman", which begins:

> Something is happening out of my eyes
> issuing streams and feathers
> a bird's wing flaps
> leaves glitter
>
> something is flickering out of my loins
> prayers, rock-steady tunes, blues
> the sunlight stops
> hope filters

The basis of this hope is his now grounded grasp of both a great heritage of African craftsmanship ("gold-weights of chameleons, lizards/bronze slipping from crucible copper") and a humane "little" tradition of religion, of something rooted, essential and earthy, imaged by clay, mud-hut, goblet. This knowledge of ground will be *suman*, talisman, protection against the spiritual bleakness which surrounds him.

"Sun Song" goes beyond "Suman" in that it grows out of an acceptance of the drought itself as an omen of impending rebirth. The dry desert wind becomes presence, spirit and muse, possessing the poet with its creative/destructive force.

> on its black crest of flesh
> the harmattan rides
> the flowers return to the fire

The ambiguous nature of this resurrected god is suggested in the dual images which depict the bush fires. The flames resemble "ears of grass", petals, even water, their opposite.

> ears of grass grow out of the crackles of paper
> rips grope where the petalled heat passes
> liquid the roar, liquid the yellow clearing
>
> consuming itself, the mouth eats air
> the dark identifies itself with every gape
> and flaring

There may be some significance in the fact that the fire consumes itself, that is, either "burns with its own energy", or, fuelled by air, "burns itself out". This fire signals the rebirth of Ogun/Shango, the lost gods of iron, fire, thunder and revolution, towards whose rediscovery *Islands* tortuously moves. The impact of the Black revolution is that Blacks begin to claim their blackness, to identify themselves. Yet the words "grope" and "gape", the latter of which refers to the open "mouth" of the fire, hint that there may be something suspect in the sudden spontaneous combustion of the skeletal landscape.

In spite of this, the gods of fire are invoked, summoned, called out of their dormancy; while the thunderstorm and hurricane, which usually succeed the Caribbean drought, are earnestly entreated to come and cleanse the land. There is, on the whole, far less doubt here than in *The Arrivants* about the necessity for, or inevitability of violent revolutionary confrontation with "the status crow". *Black + Blues,* as we have shown, grows out of the apparent hopelessness of the Jamaican situation, where drought is the reasonless drought of an unrelieved penury, of a malnutrition of body and spirit. If in "Springblade" it was the mother/muse who first went mad, here it is the child.

> craze eyed the child grows thin with thirsty
>   knowledge
> where shall his history permit my cup of penitence
>   to drip

It is this recurrent spectacle of doomed youth going slowly mad, of a peasantry little better than their own limping cattle, and of the helpless penitence of a privileged elite, among whom the poet numbers himself, which convinces the poet that the true creative possibility of his society will not be released until the people are freed from their history of hunger. The "pregnant humus" of the ground of being secretes a time bomb, whose detonation alone can create the atmosphere in which the poet can free himself of the dross of flesh, materialism and the "musty corner stones" of despair and death, and dance. It is with this realisation that he repeats the invocation to the spirit of the fire. It should be noted, though, that the fire at the end of the poem is "olodumare's conflagration", the creative spirit of God. It is a "red river of reflection", which, like the "holy fire" in Yeats's "Sailing to Byzantium", is the medium in which the ancestral sages now reside. Hence:

> i summon you from trees
> from ancient memories
> from the uncurling ashes of the dead
>
> that we may all be cleansed

The impact of the spirit of the harmattan, then, is to transform even as it destroys the trashy twittering world. In "Shango", the apocalyptic nature of the emerging god becomes clearer. This poem's epigraph ominously states that: "the god Shango was conceived in love and rises to destroy the world". The poem traces the journey from pristine love towards the destruction of the world. Between the love in which Shango (like Christ) was conceived and his ultimate manifestation (like the Christ of "Revelation") as an apocalyptic world-breaker, lies human history – that is the history of conquest, empire, violation, genocide and holocaust at whose price "progress" and "civilisation" have been won.

Shango here is not just the Yoruba deity; he is the history of the African presence in its encounter with the Western world; and the African presence, the Nummo of *Sun Poem,* is in its turn more widely representative of broad categories of being such as: the primal vision; Adamic man; radical innocence, that firstness of being which Brathwaite would later term NAM. Shango's experience of history in this encounter with the West is presented as constant loss, bruise, debasement and ordeal. He is the eternal scapegoat, but represents, in his various manifestations throughout the poem, the resurgent spirit of all the victims of history, including those whose crushed lives have been the subject of *Black + Blues.*

What is both frightening and hopeful about him is the resilience that he has developed; a sensibility which neither forgives nor forgets, but rather absorbs, lives through, and endures the twists and abortions of history. "He embraces them all" and emerges beyond them as a still living, but utterly unknown and incredible omen, the more terrifying for having survived.

> after so many turns
> after so many failures
> touch him

> he smiles
> hold him
> he rages
>
> murder him
> he shatters you
>
> your thunder has come home

Shango, finally, is the duppy of man's oppressive history and his destruction of the world is a return to its monstrous source of all the terror that has historically been visited on the oppressed. The final line of the poem, "Your thunder has come home", appeared in an earlier version as "your terror has come home".[38]

Kite

"Shango" represents an alternative possibility to the hopelessness of "Springblade". It suggests that at the imagined end of things energy and authentic personhood will not only have survived but will continuously have resurrected themselves to shatter the structures of oppression. "Kite", which precedes "Shango" in this collection, is a celebration of the triumphant resurrection of spirit from the dross of history. It differs from "Shango" in that while "Shango" moves inevitably towards headlong encounter with and prophesied destruction of the kingdom of this world, "Kite" seems to envision a state beyond catastrophe where the battered human spirit breaks free and soars in flight.

"Shango" hints at the paradox – some would argue, the impossibility – of restoring love by means of violence; of releasing creativity by means of apocalyptic destruction; of imagining a new beginning beyond the end of things. In "Kite", paradox remains and is explored in a series of ambiguous images. The chief of these is the kite itself, a flying skeleton; Krow aloft ("scarecrow of flight"); the inhuman conquistador principle perpetually on the wing, cradling in its talons bullet and neutron bomb, spreading murder and waste in the name of love ("valentine of blood").

On the other hand, the kite is a resurrection symbol; man's retrieval and recreation of his sense of the sacred and humane after the holocaust. Such is the implication of the lines:

> and the kite
> torn glass
> broken collar
> of the tribe's
> worn surrogate of god
> flying

The faith to believe that such rebirth remains perennially possible is difficult to sustain. It is, however, crucial, and has been one of the most extraordinary aspects of ordinary human life anywhere. Where it has ceased to exist, one has had sterile nihilism, the cold, cranial landscape of what Brathwaite has termed "unman" and Anthony McNeill "ungod". Against the archetype of reduced scarecrow man, cripple and mimic man, Brathwaite places that of the unshackled human spirit ("broken collar"): the emancipated divinity of man whose resurrection is the eternal responsibility of poet, prophet, shaman and singer.

Harris, in his seminal essay, "The Question of Form and Realism in the West Indian Artist",[39] observes that although artists may begin with a vision of the reduced man, they must:

> move that diminished creature through [their] work in a manner that is disturbing, so disturbing that vitality and power are realised as a very strong possibility...

Brathwaite, despite his consistent focus on images of human dereliction, shares in this aesthetics of hope, vitality and redemption, which may turn out to be the most valuable gift that the New World can offer the old.

Crab

We have been exploring the highly experimental poetry of a period of ferment, of the crystallisation of image and idea in the crucible of language. The poem becomes a kind of cryptic shorthand, hieroglyph and riddle of ambiguous process. Hence those laconic listings of word-images, the disrupted syntax, elisions, the frequent hiatuses between ideas, on the one hand, and the fluid association of ideas, images and word-echoes, on the other. At the same time, Brathwaite has retained his rhetorical style, which is fully evident in the monologues, those poems of the voice which some commentators have termed "public" poetry.

"Crab", first published as "Conqueror",[40] was the last of the original "Harmattan Poems". It is also part of a family of "Crab" poems whose genealogy might be traced from Lamming's *In the Castle of My Skin,* through Derek Walcott's "Sea Crab", Faustin Charles's *Crab Track* and many others. We see in Brathwaite's "Crab" the tendency, strong since *Islands* but implicit much earlier in his work, for images to beget other images; to split in several directions; to work with a wild energy, as well as with their own peculiarly cerebral logic. This I have called the poetry of fission, and viewed as the product of several fierce urgencies alive in Caribbean societies.

There is, first of all, the political urgency, which in Jamaica takes its most distressing form in the violence engendered through the confrontation of the legalised aggressiveness of the State, and endemic rebellion of the urban dispossessed. Such violence has an intensified effect on the spirit, because of the small island space into which it is compressed. There is "the abysmal vortex of change" in which these islands are caught. There is also the evidence of a phenomenal capacity for energy within the people. Many of our writers – particularly the Lamming of *Season of Adventure* – feel this energy; but, as Brathwaite shows in "Caliban", it is wasted rather than contained in any mold. Or it implodes like hot coals in the furnace of a locomotive, creating what Martin Carter once termed, "the strange combustion of my days". All of these things: political urgency, endemic violence, vortex of change and the people's innate life-force, give some of our new poetry – McNeill's *Credences at the Altar of Cloud* or Le Roy Clarke's *Douens* – its wild weird visionary shape, its unruliness of word. "Crab" attempts through imagery to summarise the process which brought the writing to this pass.

"Crab" is a vast summing up both of Brathwaite's journey through *Black + Blues* and the journey of Caribbean peoples through the twists and changes of history. The crab existed before the coconut took root. In the very first poem of this collection, "Fetish", we are told that "the mailed horn of the crab/was our earliest conqueror". The crab, like the spider, cripple, limbo dancer or snail of *Islands,* is the sensibility of poet, race and all the peoples. It is amphibious, born of sea and land like the people, and an apt symbol for that transition from geological to historical time which is part of the subject of *Black + Blues* and "Coral". Its journey will, therefore, be the path which the poet's sensibility has traversed, not only in this book, but from the beginning of his career as a serious poet and historian. The crab is the poem which the poet follows on its slow zig-zag journey that parallels the poet's wayward reverie as he contemplates and reclaims the past. It is the image which is created by and issues from his cramped hand.

Conventionally, the image of the guide into the unconscious is either the ghost of another poet – Dante invoked Virgil – or a bird, a spirit of the air where imagination is supposed to dwell. But in "Crab", the unconscious is thought of as ground, so the crab or the snail[41] is a more appropriate guide than the humming bird. The crab lives in the earth and knows his ground. The poem begins:

> from this cramped hand
> crippled by candlelight
> a crab scuttles

The alliteration links key words. The hand is cramped in the position of writing and because it is tired from so much writing. It is possible that the poet considers himself to be fixed in a single attitude, one type of writing – the paralysed inertia which sometimes comes over writers after a great creative effort. "Crippled" extends the meaning of "cramped" by suggesting arthritis. Given the significance of the hand in Brathwaite's poetry as an image of working, making, creating, moulding, carving or weaving, "crippled" connotes the paralysed colonial sensibility. Brathwaite makes the point that his maimed Barbadian peasant who appears as "Labourer" in *Black + Blues* and as "my father" in the "Milkweed" sequence of *Mother Poem* is:

> not simply a bajan labourer, he is a person caught in the centre of an explosion – a catastrophe – a cultural catastrophe – which this region was/is the matrix (axle) of. And all those broken fingers, the ratchets... all those images there are not only the images of contemporary exploitative technology, but are engines of a much wider cycle of destiny.[42]

On the other hand, the "cripple" has been associated in Brathwaite with Legba, the god of beginning, the pathfinder to the underworld. So the cripple is still creator; here an exhausted one, yet one whose end is perceived of as perpetual beginning and renewal.

"Candlelight" suggests that the poet sees his vision as uncertain; the light of a candle isn't particularly strong. The candle casts the shadow of the poet's hand on the page. It is this shadow, its fingers legs, that scuttles across the page and becomes the crab. So literally the crab issues from the poet's hand and from his vision's uncertain light. Its first period of recall is the age of conquest and conquistadors, hence the reference to armour, the clenched mailed fist of the conqueror, and the near obliteration of those civilisations – Arawak, Carib, Akawaio, "the lame mango leaves" – which, unable to resist, were either crippled or wiped out. The memory of their murder still shrieks with the ciçadas in the noontide forests. The phrase, "lions of grasshopper voices", seems contrived. The probable implication is that the lions of Africa, that is, the finest elements of its civilisation, shared the same grasshopper fate at the same time as the Mesoamerican peoples. That past of multiple genocide hibernates in the dried capillaries of the fossil, awaiting its appropriate tomorrow, when the mild-mannered, rocking-chair ancestors, recalled and ingathered at the Ceremony of Souls, will join the shriek of the lost tribes of forest and middle passage ("the trees' seas"). When we reconnect with these ancestors through the "contemplation [that] restores them to our time" ("Fetish") a need to enact their submerged rebellion might well be born in us.

Writing in the Jamaica of 1970, Brathwaite could already intuit the "murderous tomorrows" of springblade and ratchet and gun that the immediate future became. The omens of this future were already alive in the covert protests of Tom and Jemima. Today, in the 1990s, that intuited future has become the Caribbean present. There are more murders everywhere.

The next six lines focus on the poet on the verge of making, head filled with half-perceived dreams, ideas and images, moments of inspiration as fleeting and perhaps as insubstantial as the "fishes of birds" which he has been observing all day through crystal. Since birds and fish and indeed, flying-fish have all appeared in *The Arrivants* as images connected with the creative process, Brathwaite is certainly referring to himself in the process of making.

> and alone, my hand following
> the crab's poem, stalked
> the inheriting ghosts

To follow the crab's poem is to write with freedom, following the images wherever they lead, with the purposeful waywardness of the crab. This idea comes from Walcott's "Sea-Crab" while the notion of the "inheriting ghosts" may derive from Eliot's "Burnt Norton". When Eliot, following, not a crab, but "the deception of the thrush", the elusive and untrustworthy bird/guide of inspiration, encountered his ancestors or whatever ghosts cared to inhabit the dry inner emptiness of his garden, he was urgently entreated by the bird to avoid looking too deeply into the disillusioning reality of the self and the past ("Go, go, go, said the bird: human kind/ Cannot bear very much reality.")[43] For Brathwaite the encounter with the ancestral ghosts is far less traumatic. His ghosts are the fragments of a legend of history, which he seeks to piece together into a coherent pattern. The rest of "Crab", therefore, is a summary of how his ideas of history have developed since his return to the archipelago, as well as an examination of currents in West Indian literature during the period.

The crab's shell of memory contains the experience of encounter and conquest (sharks, white beach, filed teeth): the hardening of a vast and complex ancestral heritage ("continent of dreams") into the tough pebble of his island: the shrivelling of the ground of being and the drying up the pool of consciousness.

> pebbles became my continent of dreams
> i was content with shallow water:
> here my feet dipped
> fishing the circles of its pale fragmented mirror

Writing without a basis in an ancestral heritage, without memory, he begins his poetic career by merely paddling in the puddles by the river of history. As fisherman, he throws his feeler lines into the pool of consciousness, but finds that the river's mirror is both "pale" and "fragmented". This is so because the mirror reflects only Europe, much of whose historical record of Africa was designed to negate African personhood. The colonial sensibility, schooled into a deep self-scorn, is entrapped in the pale circles, self-alienated not only from Other, but from the several shifting fragments of its own image caught in a broken mirror.

But the colonial mind soon revolts against the image which it sees in the pale mirror, and may even question the mirror itself. The colonial historian approaches Prospero's history with an eye steeped in its otherness, and the vision of the conqueror which emerges is profoundly corrosive. There is the Commandant in Lamming's *Natives of My Person,* his dream of a New World entrammelled by his need for slaves. The music of those slaves (serenes, serenades, serenals, sirens) is an omen of doom to the Commandant's dream. This great adventure originates with Columbus in the Mediterranean as Europe pushes beyond its Western shores across the Atlantic, binding the conquered nations to Europe's vision ("bound to the vision of my sail"). But the vision of the conquistador is that of a bird of prey ("the hawk unhooded sun"). The reference here is almost certainly to Shaffer's *The Royal Hunt of the Sun.* The conquistador seeks the sun kingdoms of the New World, and finds the New World of the Dogon, the cyclic world of the Inca, spherically balanced and coherent within itself ("the world a green gourd"). This is how the hawk-man, flying into the sun's eye, finds the New World on both sides of the Atlantic. Brathwaite later develops this image of the Conquistador as bird of prey by depicting Cortez as both club-footed Atzec death-god, Akbal, and a ferocious condor insatiably scanning the Mexican terrain for its prey.[44]

But the hawk-man is seriously deficient. He is sterile ("childless"). If he is to found a really new world, he needs to be egg, life-bearer. But he is "cracked open to (his) dark of yellow stars". The "yellow stars" may be the gold which was the motive force behind the journey. The sun, the golden star which Pizzaro seeks on his royal hunt, is not the emblematic sun of the creator gods – Onyame, Osiris et al – of the Akan, Egyptian or Inca. It is, quite simply, gold. The conquistadors melted down the engraved and sculptured artifacts of Mesoamerica into bullion for their mercantile system, eliminating in one fell swoop recorded history, religion and cultural heritage; and replaced spiritual value with money-mindedness, sun's gold with materialism. The conquistador vision is really no vision at all; a vision of darkness; a dark sun. It replaces the primal, the natural and the given with the mechanical: ("eyes became astrolabes"). The dominated peoples become, like Ahab's crew, bound to the fixed, narrow obsession of the Old World. Their vision of their past grows nostalgically Edenic:

>   aouaoula was water
> was wood loving dolphins, our children of animal
>   swim

Touched by the conquistador, this dream of the past withers.

> and the dawn to have set us down here
> by the lake of invisible heritage:
> heroless savages' civilizations
> reflected in mirrorless walls

This obliteration of heritages by the inexorable laws of time and conquest embraces all civilisations:

> zimbabwe, tenochtitlan, saguenay
> mouse eaten capitols

The fact that the word is "capitols" rather than "capitals" tells us that Brathwaite is referring particularly to the Roman Empire, which he sees as the historical node out of which grew the aggressive nations of Western Europe, the remarkable wave of post-Renaissance expansionism, exploration and conquest, the emergence of a universe whose centre was commerce, money, prayer, sweat and war, and its catastrophic impact on the ancient civilisations of the non-European world. "Rome burns/ and our slavery begins", is how Brathwaite summarises this movement of catastrophe in *X-Self*.

The moment of catastrophe is suggested by the chaos of images which now crowd the crab's memory.

> to have explored the booms of cenotes
> bulls' nostrils' cisterns
> gas chambers of bud, volcanoes, emperors
> erupting from sperm into skeletone
>
> tunes of the carved year: pop, yax, kayab
> wheeling from sticks, peacocks screams of the air
> life slipping off flesh like migrations of sand
> ticking softly off tumorous dunes

In another version of the poem, it is the "ruins of cenotes" that the crab explores. Cenotes are natural wells around which the Maya built their villages and cities. Where there were no natural underground source of water, they built cisterns, or created huge reservoirs by damming up ravines. They had devised a calendar of eighteen twenty-day months plus five unlucky days. Pop, Yax and Kayab were three of those months, each of which was dedicated to a particular deity, and had its festivals. Like the Akan, the Maya played various drums, flutes and trumpets. Our knowledge of the Mayan calendar comes from their huge, intricately carved mosaics and stelae of stone, marked with the hieroglyphs in which they wrote.

What the lines under discussion seem to be saying, then, is that the Caribbean area has known both the highly advanced and balanced civilisations of the ancient world, and the horrors of the modern one, as typified by the gas chambers of Belsen or the nuclear holocaust of Hiroshima. Indeed, Brathwaite asserts that the same impulse which destroyed the ancient water sources of Mesoamerica, converting lake to dust bowl, created the gas chambers. He is, of course, well aware that the history of the New World has been the result of the interaction between the conqueror and his victims.

This awareness is demonstration by the fact that the "I" or "we" of the poem is at times conquistador and at times the voice of the vanquished tribes. Thus the crab's poem seeks to capture the ambivalence that has grown out of this strange dialectical dance of conqueror and conquered.

Emerging out of this confrontation is the scarecrow figure of the reduced, tattered muse. Simultaneously witch and prophet, she is an image of the violated anima, and is a Legba figure (limping, crooked, i.e. hunchbacked and crutched). She will reappear in "Hex" (*Mother Poem*), as a demented obeah woman who curses her children's blindness of materialism. She is what becomes of sensibility:

> dreaming of stinks
>
> kneading herbs, oracles, words
> condemning all conquerors

She is Black Sycorax, the muse of *Black + Blues,* who points him to the fact that we have "survived these terrors, cactus images and halts". Having lived through history's grim vicissitudes we have, like Shango, "embraced them all", acquiring in the process a weight and burden of knowledge. "The crab knows it all" and knows as well the responsibility that such knowledge imposes: the necessity not only to embrace, know and bear the weight of all our yesterdays, but to move beyond what we have already lived through. Like "Kite", "Crab" is about reconciliation, movement beyond and laying to rest.

Such movement beyond, however, will involve further ordeals. There is the herculean task of rebuilding the church on top of the Rockefeller building; erecting spirit on a now centuries'-old foundation of encrusted materialism, rediscovering or recreating the lost idea of the holy. The line, "petals gnashing out of the gravel", conveys the agony of the muse who bears both the burden of a knowledge of history, and the responsibility for renewing the image. It will take both the concentrated inner violence – note the force of "gnashing" – and the gentle, slow energy which drives the grass up through the cracked concrete, to survive as a poet in this age.

The poem closes with a renewed focus on the image of the crab, who is the poet with his "kernel of grit/knowledge of the eaten edges of disaster", his careful yet confident movement over the pebbles of his island. On the crab's back is etched a summary of the islands' history, the world's history, terse hieroglyphs awakened now by the poet's imagination. The "drip of my skull" is the steady trickle of his thought in a poem which is a collection of thoughts; a drizzle, rather than a stream of consciousness.

There is reconciliation and sleep in the last lines

> and the grass flesh
> and the flesh memory
> and the memory nodding

Isaiah's "all flesh is grass" is reversed here. Idea has been fleshed out by image, substance granted to the withered past. "The memory nodding" takes us back to the ending of "Tano" in *Masks*:

and my mem-

ory bends, curves, nods
head and crouches

feeding the dust at the soles
of its feet as it dances.

"Nodding" in "Crab" is both falling asleep and signalling assent and affirmation. It also seems that the ancestors have been laid to rest by the end of the poem. They are no longer the duppy omens of retribution. The mood in which the poem ends points us forward to the "calm histories" of the Barbados of *Mother Poem*.

("Songs of the Skeleton", was published in three phases: Part 1: 'The Poetry of Fission", *Trinidad & Tobago Review*, Vol. IV, No. 3 (Petit Careme 1980) and Vol. IV, No. 3 A, (Divali, 1980); Part II: "A Poetry of Dread", *Trinidad & Tobago Review*, Vol. IV, No. 5 (New Year, 1981) and No. 6 (Croptime, March/April 1981); Part III, "Flowers of the Harmattan", paper read at the Fifth Annual Conference on West Indian. Literature, College of the Virgin Islands, St. Thomas, May 25--28, 1985, and published in *West Indian Poetry, Proceedings of the fifth Annual Conference on West Indian Literature*, College of the Virgin Islands, St. Thomas, U.S.V.I., 1986, pp. 201-217).

References

1. Brathwaite, E., "Caribbean Man in Space and Time", *Savacou* 11/12, 1975, pp. 1-11.
2. Paz, O., *The Other Mexico: A Critique of the Pyramid* (New York: Grove Press, 1972).
3. Williams, D., *Other Leopards* (London: New Authors Ltd., 1963).
4. N.B. The word "stares" in *Black + Blues* (Cuba: Casa de las Americas 1976), is a misprint. See version in *Other Exiles*.
5. The issue of the miseducation of Black children was a major source of discontent in the polemic of the 1960s. This issue has been soberly documented by William Ryan in *Blaming the Victim* (New York: Vintage Books, 1971).
6. Brathwaite, E., "Negus", *The Arrivants*, pp. 222-224.
7. Ibid., "Leopard" and "Anvil", pp. 244-253.
8. Refer ibid., "Eating the Dead" (pp. 219-221), "Dawn" (pp. 236-238) for examples.

9. Jerry, Bongo, "Mabrak", *Savacou* 3/4 (1970).
10. Brathwaite, E., "Homecoming", *The Arrivants*, p. 177.
11. Refer to Curtin, P., *The Image of Africa: British Ideas and Action 1780-1850* (Wisconsin: University of Wisconsin Press, 1964). Also, Goveia, E., *A Study on the Historiography of the West Indies* (Mexico, 1956). Henriques, F., *Children of Caliban* (London: Secker & Warburg, 1974), and Herskovits, M., *The Myth of the Negro Past* (Boston: Beacon Press, 1958). (First published 1941).
12. Roach, E., "The Fighters", *Bim*, Vol. 5, No. 19 (Dec., 1953).
13. Brathwaite, E., "Sir Galahad and the Islands", *Bim* 25 (July-Dec., 1957).
14. Rohlehr, G., "Bridges of Sound: A Reading of Brathwaite's Jah", *Trinidad & Tobago Review,* Vol. 2, No. 1 (August 1977).
15. Brathwaite, E., *Mother Poem* (London: OUP 1977), p. 122.
16. See for example Tennyson's "Locksley Hall".
17. See Rohlehr, G., "My Strangled city", *Caliban,* Vol. 3, No. 1 (Sept., 1979).
18. See Chalkdust, "Uncle Sam Own We" (1980 calypso).
19. Shakespeare, *The Tempest,* Act II, Sc. ii, lines 27-32.
20. Freyre, G., *The Masters* and *the Slaves* (New York: Knopf, 1946). Originally published as *Casa Grande & Senzala.*
21. Ras Dizzy, "Ghost Riding Coffin in City," in *Rastafarians Society Watchman,* Kingston 1970 (?) No date. See also *Savacou* 3/4 (1970-71).
22. There is a reggae song about the clashing of the sevens. Culture, (J. Hill), "Two Sevens Clash", Globe Music, Jamaica, 1977.
23. Boston & the Soulites, "Starvation", Federal Records, GCS45-1.
24. White, G., "Rudie oh Rudie", *Caribbean Quarterly,* Vol. 13, No. 3 (1967) pp. 39-43; Rohlehr, G., "Sans Humanité: Violence in Jamaica", *Moko,* Nos. 8 & 9 (April & May 1969).
25. Brathwaite, E., "Springblade", in A.J. Seymour ed., *New Writing in the Caribbean* (Guyana, 1972).
26. Fynn, J.J., *Asante and its Neighbours 1700-1807* (London: Longman 1971), p. 22.
27. Quoted in Sawyer, *God: Ancestor or Creator?* (London: Longman, 1970), p. 19.
28. Rohlehr, G., "West Indian Poetry: Some Problems of Assessment", *Bim,* Vol. 14, Nos. 54 & 55 (Jan-June & Jul-Dec., 1972). "Afterthoughts", *Bim* No. 56 (Jan-June, 1973).
29. Hogg, D., Jamaica Religions: A Study in Variation, Unpublished Dissertation, Yale 1964, pp. 100-105.
30. The calypso provides hundreds of examples of such anti-feminism.
31. Brathwaite examines this contempt early in one of the sequences of "Sappho Sakyi's Meditations", *Bim,* Vol. 7, No. 26 (Jan-June, 1957) and comprehensively in "Cherries" (*Mother Poem*).
32. Compare Malik's "Pan Run II", where the Dry River image is also brilliantly developed. See Rohlehr, G., "My Strangled City", *Caliban,* Vol. II, No. 1 (Fall/Winter, 1976), pp. 79-89.
33. Brathwaite, E., "The Love Axe/1" (unpublished typescript version). For revised version, see *Bim*, Nos. 61-63, 1977/78.

34. Brathwaite, E., Transcribed from a 1975 lecture/reading at the Creative Arts Centre, UWI, Mona. For revised & abridged version, see: "Metaphors of Underdevelopment: A Proem for Hernan Cortez" in *Africa/Europe: Sixth European. Poetry Festival 1984*, Belgium, Cahier No. 48, Leuvense Schrijversaktie, 1984. (Essays & Poems selected & introduced by Eugene Van Itterbeek).
35. Brathwaite, E., "Harmattan Poems", *Black Orpheus*, II No. 7, Ibadan (1971-1972) pp. 4-12.
36. Same as #34.
37. Brathwaite, E., "Kingston in the Kingdom of this World", *Third World Poems* (Essex: Longman, 1983). Originally entitled "Good Friday 1975: Kingston in the Kingdom of this World", *Jamaica Daily News,* March 30, 1975.
38. Brathwaite, E., "Shango", *The Massachusetts Review* XV, No. 1 & 2. (Winter-Spring 1974) pp. 76-80.
39. Harris, W., "The Question of Form & Realism in the West Indian Artist", *Tradition the Writer & Society* (London: New Beacon Publications, 1967), p. 15.
40. Brathwaite, E., "Conqueror", *The Literary Half-Yearly*, XI, No. 2 (July 1970).
41. Brathwaite, E., "Dawn", *The Arrivants* (Oxford: O.U.P., 1973), pp. 235-238.
42. See note 3.
43. Eliot, T. S., "Burnt Norton" in *Four Quartets* (London: Faber, 1959), p. 14.
44. Brathwaite, E.K., "Titan" in *X/ Self* (Oxford: O.U.P., 1987), pp. 61-63.

"MAN TALKING TO MAN"
CALYPSO AND SOCIAL CONFRONTATION IN TRINIDAD 1970 TO 1984

"Social confrontation" in Trinidad has traditionally involved the indigenisation process of several migrant groups, divided by race, ethnicity, language and religion, in a country of plantations, small holdings, villages and growing towns. It has been characterised by the infighting of these groups, both among themselves and against each other. The calypso has mirrored these conflicts in the kalinda chants of the nineteenth century, calypsos about race, "small island" migrants, steelband clashes, "bad-John" violence and sexual conflict. Such calypsos share common elements of threat, challenge, boast, self-assertion and the themes of manhood and machismo which were generally connected with aggression transferred from an impoverished and degrading social system and redirected inwards or towards each other by members of the underprivileged class.

The fiercely anti-feminist calypsos of the 1940s and 1950s provide the clearest index of the way that aggression, rooted in the society, was transferred to the plane of male-female relations. Such calypsos had their predecessors in nineteenth century cariso songs, as well as the ribald music which accompanied the quelbay dancers of the 1880s and which occasioned such bitter complaint from commentators of that age.

"Race" calypsos are a special variant in that they dramatise the latent or open conflict between identifiable ethnic groups – Blacks, Whites, Chinese, East Indians. Such calypsos remind us that the process of Trinidad's social history has been punctuated by the fierce dialogue of colliding or overlapping ethnicities, each hoping vainly for private space. At times it seems that there has been no true dialogue, but rather several rudely interrupted and fragmented monologues modified by a shared forum of public platitude in which all groups can easily participate without compromising their private positions.

Race calypsos trade on racial stereotyping, and employ caricature and a humour based on the mockery of accent, music or gestures of the other race. They measure, or betray, the uncertainty with which the races have regarded each other; a latent atavistic mistrust, and the competition which has always been taking place against a background of chronic unemployment, poverty and dispossession on the part of the broad masses of people, and authoritarianism, patronage and manipulation on the part of those small elitist groups who control their destiny. Such racial attitudes are, of course, tempered by the fact that all groups partake of the same education, and are caught up in the same rush of events, cultural pressure from the metropole, and the same directionless futility of politics at home.

All these varieties of social confrontation are crystallised in the language of calypso: its hard unsentimentality which clashes with the waterish romanticism of much popular music; its cynical wit; its humour of aggression. The same spirit may permeate a calypso about urban gang conflict, one that berates the city's prostitutes and one that flays a politician for corruption or incompetence.

The political calypso emerged out of this background of conflict as a medium for articulating class struggle as well as a vehicle for transmitting images of self and potential, different from the images which had traditionally been transmitted by the prevailing order. Its emergence in the twentieth century paralleled the struggle for the localisation of politics, universal adult suffrage, and the development of the trade union movement. The calypsos of Executor, Atilla, the Growling Tiger and Beginner – to name a few – document this struggle which, as it intensified, evoked from the colonial administration the most thorough strategies of control and containment: sedition bills, armed occupation and the censorship of books, pamphlets and calypso records and performances. Calypsonians such as Atilla fought relentlessly against such controls, and the years 1937 to 1951 are an era of remarkable resistance, culminating in the amendment of a 1934 Ordinance which had given the Commissioner of Police absolute and unquestionable legal power to permit or prevent the public performance of calypsos.

The political calypsos of the 1956 to 1962 era, dominated by the phenomenal output of the Mighty Sparrow, but including singers such as Cristo, Gibraltar, Striker and Duke, were a celebration of the faith of a predominantly African sector of the working and middle classes in the new political movement led by Dr. Eric Williams. They both legitimised the party and its leader, and defended it against incipient dissent by opposition forces. Dissenting voices in 1959 criticised the clandestine marriage of Dr. Williams, which Melody in "Doctor Make Your Love" greeted with the brilliant couplet:

> I hear the Doctor married again
> Socialism must be maintained

where "socialism" suggested the difference between the party's programme of social reform and what was already beginning to look like the secrecy and elitism, the playing social of a traditional middle-class intellectual.

Sparrow defended the image and name of Williams in his "Leave the Damn Doctor". The Growling Tiger, who also sang about the marriage, was forced to quit the tent early in the 1959 season.

The infamous Solomon incident[1] marked a turning point, evoking in 1965 both defence and trenchant criticism of the behaviour of Solomon and Williams's high-handed treatment of the affair. Sparrow's "Solomon" and "Get to Hell Outa Here" are justly famous. Less well known is Blakie's really irreverent "De Doctah Ent Deh" (1965) or Leveller's "How to Stop Delinquency" (1966), a calypso whose burden was that a government of intellectuals had achieved no fundamental change, and was now involved with analysis divorced from action, and the gimmickry of youth rallies which could not conceal the reality of unemployment.

> You could tear down the barrack-yard
> Augment the local guard
> Appoint ten committees
> Promote big youth rallies
> To camp down Nelson Island
> But employment is the key
> For kink-head and company
> That is so evident
> Still the dilly-dallying
> From our intellectual government

Alongside this equating of intellectuality with impotence was the notion of the typical postcolonial politician as a parvenu up-from-slavery hustler whose main concern in gaining power was feathering his own nest, and who therefore had a vested interest in dishonesty. Sparrow gave us this image in his 1966 calypso, "Honesty", signalling in the process that little had changed in people's fundamental attitudes and assumptions. The paradoxical task of loyalist calypsonians over the next decade (1966-1976) would be to maintain the party's ideal image of integrity, and particularly to preserve the sheen on the charisma of the maximum leader, in an atmosphere of collapse and terrible disorganisation at almost every level of social life.

One device for doing this was the patriotic calypso, a genre which surfaced early in the twentieth century and gave us the cliché "Trinidad is nice/Trinidad is a paradise". It gained great currency, as one would expect, around Independence time in 1962 and found its perfect expression in Sniper's beloved "Portrait of Trinidad" (1965). As younger singers such as Leveller (1966) and, two years later, Chalkdust (1968) began to chronicle the regime's shortcomings, loyalist singers such as Duke (1967) added to the patriotic calypso a celebration of supposed PNM achievements.

> They taught us both the black and white
> In Trinidad have equal right
> The rich and poor the big and small
> Opportunity is here for all

> Trinidad and Tobago
> Is the land of calypso
> Our chief products are sugar and oil
> With the pitch lake where so many toil
> We practise true democracy
> With a very sound economy
> And a group of men who are efficient
> To lead a proper government

The next year, Sparrow, in a newspaper interview with the *Trinidad Guardian*, explained why he had (temporarily it turned out) ceased to function as a political commentator. The media, he said, anticipated the calypsonians in presenting and interpreting news, and thus rendered his role as commentator irrelevant. Besides there was nothing to criticise.

> Picong is fine and most of the people like picong on the Government. But there is very little to laugh at in this Government. This is a serious Government. There was a time when the role of the calypsonian was to expose private affairs, a scandal; and generally to act as town crier. If this is what people are afraid of there is no need; for this no longer the case.
>
> The calypsonian today is not satirical; he is there for one purpose: to entertain. He does his best to please his listeners and his audience[2]

Sparrow was, like Duke, Gibraltar and others, reluctant to attack what he had fervently supported. The claim that Trinidad had few issues worthy of protest, around 1968 and 1969, was little more than a mask to hide the uneasy sense that matters were coming to a head. Bomber in a 1970 calypso called "Political Wonder", eulogised Dr. Williams in adulatory 1956 terms, but wondered whether he would die like Gandhi or Martin Luther King, neither of whom died in bed. Bomber's calypso was clearly a projection of those ill-concealed ominous fears that the society, now chronically involved in demonstrations, strikes, Black Power rhetoric and anti-PNM polemic, might be caught up in an irreversible process which could result in violence and even assassination.

The Political Calypso 1970-1984

It has been claimed by Frank Manning in 1984 that the rise of highly rhythmic, celebratory but verbally simplistic "Soca" tunes has led to a depoliticisation of the Trinidad calypso. I have not found this assertion to be true of the years 1970 to 1984, and have compiled a shortlist of nearly two hundred and fifty calypsos from this period which contain extensive political or social commentary. So close, so fine, so meticulous has been the political seeing in these calypsos that I intend to write a long book dealing exclusively with them and what they reveal of a continuum of overlapping and often contradictory attitudes, stretching between total acceptance of the PNM regime, through total rejection of the political disorder which it represents, to vague intimations of an alternative.

In this paper I confine myself to three main concerns. First, the images of Dr. Williams and the PNM which emerged during the period and how calypsonians' perception of the man altered over the period; second, what images of the citizen's roles and responsibilities could be discerned, and third, the roles that calypsonians have adopted and performed in the political life of their country.

Images of Dr. Williams

The traditional 1956 image persisted among loyal party diehards such as Gibraltar ("Politics", 1971), Bomber ("Political Wonder", 1970), Vallee, the Pretender ("Black Power", 1971). Williams is seen as benefactor, patron, reformer and builder. Such singers emphasise the positive achievements of the party – houses, roads, education – and view them as personal gifts from a loving paterfamilias, and accuse the youth or the opponents of the party of ingratitude to the unappreciated father of the nation.

There are several calypsos which acknowledge Williams as the undisputed leader of the nation, recognise his power, but also insist on his responsibility to set things right. Calypsos of this kind are Chalkdust's "Answer to Black Power" (1971) which warns Williams of the difference between a negative policy of controlling and containing social unrest, and positive creative legislation which could tackle some of the rooted problems facing the youth. Valentino's "No Revolution" (1971) both acknowledges Williams's power and criticises him for what he regards as its unjust use during 1970. Duke's "Lock them Up Dr. Williams" (1974) appeals to him to adopt a hard line with black marketeers and profiteering businessmen. Maestro's "To Sir With Love" (1974) also acknowledges Williams as leader, but is a devastating frontal attack on Williams from the point of view of a disgruntled proletarian. Maestro stresses Williams's air-conditioned distance from the people and the day-to-day issues. This portrait of Williams is reinforced by the calypsos in which he is portrayed as "Deafy"; one whose real deafness has become symbolic of his egoism, isolation, remoteness and tendency towards a one-way communication from himself to the people.

Calypsos which allude to Williams's deafness are Chalkdust's "Two Sides of a Shilling" (1971), "The Answer to Black Power", i.e. the Dimanche Gras (1971) version which contains the line, "Ah hope your hearing aid working"; Valentino's "Barking Dogs" (1973), in which the commands "fix your hearing aid" and "wipe your glasses" appear; Relator's "Deaf Panmen" (1974), Chalkdust's "Deafness or Dr. Aziz" (Dimanche Gras 1974); Black

Stalin's "Piece o' de Action" (1976) in which the line, "Mr Divider, like the switch ain't working", expresses the exasperation of the citizen who is trying to make contact with Godot. These kaisos all signal a desire on the part of the citizen to be heard; an insistence on the need for participation. Valentino begins his "Barking Dogs" with the declaration:

> This word is mine I am this word
> So let my voice be heard,

which, incidentally, parodies and reverses the arrogance of the Williams/persona in Sparrow's "Get to Hell Outa Here" (1965) who is made to declare:

> This land is mine, I am the boss
> What I say goes, and who gets lost.

Stalin in "Piece o' de Action" ends his first stanza with the manifesto

> Mr. Divider listen to me
> This is man talking to man

Relator's "Deaf Panmen", the cruellest and most corrosive calypso of this type, portrays a nation of deaf masqueraders led by Dr. Williams whose name the band bears and who insists that only deaf people must be in his band. The characteristic quality of the band is its incoherence and disharmony;

> Some playing B-flat, some playing F
> They can't hear a thing because they deaf
> But still they come out to jam
> And the name of the band is Dr. William
> Ah hope you understand the masquerade
> Panmen with dark shades wearing hearing aid.

The last two lines are subtly ironic. First of all, they view Williams' politics as an odd mixture of blindness and masquerade. They, however, suggest that if one tried one could "understand the masquerade", the street theatre of politics. But they also imply that such a masquerade, a "deaf pan man panorama", is incomprehensible.

Satirised is Williams's encouragement of sycophancy (he wants only deaf people in his band), his creation of a system based on the non-participation of the people and the remoteness of the leader. In the final stanza scatological imagery is applied to the regime, which has messed its pants, reducing a nation to faeces. The deaf panmen play their discordant music in B-flat, F, GCE and finally W.C. Surdity, then fulfilling itself in absurdity, has ultimately produced turdity.

It is, possibly, the demoralisation which arose after Dr. Williams resigned in 1973 – in order to identify and demolish a younger clique of rival politicians within his party – that led to the fierce irreverence of Relator's calypso. Chalkdust in "Two Sides of a Shilling" (1971) had prepared the ground for this line of attack by characterising him as a deft role-playing manipulator of images; one who masked as a benevolent and aggrieved paterfamilias, but was, in fact, a rigid authoritarian, a maker and breaker of men, one who extended or withheld patronage to a menagerie of time-serving, self-seeking sycophants whose flattery he simultaneously needed and scorned; one who had compromised with big business at the expense of the poor and tolerated corruption among his followers.

It was a short step from this grim portrait to Chalkdust's image of Williams as madman ("Somebody Mad", 1973). This image was a direct response to the bewildering paradoxes of civic life; the inconsistencies between proclamation and behaviour. The notion of madness was foreshadowed by Blakie's 1965 calypso, "De Doctor Ain't Deh", where Blakie, seeking his leader and not finding him in the various ministries, tries the hospital, the madhouse and the jail. When he enquires at the jail

> The officer started to fret
> I am sorry Blakie, but the Doctor ain't reach up here yet

There was a belief current in the early seventies that Williams suffered from bouts of mental depression and even breakdown. Such rumours were totally unverified but they remained in the public mind. Reflections on the rumoured madness of the leader would eventually become contemplation of the literal madness visible on the streets; so after the mid-seventies we have Terror's "Madness" (1978) which focuses on the plight of the youth, and several calypsos noting the serious growth in drug abuse. (e.g. Creole's "Ah Want to Be Tight" (1976); Sparrow's "He Went Off on Dope"). All of these meet and find their tragic political metaphor in Stalin's "Breakdown Party" (1989).

After the oil windfall, the image of Dr. Williams underwent a change. It became even more contradictory because Dr. Williams was now being seen simultaneously as a man who had been endowed with an enormous power of patronage and as an old, capricious and incompetent eccentric. For Stalin in "Piece o' de Action" (1976) and "Breakdown Party" (1980) he had become "Mr. Divider", the dispenser of "oil bread" to all and sundry. Swallow may have applauded Williams's generosity towards his impoverished Caribbean neighbours in "The Trinidad Godfather" (1980), but many Trinidadian felt that all sorts of improvements were necessary at home, and grew bitter at the fact that the nation had attained a negative image among its Caribbean neighbours as being arrogant and extravagant.

In many calypsos of the post-1976 period there is a latent mistrust of "money" as the mammon of unrighteousness. A shortlist of these includes Stalin's "Money" and "Breakdown Party" (1980); Shorty's "Money No Problem" (1979); Chalkdust's "Trinidad Dollar", Sparrow's "Neurosis of the Rich" (1975) and "Capitalism Gone Mad" (1983); Chalkdust's "De Spirit Gone" (1979), which observes the impact of commercialism on a Carnival reduced to colour and gesture without spirit. Money also becomes an evil in King Austin's "Progress" (1980). It "makes egos inflate". Stalin declares in Money:

> Money today change up so much life
> Calculators take the place of wife

Dr. Williams, as Mr. Divider, was seen as presiding over a dispirited kingdom of collapse. His performance in CARICOM was scathingly satirised in Chalkdust's "Three Blind Mice", which was strangely misinterpreted by one Trinidad commentator as a moment of softening towards Dr. Williams. The persona which Chalkdust in fact presented was that of an arrogant comprador Godfather, falsely secure in the sentiment:

> Tell Burnham and Manley I got oil
> Let Barrow kiss me tail, oil don't spoil

The blindness which Williams points out in his CARICOM partners, whom he accuses of supporting Venezuelan hegemony in the Caribbean Basin, is at least equalled by his own in feeling that he could afford to treat them with contempt. The calypso ends with the observation that Williams's behaviour in the region was an attempt to extend the authoritarianism which he had been allowed to practise by his faceless colleagues in the party.

> Dem three deputies that he have is the oil
> Three faceless men of straw got he spoil

Throughout the seventies the calypso had been chronicling the disintegration – Sparrow's "Ah Digging Horrors" (1975) – and predicting the collapse of the regime. By the late 1970s, the regime remained alive but was perceived as being spiritually dead. Indeed in "Somebody Mad" (1973) Chalkdust had used images of carrion to symbolise the regime's acts of patronage towards the people:

> Suppose I take a dead dead dog
> And throw it dong Frederick Street
>
> Chorus
>
> I say you mad
> I say you mad mad mad
>
> And if I give a dead corbeau
> To everyone I meet
>
> Chorus
>
> I say you mad
> I say you mad, real mad

He was alluding to the building of flats in Shanty Town which coincided with the establishment of a more elaborate and nauseous rubbish dump opposite the flats.

By the late 1970s, Williams the man had ceased to be important. Stalin in "Breakdown Party" (1980) answers criticisms made by a UWI academic that his "Caribbean Unity" (1979) was "sexist and racist", as well as Williams' criticism of Stalin's definition of Caribbean identity in Black nationalist terms, by depicting Williams as a sort of incompetent sorcerer's apprentice, unable to stop or control a process of squandermania which he, borrowing his master's book of spells, had set into motion. The attack was on inflated salaries, and the money circulating in the society, as well as on the large-scale industrial projects which had been undertaken, as Williams attempted to enter the big league of iron and steel,

> Mr. Divider start the habit
> Brother all Trinidadian love it
> Now he trying he utmost best to stop it
> Brother I took a look around
> From the country right into town
> And is a total breakdown fête going on

The society seems caught in a process of irreversible entropy, and many post-1980 calypsos will become involved with this process. Here the words "breakdown" and "party" are both employed in two senses – that of a fantastically successful and totally enjoyable fête and that of economic, mental, moral and societal collapse engineered by crazy administration. The irony engendered between the two meanings can only be described as violent and anguished and there is the strong suggestion that the issue will be resolved only by violence.

> But if this had been my party
> Ah woulda stop the thing already
> When I say "Stop!" Stop the jam!
> Else I break a DJ hand!

The final portraits of Williams come from Chalkdust and Relator. Chalkdust, searching in vain for a sane explanation of Trinidad politics towards the eighties, concluded that Williams existed only to provide material for Chalkdust's calypsos. In "Eric Williams Loves Me" (1980), he sings

> I've read books by Hobbes and Plato
> But I never see a Prime Minister so
> Must be calypso he want Chalkie sing

Such witheringly comic reduction to nothing came at a time when Williams was ostensibly at the apex of his high, the crest of his cloud. Yet the calypsonians had described an absurd, hollow figure and were now more concerned with the drastic measures which would be necessary to set the country in order. Chalkdust was calling for an "Ayatollah" in 1980, whose stringent controls and vicious punishments alone would impose order on the nation's public affairs.

Relator's final portrait of Williams is of "a horse that is tired and almost lame" (1980), whom it is now pointless to blame even if he is indeed at fault. Relator advised the Prime Minister and his party to take a rest, and foresaw the possibility of Williams simply dropping dead on the job. Delamo, too, in "Apocalypse" (1981) saw the nation as a headless horse galloping towards the Lapeyrouse Cemetery, the last runner in the international derby.

Definitions of the Citizen

The political calypsos of the post-1970 period defined the citizen in several ways. The citizen is a node of resistance to wrong and corruption regardless of the consequences, in Valentino's "No Revolution" (1971). The "good" citizen is transgressor, oppressor, exploiter and crook in Sparrow's "Good Citizen" (1972). We have pictures of the citizen as articulate dog in the face of contemptuous authoritarianism in Valentino's "Barking Dogs" (1973); the citizen as "as a man out for change", a committed antagonist of the system and thus a man on the firing line, for whom life has become a hazardous game of chance, and nothing is strange in Stalin's "Nothing Ent Strange" (1975). In Valentino's "Liberation" and "Dis Place Nice" (1975), the citizen is an absurd puppet, a deaf panman, a mindless follower in the politics of absurdity, as revolutionary-in-the-making, the end product of a politics in which he has remained a mere object of the manipulation of the powerful. In Maestro's "Mr. Trinidad" (1974), the citizen is the one who is ultimately responsible for the "political confusion" and paralysis in which the country finds itself; as a lover of "plenty mamaguy", he is a not-too-smart smartman who ends up by tricking himself, because he has chosen no path towards change and invested his faith in no alternative.

In Stalin's "Steelband Gone" (1973) and "De Jam" (1980), and in Chalkdust's "De Spirit Gone", the citizen is described as a dispirited product of a predatory commercialism that has defined his tastes, fed on his true life-force and ultimately rendered him a shell, emptying his most creative expressions of their soul and meaning is described. An extension/intensification of this definition has been Chalkdust's "Uncle Sam Own We" (c. 1978), which sees the Caribbean as having almost willingly abandoned its cultural identity to the hegemony of US commercialism. The Caribbean becomes a dumping ground for American cultural refuse – its clothes, eating habits, music and style. Relator's "Radio Stations" and

Chalkdust's "Cultural Heritage" also make this point. Lancelot Layne bluntly and aggressively attacks these tendencies in his "Get Off the Radio" (1982).

The citizen is also depicted as a potential agent of retribution, a grim reformer, a troubleshooter in a world of political cowpokes. Listen to Chalkdust's "Ah Put on Me Guns Again" (1976), "Shango Vision" (1977), and "Ayatollah" (1980). At another level, the vision of retribution appears in several of Shadow's calypsos, in Delamo's fundamentalist visions of "Apocalypse" (1981) and "Armageddon" (1984); Explainer's "Tables Turning" (1980) and Johnny King's "Nature's Plan" (1984).

In these calypsos we find a yearning for reversal, for an equalling of the scales, a turning of the wheel. Most of these dreams involve a hope for *deus ex machina* solutions – an expectation that the state of things will suddenly change as the medieval wheel of fortune mysteriously turns. Beneath such dreams often lies an unacknowledged sense of individual helplessness in the grip of historical process; an absence of political or existential will; the bewildered apathy of the weak and powerless. One of the future tasks of creative politics will undoubtedly be to convert the dream of retribution into a positive force for the willed and conscious transformation of society.

Some calypsonians have begun to grope their way towards a vision of the new politics of "man talking to man". They have, however, made it clear that such dialogue can only occur on a basis of honesty and trust, which are precisely the elements that have been destroyed in most of our public and much of our private affairs. A number of calypsos by Black Stalin – "De Ole Talk" (1974), "More Times" (1979) and "Vampires" (1981) – have accepted as their premise the idea that dialogue is no longer possible in a society permeated by mistrust. Acutely conscious of politics as manipulation, Stalin has articulated the necessity for cunning and evasiveness. Such cunning is particularly necessary when one is approached by people seeking office, be they academics, trade union leaders, priests, lawyers or whosoever. Stalin has raised the question of who is to speak for or represent the people, but his negative list seems to have included almost everybody. Everyone is classified as a "headhunter", that is, a person who tinkers with people's minds in order to secure their loyalties, and then abandons the people to the anguish of their condition. Stalin, like Struggler, another calypsonian who has embraced Rastafarianism, recommends that the righteous put distance between themselves and all potential manipulators:

> Now whether morning, noon or night lately time
> Don't you know people come out so for your mind
> If they couldn't get it all, just a piece would do
> But their greatest wish in the world is to have control of you
> So when I see them headhunters come walking my way
> I does simply humble myself, take aside and say
> More times, more times, etc.

"More time" is the Rastafarian way of saying "goodbye see you later", and is the only conversation Stalin recommends when the "head-hunters" are on the prowl. Headhunters come in various disguises and while their aim is not to kill physically, it is to reduce the person to a puppet. Stalin's retreat, then, is a positive act in that it signals the existential refusal of the person to be reduced to an object, and is the beginning of Freire's "critical consciousness", the very basis and precondition for any new politics in the Caribbean. Stalin, when he sang "More Times", had already recognised the extreme danger implicit in the citizen's refusal to become dumb object, robot, puppet. The burden of "Nothing Ain't Strange" (1975) was that such refusal immediately imperils the life of the citizen who has by that act of will transformed himself into a political guerilla:

> Because you won't let people talk for you
> Or do the things that they want you to
> Your life ain't safe whether night or day
> Because, any number can play.
> Nothing! Nothing! Nothing ain't strange
> In the life of a man out for change.

Understanding, then, the dreadful possibilities which the new politics will open up, the severity with which the old system will seek to maintain itself, Stalin has recognised that none of the people offering themselves today for high political office is capable of providing the leadership necessary. These people he characterises, employing Peter Tosh's "Buckingham Palace" metaphor, as "vampires":

> They telling you that they care
> About your welfare
> See them with their mouth cock
> Waiting for their suck
> So keep the chalice smoking
> Vampires passing

But if everyone is unworthy, what are the righteous brethren to do in the interim between this moment and the second coming? Stalin seems to suggest that the retreat of the righteous is a means of creating a space outside of the prevailing prison of the system, within which the brethren can contemplate and responsibly attend to the really crucial issues of life and death which confront them every day.

> Now children dying in ghettos every day
> So much o' food shortage ah seem to say (?)
> Ah got to do something; tears in mankind eye
> So if you ain't making sense say nothing to I
> I man got to go, so you stay and rap
> Look ah just moving on and ah done wid that.

The citizens, then, need to set about the business of rescuing themselves and their children from the slow or sudden death which is being visited on them, and will have to do it themselves.

Functions of the Political Calypsonian 1970-1984

Valentino claimed in the mid-seventies that the calypsonian was the only true opposition, while Chalkdust in his "Message to George Weekes" (1976) said that the calypsonian had a far greater freedom to articulate protest than anyone else in the society. The political calypso created in the period under observation a forum where popular disaffection found constant expression. NJAC was a prime force in providing important singers such as Black Stalin, Chalkdust, Valentino, Relator, Composer and a host of others year-round exposure to their public in a series of concerts which were, in fact, an important alternative to the Carnival calypso tents. What those NJAC-sponsored concerts did was to enable the protest singers to recognise themselves as a potential solidarity; to rescue them from their solitude.

The political calypso as alternative forum for opposition politics was even more necessary in the light of the impotence of the official opposition party. While it is impossible to measure what impact political calypsos have had on people's consciousness, it is certain that their importance has been recognised. They receive very little air-play; the managers of radio stations act as unofficial censors who, apprehensive of dangers which may occur to their jobs on government-controlled media, are careful not to transmit to the public any but the safest sort of opinion. This absence of exposure probably affects the sale of records, and makes protest singers unsafe business risks. It is, therefore, a powerful method of control and containment.

The Calypso King Competition has at times functioned in the same way, and in some years singers of impressive but critical songs have been omitted from the finals, while weaker, emptier songs have been promoted; although this has not happened all the time. Constant protests were made by Chalkdust, Shadow and others about the criteria for judging the calypsos and, in 1976, it was actually specified that at least one of the songs in the competition should be on a political theme. Kitchener, in turn, protested against this innovation, arguing that the Dimanche Gras Show should be exclusively for the entertainment of an audience who needed to be instilled with the celebratory spirit of Carnival. This issue has not been resolved, but one notices that in recent years points are being awarded in the competition for the "spirit of carnival". So Chalkdust and others have had to sing their political calypsos in an up-tempo rhythm which could conceivably clash with the mood of their song.

Another technique employed between 1972 and 1973 was that of discrediting or attempting to discredit Chalkdust as a political singer. He was accused by the Public Relations Officer of the People's National Movement of having applied to join the party, an act which would, of course, have nullified his effectiveness as a critic of the party. The PRO produced signatures which he claimed were Chalkdust's. Chalkdust denied the accusation and promptly composed a calypso explaining why his presence in the PNM would have to be resisted. He would expose all the inner scandals to the public glare. Far from being discredited, Chalkdust used the issue to launch even fiercer attacks in "Somebody Mad" and "Somebody in PNM Loves Me" (1973) on the party and its leader. No further attempts were made to control him through discredit.

Another function of the political calypso has been that of political recall. In a country where political events occur at a bewildering pace, one frequently either forgets entirely what has been taking place, or confuses event with event. The political calypso often provides one with catalogues of current political events and assesses current events in the context of past events which may now be forgotten. This is a crucial need in a society where one forgets so easily; where there is little respect for history, research and archives: no memory, only a sort of blankness, breeding indifference to present, past and future.

The political calypsonian functions as an investigative reporter of political events in a special sense. He weighs the "official version" of an event against "inside information" which generally means gossip, scandal, unverified hearsay. This is a potentially dangerous role, in that the political calypsonian may fail to distinguish between truth and rumour, and may therefore not rise above the yellow journalism of the weekly tabloids.

On the other hand, what this sort of "investigative" calypso does is to keep alive the spirit of popular scepticism, to feed a mistrust of surfaces, a doubt of the "official version" which is generally well founded. Researchers into business, industry or state-owned corporations have often complained of the difficulty they experience in getting data. Such information is carefully controlled, or shelved, so that the official version of anything is a cleaned-up and carefully arranged reconstruction of events. By keeping alive our mistrust of such things, the political calypsonian invites us to look for alternative versions of events.

The political calypsonian "takes the sheen off the charisma" of public figures whose egos may have become elephantine. His role here is one of social control through humour, picong, reductive commentary. This is, in fact, a traditional role of the artist in West Africa societies and its survival in Trinidad has been something of a miracle. The period under study has been characterised by a closeness and severity of seeing, in which public figures have been placed under a microscope that has magnified and at times distorted the tragic-comic pettiness of their activities.

We have already discussed some of the reactions that have taken place to such fierce scrutiny; the subtle attempts at control, the encouragement of a self-censorship which prevents the state from provoking the unpopularity which would result from open censorship. Some calypsos are permitted because it is believed that the criticisms which they contain are harmless to the system; others because all past attempts at censoring calypsos have simply drawn them to the attention of the public in a special way, and thus enhanced their popularity and impact.

The political Calypso keeps open one area of freedom – freedom of expression – by the vigorous exercise of this freedom. Between 1970 and 1984, freedom has been a consistent theme in the political calypso, and the indivisibility of the various freedoms has been recognised.

Finally, the political calypsonians have been the poets of a nation in search of its soul; in search of a way of moving beyond machismo towards the inclusion of a larger measure of feeling and compassion in our personal and civic consciousness. This struggle has been evident, and has led to revitalisation of the minor modes of the traditional kaiso in a growing number of contemporary calypsos. The calypsonians have kept open a vein of desperately sane reflectiveness on the chaos of our civic life, and in the process have inched an art form rooted in conflict, celebration and the catharsis of light entertainment, towards the deeper qualities of anguish and compassion.

(Conference paper read at the Research Institute for the Study of Man, Conference on Caribbean Studies, New York, (August 28-Sept. 2, 1984); published in *Caribbean Quarterly* ,Vol. 31, No. 2, (June 1985) pp 1-13.)

References

1. As Minister of Home Affairs, Patrick Solomon went to a police station and arbitrarily removed his stepson from custody.
2. *Trinidad Guardian*, Saturday, 2 November, 1968.

ACKNOWLEDGEMENTS

I owe a debt of gratitude to my wife Betty Ann Rohlehr, whose skill, patience and dedication in typesetting this book, know no bounds. Thanks are also due to Martin Carter, whose poem "Not Hands Like Mine" supplied the epigraph from which the title-essay of this volume derives its name; to *Tapia* and the *Trinidad and Tobago Review* whose generous and enlightened editorial policies over the years have been reflected in the extraordinary space which these journals have made available to intellectual discourse; to the staff of UWI Library, St. Augustine for their cooperation over these two decades.

"Articulating a Caribbean Aesthetic, the Revolution in Self-perception" was originally presented as a paper at the Conference on "Caribbean Expressions: African Diaspora in the Americas" sponsored by the Visual Arts Research and Resource Center Relating to the Caribbean, New York, September 18, 1979. It was first published in *Caribe: Caribbean Expressions Festival I*, New York, 1980, pp. 7-15.

"History as Absurdity" was first published in *Tapia* No. 11 (Nov. 29, 1970) and *Tapia* No. 12 (Dec. 20, 1970). An edited version was published in Coombs, O., (ed) *Is Massa Day Dead?* (New York: Doubleday/Anchor, 1974), pp. 69-108.

"Literature and the Folk" was originally a paper read at the ACLALS Conference, UWI, Mona, Jamaica, January, 1971. It was first published in *Tapia*, (December, 1971) and (January, 1972). Two excepts appeared in Baugh E., (ed.) *Critics on Caribbean Literature* (London: George Allen and Unwin, 1979).

"Sounds and Pressure" was originally published in *Moko* No. 16, (Fri. June 6, 1969) and No. 17, (Friday June 20, 1969).

"Once in a Blue Sun" was published as "Review of *The Harder They Come*" in *Tapia*, Vol. 3, No. 24, (June 17, 1973).

"West Indian Poetry: Some Problems of Assessment" was first published in *Tapia* No. 20 (Aug. 29, 1971) pp. 11-14. It also appeared in *Caribbean Quarterly* Vol. 17, Nos. 3 & 4 (Sept- Dec., 1971) pp. 92-113 and in *Bim* Vol. 14, No. 54 (Jan-June, 1972) pp. 80-88 and No. 55 (July-Dec., 1972) pp. 134-144.

"Afterthoughts" was first published in *Tapia* No. 23 (Dec. 26, 1971). It was republished in *Bim* Vol. 14, No. 56 (Jan-June, 1973) pp. 227-232

"Blues for Eric Roach" was published in *Tapia*. Vol. 4, No. 21 (May 26, 1974).

"A Carrion Time" was first published in *Tapia* Vol. 4, No. 24 (June 1973) pp. 5-8 and p. 11. It was republished in *Bim* Vol. 15, No. 58 (June 1975) pp. 92-109.

"My Strangled City" was first published in Roberto Marquez (ed.) *Caliban* Vol. II, No. 1 (Fall/Winter 1976) pp. 50-122. Two sections appeared in John Hearne (ed.) *Carifesta Forum*, Kingston 1976. It was also serialised as "Poetry, Politics and the February Revolution", in *Trinidad & Tobago Review* Part I Vol. 2, No. 4 (Dec 1977) pp. 7-8: 33 Part II, "Transition of Sadness", Vol. 2, No. 5 (Jan. 1978) pp 8, 33-34; Part III, "The Mind Musicians", Vol. 2. No. 6 (Feb., 1978) pp 1215; Part IV, "Prophet and Singer", Vol. 2, No. 8 (April, 1978) pp. 12-14, p. 16; Part V, (a) "Between Timber and Termites", Vol. 2, No; 9 (May 1978) pp. 8, 17-18; Part V (b), "Between Timber and Termites", Vol. 3, No. 10 (June 1978) p. 8, 17; Part VI, "Icy Intuitions", Vol. 2, No. 11/12 (July/August 1978) pp. 12, 14, 21, 26; Part VII, "Valedictory", Vol. 2, No. 13 (Sept. 1978) pp. 8, 13; Part VIII, "Future Mornings", Vol. 3, No. 1 (March 1979) pp. 8, 17.

"Songs of the Skeleton" was published in three phases: Part I "The Poetry of Fission", in *Trinidad & Tobago Review* Vol. IV, No. 3 (Petit Careme, 1980) and Vol. IV, No. 3A (Divali 1980); Part II, "A Poetry of Dread", in *Trinidad and Tobago Review*, Vol. IV, No. 5 (New Year 1981) and Vol. IV, No. 6 (Croptime, March/April 1981); Part III, "Flowers of the Harmattan", paper read at the Fifth Annual Conference on West Indian Literature, College of the Virgin Islands, St. Thomas (May 25-28, 1985) and published in *West Indian Poetry: Proceedings of the Fifth Annual Conference on West Indian Literature*, College of the Virgin Islands, St. Thomas, U.S.V.I. 1986, pp. 201-217.

"Man Talking to Man: Calypso and Social Confrontation in Trinidad 1970 to 1984" was originally a conference paper read at the Research Institute for the Study of Man Conference on Caribbean Studies, New York (August 28 - Sept. 2. 1984). It was published in *Caribbean Quarterly* Vol. 31, No. 2 (June 1985) pp. 1-13.

INDEX

Absurdity and rebellion in *A House for Mr Biswas*, 36
Abyssinians, "Satta Amasa Gana", 93, 106
Africa, rediscovery of in N.E. Cameron's work, 12
African religious survivals, 10
Afro-Saxon psyche, the 39
Akan cosmology, 13
Alphonso, Roland, 80
Anansi stories, 62, 67
Armstrong, Louis, 69
Army mutiny, Trinidad, 7
Atilla the Hun (Raymond Quevedo, calypsonian), 62, 74, 222, 280
Autobiography of Malcolm X, 180
Baldwin, James, 15; *Go Tell it on the Mountain*, 186
Barrett, Lindsay, *Song for Mumu*, 107
Bassies, "Things a Come up to Bump", 86
Bastien, Elliot, 150, "And Here You Are Now", 157
Beddeau, Andrew, 214, 252
Bennett, Louise, 12, **65-77**, 109; attack on class and colour snobbery, 66-67; Anansi stories, 67; rejection of fixed class identities, 67-68. Poems: "Bans O' Killing", 66; "Suffrage", 68; "Candy-Seller" and "South Parade Peddler", 69; comparison to quarrel calypsos: "Cuss-Cuss", 69; physical caricature, 70; proverbial wisdom and moralising in: "Dutty Tough", 70-72; political commentary: "Problem", "White Pickney", 72-75, irony and anti-racist and anti-misogynist logic in; "Pass for White", 75-76; commitment to Jamaican identity: "Back to Africa", 73; comparison with Walcott in attitude to mulatto consciousness, 76; Bennett's poems as performative, improvisations in tonal range, 76-77; Anancy stories and oral performance, 77; *Jamaica Labrish*, 98
Best, Alec, "Memorial Blues for Billie Holiday", 178
Best, Lloyd, 149
Bhajan, Selwyn, *Season of Songs, Quest*, 150; poetry of rural images and transcendental meditation, 227-228
Black Power, 18, 48; uprising, Trinidad, 7; US influences transformed by Trinidadian cultural expression, 48-49
Black Stalin (calypsonian), 11, 150; "Piece o' de Action", 284; "Breakdown Party", 285, 287; "Mr Divider", 285; "Money", 285, 286; "Steelband Gone", "De Jam", 288; "De Ole Talk", "More Times", "Vampires", 289-290; "Nothing Ain't Strange", 290
Black stereotypes, 9
Blackman, Peter, 14
Blakie (calypsonian), "De Doctah Ent Deh", 158, 281, 285
Blyden, Edward Wilmot, 12
Bogle, Paul, 106, 111, 249, 252
Bolom myth, 129, 155, 218, 256, 262
Bomber (calypsonian), "Political Wonder", 282, 283
Bongo Jerry, "Sooner or Later", 109-110; "Mabrak", 102, 108, 140-141, 240; rhetorical style, 108; tribute to Don Drummond, 106-107; cryptic imagery in, 112; Morris's enlightenment on hearing poem, 112
Bongo, derivation of word and counter-uses, 110
Brathwaite, Kamau: 14, 66, 118; on Walcott's terror of peasant poverty, 57; poems of hope, 234; influence on younger poets, 157. Poetry: *Rights of Passage*, 9; *Masks*, 13, 239;

"The Making of the Drum", 188; "SunSum", 196; "Kumasi", 251-252; "Tano", 276; *Arrivants*, 11, 19, 239: "The Spades", 107, "Wings of a Dove", 107-108, 216, 249; "Francina", 216; "Trade Winds", 129; "Wake", 36; *Islands*, 239; "Ananse", 197; return of the stranger in "Homecoming", 241-242; "Negus", 265; *Other Exiles*, 20; "Jazz Portraits", 178; *Black + Blues*, 20, **234-278**: poems responding to contemporary ravages of political defeats and fragmentation, 234; on drug addiction destroying black communities, "Glass", 20, 237-239, 258; on street violence in "Springblade", 215, 234, 246, 250-259, 265, 266; "Eating the Dead", 234; "Conqueror, 234, 235-236, 258; "Fetish", 234, 235; the ominous in "Starvation", 234, 247-250; "Moor", 234; "Trane", 234; images of drought, allusions to Othello and Roach's "The Fighters" in "Caliban"; 21, 234, 240-244; energy as creative or destructive, 245; as Dahomean cripple god, 246; as Shakespeare's holiday fool, 247; "Manchild", 253-254; "Krow", 260-262, 263; "Bread", 264; "Labourer", 264, 271; "Harmattan Poems", 262-264; "Sun Song", 250, 262, 263, 264-266; "Kite", 264, 268-269; "Suman", 265; "Shango", 267-268; "Crab", 269-276; *Mother Poem*, 244, 265: "Milkweed", 271; "Hex", 275; *Third World Poems*: "Kingston in the Kingdom of this World", 263; *Sun Poem*, 267. Essays and criticism: "Sir Galahad and the Islands", 14, 56, 128; "The New West Indian Novelists", 57-58; CAM and *Savacou*, 98; on artist as participant and servant, 197; "Caribbean Man in Space and Time", 235; critique of growing solipsism in Caribbean fiction in "The New West Indian Novelists", 136-137; "Art and Society", 137-138

British royalty and Caribbean attitudes, 39

Brooks, Baba, 80

Brooks, Gwendolyn, "The Mother", 250

Brown, Wayne, 101, 103; *On the Coast*, 150, 151; as Walcott echo, 144, 147; Roach's review of as Tribe Boys vs. Afro-Saxons, 151; Walcott on Brown's "confused shorthand", 156; Brown's attack on turn to Africa as "hunchbacked Blackness", 173; "Soul on Ice", seen as having close verbal resemblances to Walcott's winter poetry, 211; Brown's continuing of the cultural quarrel over *Savacou* 3/4 in a personally abusive poem, 131-132; Brown's stand seen as an echo of Walcott's abusive rhetoric in *Another Life*, 132-133; Brown's self-righteous simplification of Walcott's complexity", 133-134; Rohlehrian picong on Brown, 134, 144; Brown as dismisser of Brathwaite's *Rights of Passage* and *Masks* as mere prose, 134; echoes of Roach's criticism of Savacou 3/4, 135-136; view of Caribbean artist as alienated Western man, 135-136; GR locates Brown's position on one side of an on-going argument involving early Lamming and Kamau Brathwaite concerning artist as isolato and part of his/her community, 137-138; Brown's echo attack on Bongo Jerry and "Mabrak", 139; inconsistencies of Brown's position on pose of artistic alienation, 140; Brown's trivial treatment of Roach's poetry in earlier essay, 144; attack on Syl Lowhar and Gordon Rohlehr over their eulogies for Eric Roach, as "carrion", "treachery", 131; answered by Rohlehr, **131-148**: untruths about Roach's relationship to younger poets and the sources of his despair, 141-142; praise for Anthony McNeill but dismissal of Brathwaite, despite McNeill's deep appreciation of Brathwaite, 146

Burnham, Forbes, 23

Butler, Tubal Uriah Buzz, 48, 54, 59, 129

Byles, Junior, "Beat Down Babylon", 89

Calliste, Leroy, *474 Years of Pain and Suffering*, 150; psychic breakdown, lost innocence and rural retreat, 178; "South Trumpeter" (see also poems on Don Drummond's death), 178-179, 216

Calypso, 11, 59-60; ethnic stereotypes in, 60-61; secular absence of folk-religious roots, 71; comparison with reggae, 121-122; suffering from Trinidad's neo-colonial openness to every external cultural influence, 123; calypso and politics in Trinidad, 121, **279-293**: bad-john violence, 279; anti-feminist calypsos, 279; "race calypsos", 279-280; political calypsos, 280-282; 1934 censorship ordinance, 280; patriotic calypsos, 281; absence of protest from old school, 282; soca and politics, 282; images of Eric Williams, **283-288**; on state's failure to deal with drug's crisis, 285; on misuse of oil revenues, 285-286; on citizen's duties: 288-291; the political calypsonian 1970-1984, 291-293; absence of radio air-play, 291; politics vs entertainment, 291-292; importance for maintaining freedom of expression, 293

Cameron, Norman, *The Evolution of the Negro*, 12-13, as a pioneer of African consciousness in Caribbean, 13

Camus, Albert, *Resistance, Rebellion and Death*, 166

Carew, Jan, 52

Caribbean aesthetics, **9-21**

Caribbean Artists Movement, 98

Caribbean Quarterly: Anthology of West Indian Poetry, 98

Caribbean writers in Africa, 14

Carlyle, Thomas, 49

Carnegie, James, 48

Carpentier, Alejo, 20, 33

Carter, Martin, 21, 116, 117, 121, 138, 149; "Black Friday 1962", 35, 152; "Poems of Shape and Motion", 118; "University of Hunger", "I Come from the Nigger Yard", 154; "After One Year", 182; "Not Hands Like Mine", 200-201

Césaire, Aimé, *Cahier d'un retour au pays natal*, 26, 33, 126-127; *Discourse on Colonialism*, 212

Chalkdust (calypsonian), 11, 150, 177; "Massa Day Must Done", 100; "Ah Fraid Karl", 204; "Answer to Black Power", 283, "Two Sides of a Shilling", 283, 285; "Deafness or Dr Aziz", 283; "Somebody Mad", 285, 286; "Trinidad Dollar", 285; "De Spirit Gone", 286, 288; "Three Blind Mice", 286; "Caribbean Unity", 287; "Eric Williams Loves Me", 287; "Uncle Sam Own We", 288; "Cultural Heritage", 289; "Ah Put on Me Guns Again", "Shango Vision", "Ayatollah", 289; "Message to George Weekes", 291; "Somebody in PNM Love Me", 292

Charismatic political leadership and manipulation, 19

Charles, Faustin, *The Expatriate*, 98, 151: "Black Cat", 178; biological vision in *Crab Track*, 226, 269; influences of Harris and Walcott, 226-227

Churchill, Winston, 37

Clarke, Le Roy, *Douens*, 270

INDEX

Cliff, Jimmy (*The Harder They Come*), 90; "Sufferers in the Land", 254
Collymore, Frank (*Bim*), 12, 98
Coltrane, John, 11, 123, 159, 162, 163, 164, 239
Conrad, Joseph, *Heart of Darkness*, 27, 34, 56; *Nostromo*, 252; *The Nigger of the "Narcissus"*, 135
Convince cult, 110
Coombs, Orde, *Is Massa Day Dead?*, 192
Corlit, 150
Corsbie, Ken, 143, 150
Coulthard, Gabriel, *Race and Colour in Caribbean Literature*, 15
Crab imagery in Caribbean poetry, 269, 270
Craig, Susan, 149
Creole (calypsonian), "Behind the Bridge", 100; "I Want to be Tight", 285
Creolisation as colonial self-contempt, 59; as violation in *The Mimic Men*, 62
Cristo (calypsonian), 280
Crowley, Daniel, 14
Damas, *Pigments*, 27
Daniel Heartman, Ras, 48; *Daniel in the Lion's Den*, 113
Danquah, J.B., 255
Dante, *Inferno*, 185, 270
Darbeau, Dave, 142; on Carmichael and Hamilton's *Black Power*, 162
Davidson, Basil, *Old Africa Rediscovered*, 12
Davis, Basil, 195
Davis, Wayne, *Old Oracle, Timeless Dream*, 150; **174-178**; UMROBI, 174; jazz influences, in "Kaleidoscope", 174; political detention, 174-175; on the alienated city in "Squares" and "Dawn", 175; sadism, madness and scatological imagery in "Prison House Blues", 175-178, 185, 223
Dawes, Neville, 52
Defoe, Daniel, 32
Dekker, Desmond, "007", 85; "Poor Me Israelites", 86

Delamo (calypsonian), "Apocalypse", 288, 289; "Armageddon", 289
Discontinuities in Black struggle, 20
Dostoyevsky, *Notes from Underground*, 163
Drummond, Don, 77, **80-87,** 105-106, 107, 249; musician of the inferno of Kingston, 80-81; roots in Rastafari and Pukkumina, 81; political expression in "Marcus Junior", "The Reburial", "Fidel", 82; worksong call-and-response patterns, 112; Black consciousness in, 113; desolation and sorrow in solos, 82-83; Rastafari connections in "Addis Ababa", "Beardman Ska", 82-83; esteem amongst musicians, 83; McNeill's appreciation of, 102-103; Morris's elegy, 108
Du Bois, W.E.B., 9, *The Souls of Black Folk*, 12
Duke (calypsonian), 280, "They Taught us both the Black and White", 282; "Lock them up Dr Williams", 283
Eccles, Clancy, "Rod of Correction", 89
Ecological catastrophe, 20
Elder, Dr J.D., 198
Eliot, T.S., *The Waste Land*, 65; "Ash Wednesday", 265; "Burnt Norton", 272
Ellison, Ralph (*Invisible Man*), 9, 163, 192, 199
Embryo, 142, 150, 162
Ethiopians, "Everything Crash", 86
Ethnic conflict, 18
European history, meaning of, 20
Executor (calypsonian), 280
Explainer (calypsonian), "Tables Turning", 289
Expression 1971 (PNM cultural jamboree), 115
Fanon, Frantz, *Black Skin, White Masks*, 9
Federation, 14
Figueroa, John, *Love Leaps Here*, 98;

as editor of *Caribbean Voices*, vols 1 & 2, 98
Fitzgerald, Ella, 69
Folk in Caribbean literature, **52-79**; Lamming's class analysis, 52; novelists as "peasant", 52-53; definitions of peasant, 53; contrast between folk and urban, 53; Rohlehr's critique of the peasant thesis, 55-56; Rohlehr's critique of Lamming regarding fluidity of Caribbean class boundaries, 53-54, 57; living existence of peasant society in self-activity, not literature, 54; writers as reflecting, not restoring, 54; critique of Lamming's simplifications of Selvon as "peasant", 55; *In the Castle of My Skin* concerned with both fragmentation and fluidity, 55-56; Brathwaite on the "folk" and distinction between "peasant" and "folk", 56-57; Brathwaite's concept of the "urban village", 57; ethnic divisions within the "folk", 60-62; Selvon and the oral tradition, 63-64; Selvon's "boys" and immaturity, 64-65; group consciousness and literary sophistication in architecture of "peasant" novels, 65; Louise Bennett, as exemplar of folk-urban continuum, **66-77**; as poet of folk-urban transitions, 68; use of nation language, 68-69
Folk-tales and proverbs, survival and renewal of, 11
Fraser, Alfred, 142, **159-167**, 204; evolution from isolation to political commitment, 166-167, 180. Poems: "Woodford Square, Port of Spain", 159; "The West Indian", traumatic movement from tribal village to diasporic city, 159-160; "Between Histories", search for artistic mentors, 160; rejection of group consciousness, "A Simple Nihilistic Philippic", 161-162; influence of jazz aesthetics in "John Coltrane Is Dead", 162-163; theatre of the absurd in "Protoplasmic Consciousness", 163-164, (see also Walcott "A Village Life"), 165, 196; existentialism and conversion to Fanonian violence, in "Existentialism, Revolution and Death", 166
Freyre, Gilberto, 247
Froude, James, 49
Fuentes, Carlos, 20
Gandhi, Mahatma, 38
Garvey, Marcus, 11, 12, 13, 14, 18, 82, 83, 106, 111, 124, 249, 252; *Philosophy and Opinions*, 12, 13
Gay, John, *The Beggar's Opera*, 84
Gibraltar (calypsonian), 280, "Politics" 283
Gomes, Albert, 24, 59-60
Gonzalez, Anson, 142, 157; critique of political masquerade in "Cadence", 99, 167-168; *Score*, 150, 151; *The Love Song of Boysie B*, 150, 151; critique of revolutionaries and Black Power, 168; "Decision", 168; "Who Killed My Son", 168; "Hey Alfie", 168-169, 216; "Nation's State", 169-170
Goveia, Elsa, 15, 25, 33; *A Study on the Historiography of the British West Indies*, 33, 50
Granger, Geddes, 116, 171
Growling Tiger (calypsonian), 280, 281
Guerrilla warfare in Trinidad, 170
Guillen, Nicholas, 99
Hackett, Winston, 151, "Survival", 195, 198
Harris, Wilson, 16-17, 65, 138; *Guyana Quartet*, 17; *Palace of the Peacock*, 20, 236; "The Question of Form and Realism in the West Indian Artist", 269
Hendricks, A.L., 101; *On This Mountain*, 98
Hendrix, Jimi, 238
Henzell, Perry (*The Harder They Come*), 88

Hercules, F.E.M., 14
Herskovits, Melville and Francis, 14
Hill, Errol, *Whistling Charlie and the Monster*, 176
Hinds, Justin, "Carry Go Bring Come", 83; political commentary as proverb, 109
Historical processes, on destructiveness of in Caribbean, 16; variant Caribbean attitudes to, 16
Hogg, Donald, 10, 110
Holiday, Billie, 238
Hope and despair in history, 21
Hopkinson, Slade, "Mad Woman of Papine", 254-255
Horowitz, Michael, *The Children of Albion*, 164
Hughes, Langston, "The Negro Speaks of Rivers", 173
Hughes, Ted, "Crow", 260
Indians in the Caribbean, 16
Irony and the colonial experience, 27-28; as mingled love and hate, 30; irony as probe, irony as self-reassurance, 39
Jagan, Cheddi, 54
Jagessar, Ramdath, "The New Discrimination", 162
Jahn, Janheinz, *Muntu*, 15
Jamaica: Afro-Protestantism in cultural expression, 124
James, C.L.R., fall-out with Williams, 36, 38; *Minty Alley*, 11, *Toussaint L'Ouverture*, 11; *The Black Jacobins*, 13, 33, 43
Jazz in West Indian poetry: See Brathwaite, Shake Keane, Wayne Davis, Mervyn Morris, Alec Best and Anthony McNeill, 178
John, Frank, *Black Songs*, 98
Johnny King (calypsonian), "Nature's Plan", 289
Johnson, Astor, 150
Jones, LeRoi (Amiri Baraka), 71
Joseph, Daniel Samaroo, "Taxi Mister", 62
Joyce, James, 27, 137; *Portrait of the Artist*, 57

Kairi House group, 143, 150, 204; "Iswe", 143
Kairi, 150
Kalinda, 12
Keane, Shake, 118, "Shaker Funeral" and "Calypso Dancers", 178
Keens-Douglas, Paul, 11
Keil, Charles, 71
Killer (calypsonian), 60
King Austin (calypsonian), "Progress", 286
King, Martin Luther, 18
Kingsley, Charles, 103-104
Kingstonians, "Sufferer", 86, 254
Kissoon, Freddie, 143
Knibb, Mrs Mary (Miss Married Knibbs), 68
Kwesi, Lasana (Winston Daniel), *Giving Back to My People, Poems of Rebellion*, 138, 150
La Rose, John, *Foundations*, 98
Laird, Christopher 150; "The Road", 167, 222-223; "In Memory of Future Mornings", 222
Laird, Judith, 150
Lamming, George, 118, 193; writer as alienated existentialist, 135, 136; attitudes to land, national differences, 54-55; "The Negro Writer and his World", 15; *Of Age and Innocence*, 18, 19, 208; *In the Castle of My Skin*, 18, 35, 55-56, 65, crab imagery in, 269; influence of Conrad, 56, 135; characters as fragments of a single consciousness, 56; *Water with Berries*, 20, 137; *Natives of My Person*, 20, 273; *New World of the Caribbean*, 26; *The Pleasures of Exile*, 52-55; *Season of Adventure*, 125
Lancelot Lane (calypsonian), "Get off the Radio", 289
Laurence, K.O., 24
Leavis, F.R., 126
Lee, Byron (as middle-class appropriator of ska), 82
Legba, 209, 246, 256, 271, 275

Leveller (calypsonian), "How to Stop Delinquency", 281
Little Roy, "Bongo Nyah", 110-112
Lord Fluke (calypsonian) 168
Lord Kitchener (calypsonian), 65, 292; "No Freedom", 204; "The Road", 222
Lord Melody (Fitzroy Alexander), "Peddlars", 62; "Sparrow's Sister", 69
Lord Shorty, "Fat Pants Fathers", 70
Love, Robert, 13
Lovelace, Earl, 142, 150
Lowhar, Syl, 142, **170-174**; founder member of Tapia, 171; revolutionary role and internment, 171-172; advocate of freedom, 171; poetry: "Bureaucracy, 172; "To Martin Carter", 172-173; from rural to urban in "Shantytown", 173; spiritual drought in "Dry River", 173-174.
Maestro (calypsonian), "To Sir with Love", 283; "Mr Trinidad, 288
Mais, Roger, 52, 55, 176; *The Hills Were Joyful Together*, 55, 216, 256; *Brother Man*, 65, 257; *Black Lightning*, 240
Malcolm, Carlos, 80
Malik, Abdul (Delano De Couteau), 11, 99, 138, **179-193** 220; cofounder of Trinidad Black Panthers; confined as political detainee, 180; *Black Up*, *Revo*, 150, 156; "Afro-Saxon", 176; "The Bad Poet" performance, 180-181; New World Black as "The Zebra", 181-182, 186; "Pan Run I & II", **182-193**; as a richly allusive dramatic poem on the betrayal of black hopes by Afro-Saxon political elite, on bad-johnism trapped in history, 182-183; anatomy of the poverty and class oppression that produced 1970, 185-186; pan as the symbolic womb of resistance, 188; symbol of drum, 188; pan and anti-Indian political violence, 189;

pan-man as a persona who straddles Africa, Trinidad and rural-urban "divides", 193; notes of affirmation, 193; "Motto Vision", 221; "Fireflies for Beverley", "Climb to Freedom", 222
Maloney, Arnold H., 14
Manley, Michael, 89
Manning, Frank, 282
Maraj, Jagdip, 228
Marley, Bob, "Duppy Conqueror", 89, 124-125, 254, 256; "Small Axe", 125
Maroonage, 9
Marshall, Woodville, 53-54
Marxism-Leninism, 19
Massy, Alvin, geographical visions in "Tourist Brochure", 225-226, echoes of Césaire, 226
Matthews, Marc, 143; "For Cuffy", 102, 125-126; Dem Two/All a We, 143, 150
Max Romeo, "Babylon's Burning", 254
Maxwell, Marina, "Bongo Man a Come", 124
Maytals, "54-46 That's My Number", 86; "Scare Him", 86
McCook, Tommy, 80
McFarlane, Basil, 146
McKay, Claude, 11
McNeill, Anthony, 21, 95; "Saint Ras", "Ode to Brother Joe", 102-103; "Rimbaud Jungle", 103; "The Children", 146; ungod, 269; *Reel from the "Life Movie"*, 144: "Who'll See Me Dive", "The True Gage", "Suicide's Girlfriend", 145; *Credences at the Altar of Cloud*, 270
McTair, Dionne, 142
McTair, Roger, 142; "Corners without Answers", 99-100, 149, trapped hopelessness, **157**; on *Savacou* controversy, 151; Walcott on, 156; on links between Black Power and Soul Culture, 158; 162-163; "Notes Towards a Final Belief", 167; "March-February Remembering", 181, 222, 223-224

Melody (calypsonian), "Doctor Make Your Love", 280
Mendes, Alfred, 11
Mighty Dictator (calypsonian), "Moonia", 61
Mighty Duke, the (Kevin Pope), 69
Mighty Sparrow, "Jean and Dinah", 71, 190; "Gunslingers",91, 183; "Rope", 91; "Get to Hell Outa Here", 158, 281, 284; "Sedition", 204; 282; "Leave the Damn Doctor", 281; "Solomon", 281; "Honesty", 281; "He Went off on Dope", 285; "Neurosis of the Rich", "Capitalism Gone Mad", 286; "Ah Digging Horrors", 286; "Good Citizen", 288
Mighty Spoiler (Theophilus Philip), 66
Miles, Judy, 150, 215; urban desert in "The Holocaust", "Lunch Hour", 158-159, 166; "Suicide?", 210; "Black Out", 210-211
Millette, James, 149
Milner, Harry, on *The Harder They Come*, 91-92
Mittelholzer, Edgar, 52
Mohammed, Kamal, 49
Moralising and didactic element in popular culture, 11
Morris, Mervyn, 66, 112; *Seven Jamaican Poets*, 98; "Valley Prince", 108
Mulatto consciousness (Walcott), 17
Multi-ethnic societies, complexities of, 18
Murphy, Audie, *To Hell and Back*, 183
Murray, Dave, 142
Muslimeen attempted coup 1990, 7
Muttoo, Henry, 150
Mystical Revelation of Rastafari (Count Ossie), 123-124
Naipaul, Seepersad, *Gurudeva and Other Indian Tales*, 12
Naipaul, V.S., 15, 33, 105; at Oxford, 30-31; on culture of cinematic mimicry in Trinidad, 184; differences between Naipaul the novelist and social commentator, 49. Works: *Miguel Street*, 64; *The Middle Passage*, 35, 40, 47, 153; *A House for Mr Biswas*, 30, 36; *The Mimic Men*, 16, 20-21, 62, 167
Nationalism, 19
Neocolonialism, 36-37
Nettleford, Rex, 66, 76
Newton, Selwyn, *474 Years of Pain and Suffering*, 150
Niney the Observer (Winston Holness), "Blood and Fire", 254
NJAC (National Joint Action Committee), 115, 138, 142, 143, 149, 167, 150, 170, 291
Nuttal, Jeff, 183-184
Nyabingi, 111, 249
Ogun, 21, 190, 241, 244-245, 266
Oliver, Paul, *The Meaning of the Blues*, 80-81; submission and rebellion in, 81
Oral and scribal traditions, 65-66
Outsider positions, 17
Owens, R.J., as example of expatriate white liberal criticism on Carter and Roach, 117-118
Paddington, Bruce, 180
Padmore, George, 13
Panther (calypsonian), "Taxi Drivers", 63
Pantomime, in Jamaica, transformation of in 1970s, 94
Parker, Charlie (Bird), 11, 238
Patterson, Orlando, 107
Paz, Octavio, 235
Pearse, Andrew, 14
Pelican, 167
People's National Movement (PNM), 23, 37, 38, 50, 190, 216, 281, 283, 292
Picong, 12, 37, 60, 62, 69, 89, 117, 194, 282, 292
Pivot, membership, 142; the movement from art to politics, 142-143; 150
Planno, Ras Mortimo, 108
Poetry, Caribbean: 1960s-1970, **98-119**
Prince Buster, 83, "Prince Buster

Fabulous", 85; ambivalence of "Judge Dread", 85-86; "Pharoah House Crash", 254

Psycho (calypsonian), "Jail Them", 100

Pukkumina, 10, 81, 82, 110, 124, 126, 257

Questel, Victor, 7, 21, 143, 176, 181, **194-210**; as critic, 151; punning, 157, 195, 200; founder member of Pivot, 194; poet of wit, control and dry humour and consistent development, 194; on the quest for ancestors; relationship to Walcott and Brathwaite, 195, 199-200, 202; connections with work of Martin Carter, 200-201; writing from within the working class heart of the city, 195; steelband as ambivalent echo of Africa, 199; writing in a climate of fear, 203-204. Poetry: "Downbeat", 99, 103; *Score*, 150, 151, 195; "Torn", 194-195; on the need for community in, "Words and Gestures", **196-206**; "The Epileptic Boy of February", 198; crab and snail images, 198; "Prelude", 201, Crusoe and Adamic allusions, 202-203; *The Doctor He Dead* (play), 204-205; "Only Believe", 206; "Near Mourning Ground", as hesitant movement towards Spiritual Baptists as folk and to the figure of the cult leader: 195, 206-210

Quevedo, Raymond (Atilla the Hun), 74-75

Ramchand, Kenneth, 98

Ramon-Fortune, Barnabas, 142

Ras Dizzy (Bongo), 105, 248-249

Rastafari, 10, 48, 68, 105; symbolism, 107; dread/ness, 108, 113-114, 122; hymns of 121-122

Rebellion and resistance of enslaved, 10

Redfield, Robert, definitions of peasant society, 53

Reggae, 68; songs of sufferation and rebellion, 86-87; comparison with more sophisticated language of calypso, 86-87, 123; proverbial wisdom in, 87; dread in, 240, 254

Reid, V.S., 52; *The Leopard*, 14

Relator (calypsonian), "Deaf Panman", 283, 284, 288; "Radio Stations", 288

Reynolds, Mallica (Kapo), 137-138, 197

Rhone, Trevor (*The Harder They Come*), 88, 92; *Smile Orange*, 96

Rhys, Jean, 33

Riviere, Bill, 149

Roach, Eric, 14, 21, 57, 154; barrier to appreciation without having collected, published work, 128; despair over collapse of Federation and drying up of work in 1960s, 154; involvement with younger writers in Trinidad, 154; Roach as attender of Pivot meetings, 141-143; appreciation of by Brathwaite, Walcott and Lamming, **128-130**; study of by Cheryl Williams, 128-129, 151; poet of landscape and peasantry, 129; images of death in later poetry, 130-131; Roach's rejection of *Savacou* 3/4, 219. Poetry: "I am the Archipelago", 116-117; "Frigate Bird Passing", 128; "He Juggles Images", 130; "For Frank Collymore", 130; late work 1970-1974: **215-221**; "Growing Up in Tobago", 215-216, 219; visions of urban dereliction in "Poem for This Day", 216; "The Homestead", 216-217; "City Centre '70", 217-218; "Hard Drought", 218; "Verse in August", 218, 220-221; "The Ballad of Canga Brown", 218; poems of faith in the islands, "Fugue for Federation", "Love Overgrows a Rock", 141, 221; "The Fighters", 244-245

Robber-talk, 37, 117

Rocksteady, emergence from ska, 83

INDEX

Rodney, Walter, 7; *A History of the Upper Guinea Coast*, 33
Rodriguez, Rico, 83
Rohlehr, Gordon, personal history, 7, 8; pessimism, 120; tastes, 100; on politics and art, 120-121; mission to integrate, not separate, 143; on work on calypso, *From Attila to the Seventies*, 143; on duties of the critic, 151-152
Rudie songs, 83-86; anarchist stance: "Tougher than Tough", "Dreader than Dread", 84; comparison to bad-john calypsos, 84; trials in, 84, 85-86; Judge Dread, 85, 113, 263; Prince Buster's critique of Black on Black violence, 85-86
Salkey, Andrew, 52, 98; *A Quality of Violence*, 263
Sanders, Pharoah, 11, 123
Sans humanite picong, 12, 37, 60, 69, 117; self-contempt in, 62
Savacou 3/4, contents and editorial issues, 99; Jamaican biases, absent Trinidadians, 99; Eric Roach's critical attitude to experiment and appreciation of traditional, 100-101; Roach's criticism of alleged fanatical racial assertion, 103; Syl Lowhar's response, 101; Rohlehr's areas of agreement and disagreement over Roach's premises, 101-102; over Roach's failure to deal with blending of scribal and oral, 103-104; over Roach's apparent Afro-phobia and Eurocentrism, 103-104, 219-220; over failure to confront totality of Caribbean history, 105; critique of Roach's one-sided reverence for English verse tradition, 115-116; inconsistency between Roach as poet and critic, 116
Scatting, 69
Scott, Dennis, 21, 66, 103; "No Sufferer", 182
Seaga, Edward, 89

Sealey, Clifford, *Voices*, 98, 142, 150
Selvon, Samuel, 52, 55, 57, 118; language distinctions in *A Brighter Sun*, 58-59; Brathwaite's distinction between Selvon's different worlds: peasant: *A Brighter Sun*, 57, 58, *Turn Again Tiger*, 57-59, 61, 62, 64; "Cane is Bitter", 57; *The Plains of Caroni*, 58; urban stories: "Down the Main", "Wartime Activities", "Calypsonian", 58; urban novels: *The Lonely Londoners, The Housing Lark*, 58, 64-65, 68; of the soul-searching middle-class: *An Island is a World*, 58
"Sergeant Pepper" (The Beatles), 65
Sewell, William, *Ordeal of Free Labour*, 43, 53
Seymour, A.J. (*Kyk-over-Al*), 12, 98, 118; anthology, *Kyk* 22, 1957; *Selected Poems*, 98.
Shaffer, Peter, *The Royal Hunt of the Sun*, 273
Shango (god), 244, 245, 264, 266, 267, 268, 275
Shango (worship), 81, 102, 172, 189, 193, 208, 214, 236, 289
Shepp, Archie, 95
Shorty (calypsonian), "Money No Problem", 285
Simpson, George Eaton, 14
Ska, origins of, 81-82; sexuality in, and difference from calypso, 81
Skatalites, 82
Slavery and the plantation system, 9
Smith, M.G., 14
Smith, Raymond, 14
Smith, Slim, "The Time Has Come for I", 83
Sniper (calypsonian), "Portrait of Trinidad", 281
Sons of Negus, 84-85, 121-122
Spiritual Baptists, 10, 206, 208
Striker (calypsonian), 280
Swallow (calypsonian), "Trinidad Godfather", 285
Swift, Jonathan, satire on British

imperialism, 27; colonial ambition and self-contempt (seen as parallel to Williams' psyche), 28; *A Modest Proposal*, 28; *Gulliver's Travels* as critique of Europe, 28-29, 31
Syncretism in religious practice, 10
Tacky, 252
Tapia, 142, 150
Taylor, Jeremy, 180,181
Taylor, Lloyd, 142
Terror (calypsonian), "Madness", 285
The Harder They Come (film), **88-97**, 183; made for Jamaicans and rooted in Jamaican reality, 88-89; obstacles to showing in Trinidad, 89, 91; political context of film, 89-90; patterns of violence and reprisal in Jamaican society, 90; synopsis, 90-91; performances in, 96-97; hero as fantasist, comparison with Sparrow's "Gunslingers", 91; critiques of film in Jamaica located in class complacency, 91-93; as a film which locates the violence in music to the streets, 95; market capitalism shown as exploiter of talent, 95-96
The Pioneers, "Starvation", 254
The Tempest (Shakespeare), 246-247
Themes, 150
Thomas, J.J. *Froudacity*, 49
Tosh, Peter, 11, 254; "Buckingham Palace", 290
Trickster figures, 62-63
Trinidad Theatre Workshop, dramatization of Selvon's stories, 143
Trinidad, as a fragmented society, 123
Trinidadian poetry 1964-1975 and Black Power uprising, **149-233**; cross-talk, 151; the *Savacou* debate, 151; influence of Brathwaite's *Arrivants*, 156-157
Trollope, Anthony, 103
Twain, Mark, 118
U Roy, 69, 108; "Babylon Burning", 86
Unit 16, 150, 161

University of the West Indies, former neo-colonial English literature curriculum and denial of Caribbean cultural resources, 117, 126
University of Woodford Square, 24, 37-38, 159, 217
Valentino (calypsonian), 11, 150, 223; "No Revolution", 283, 288; "Barking Dogs", 283, 284, 288; "Liberation", "Dis Place Nice", 288
Vallee, the Pretender (Calypsonian), "Black Power", 283
Virgil, 270
Vodun, 10
Walcott, Derek, 21, 118; creative schizophrenia", 76; on politics and art, 121; Walcott's newspaper articles and reviews, 133-134, 151; dramatisation of Brathwaite's "Wings of a Dove" and "The Dust", 143; criticism of black urban culture, 191; criticism of false pastoralism of Better Village competitions, 192. Poetry: *In a Green Night*, 154, "Steersman My Brother" 158; "Choc Bay", 195; *The Gulf*, 153, 154; "Landfall Grenada", "Statio Haud Malefida Carinis",103, "Blues"; *The Castaway*, 203: "Laventille", 154-155, 193, 216, and its influence on other poets, 173,175, 186; political despair of "The Swamp", 155; criticism of preoccupation with blackness and Africa, 156; "A Village Life", allusions to by other poets, 195, 196; ambivalence over theatre of the absurd in "A Village Life", 165; masquerade in "Mass Man" and Junta", 167, 200, 205, 217; "A Patriot to Patriots", 170; "The Glory Trumpeter", 178; "Greenwich Village, Winter", "The Flock", "God Rest Ye Merry Gentlemen", influences on Wayne Brown, 211; "Sea Crab", 269, 272; turn to vituperation against the

turn to Africa and fellow artists, academic and historians in *Another Life*, 213-214; rejection of a political role in "A Patriot to Patriots", 214-215; "At Last", 215; "The Wind in the Dooryard", for Roach, 215. Plays: *Dream on Monkey Mountain*, 16, 40, 212-213; *Ti Jean and his Brothers*, 256; *The Charlatan*, *In a Fine Castle*, *The Joker of Seville*, 151, 203. Criticism: "The Muse of History", 16, 191; "What the Twilight Says: An Overture", 100

White, Garth, "Rudie, Oh Rudie", 84, 113

Williams, Cheryl, on Roach, 143-144, 151

Williams, Denis, 14; *Other Leopards*, 235

Williams, E.E. (Eric), 14, 59, 280; *Capitalism and Slavery*, 15, 26-27, 32; *From Columbus to Castro*, 23-51; failure to provide references, 32-33; Williams as philosopher-king, historian-politician, 23; *History of the People of Trinidad and Tobago*, overstatements, partisanship and omissions, 24-25, 49; *British Historians and the West Indies*, Goveia's critique of, 25; unfair criticism of other WI historians, 26; fact-accumulating historical method, 26-27, 32, 33; *The Negro in the Caribbean*, 26, 30; *Inward Hunger*, 27-28, 36; appreciation of Swift, Shaw and Joyce, 27-28 and resemblances to Swift's psychic divisions, 29, 31; fighting the white elite at Oxford, 29-30; Williams as polemical pamphleteer, 32; absence of human dimension, 34; failure to explore the dynamics of revolt and submission under slavery, 34; Caribbean history as absurdity, 36, 40, resemblances to V.S. Naipaul, 40, 47, 48; as historical grand inquisitor, 40-41; failure to engage with later historians of Abolition, 40-41; hypocrisy over issues of popular power and democracy in critique of Wilberforce, 41-42; Williams and repressive laws against dissent, 42; verbatim uncritical use of earlier books, 42, 43-44; failure to deal with the political unrest of 1960s and 70s, 43; ambivalence over the Cuban revolution, 45-46; absence of social history and contemporary economic dimensions, 44-45; failure to engage with need for educational reform and repression of academics, 46; Williams' despair over Caribbean identity and confusions between economic and cultural dependence, 47, 48-49; *My Relations with the Caribbean Commission*, 36; *Massa Day Done*, 36-39; *Education in the British West Indies*, 46

Williams, John A., *The Man Who Cried I Am*, 161-162

Williams, Sylvester, 13

Wilson, Delroy, "Better Must Come", 89

"Woman a Hebby Load", 112

Wright, Richard, *Black Boy*, 15

Wyke, Marguerite, 142, 150; "History Leaves No Memorials", "Guyana", "On Remembering Immortelles", 152-153; on history and search for sanity in an insane world, 153-154; "A Plume of Dust", 167; "Tonight the Soucouyant", 199

Wynter, Sylvia, 27, critique of metropolitan white liberal attitudes to Caribbean writing, 27

Yeats, W.B., "Sailing to Byzantium", 267

Zion revival, 10

ABOUT THE AUTHOR

Gordon Rohlehr is Emeritus Professor at the University of the West Indies at St Augustine. Unquestionably one of the Caribbean's finest critics and thinkers, his territory covers both literature and popular culture, particularly calypso. His publications include: *Pathfinder: Black Awakening in "The Arrivants" of Edward Kamau Brathwaite* (Tunapuna: College Press, 1981); *Cultural Resistance and the Guyana State* (Casa de las Américas, 1984); *Calypso and Society in Pre-Independence Trinidad* (Port of Spain, 1990); *My Strangled City and Other Essays* (Longman Trinidad, 1992); *The Shape of That Hurt and Other Essays* (Longman Trinidad, 1992); *A Scuffling of Islands: Essays on Calypso* (Lexicon Trinidad Ltd, 2004); *Transgression, Transition, Transformation: Essays in Caribbean Culture* (Lexicon, 2007); and *Ancestories: Readings of Kamau Brathwaite's "Ancestors"* (Trinidad: Lexicon, 2010) and *My Whole Life is Calypso: Essays on Sparrow* (2015).

ALSO BY GORDON ROHLEHR

Perfected Fables Now: A Bookman Signs off on Seven Decades
ISBN: 9781845234508; pp. 289; pub. 2019; £19.99

Since the mid-1960s, Gordon Rohlehr has been an incomparable recorder and analyser of Caribbean literature and culture and their intersection with history and politics. His work on the emergence of Caribbean writing from its colonial shell and his analysis of calypso as the voice of Trinidadian consciousness establishes him as essential to our time as William Hazlitt was to the early 19th century in documenting and characterising the turbulent spirit of his age. Radical, but never willing to compromise his sense of what was fraudulent or power-seeking amongst his fellow travellers, Rohlehr is the best touchstone we have for both what the Caribbean has achieved and of its struggling, neo-colonial fragility in the face of the new imperialism of economic and cultural globalism.

Now – though who knows? – in putting together what he says is his last book, Gordon Rohlehr doffs the costume of the carnival figure of the "Bookman", the recording Satan of the devil band, who walks with his book in which he writes down the names of the damned. And here we have the clue to the fact that along with the serious analysis of calypso, his summing up of what is essential in the work of Derek Walcott, Earl Lovelace and V.S. Naipaul, and the essays of remembrance for those like Walcott, Lloyd Best, Pat Bishop, Tony Martin and others who have made their earthly exits, there is a devilish humour at work. This comes out particularly in an essay that joyfully demolishes an attempt to characterise the Caribbean in any other than its own terms – as a new Mediterranean, for instance – and the subservience of Trinidad's rulers to the neo-colonialisms of tourism, visiting American ships and the U.S. embassy. What is often salutary, if uncomfortable, is to be reminded by the long span of Rohlehr's observations that problems seen as contemporary were being identified by the nation's calypsonians sixty years ago.

Rohlehr's voice is always distinctively personal, though the Bookman has rarely revealed much of himself, but in one of the concluding essays he writes about his Guyanese upbringing from the 1940s to the 1960s in a way that is both very funny and sad and gives an understanding of what has shaped his vision.